THE HAUNTED WOOD

THE HAUNTED WOOD

Soviet Espionage in America—
the Stalin Era

ALLEN WEINSTEIN
ALEXANDER VASSILIEV

THE MODERN LIBRARY
NEW YORK

2000 Modern Library Paperback Edition

Copyright © 1999 by Allen Weinstein and Alexander Vassiliev

All rights reserved under International and Pan-American Copyright
Conventions. Published in the United States by Random House, Inc., New York,
and simultaneously in Canada by Random House of Canada Limited, Toronto.

MODERN LIBRARY and colophon are registered trademarks of Random House, Inc.

Originally published in hardcover by Random House, Inc., in 1999.

Library of Congress Cataloging-in-Publication Data
Weinstein, Allen.
The haunted wood: Soviet espionage in America—the Stalin era/
Allen Weinstein and Alexander Vassiliev.
p.   cm.
Includes bibliographical references and index.
ISBN 0-375-75536-5
1. Espionage, Soviet—United States—History—Twentieth century.
2. Spies—Soviet Union.   3. Spies—United States.   4. United States—
History—1933–1945.   I. Vassiliev, Alexander.   II. Title.
UB271.R9W45   1999   327.1247073—dc21   98-11801

Modern Library website address: www.modernlibrary.com

Printed in the United States of America on acid-free paper

2 4 6 8 9 7 5 3 1

Book design by Carole Lowenstein

To Adrienne, Dena, Andrew, David, and Alex
and
To Helen and Ken
For their love — and patience

All the conventions conspire
To make this fort assume
The furniture of home;
Lest we should see where we are,
Lost in a haunted wood,
Children afraid of the night
Who have never been happy or good.

—W. H. AUDEN, "September 1, 1939"

To be excited by the same dispute, even on opposing sides, is still to be alike. This common stamp, deriving from common age, is what makes a generation.

—MARC BLOCH, *The Historian's Craft*

ACKNOWLEDGMENTS

The authors are deeply grateful, above all, for the humane balance, insights, and editorial skill of Robert D. Loomis, Random House's executive vice president and senior editor. He read successive drafts of *The Haunted Wood* and significantly improved every page. As a result, he is greatly responsible for the book's strengths, while its flaws remain entirely attributable to the authors.

This narrative history of major Soviet intelligence operations in the United States during the Stalin era, the first to be based upon an examination of files in the KGB archives, began as part of a larger Random House project a half-decade ago. Alberto Vitale, the company's president, negotiated an agreement with the KGB's retired agents' group, as a result of which the Russian Foreign Intelligence Service, a KGB successor agency, allowed a small group of Western and Russian scholars—among them the authors of *The Haunted Wood*—access to previously unavailable Soviet intelligence files. We remain indebted to Mr. Vitale's initiative.

Several authors working under the umbrella of this agreement on other books—the late John Costello, Timothy Naftali, and David Murphy—also participated in an informal dialogue and exchange that provided critical help in developing our book.

At its inception and for several years thereafter, the editorial gadfly and ringmaster of the entire project was James O'Shea Wade, to whom we remain deeply appreciative. Both John Hawkins, representing Alexander Vassiliev, and Bob Barnett, representing Allen Weinstein on this book, have provided timely and sensible counsel.

Without Donna Gold's unstinting efforts in editing and preparing the manuscript, this book might never have been completed. No acknowledgment or expression of thanks can adequately compensate Ms. Gold for the devotion and time she has contributed to *The Haunted Wood*. Our thanks also to production editor Dennis Ambrose for his precise and thoughtful handling of this book on the road to publication. Every page of the book reflects also the sensitive copyediting done by Jane Herman and the proofreading by Adrian Wood.

Strongly supportive of this project from the beginning, though probably not of every specific conclusion in *The Haunted Wood*, were then–Russian Foreign Intelligence Service (SVR) Director Yevgeny Primakov, now Russia's Prime Minister, and two other SVR officials who have contributed to better Russian-American understanding: General Vadim Kirpichenko, who coordinates the senior counselors' group of retired officers within that service, and General Yuri Kobaladze, head of the SVR's press bureau.

The archivists, historians, and officials of the Russian Foreign Intelligence Service, with whom the authors dealt during their research, especially the following (in addition to those previously mentioned), deserve our appreciation for cooperating in this unprecedented opening of materials in the KGB archives for this book: Serguey Guskov, Vladimir Karpov, Boris Labusov, Tatiana Samolis, and Oleg Tsarev. In similar manner, we appreciate the efforts of archivists and historians at the Central Intelligence Agency and National Security Agency—specifically Robert Louis Benson, Brian Latell, Michael Warner, and their colleagues—for their work on processing the VENONA intercepts for release. These two sets of concordant materials—dispatches read first in Moscow from the KGB archives and later found in deciphered versions in the VENONA materials—appear in tandem for the first time in *The Haunted Wood*.

Finally, over the past five years, three young Russians who served as assistants and translators—Julia Astashkina, Alexander Kravtsov, and Sergei Stepanov—helped to bridge the cultural gap between our two societies, for which the American co-author, whom they assisted so ably, will always be grateful.

—ALEXANDER VASSILIEV, *Western Europe*
—ALLEN WEINSTEIN, *Washington, D.C.*

CONTENTS

ACKNOWLEDGMENTS		*xi*
INTRODUCTION		*xv*
CAST OF CHARACTERS		*xxi*

PART ONE: Burden of Innocence: The New Deal Years — 1

1 Communist Romantics, I: The Reluctant Laurence Duggan — 3
2 Creating the Soviet Networks: Hiss, Chambers, and Early Recruits — 22
3 Love and Loyalties, I: The Case of Martha Dodd — 50
4 Communist Romantics, II: The Exuberant Michael Straight — 72
5 Love and Loyalties, II: Elizabeth Bentley and Jacob Golos — 84
6 Double Agent/Hollywood Hustler: The Case of Boris Morros — 110
7 "Crook": A Soviet Agent in Congress — 140

PART TWO: The Third Front: Soviet Espionage in the Second World War — 151

8 Harvest Time, I: The Silvermaster Network in Wartime Washington — 153
9 Atomic Espionage: From Fuchs to the Rosenbergs — 172
10 Harvest Time, II: The Perlo Group — 223
11 OSS and NKGB: Penetration Agents — 238
12 Harvest Time, III: Hiss, Glasser, and Warning Signs — 265

PART THREE: Discovery: Cold War Confrontation   281

13   Flight from Exposure, I: The Washington Sources   283
14   Flight from Exposure, II: The Atom Spies   311

EPILOGUE: Aftermath and Legacy   339

NOTES   345
BIBLIOGRAPHY   377
INDEX   383

INTRODUCTION

❖❖❖

Tucked into a quiet side street a few blocks from Moscow's notorious Lubyanka prison and the grimy buildings of the Soviet Union's KGB stands an unmarked four-story house, until recently the Press Bureau of Russia's Foreign Intelligence Service (or SVR). From 1994 to 1996, my Russian co-author, Alexander Vassiliev, and I pursued research on *The Haunted Wood* in this sanctum of secrets through a unique 1993 agreement between Random House and the SVR's "old boy" organization of former KGB agents, the Association of Retired Intelligence Officers (ARIO).

In return for payments made to that group, the SVR agreed to permit Vassiliev, a journalist who had once worked for Soviet intelligence, and me substantial and exclusive access to Stalin-era operational files of the KGB and its predecessor agencies.

Our contract allowed Vassiliev, who had retired from the KGB in 1990 because of his opposition to Soviet leadership, to review archived documents and to make summaries or verbatim transcriptions from the files, including their record numbers. The documentary material, organized into topical areas, was then submitted to a panel of the SVR's leading officials for review and eventual release. Throughout this process, I worked alongside Vassiliev during more than two dozen visits to Moscow: monitoring the information found, prodding the SVR to expedite release of material submitted, and organizing Western primary and secondary research data essential to the book.

As relations between the United States and Russia grew strained, the SVR became less cooperative about providing timely release of the reviewed documentary materials. By late 1995, there were no more releases, and SVR officials had begun to express concern about the extensive and revealing data previously turned over: "The problem is that you know too much," one leading official told me while examining a gift copy of an earlier book of mine, *Perjury: The Hiss-Chambers Case*. In 1996, Alexander Vassiliev accepted a journalist's assignment abroad and moved with his family to England.

By that time we had received a critical mass of the released KGB material. Using Vassiliev's initial draft and translations while incorporating new Western documentation, I wrote the English-language manuscript, and Vassiliev is now preparing *The Haunted Wood*'s Russian-language edition. The book was not submitted for SVR scrutiny before publication.

During many visits to Moscow, I benefited also from the SVR's hospitality, which increased my knowledge of Soviet intelligence practices. Often, I was hosted in the Press Bureau's plush upstairs dining and reception rooms by General Vadim Kirpichenko, head of the senior officials' influential advisory group to then–SVR Director Yevgeny Primakov (now Russia's Prime Minister) and by General (then Colonel) Yuri Kobaladze, chief of the Press Bureau and Russian intelligence's public relations mastermind. Occasionally, Director Primakov himself would join these luncheons or dinners, which always provoked spirited discussion of current Russian-American relations.

Sometimes there were surprise guests. On one occasion, convicted Soviet agent George Blake, who had escaped from an English jail to KGB sanctuary in Moscow, proved a fluent and gracious dinner partner. On another evening, General Kirpichenko escorted me to a nearby SVR hospital for a rare visit with the aged and ailing Morris Cohen (a.k.a. Peter Kroger) who, along with his wife, Lona Cohen, served Soviet intelligence both in the United States (Lona was a courier in the atom spy ring) and later as an active agent in England. Cohen, who died shortly after this visit, provided fascinating stories of his life as an American Communist.

In 1993, during the brief honeymoon period of Russian-American intelligence relations prior to the exposure of Aldrich Ames, both Kirpichenko and Kobaladze—joined by another Soviet general, Konstantin Gueyvandov, the head of ARIO—visited the United States as my guests. Their meetings included a private talk with then–CIA Director R. James Woolsey at my home; a visit, hosted by former CIA Director William Colby, to the New York office of OSS founder General William "Wild Bill" Donovan (whose personal and agency entanglements with Soviet intelligence are described in these pages); and conversations with leading CIA and FBI counterintelligence officials at the request of those officials.

In Moscow, meanwhile, a great deal of additional and important unreviewed KGB material reached us informally from other, non-KGB sources during our research and has been incorporated into the book. We thank those responsible for this help and have honored their requests for anonymity.

Adding to the SVR's evident distress concerning this book, the release in 1995–96 of the previously classified VENONA cables—2,900 translated intercepts sent by Soviet agents in the United States to Moscow about their intelligence efforts during World War II—allowed us to corroborate further a number of episodes in *The Haunted Wood*. Over forty intercepted VENONA cables that match those found in the KGB archives in Moscow are quoted in text footnotes to allow readers to compare the two versions, and dozens of additional VENONA cables are cited where appropriate in the backnotes. Much of the inside history of Soviet espionage in the United States, until now seen (if at all) through a glass darkly, thus emerges with fresh clarity in these pages.

Readers with an ideological axe to grind regarding Soviet espionage will find little comfort in *The Haunted Wood*. The book neither denounces nor defends Moscow's American espionage in the overheated manner that has characterized much Cold War literature on this subject. Rather, we have tried simply to relate the story found in the KGB archives' documents themselves. The Soviet records are filled with struggles for control among contending operatives, love affairs among the agents, dramatic personality conflicts, and occasionally even vivid accounts of plotted or actual murders. In the end, the underground world that emerges was far more contentious, chaotic, and confused than previous accounts by both Russian and Western writers would suggest.

A small sampling of the Americans who served as Soviet agents and sources during this era, described in these pages, would include:

· the passionate daughter of the American Ambassador to Nazi Germany;
· an influential (and surprising) member of Congress;

- one of President Roosevelt's personal assistants;
- a close family friend of Eleanor and Franklin Roosevelt (who had been recruited for Soviet intelligence by members of England's "Cambridge ring");
- the leader of a group of agents—all U.S. government officials—who shared his wife with one of his sources in a ménage à trois; and
- the head of the American Communist Party, who also served as an agent and recruiter of other covert sources.

Soviet operatives in the United States during these years ranged from many who were highly sophisticated practitioners of tradecraft to bumbling amateurs. One steered Moscow into a Hollywood producer-source's music publishing company while others considered similar "joint ventures" with the producer in various film projects. One hapless Washington station chief spoke almost no English while another operative plotted "cover" identities in the business world and a third worked both as station chief and as Soviet Ambassador to the United States!

But "the haunted wood" normally experienced far more tragedy than comedy. Thus, while hounded by both Soviet and U.S. intelligence operatives, one troubled former American agent of Moscow's jumped (or fell) to his death at his office building. During the bloody 1936–39 purge years in the USSR, several loyal station chiefs and operatives obeyed instructions to return home despite their recognition that arrest, torture, and execution probably awaited them. Others stalled and remained at their posts in the United States, thereby saving their lives. For those, whether in Western Europe or in the United States, who defected from Soviet intelligence and refused to suffer voluntarily Stalin's vengeance, assassins were sent to hunt them down—successfully sometimes, as in the murder of station chief–in–hiding Ignatz Reiss in Switzerland, and sometimes not, as in the failure to eliminate American defectors Elizabeth Bentley and Whittaker Chambers.

Normally, Soviet operatives and their American agent-sources pursued valuable (occasionally breakthrough) information—scientific, technical, military, and governmental—while, on occasion, their assignments approached the bizarre. Stalin was obsessed, for example, with a need to infiltrate every small and pathetic Russian pro-monarchist group in the world two decades after the overthrow of the Romanovs, and years after Soviet intelligence succeeded in killing his arch rival Leon Trotsky, the pursuit of Trotskyists continued unabated.

For the most part, however, Soviet operatives and their American agents collected during the 1930s and 1940s a remarkable range of material on U.S. industrial and military production culminating in the data provided by its sources within the atomic research program during World War II. Moreover, during the New Deal and war years, the Soviets benefited from a voluminous amount of information coming from its key agents in a range of U.S. government agencies, including the Office of Strategic Services (OSS), America's major foreign intelligence agency from 1942 to 1945.

Often the most insightful personal material on its American agents was contained in the "autobiographies" Moscow requested from these individuals for inclusion in their personnel files, and which are quoted throughout this book. The "cast of characters" will provide readers with some indication of the range of remarkable, occasionally improbable, people whose human dramas crowd the following pages. Their intersecting stories, drawn from the archives of the KGB, form the narrative heart of *The Haunted Wood*.

Notwithstanding the significant amount of previously unknown material, this account does not claim to be a definitive history of Soviet espionage in the United States during the Stalin era. That book awaits unlimited access not only to Soviet archives but to still-restricted British and American intelligence files. Only then can a complete, dispassionate, and multiarchival history of the subject be written.

In the end, research for this book benefited enormously from the fact that from 1993 to 1995, before they shut down, Russia's intelligence archivists and officials often released pivotal files that more attentive guardians might have withheld. Fortunately, the archivists who assisted us appeared to be as unfamiliar with the history of Soviet intelligence during the Stalin era as were those FBI agents who reviewed Bureau records at my request in the mid-1970s concerning the Bureau's earlier history. (With help from the American Civil Liberties Union, in 1974, I won the first Freedom of Information Act lawsuit concerning historical records requested from the FBI.)

Or did some historically minded archivists in Moscow actually wish to assist the authors in producing a more complete and accurate account of Soviet intelligence than the one found in the existing literature of both countries? That, after all, has been, from the start, our major reason for writing *The Haunted Wood*.

—Allen Weinstein

CAST OF CHARACTERS

❖

In *The Haunted Wood*, readers will encounter a number of people—Americans, Russians, and Western Europeans; many well known, others less familiar. In order to introduce the cast of characters portrayed in the following pages, the authors have provided a listing that includes the real name and (if appropriate) Soviet intelligence code name(s) and a brief description of the individual's role in the book's framework. The listing has been broken down into six categories:

1. American Agents and Sources
2. American Public Figures
3. English/European Agents and Sources
4. Soviet Operatives in the United States and Europe
5. Soviet Operatives in Moscow
6. Soviet Public Figures

Virtually all of the individuals who figure in the story that emerged from our scrutiny of the KGB archives can be found in one of these categories.

I. AMERICAN AGENTS AND SOURCES

"Arena": official of the Civil Service Commission and U.S. Navy, an agent of the New York "illegal" and Washington "legal" stations.

Barr, Joel ("Meter"): a source in Julius Rosenberg's agent group.

Bentley, Elizabeth ("Miss Wise," "Myrna"): courier and group handler in the 1930s and 1940s.

Brothman, Abraham ("Constructor," "Kron"): a scientific-technical source of the New York "legal" station in the 1940s.*

Browder, Earl ("Helmsman," "Shaman"): leader of the U.S. Communist Party and an informal group handler for Soviet intelligence.

"Buck": an official of the War Production Board and the United Nations and a member of Silvermaster's agent group.

Chambers, Whittaker ("Karl"): a group handler in the 1930s, later a defector.

Coe, Frank ("Pick"): a U.S. Treasury official and a source of the New York "illegal" station in the 1940s.

Cohen, Lona ("Leslie"): an agent of the New York "legal" station in the 1940s, wife of Morris Cohen.

Cohen, Morris ("Volunteer"): an agent of the New York "legal" station in the 1930s and 1940s.

Coplon, Judith ("Sima"): a source in the U.S. Justice Department in the 1940s.

Currie, Lauchlin ("Page"): an assistant to President Franklin Roosevelt and a source of the New York "illegal" station in the 1940s.

"Dan": a source in the U.S. War Production Board and the Soviet section of the OSS.

Dickstein, Samuel ("Crook"): U.S. Congressman and agent of the New York "legal" station.

Dodd, Martha ("Liza"): daughter of the U.S. Ambassador to Berlin in the 1930s, an agent from the 1930s to the 1950s.

Dodd, William ("Boy," "President"): Martha Dodd's brother, an agent of the New York "legal" station in the 1930s and 1940s.

Duggan, Laurence ("19," "Frank," "Prince"): U.S. State Department official, a source of the New York "illegal" station in the 1930s and 1940s.

Field, Noel ("Ernst"): U.S. State Department official, a source of the New York "illegal" station in the 1930s.

Fitzgerald, Edward ("Ted"): a source in the OSS.

"Fogel" ("Persian"): a source on atomic problems in the 1940s.

Glasser, Harold ("Ruble"): a source in the U.S. Treasury Department in the 1940s.

---

* "Legal" was the term Moscow used in relation to its agents in the United States as journalists or as part of the diplomatic corps. "Illegal" agents were those operating outside of diplomatic or journalistic cover identities.

Gold, Bella ("Acorn"): a U.S. Commerce Department official and a source of the New York "illegal" station in the 1940s.

Gold, Harry ("Goose," "Arno," "Mad," "Raymond"): Soviet source on chemical problems, later handler and courier for Klaus Fuchs.

Gold, Sonya ("Zhenya"): Bella Gold's wife, a U.S. Treasury official and a source of the New York "illegal" station in the 1940s.

Golos, Jacob ("Sound," "John"): Soviet group handler in the 1930s and 1940s in New York.

Greenglass, David ("Bumblebee," "Caliber," "Zinger"): a Soviet source on atomic problems.

Greenglass, Ruth ("Wasp," "Ida"): courier for her husband, David Greenglass.

Gumperz, Hedda ("Redhead"): an operative of the New York "illegal" station in the 1930s.

Hall, Theodore ("Mlad"): a source of the New York "legal" station on atomic problems in the 1940s.

Halperin, Maurice ("Hare"): a source in the Latin American section of the OSS.

Hiss, Alger ("Lawyer," "Ales"): U.S. State Department official, a GRU source in the 1930s and 1940s.

Joseph, Julius ("Careful"): a source in the OSS.

Katz, Joseph ("X"): an agent of the Washington "legal" station in the 1940s.

Kramer, Charles ("Mole," "Lot"): a U.S. congressional staff member and a source of the Washington "legal" station in the 1940s.

Lee, Duncan ("Kokh"): a source in the OSS.

Massing, Paul: Hedda Gumperz's husband, an operative of the New York "illegal" station in the 1930s.

Morros, Boris ("Frost," "John"): Hollywood producer, Soviet agent from the 1930s to 1950s, FBI informer in the 1940s and 1950s.

Neumann, Franz ("Ruff"): a source in the German section of the OSS.

Perlo, Victor ("Eck," "Raid"): an official of the War Production Board and a group handler.

Peter, Joszef ("Storm"): head of the U.S. Communist Party underground network in the 1930s.

Price, Mary ("Dir"): an agent, Duncan Lee's courier and lover.

Rosenberg, Ethel: Julius Rosenberg's wife.

Rosenberg, Julius ("Antenna," "Liberal," "King"): Soviet source on radio-electronics and group handler, later the Greenglasses' handler.

Sax, Saville ("Star"): a courier for Theodore Hall.

Silverman, David ("Eleron"): an official of the U.S. Aviation Department and a member of Silvermaster's agent group in the 1940s.

Silvermaster, Helen ("Dora"): wife of Nathan Gregory Silvermaster and an agent of his group in the 1940s.

Silvermaster, Nathan Gregory ("Pal," "Robert"): a U.S. Treasury official and a group handler in the 1940s.

Slack, Alfred ("Al"): a source of the New York "legal" station on scientific-technical issues in the late 1930s and early 1940s.

"Slava": agent of Jack Soble's "illegal" station in the U.S. State and Defense Departments.

Stern, Alfred ("Louis"): Martha Dodd's husband, agent of the New York "legal" station.

Straight, Michael ("Nigel"): a U.S. State Department official and a source of the New York "illegal" station in the 1930s.

"Tan": an official of the War Production Board and Trade Department and an agent of the New York "illegal" station.

Tenney, Helen ("Muse"): a source in the Soviet section of the OSS.

Ullman, William Ludwig ("Polo," "Pilot"): an official of the U.S. Aviation Department and a member of Silvermaster's agent group in the 1940s.

Weisband, William ("Zhora"): a source in the U.S. Army Signals Security Agency in the 1940s.

Wheeler, Donald ("Izra"): a source in the OSS.

White, Harry Dexter ("Lawyer," "Richard," "Reed"): a U.S. Treasury official and a member of Silvermaster's agent group.

Zelman, Franklin ("Chap"): an agent of the New York "legal" station in the 1930s and 1940s.

II. AMERICAN PUBLIC FIGURES

Barkley, Alben: U.S. Vice President, 1949–53.

Berle, Adolf: U.S. Assistant Secretary of State in the Roosevelt Administration.

Bullitt, William: U.S. Ambassador to France and to the Soviet Union in the 1930s.

Chaplin, Charles: actor

Clay, General Lucius: commander of the American occupation zone in Germany in the 1940s.

Dean, General John: head of the U.S. military mission in Moscow in the 1940s.

Dewey, Thomas: New York Governor, Republican presidential candidate in 1944 and 1948.

Donovan, William: Director of the OSS.

Dulles, Allen: OSS station chief in Switzerland.

Eisenhower, Milton: brother of General Dwight D. Eisenhower.

Harriman, Averill: U.S. Ambassador to the Soviet Union during the Second World War.

Hemingway, Ernest ("Argot"): writer.

Hoover, Herbert: U.S. President, 1929–33.

Hoover, John Edgar: Director of the Federal Bureau of Investigation.

Kaufman, Irving: presiding judge at the Rosenbergs' trial.

Knox, Franklin: Secretary of the Navy in the Roosevelt Administration.

McCarthy, Joseph: U.S. Senator.

Morgenthau, Henry ("Nabob"): U.S. Treasury Secretary in the Roosevelt Administration.

Oppenheimer, Robert ("Chester"): American scientist.

Robeson, Paul: singer and Communist Party member.

Roosevelt, Eleanor: wife of Franklin Roosevelt.

Roosevelt, Franklin D. ("Captain"): U.S. President, 1933–45.

Shipley, Ruth: head of the State Department's passport bureau in the Truman Administration.

Spellman, Cardinal Francis: influential Catholic leader from New York City.

Stettinius, Edward: U.S. Secretary of State, 1944–45.

Truman, Harry ("Sailor"): U.S. President, 1945–53.

Truman, Margaret: daughter of Harry Truman.

Wallace, Henry: U.S. Vice President (1941–45), U.S. Secretary of Commerce (1945–46).

III. ENGLISH/EUROPEAN AGENTS AND SOURCES

Blunt, Anthony ("Maurice"): an agent of the London "illegal" station in the 1930s and 1940s.

Burgess, Guy ("Mädchen," "Daughter"): an agent of the London "illegal" station in the 1930s and 1940s.

Cairncross, John ("List"): an NKVD agent in London.

"Eric": a source on atomic problems in London in the 1940s.

Fuchs, Klaus ("Rest," "Charles," "Bras"): Soviet source on atomic problems in Great Britain and the United States.

Kuchinsky, Urgen ("Karo"): Soviet agent in London.

Maclean, Donald ("Homer"): an agent in the British Foreign Office and in the British Embassy in Washington in the 1940s.

Philby, Harold "Kim" ("Söhnchen," "Son"): Soviet agent in London and Washington during the Second World War.

"Tina": a source on atomic problems in London in the 1940s.

IV. SOVIET OPERATIVES IN THE UNITED STATES AND EUROPE

Akhmerov, Itzhak ("Yung," "Bill," "Mer," "Albert," "Michael Green"): New York "illegal" operative and station chief in the 1930s and 1940s.

Barkovsky, Vladimir: London "legal" operative in the 1940s.

Bazarov, Boris ("Nord"): New York "illegal" station chief in the 1930s.

Borodin, Norman ("Granite"): New York "illegal" operative in the 1930s.

Deutsch, Arnold ("Stephan"): London "illegal" operative in the 1930s.

Dolbin, Grigory ("Grigory"): Washington "legal" station chief in the 1940s.

Feklissov, Alexander ("Kalistrat"): an operative of the New York and London "legal" stations.

Gorsky, Anatoly ("Vadim"): Washington "legal" station chief in the 1940s.

Gutzeit, Peter ("Nikolai"): New York "legal" station chief in the 1930s.

Heifetz, Grigory ("Kharon"): San Francisco "legal" station chief in the 1940s.

Krivitsky, Walter ("Enemy"): Soviet operative turned defector.

Krotov, Boris ("Bob"): Washington "legal" operative in the 1940s, New York "legal" station chief in the late 1940s and early 1950s.

Kurnakov, Sergei ("Beck"): a journalist for the *Russian Voice* and an agent of the New York "legal" station in the 1940s.

Kvasnikov, Leonid ("Anton"): scientific-technical station chief in New York in the 1940s, later a leading operative of Soviet scientific-technical intelligence.

Lowry, Helen ("Nelly," "Stella," "Elsa"): wife of Itzhak Akhmerov, New York "illegal" operative in the 1930s and 1940s.

Markin, Valentin ("Davis," "Herbert"): New York "illegal" station chief in the 1930s.

Mally, Theodore ("Man"): London "illegal" station chief in the 1930s.

Ovakimyan, Gaik ("Grigory," "George," "Guennady," "General Alexander Ossipov"): New York "legal" operative in the 1930s, station chief in the late 1930s–early 1940s, leading official of the NKVD intelligence service in the 1940s.

Panyushkin, Alexander ("Vladimir"): Soviet Ambassador to Washington and NKGB Washington "legal" station chief in the late 1940s, head of the KGB intelligence service in the 1950s.

Pastelnyak, Pavel ("Luka"): New York "legal" station chief in the early 1940s.

Pravdin, Vladimir ("Sergei"): New York "legal" station chief in the 1940s.

Reiss, Ignatz ("Raymond"): "illegal" operative in Europe in the 1930s.

Semyonov, Semyon ("Twen"): New York "legal" operative in the 1930s and 1940s.

Soble, Jack ("Abraham," "Czech"): Soviet "illegal" station chief in the 1940s and 1950s.

Soble, Myra: Jack Soble's wife, "illegal" operative.

Vinogradov, Boris ("Alexander"): Soviet diplomat, Martha Dodd's recruiter and lover.

Yatskov, Anatoly ("Alexsey"): New York "legal" operative in the 1940s.

Zarubin, Vassily ("Katya," "Maxim"): "illegal" operative in Berlin in the 1930s, New York "legal" station chief in the 1940s.

Zarubina, Elizabeth ("Vardo," "Helen"): wife of Vassily Zarubin, "illegal" operative in Berlin in the 1930s, "legal" operative in New York in the 1940s.

Zborovsky, Mark ("Tulip"): a Soviet agent in the American Trotskyist groups during the 1940s.

V. SOVIET OPERATIVES IN MOSCOW

Fedotov, Peter: the head of the NKGB intelligence service in the late 1940s.

Fitin, Pavel: the head of the NKVD intelligence service in the 1940s.

Graur, Andrei: the chief of the NKVD intelligence's Anglo-American section in the 1940s.

Korotkov, Alexander: the head of the NKGB intelligence service's "illegal" department in the 1940s and 1950s.

Passov, Zinovy: the head of the NKVD intelligence service in the late 1930s.

Sakharovsky, A.: the head of the KGB intelligence service in the 1960s.

Savchenko, Sergei: the head of the NKGB intelligence service in the early 1950s.

Slutsky, Abram: the head of the NKVD intelligence service in the 1930s.

VI. SOVIET PUBLIC FIGURES

Abakumov, Victor: USSR Minister for State Security.

Beria, Lavrenty: the head of the NKVD (1938–53), Soviet Deputy Prime Minister (1941–53).

Bulganin, Nikolay: USSR Deputy Prime Minister and Defense Minister (1953–55), USSR Prime Minister (1955–58).

Gromyko, Andrei: Counselor at the USSR Embassy in Washington in the early 1940s, USSR Ambassador to Washington (1943–46), USSR Foreign Minister beginning in 1957.

Khrushchev, Nikita: First Secretary of the Communist Party of the USSR (1953–64), Soviet Prime Minister (1958–64).

Litvinov, Maxim: People's Commissar for Foreign Affairs (1930–39), USSR Ambassador to Washington (1941–43).

Lozovsky, Solomon: Chairman of Sovinformbureau in the 1940s.

Malenkov, Georgy: USSR Prime Minister (1953–55).

Merkulov, Vsevolod: People's Commissar for State Security in the 1940s.

Molotov, Vyacheslav: USSR Prime Minister (1930–41), USSR Foreign Minister (1939–49, 1953–56).

Shelepin, Alexander: KGB Chairman (1958–61).

Stalin, Joseph: Secretary General of the USSR Communist Party (1922–53), USSR Prime Minister (1941–53).

Trotsky, Leon ("Tuk," "Old Man"): a leader of the October Revolution in 1917, the leader of the anti-Stalinist opposition abroad (1929–40).

Troyanovsky, Alexander: Soviet Ambassador to Washington in the 1930s.

Umansky, Konstantin: USSR Ambassador to Washington in the early 1940s.

Voroshilov, Kliment: People's Commissar for Defense (1925–41), Chairman of the Presidium of the Supreme Soviet (head of state) (1953–60).

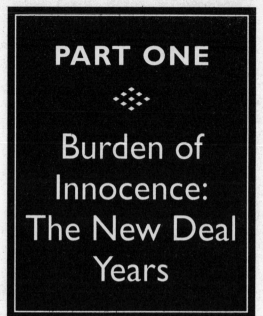

PART ONE

❖

Burden of
Innocence:
The New Deal
Years

CHAPTER I

❖❖❖

Communist Romantics, I:
The Reluctant
Laurence Duggan

WHO WAS LAURENCE DUGGAN and why was he targeted for recruitment as a Soviet intelligence agent? Officials in Moscow
might well have asked that question in 1934 when word came from one
of their Washington, D.C., operatives that Duggan had been approached.

He had come to town the previous year along with thousands of
other Americans, many—like Duggan—in their twenties, to work in
Franklin Roosevelt's "New Deal" government. Most were liberals,
committed to the Administration's experimental plans for achieving
economic recovery from the catastrophic depression. Some favored a
more radical solution comparable to the Communist experiment in
state economic management underway in the Union of Soviet Socialist Republics since the Bolshevik Revolution.

Soviet intelligence operatives resident in the United States sought to
identify and involve in espionage people sympathetic to the USSR and
for whom covert activity might seem exciting but who were, at the
same time, innocent and morally committed. Especially after Adolf
Hitler and his Nazi cohort took power in Germany in 1933, "doing
something" concrete (and secret) to help the struggle against fascism, a
battle in which the Soviet Union claimed the leadership of "progressive forces," attracted a number of the more adventurous spirits in
Washington's new reformist political class.

The professional and social relationships that linked individuals in the New Deal often blurred their political differences. Avowed or covert Communists, democratic socialists, farmer-labor activists, and Roosevelt Democrat loyalists found common ground within the many new agencies and older departments of FDR's government. This intermingling of related but distinct political agendas did not usually trouble the youthful bureaucrats crowding into Washington, which had been until then a far smaller and less-important governmental capital.

Soviet intelligence files document the mixture of accidental encounters, underlying ideological beliefs, romantic antifascist views, and Soviet persistence that led some New Dealers on the Left at the time to become espionage agents. The case of Laurence Duggan illuminates a pattern that affected a number of Soviet sources in the New Deal, including a few of his colleagues. Duggan moved willingly into the Moscow underground during the 1930s only to struggle later and without complete success to free himself from its orbit.

A 1934 memorandum by one Soviet operative urging Laurence Duggan's recruitment described "his character [as that of] a very soft guy . . . under his wife's influence, a very lively, energetic and joyful woman. Laurence is cultural and reserved."[1] Duggan's father headed the prestigious Institute of International Education, a major organizer of teacher and student exchanges. The younger Duggan was an official in the State Department's Latin American Division when he and his wife, Helen Boyd, first attracted Soviet interest. Boyd—described in a station cable to Moscow as an "extraordinarily beautiful woman: a typical American, tall, blonde, reserved, well-read, goes in for sports, independent"—had been cultivated as a friend by the anti-Nazi exile and NKVD agent Hedda Gumperz ("Redhead").[2]

Peter Gutzeit, who ran Moscow's "legal"* cover station from the Soviet Consulate in New York, reported home on October 3, 1934, that he had begun recruiting Duggan, who "is also interesting to us because through him one will be able to find a way toward [Noel] Field . . . of the State Department's European Department with whom Duggan is friendly."[3] (The European Division's information was a priority interest of Moscow's throughout the decade, and Field, too, would later launch a covert career as a Soviet agent through Gumperz.)

Concerned lest a Soviet diplomat be exposed recruiting spies only a

---

* "Legal" was the term Moscow used in relation to its agents in the United States as journalists or as part of the diplomatic corps. "Illegal" agents were those operating outside of diplomatic or journalistic cover identities.

year after formal U.S. recognition of the USSR, in 1935, Moscow reassigned contacts with Duggan from Gutzeit to Hedda Gumperz.[*]
Throughout 1935 and early 1936, social exchanges and prerecruitment talks on the Soviet Union continued between Gumperz and both Field and Duggan. Both men held key posts at State, a department the NKVD had code-named "Surrogate." Both were considered likely candidates for advancement in rank and responsibilities.

In April 1936, however, an encounter occurred involving Noel Field (code-named "Ernst" at the time) that, a decade later, would affect gravely both his life and Duggan's. The story emerged in a memorandum that month from Hedda Gumperz to her superiors concerning her efforts with Field. She informed them that a week before the latter's departure for Europe to attend a London conference representing State, he was approached by another New Deal friend, Alger Hiss,[*] then completing an assignment at the Justice Department and scheduled to join State that fall: "Alger let him know that he was a Communist [Gumperz's memo continued], that he was connected with an organization working for the Soviet Union and that he knew [Field[†]] also had connections but he was afraid they were not solid enough, and probably, his knowledge was being used in a wrong way. Then he directly proposed that [Field] give him an account of the London conference."

Field described himself and Hiss, according to Gumperz's memo, as "close friends," hence Field's willingness to discuss the subject of espionage. (Gumperz used Alger Hiss's actual name in her memo because she obviously did not know his code name.) Noel Field told Hiss that he was already reporting to his *own* Soviet NKVD contacts on the conference.

Hiss was then a member of a Soviet military intelligence (or GRU) network headed by Harold ("Hal") Ware, a group that had been energetic in recruiting new "believers"—especially friends—into its work.[‡] Hiss was not dissuaded by Noel Field's initial refusal to cooperate.

Gumperz's memo chronicled Field's account of the subsequent discussion, which at times seemed almost like a polite debate over joining competing college fraternities:

---

[*] See Chapter 2 for a fuller discussion of Alger Hiss's role as a Soviet agent in the 1930s.

[†] Here and throughout the book, the authors have inserted the subject's real name [in brackets] in place of the code names used in the cables.

[‡] On Hiss and the Ware Group, see Chapter 2.

Alger kept insisting on the report, and [Field] was forced to tell him that he needed to consult his "connections."

In the next couple of days, after having thought it over, Alger said that he no longer insisted on the report. But he wanted [Field] to talk to Larry and Helen [Duggan] about him and let them know who he was and give him [Alger] access to them. [Field] again mentioned that he had contacted Helen and Larry. However, Alger insisted that he talk to them again, which [Field] ended up doing. [Field] talked to Larry about Alger and, of course, about having told him "about the current situation" and that "their main task at the time was to defend the Soviet Union" and that "they both needed to use their favorable positions to help in this respect." Larry became upset and frightened, and announced that he needed some time before he would make that final step; he still hoped to do his normal job, he wanted to reorganize his department, try to achieve some results in that area, etc.*

Evidently, according to [Field], he did not make any promises, nor did he encourage Alger in any sort of activity, but politely stepped back. Alger asked [Field] several other questions; for example, what kind of personality he had, and if [Field] would like to contact him. He also asked [Field] to help him to get to the State Department. Apparently, [Field] satisfied this request.

When I pointed out to [Field] his terrible discipline and the danger he put himself into by connecting these three people, he did not seem to understand it. He thought that just because "Alger was the first to open his cards, there was no reason for him to keep a secret." Besides, Alger announced that he was doing it for "us" and because of the fact that he lived in Washington, D.C. . . . and, finally, [since] I was going to go out of the country for a while, he thought it would be a good idea to establish contact between us.[5]

Since Hedda Gumperz was then trying to cultivate both Laurence and Helen Duggan as well as Noel Field for her NKVD cohort, she was deeply troubled by this apparently casual interlocking of agents from two completely distinct networks (supposedly unfamiliar with each other). Alger Hiss, assigned the code name "Lawyer," had as-

---

* Other Soviet operatives found Duggan far more restless in his ordinary work at State and, as a result, more strongly motivated to assist in gathering information for them.

sumed the self-appointed and unwelcome role of recruiter of fellow officials such as Field and Duggan. Gumperz had at once informed her Soviet superior, an "illegal" station chief named Boris Bazarov, who had the unpleasant task of notifying Moscow (in an April 26, 1936, dispatch) that the whole Gumperz-Duggan-Field-Hiss situation had become something of an unseemly tag team match among agents, actual and potential:

> The result has been that, in fact, [Field] and Hiss have been openly identified to [Laurence Duggan]. Apparently [Duggan] also understands clearly [Gumperz's] nature. And [Gumperz] and Hiss several months ago identified themselves to each other. Helen Boyd, [Duggan's] wife, who was present at almost all of these meetings and conversations, is also undoubtedly briefed and now knows as much as [Duggan] himself. . . . I think that after this story we should not speed up the cultivation of [Duggan] and his wife. Apparently, besides us, the persistent Hiss will continue his initiative in this direction. In a day or two, [Duggan's] wife will come to New York, where [Gumperz] will have a friendly meeting with her. At [Field's] departure from Washington, Helen expressed a great wish to meet [Gumperz] again. Perhaps Helen will tell [Gumperz] about her husband's feelings.[6]

NKVD Moscow pressed for continuing efforts to bring the Duggans on board, however, and a May 3, 1936, cable responding to Bazarov complained about Gumperz's handling of the situation (unfairly since Gumperz, too, had protested Hiss's having crossed over to other networks in search of recruits): "We do not understand [Gumperz's] motives in having met with [Hiss]. As we understand, this occurred after our instruction that [Hiss] was 'the neighbors' man' [working with military intelligence], and that one should leave him alone. Such experiments [as Gumperz's meeting] may lead to undesirable results."[7]

Moscow instructed Bazarov to be certain that none of his agents undertook similar meetings across jurisdictional boundaries "without your knowledge," especially not Hedda Gumperz, "knowing that her drawbacks include impetuousness." As for "how to untangle" the interwoven agents, Moscow was similarly practical:

> [Field] left [for Europe], which isolates him to a certain degree, and [Hiss] will gradually forget about him. As for how to save [Duggan] and his wife [completing their agent recruitment], [Duggan] may be of interest to us, taking into account his status in "Surrogate" [the State Department]; his wife, also, taking into

account her connections. Therefore, we believe it necessary to smooth over skillfully the present situation and to draw both of them away from [Hiss]. As an extreme measure, [Duggan] could tell [Hiss] that "he is helping the local compatriots [the American Communist Party] and that the latter suggested that he not get in contact with anyone else." It is our fault, however, that [Field], who is already our agent, has been left in [Gumperz's] charge, a person who is unable to educate either an agent or even herself.[8]

Another Soviet operative then active in Washington, Itzhak Akhmerov, responded to Moscow's May 3 instructions with his own account of the background of the Gumperz-Hiss meeting that troubled NKVD officials at home. His version was milder than Bazarov's. Akhmerov shed light on Soviet intelligence's sudden embarrassment of American agent riches, a recent bonanza of antifascist romantics that at times caused different networks to stumble across one another:

[Gumperz] met with [Hiss] only once during her stay in this country [Gumperz herself had left for Europe by then], and it was last winter. She went to this meeting with Comrade [Bazarov's] consent. After you informed us that he had a liaison with the neighbors, we did not meet with [Hiss]. . . . [However, Hiss], after meeting [Gumperz] at the flat of [Noel Field] and his conversation with her, undoubtedly informed his command about this meeting. By an accidental coincidence, a brother organization's worker connected with [Hiss] knew [Gumperz] well. . . . This brother worker,* whom we know as "Peter," . . . at one of his rare meetings with [Gumperz] told the latter: "You in Washington came across my guy [Hiss]. . . . You better not lay your hands on him, etc. . . ."[9]

Before Hedda Gumperz rejoined her husband and fellow agent Paul Massing in Europe, however, Bazarov assigned her to continue cultivating Laurence Duggan and his wife. She held several social meetings with him in May 1936, which appeared to have deepened Duggan's interest in helping.[10] As Bazarov informed Moscow later that spring, Duggan rejected the idea of cooperating with other New Deal radicals (including Frederick Vanderbilt Field—no relation to Noel— whom his friend Alger Hiss had recommended as a contact). Instead,

---

* A reference to the Comintern agent Joszef Peter, who crisscrossed the Soviet underground world in America during the 1930s.

Duggan "said he preferred . . . being connected directly with us (he mentioned our country by name) [because] he could be more useful . . . and that the only thing which kept him at his hateful job in the State Department where he did not get out of his tuxedo for two weeks, every night attending a reception (he has almost 20 countries in his department), was the idea of being useful for our cause."*

Duggan defined with some care, according to Bazarov's memo, his conditions for launching an underground liaison: "It is true that he is widely known as a liberal, a typical New Dealer. . . . But that is not a problem. For the sake of security, he asked us to meet with him once a month, and he would like very much if our man knew stenography. He cannot give us documents yet, but later, apparently, he will be able to. . . . He asked us not to tell his wife anything about his work and revealed an understanding of contact technique. . . ."[11]

Bazarov, in turn, assigned a novice Soviet "illegal," Norman Borodin (code-named "Granite"), as Duggan's contact after Hedda Gumperz left for Paris, since Akhmerov was overburdened with other agents to manage.[12] At his initial meeting with Borodin, Duggan continued to be extremely reluctant to cooperate despite his earlier avowals: "his wife was pregnant, and he had to think about his family's well-being," Borodin reported. "Sooner or later . . . the authorities would discover his meetings with me, and then he would be fired from the State Department and blacklisted." Nevertheless, Duggan agreed to further meetings at two-week intervals, "sometimes in his car (we went to the countryside), sometimes at his residence as he was ill several times."[13]

By midsummer, Duggan had begun turning over documents to Borodin at these meetings, and as Borodin reported to Moscow on August 19, 1936: "my relations with [Duggan] have become quite friendly."[14] Initially, the materials received from Duggan were "insignificant" papers on subjects in which the Soviets were utterly disinterested, such as U.S.-Argentina trade relations.[15] Soon, however, he delivered more relevant materials, among them U.S. diplomatic dispatches from European embassies, reports on State Department perspectives on the Spanish Civil War, and a confidential cable from Ambassador Bullitt in Moscow recommending reforms at State in the event of a new world war. "Our relations with [Duggan] continue being friendly," Borodin informed Moscow in mid-October 1936. "He would like very much to give us more urgent stuff, but asks us to rec-

---

* A different attitude toward his State Department work than the one Duggan had displayed earlier in the year to Hedda Gumperz.

ognize his more or less isolated position [at State] with regard to the materials in which we are interested."[16]

Moscow was patient, instructing Borodin the following month (on November 14) that Duggan should continue collecting documents related to his Latin American responsibilities: "Simultaneously, the goal in developing [Duggan] must be to broaden his possibilities in [State] outside his department and to receive from him the exact scheme of work for all of [State's] stations both inside and outside the country."[17]

Duggan obliged by giving to Borodin a recently issued State Department employee handbook and personnel list, which Bazarov forwarded home, noting Moscow's various agents, including "[Duggan] and many of our 'correspondents.' "[18] The Soviet operative recommended that Moscow dispatch "a proper recruiter" to assist with developing agents at State: "through some of these talent-spottings one can come to valuable people." Bazarov commented on one employee already deeply involved who appeared in the State Department's registry: "There was [Alger Hiss]—but the neighbors stole him according to your information. (Having [Hiss], one does not need others.)"[19]

While Laurence Duggan continued providing State Department documents to the NKVD throughout 1937, as attested by the cable traffic between Moscow and its American stations, a high-ranking defector from Soviet intelligence in Europe threatened to reveal not only Duggan's role as an agent but that of many other operatives and sources throughout Western Europe and the United States. Ignatz Reiss (code-named "Raymond"), the head of NKVD operations in Europe based in Paris, had broken his ties to Moscow in July 1937 because of the threat to his security and that of his family posed by Stalin's ever-expanding purges in the USSR, which had even reached into the foreign intelligence networks.

Hedda Gumperz and Paul Massing, after leaving the United States, had worked for Reiss. Through their briefings, Reiss had been informed about various American agents of the NKVD. Itzhak Akhmerov responded on August 15, 1937, to his superiors' inquiry about American sources known to Reiss by noting that "[Reiss] knew about [Duggan] and his wife. . . . [Also,] apparently, [Reiss], being at your place at home [NKVD headquarters in Moscow], became acquainted with personnel files of our network." The Reisses, Akhmerov continued, had also socialized with Noel Field and his wife, Herta, in Switzerland through introductions by the Massings: "Also, take into account that [Field] is a friend of [Duggan's]. It is very important to keep [Field] in our hands. If [Field] is compromised in connection with [Reiss's] disclosures, apparently [Duggan] will be frightened and will want to break contact with us. In his time, [Field] recommended [Duggan] to us."[20] Protecting Soviet agents in the U.S. government as well as in Europe, therefore, required killing Ignatz Reiss before he denounced figures such as Duggan and Field.

Shortly before defecting with his wife and children, Reiss had delivered a letter to the Soviet Embassy in Paris addressed to the USSR's Central Committee in Moscow. The defector stated that he was "returning to freedom—back to Lenin, to his teachings and his cause," in short, breaking with Stalin's leadership. It took two months of diligent pursuit before a pair of NKVD assassins caught up with Reiss at a restaurant near Lausanne, Switzerland. On September 4, 1937, Reiss's pursuers seized him, shoved him into their car, and (according to NKVD official Pavel Sudoplatov's later account) promptly ended his life: "Three miles from the restaurant they shot [Ignatz Reiss] and left him on the roadside."[21]

On September 11, 1937, NKVD officials in Moscow informed Akhmerov: "[Reiss] is liquidated, [but] not yet his wife. So far, we do not know to what extent she knows about [Duggan] and what steps she will take in future. Now the danger that [Duggan] will be exposed because of [Reiss] is considerably decreased."[22]

Soviet intelligence had begun to depend upon well-placed agents within the State Department, such as the NKVD's Laurence Duggan and Noel Field and the GRU's Alger Hiss, to provide vital information from America's "neutral" diplomatic outposts regarding the capabilities and intentions of Germany and Japan. The Soviet Union understandably viewed both countries as its potential "main enemies" in an Atlantic-Pacific war, the approach of which Moscow believed probable if not yet inevitable.

Duggan in particular proved extremely helpful at this time. At a March 19, 1937, meeting, he gave Borodin a letter he had received recently from Joseph C. Green, head of State's Office of Arms and Munitions Control, which Green in turn had received from the Navy Department: "This letter said the navy knew that U.S. plants were now receiving large war orders from many countries," Borodin reported to Moscow, "in particular the USSR and Turkey. . . . In principle, the navy does not object to filling the orders . . . but it categorically objects to carrying out war orders for the USSR since it reckons that the latter is a potential enemy."[23]

The following month, Duggan provided information from Green's files on foreign war orders in the United States, which elicited this rare compliment from Moscow: "We can ascertain your success in working with [Duggan],"[24] who by then was becoming fearful of continuing to pursue departmental information in areas other than his direct Latin American responsibilities, as Borodin informed Moscow in late May: "[Duggan] thinks that now trying to acquire similar folders with German, Japanese, and British or Italian orders would be like 'playing with fire.' We'll see in future, but now, in his opinion, Green must be left in peace. We completely approved his point of view. . . ."[25]

That same month, however, Duggan passed other documents to Borodin, including some dealing with arms purchased by Spanish government officials in Mexico and a copy of a U.S. Embassy report from Berlin.[26] He also described confidential discussions of peace prospects undertaken on Roosevelt's and Secretary of State Cordell Hull's behalf in Europe by an American diplomat.[27]

For whatever reason, Moscow decided that same year that its primary sources in the United States—mainly romantic ideologues committed to Communist dogma and the Soviet Union's success—should be rewarded with special gifts. Thus Whittaker Chambers, under instructions from GRU station chief Boris Bykov, acquired and delivered four Bokhara rugs to key operatives in his network, including Alger Hiss. When Soviet intelligence in the spring of 1937 raised the question of a possible monetary payment to Laurence Duggan, however, Bazarov immediately objected and reminded his superiors of Duggan's motives in cooperating:

> You ask whether it is timely to switch him to a payment? Almost definitely he will reject money and probably even consider the money proposal as an insult. Some months ago [Borodin] wanted to give [Duggan] a present on his birthday. He purchased a beautiful crocodile toiletries case with [Duggan's] monograms [engraved]. The latter categorically refused to take this present, stating that he was working for our common ideas and making it understood that he was not helping us for any material interest.[28]

What romantic radicals such as Duggan sought most from their Soviet intelligence contacts was not funds but frankness, not cash but candor. Both were in extremely short supply among Soviet citizens in the 1936–39 purge years, when millions were imprisoned, tortured, and executed. Duggan raised the question of the purges with Norman Borodin on July 2, 1937, according to the latter's memorandum to Moscow on the discussion, which suggested the State Department official's troubled reaction to recent events in the Soviet Union:

"[Duggan] cannot understand events in the USSR . . . the disclosure of Trotskyite-fascist spies in almost all the branches of industry and in the state institutions embarrass him enormously. People he has learned to respect turn out to be traitors to their motherland and to the socialist cause . . . all this seems to him 'a remote, incomprehensible nightmare.'"

Duggan drove the point home, since it directly affected his own willingness to cooperate: "What will happen to him if in the institution to which his information is sent [the NKVD] there is a fascist spy? It seems more than impossible, but two months ago the same could have been said about the nine [arrested Soviet] generals. . . . He repeats again and again: he cannot understand it, he is embarrassed, he cannot sleep." As a result, Duggan proposed breaking off relations with the NKVD and retreating into work with the American Communist Party: "he does not want to work for a country where something happens that he does not understand."[29] After long discussion, however, Borodin persuaded Duggan to continue his work. Nevertheless, he remained anxious that materials he handed over to the Russian might somehow reach "the enemy through the spies"—and his name with it.

Duggan asked to meet with Hedda Gumperz, who had launched his NKVD career, "to discuss all of his doubts with her."[30] But Itzhak Akhmerov, by then station chief and Borodin's superior, strongly opposed reinvolving the mercurial Gumperz in Duggan's life. Duggan was told eventually that such a meeting would compromise his security.[31] By that time, he had become even more important to Moscow. His promotion to head of State's Latin American division meant that Duggan had begun to receive (if only as secondary "information copies") virtually all important cables coming into the department, selections from which he, in turn, agreed to transmit to Borodin: "From the beginning," Akhmerov reported to Moscow on August 15, 1937, "we will be receiving [them] once a fortnight, and then [Duggan] will try to make more frequent our receipt of these cables."[32]

Considering his increased importance to Soviet intelligence, Moscow instructed Duggan's handlers in the United States to redouble their efforts at ideological education, addressing his declared doubts regarding the purges and Soviet leadership: "One must systematize the political work with [Duggan]. All the puzzling questions from [Duggan] must receive exhaustive answers from you. Leave nothing unclear and not satisfied. Always note the issues [Duggan] is interested in and inform us. . . . We cannot lose him for any reason."[33] Throughout these months, Duggan was a reliable source of State Department documents, which his contacts photographed and returned. The procedure was comparable to the one used by GRU courier Whittaker Chambers with *his* State Department sources, Alger Hiss and Henry Julian Wadleigh, during the same period. Still, Moscow pressed for more urgent attention to Duggan's importance: "Cable us his agent information immediately, since all this is exceptionally urgent material."[34] Because Akhmerov and his colleagues had to provide translations into Russian before sending along documents and other information, the process was extremely laborious.

Duggan's new eminence as a Soviet source led Akhmerov to decide it was time he met with him. The meeting took place on August 23, 1937, after which the Russian reported candidly to his superiors:

> Ideologically [Duggan] is not our solidly formed man yet. He lives and circulates in the circle of [State Department] officials who represent a privileged and conservative caste in Washington. He reads mainly newspapers of the anti-Soviet kind and, being exceptionally busy, he cannot read Marxist literature or our brother press. Undoubtedly, these circumstances play a major role in his vacillations, which, thus far, have not disappeared.

Despite his concerns about the relationship, Laurence Duggan continued to meet Akhmerov and hand over documents. At an August 30 liaison, for example, "he passed me [State's] cables for over an hour, approximately 60 pages, which I photographed and include in this mail. The second part of the documents, about 100 pages, he gave me at a third meeting on September 13. . . . Thus far I meet with him to receive documents about once a fortnight." Duggan, according to Akhmerov, gave him not only diplomatic cables but also Navy Department materials, information copies of which had been sent to State.

Akhmerov now pressed Duggan for weekly meetings and additional document deliveries. Duggan refused, explaining that his busy schedule made this impossible since he "cannot be absent from [State] without being noticed": "These materials are in his hands only during the working day. By the end of the day, they return to the chief archivist's office. The Secretary of State or his assistant summon [Duggan] very often, and, also, [Duggan's] working day's schedule is known to the secretary of his department."[35]

When Duggan announced that he was going on a vacation to Mexico in October, Akhmerov pressed him about information that State might have concerning Leon Trotsky ("Tuk"), who was then an exile in that country. Duggan reported that State's files contained nothing but a few stray items. He then stirred Akhmerov's fears by noting that the painter Diego Rivera, "in whose house [Trotsky] lives, is an old friend. Apparently, [Duggan] will go to see Rivera and, possibly, will meet [Trotsky] there." Akhmerov cautioned Duggan against being taken in by the Trotskyist leader. The diplomat brushed aside the idea, changing the subject to some incoming cables he had seen from Ambassador Bullitt regarding a possible French cabinet shake-up that could lead to annulment of the Franco-Soviet mutual assistance pact.[36]

When Duggan returned from Mexico in November, he continued meeting Akhmerov twice monthly, again declining to come weekly because of his workload at State.[37] By year's end, however, Duggan's doubts had reappeared even more strongly. "He claims he cannot digest events in the Soviet Union," Akhmerov cabled Moscow about a January 3, 1938, meeting with Duggan. "He thinks something is fundamentally wrong, since there cannot be so many members of the Right and Left oppositions who became traitors."[38] Duggan knew personally some of the Soviet diplomats who became victims of repression in the purges, he told Akhmerov, and did not question their devotion to the USSR.

Akhmerov's superiors blamed him for the difficulties with Duggan. The deputy chief of the NKVD's foreign department, Michael Spiguelglass, proposed replacing Akhmerov with Arnold Deutsch, a Soviet "illegal" operative, then working with the "Cambridge group" in England.[39] That never happened, nor did Moscow apparently approve Akhmerov's suggestion that, as an act of friendship, he purchase a painting depicting workers' lives to present to Duggan.[40]

Duggan expressed his concerns plainly in meetings with Akhmerov at this time. Above all, he feared exposure and its impact on his family. He pointed out early in March 1938 that the Deputy Secretary of State had summoned him to a meeting and warned him to "be exceptionally careful in your contacts," and using information presumably gathered by a counterintelligence search of Duggan's home, noted that "it does not befit a person of your status to have Marxist books." Security procedures were being tightened at State, Duggan informed his Soviet handler. Above all, Akhmerov relayed to his superiors, Duggan "fears that such traitors as Yagoda [the former head of Soviet intelligence who was executed in the purges] and others could expose his cooperation with us."[41]

Akhmerov agreed to Duggan's insistence on a three-month pause in their contacts, if only to forestall a complete rupture. When they met again on June 1, Duggan wanted to continue the break. He was about to be promoted but felt that this might not happen because of his superiors' concerns over the security situation. Three hours of intense discussion, Akhmerov reported to Moscow, could not change Duggan's mind.[42]

By that time, at the height of the purges, more paranoid figures in the NKVD leadership had concluded that Duggan was a Trotskyist sympathizer, a judgment with which Akhmerov disagreed.[43] Despite his anxieties, in fact, Duggan continued to convey State Department reports to his Russian contact, including two September 1938 cables (one on Nazi and Italian Fascist activity in the American republics) that the NKVD considered important enough to send on to Stalin, Molotov, and Marshall Voroshilov.[44] Duggan's activity as an agent remained sufficiently extensive for Akhmerov to describe their usual contact procedure in a late-1938 memorandum for Moscow:

> I would meet [Duggan] in the evening in a decent quiet bar, or he very often picked me up in his car. We drove to a dark area and talked in the car. [When delivering documents, State's] cables with which you are familiar, he would pass them to me in the afternoon on his way to lunch. I would photograph them in about an hour and a half and pass them back. That was due to the fact that he had to return them to [the State Department] archive on the same day.[45]

By the spring of 1939, Akhmerov and Duggan met less frequently. Duggan informed Akhmerov at a late-April meeting that "materials from other departments were not coming to him anymore, and he was learning about events in Europe and the Far East only from the press and from casual conversations with his colleagues." Still, he turned over at that same meeting a personal briefing on Lawrence Steinhardt, the new U.S. Ambassador to the Soviet Union.[46]

Five months would pass before the next Duggan-Akhmerov meeting, which took place on October 2, 1939. Duggan appeared extremely shaken: "He came to the meeting without his car, very gloomy and brokenhearted," Akhmerov reported. "He said he left his house through the back door, took a taxi and went to a movie theater before coming to meet me." According to Duggan, a State Department aide to the Department's chief security officer (the latter code-named "Mechanic") had approached him asserting that "[State] had information that he had cooperated with [Soviet intelligence], providing the latter with secret materials and secret information. Further, the assistant claimed that it would be better for him if he found another job. . . . [Moreover,

Duggan] said he is absolutely isolated in [State] and put in intolerable conditions. He says he is already looking for another job."*

Duggan blamed Soviet intelligence, and specifically the NKVD, for his problem: "He says that, apparently, someone in our chain turned out to be a traitor, and this traitor reported on him." Although Akhmerov assured Duggan that only a few leading officials, two or three, knew about him and that his name was never used, "he persistently and resolutely asked to break any connection with me." Akhmerov suggested another three-month pause in their meetings, but Duggan continued to insist that, henceforth, he would only work openly within American leftist circles and, therefore, "he was not walking away from the movement forever." Akhmerov appeared genuinely touched by the encounter: "We said goodbye as close friends."[47] Soon afterward, early in 1940, Akhmerov returned to Moscow, while Duggan, despite the threats from State's security section, not only continued to work in the Department but had been appointed a personal adviser for Latin America to Secretary of State Cordell Hull.[48]

When the NKVD learned about Duggan's more prominent post, Moscow promptly assigned a Washington agent to try and resume contact. After some failed attempts, a Soviet operative known in the files only by his code name, "Glan," met with Duggan in 1940 at the latter's suggestion at 10:35 P.M. in that most unsecretive of Washington locations, the Cosmos Club. The two then proceeded to a local restaurant and held an unsatisfactory conversation, which "Glan" reported to his superiors. Duggan stated bluntly that "he had ceased working with us due to the fact that . . . at the office he is not trusted, and his position there is not stable." In his new post, he was detached from the Department's important work and had no staff. Nor did anyone seek his advice, despite his title, or so he informed "Glan," perhaps to dampen his former NKVD associates' interest in him. "Glan's" memo showed that Duggan's position was the same as it had been at his last meeting with Akhmerov:

He asks us to believe that his attitude toward us has not changed, that he does not mind in principle returning to work, but he states

* The warning to Duggan had probably come from an aide to Assistant Secretary of State Adolf Berle, who oversaw State Department security matters. Berle had met the previous month, on September 2, with Whittaker Chambers, a GRU courier who had defected the previous year. Chambers had named Duggan, among others—including Alger Hiss—as an active Soviet source within the government. The episode is described in detail in Chapter 2.

firmly that, to date, he does not see any sense in it, that he cannot be useful and does not want any more meetings, at least for all of 1941. . . . He was disappointed by the fact that when he started work with us he was guaranteed full security, but the time he was summoned to [State's] top brass convinced him that there was a leak somewhere in our line.

Before leaving, Duggan asked "Glan" not to call again. He observed that all Washington telephones were wiretapped—despite the fact that, on counterintelligence issues, FBI agents were like "boys lost in the forest."[49]

In early 1942, the task of bringing Laurence Duggan back into the fold once again fell to Itzhak Akhmerov. On February 25, after his return to the United States, Akhmerov reported to Moscow that he had been in contact with Duggan, who repeated what "Glan" had reported the previous year: that he was ready to help Soviet intelligence but, at present, saw no possibilities for such assistance. The previous month, Duggan told Akhmerov, one of his leading State Department colleagues and a fervent anti-Communist, Assistant Secretary Adolf Berle, a bit drunk at the time, had hinted to him that he recalled his colleague's links to "Left elements," possibly a reference to Whittaker Chambers's naming of Duggan as an active Communist at his 1939 meeting with Berle.[50]

Akhmerov had other sources to supervise in both New York and Washington, but he managed to persuade Duggan to resume regular monthly meetings. Duggan kept deferring the encounters, however, blaming the demands of his job, and the relationship never revived despite the Russian's admiration for his source: "He is a sincerely progressive American, sympathizes with us, understands our role in this war, and, at the same time, is a 100 percent American patriot. . . . Being scalded once, he is inclined to exaggerate the danger considerably. Earlier he brought me piles of the most interesting things from his office. Now, he avoids even referring to the source when he tells me something."[51]

But Akhmerov's Moscow superiors were unimpressed with his handling of Duggan, criticizing his efforts as "unsatisfactory" in a November 26, 1942, cable on the situation. They pointed out that Duggan "undoubtedly has access to many materials of paramount interest for us" and could also provide "valuable oral information" based on discussions with his leading colleagues at State: "You should take a firmer stand toward [Duggan]. Let him understand that he is really our agent, that he has been working with us for several years, that in the past he gave us valuable documentary materials, and we have a right to demand from him at present at least valuable oral information on the most important issues."

Essentially, Moscow demanded that Akhmerov remind Duggan of his "moral commitments" to Soviet intelligence, although, "of course, we do not mean to blackmail him with the fact that in his time he gave us documentary materials."[52] But had Akhmerov followed Moscow's instructions and insisted that Duggan meet weekly and deliver "valuable . . . information," the implied threat to expose him would have been obvious.

Akhmerov was then given a long letter sent from Moscow by Duggan's earliest Soviet handler, Norman Borodin, a not-especially-subtle reminder of his past relationship with Borodin. The letter urged Duggan to resume his covert activities "to help your own country by helping us win the all-out war we are waging."[53]

Akhmerov decided that Borodin's letter would not help persuade Duggan (to whom he now assigned a new code name, "Frank"), reminding Moscow on February 2, 1943: "[I]deological links and personal friendship are the mainsprings in our connections with [Duggan]. . . . Could we scare him and make him work? Of course not. He knows we will never compromise him deliberately. Besides, he knows we have nothing we could compromise him with." Akhmerov continued in his determined campaign of "persistent influence on [Duggan's] conscience so he will help us more actively and developing our personal friendship."[54] In the end, occasional tidbits of State Department information was the most the Soviet operative gained from his rare meetings with Duggan during this period.*

In July 1944, confronted by continuing pressure from the Department's security officials, Laurence Duggan resigned his post at State and joined the newly organized United Nations Relief and Rehabilitation Administration as a diplomatic adviser. In his final memorandum on the subject, on July 10, a surprised Akhmerov advised Moscow that he had not expected this move, although Duggan "told me quite often about his troubles and his status there."†[55]

---

* Some of Duggan's information during this period, however, may have proved valuable to Soviet intelligence, as in this June 30, 1943, cable from the New York station to Moscow: "[Laurence Duggan] reports the following: 1. In the near future the [United States] and [Great Britain] will land strong forces in ITALY and on her islands with the aim of seizing the whole of ITALY." The cable provides details of preparations for the landings. Nos. 1025, 1035–36, VENONA files.

† Duggan continued to deliver information to Akhmerov virtually up to the day he left the State Department. See, for example, the following VENONA cables dealing with Duggan's data: March 28, 1944, No. 380; June 28, 1944, No. 916. Zaru-

Nor did Moscow's interest in Duggan (who in addition to "Frank" had also acquired a third code name, "Prince") end there. After the war, Duggan replaced his father as the director of the Institute of International Education (IIE) and became a strong supporter of student exchanges with all major countries including the Soviet Union.[56] His former NKVD handler, Norman Borodin, urged Moscow in a March 1948 memorandum to consider recruiting Duggan for intelligence activities once again through the IIE because of "the possibility of legalizing entry into the U.S. of our illegals from Europe as students and their subsequent legalization in the U.S. and other countries. It seems to me that [Duggan] will not be afraid to resume work with us . . . now that he does not work in a state institution and, therefore, will not be afraid of being identified as a 'disloyal' American, provided of course that a sensible conversation is held with him."[57]

Although Borodin may have had himself in mind as the obvious interlocutor, his superiors recommended instead that their Washington station chief, Ambassador Alexander Panyushkin, use an official meeting with Duggan to clarify their prospects. "One may presume," Moscow informed Panyushkin on May 7, 1948, "that the Institute's activities are guided directly by the State Department and, at the same time, apparently are actively used by American intelligence in its work preparing and sending agents to all the countries it is interested in." Thus, sending a "legal" Soviet operative in Washington, code-named "Saushkin," to see Duggan could determine whether he was willing to resume his work as a Soviet agent, "possibly receiving from him talent-spotting on people working in the State Department, using him to legalize our operatives, and possibly acquiring information about how American intelligence uses student exchanges in its work against us." Nevertheless, Moscow cautioned the ambassador to take into account Duggan's past vacillations "and a persistent urge in the past to break all relations with us" and thus "be very careful with him not to expose our worker ["Saushkin"] or to push [Duggan] away by our sharply expressed interest in him."[58]

A forty-minute meeting between Duggan and "Saushkin" took place at the Institute's offices on July 1, 1948. The Soviet agent's report high-

bin commented to Moscow in a July 1944 cable of the situation: "[Duggan] will resign from [the State Department] allegedly for 'personal reasons.' Details and prospects for the future are being looked into." July 22, 1944, No. 1015, VENONA files.

lighted Duggan's refusal to be engaged in a compromising conversation: "He received me politely . . . [and] talked in detail about the Institute's work, showed me the office and, having done this, led me to the exit. . . . He did not want to talk about any other issues except the Institute and tried to be official throughout. I got the impression [that] he was on the alert all the time, expecting an unexpected question from me."[59]

On December 11, Duggan was questioned by FBI agents about Whittaker Chambers's allegations concerning Alger Hiss's Communist past, a probe then reaching its climax before a New York grand jury. Four days later, "Saushkin" called Duggan at his office, leaving a message for the absent official that was never answered. On December 20, 1948, Laurence Duggan either jumped or fell to his death from the sixteenth floor of his office building, tragically terminating his long, anguished, and ambivalent association with Soviet intelligence.[60]

Other American sources with whom the NKVD developed relationships in the 1930s proved more compliant and less sensitive to the brutal abuses of Soviet power than had Duggan, cheerfully maintaining covert links to Moscow in the antifascist climate of the depression decade.

CHAPTER 2

❖❖❖

Creating the Soviet Networks: Hiss, Chambers, and Early Recruits

RECOGNITION

IN THE MONTHS FOLLOWING Franklin D. Roosevelt's November 1932 election as President, leaders in Moscow anxiously awaited word that the incoming head of the American government would abandon his predecessors' policy denying formal diplomatic recognition to the Soviet Union. Moscow instructed its few intelligence operatives at the GPU's* New York station to focus on learning Roosevelt's views and his probable course of action. The station responded with a steady flow of published news stories, rumors, and reports of private discussions with pro-Soviet Americans, all of which suggested a likely decision to establish diplomatic ties. Nevertheless, the station cautioned in a January 3, 1933, cable and in other dispatches that nothing was settled: "the activities of the USSR's enemies have intensified at present because of the possibility of Washington's change in policy toward Moscow . . . [after] the change of government in March [1933]."[1]

---

* The Soviet Union's state security agency changed names (and acronyms) regularly; hence the varied references in these pages to what would eventually become the KGB. Initially (starting in 1917) the Cheka, it became the OGPU or GPU (1923), the NKVD (1934), the NKGB (1941), and, after several additional adjustments in nomenclature, the KGB in 1954.

Months of secret negotiation between Soviet and American diplomats preceded President Roosevelt's 1933 decision to accord diplomatic recognition to the Soviet Union. Even many U.S. business leaders and conservatives supported the move in that time of high unemployment and collapsing markets, at the virtual trough of the worldwide Great Depression, on grounds that (in historian William Leuchtenberg's words) it "would lead to a revival of trade with the world's largest buyer of American industrial and agricultural equipment." Many within the American labor movement, the Catholic Church, and others remained opposed. But the economic collapse of the Hoover years, which led a million Americans in 1932 to vote for either the Communist or Socialist presidential candidates, had left large numbers agreeing with newspaper tycoon Roy Howard that "the menace of Bolshevism in the United States is about as great as the menace of sunstroke in Greenland or chilblains in the Sahara."[2]

After nine days of negotiations between Soviet envoy Maxim Litvinov and American officials, FDR and Litvinov exchanged documents on November 16, 1933, that accorded diplomatic recognition. In the years ahead, Roosevelt's expectation that his "New Deal" Administration would now enjoy greatly enhanced trade with the USSR did not materialize. For its part, the Soviet government failed to keep its commitment to curb Communist propaganda in the United States. But recognition brought the United States into line with other great powers that had opened diplomatic ties to Moscow years earlier. In one respect, however, Leuchtenberg's dismissal of recognition as "an event of monumental unimportance" proved inaccurate.

Recognition provided the Soviet Union's floundering intelligence-collection efforts in the United States with a number of previously unavailable opportunities. Over fifteen years had elapsed since the October 1917 Revolution brought the Bolsheviks to power. And during this period, Soviet agents in the United States sometimes had to depend upon personal relationships between the USSR's leaders and radical Americans—for example, the father-son team of entrepreneur-agents Julius and Armand Hammer. At other times, the USSR created state-run trading companies—such as AMTORG—that, as in the case of the Hammers, combined legitimate business activity with espionage.

Now, with diplomatic recognition, both wings of Soviet intelligence—the "civilian" GPU and "military" GRU—could function under legal cover through station chiefs in Washington's Soviet Embassy and at Soviet Consulates in New York and San Francisco. Such

"legals" could be found in most major-power diplomatic establish-
ments of the era except for those of the United States.

Older anxieties, however, accompanied these new opportunities.
Thus, Moscow urged Peter Gutzeit, the GPU's New York station chief,
to proceed cautiously: "Taking into account the categorical need to
avoid everything that could complicate our relations with the masters
of your country, I order [you to] (1) renounce the methods of mass recruitment [of agents]; (2) under no circumstances carry out recruitments without the station chief's sanction."[3] On September 14, 1935,
Gutzeit was reminded of a recent directive from the Soviet Communist
Party's Central Committee, which

> obliged us not to commit any failure in your country under any
> circumstances, since the slightest trouble in this direction can
> cause serious consequences of an international character affect-
> ing relations not only between us and the country of your
> residence. . . . The work demands particular operational charac-
> teristics:
>
> a. maximum caution;
> b. observation of the rules of security;
> c. caution and purposefulness in the selection of agents.[4]

Nor were the newly arrived station chiefs especially well-informed
about work already being performed by agents recruited by their predecessors or by "the neighbors" (a euphemism used to describe military
intelligence—the GRU).[5] During the early years following formal
U.S.-Soviet recognition, the USSR's underground operatives in the
United States functioned under frequently repeated instructions from
Moscow to concentrate on three crucial areas of information collection: scientific and economic secrets from U.S. industries with potential value to the industrialization process under way in the Soviet
Union; policy documents related to Japanese and German military
threats to the Soviet regime (the "listening post" rewards of American
recognition); and information on individuals and groups in the United
States supporting either the exiled Soviet leader Leon Trotsky or the
various small pro-monarchist organizations of so-called Whites (designated thus, of course, as opponents of the "Reds"). These "anti-Soviet"
activists preoccupied Joseph Stalin and the uneasy cabal that supported his leadership in the USSR.

In Washington, beginning in 1934, Soviet operatives and a number
of freshly recruited U.S. agents within the New Deal joined existing

sources, largely in New York and San Francisco, supplying Moscow's expanding appetite for secret information and documents from America's thoroughly unsecretive society. Gathering scientific and technical data interested Soviet "legal" operatives stationed at the embassy and consulates under diplomatic cover: "Nowhere in the world are techniques in every industry so highly developed as in America," ran one typical Moscow directive. "The scale of manufacturing in America most corresponds to our own . . . ; this makes technical intelligence in the U.S. our main center of work."[6]

ECONOMIC AND MILITARY ESPIONAGE

Goals for economic intelligence were extensive and precise. A 1934 directive specified the information Moscow sought concerning certain major corporations and international markets:

- Standard Oil's global competition and its policies toward the Soviet government and oil products, as well as exposure of Soviet citizens who act as informants for the company;
- General Electric's activities and its Soviet "sources"; and
- the activities of the Chicago Bread [Wheat] Exchange, the furs market, and Soviet trading institutions abroad.[7]

During the years that followed, and based upon instructions such as these, Soviet operatives collected data and documents—whatever their degree of usefulness—from agents in American industries ranging from defense plants to cosmetics firms. Informants were normally paid, not a practice followed with Moscow's more ideologically driven Washington sources of political or governmental data.

Those activities that did not require intelligence cover were still assigned to operatives. For example, the wife of Stalin's close associate Vyacheslav Molotov, one Polina Zhemchuzhina, headed a Soviet state-owned cosmetic company TEZHE. She used a U.S. visit in January 1937 to acquire the formulas for two dozen products made by an American company, shipped to her through the NKVD's New York station![8] Normally, such intelligence probes involved accomplices working in American heavy industries and defense production, with payments for their services amounting to hundreds and sometimes thousands of dollars, a considerable amount in that depression decade.[9] Occasionally, operatives dangled before possible sources offers of trips to the Soviet Union, and in the case of one aviation engineer being cultivated, code-named "Taran," actually arranged an NKVD-sponsored lecture tour of the USSR during which (according to his escort's report) the engineer "apparently liked having a good time with women, mainly young girls."[10]

As the crisis in Europe intensified and war drew closer, understandably the interests of Soviet intelligence focused on defense-related industries. Thus, in 1937, a Moscow cable conveyed to its American stations these instructions on what information or plans to seek out:

1. Aviation: high-speed planes with powerful armaments and the plane's controlling equipment;
2. Navy: high-speed battleships and cruisers, armor, armaments, controlling and navigation equipment, accumulators for submarines;
3. tanks: engines, armor, armaments, equipment;
4. chemistry: new war chemicals;
5. . . . telemechanics; equipment for seeing in the dark.[11]

The responses to such instructions were varied and occasionally even exotic. One agent reported on a new variety of chemical warfare supposedly being developed by Nazi scientists—"parrot illness or so-called psitacosis. . . . The death rate among those contaminated by this microbe is 100%."[12] Of a more practical nature was the work of an operative named Shumovsky (code-named "Blerio"), whose assignment was to obtain aviation industry data and who concentrated on the Northrop and Douglas plants in California. One agent he recruited, Jones Orin York,* a Northrop inventor (code-named "Needle") who needed funds to open his own business, provided Shumovsky in 1935 with plans for a new engine of his own design[13] and, in that same year, with documents on the newest Northrop fighter plane.[14] York's value to Moscow was quickly recognized: "[York's] attitude toward work is excellent," the San Francisco station cabled Moscow in April 1936. "He fulfills all our assignments precisely and accurately."[15] Apparently the inventor continued to produce material of significant value since, in the fall of 1937, Shumovsky's Soviet controllers told him that they planned to create a special research commission in Moscow to study

---

* Jones Orin York ("Needle") told the FBI in 1950 that he had given secrets to Soviet intelligence since the mid-1930s while a West Coast aircraft worker. Robert Louis Benson and Michael Warner, eds., VENONA: Soviet Espionage and the American Response, 1939–1957 (Washington, D.C.: National Security Agency & Central Intelligence Agency, 1996), p. xxviii.

and implement York's various plans.[16] But another Soviet agent reported to Moscow in the summer of 1939 the embarrassing news that York ("according to his former wife") had disappeared with an unknown woman.[17]

Meanwhile, Shumovsky had developed other contacts in the industry but with less productive results. Code-named "Gapon," a Douglas specialist on high-altitude flights tempted the Soviet agent with information and documents related to allegedly "secret" tests, only to suggest that Shumovsky approach Douglas officially if he wished to pursue the relationship.[18] He had similar bad luck with another Douglas employee, a draftsman code-named "Falcon," who promised (but apparently never delivered) "many interesting things for Soviet aviation."[19]

At the Marietta Company in 1936, then producing four-engine "flying boats" under contract to the Soviet Union, Shumovsky met a young engineer code-named "Lever" with whom he became friendly. "Lever" switched employers later that year, transferring to the National Aeronautics Center at Wright Field in Dayton, Ohio. He told Shumovsky that he now enjoyed access to reports from U.S. military attachés in Europe regarding the performance of planes various countries were using in the Spanish Civil War. Pointing to the counterintelligence surveillance of Wright Field employees, however, "Lever" declined the Soviet agent's request for this and other material, postponing another meeting for several months, at which "Lever" continued to refuse Shumovsky's requests for classified information.[20]

In 1938, the NKVD assigned another courier, a young underground operative named Harry Gold (then code-named "Goose"), to meet with the Wright Field engineer. "Lever" later insisted that he had rebuffed all advances made by Gold and other Soviet agents. Their relationship ended in 1940, when "Lever" informed Gold that if Gold had not also been Jewish, he would have told the FBI about him when they first met![21]

Elsewhere, Soviet intelligence appeared more successful, although one valuable source who had been removing secret documents from the Navy Department, described only as "C-II" in the Moscow files, ended her efforts in the summer of 1940 when U.S. counterintelligence inquiries threatened exposure.[22] Another Navy Department source, code-named "Chita," provided documents on various military ships, including submarines, and—according to the NKVD file report on his work—"seriously wants to help us for ideological reasons not having any material interests. The only reward he expects is to move at some point to the Soviet Union to work there . . . he doesn't want to bring up his three sons in the conditions of capitalist America. . . ."[23]

One recruited agent, code-named "Magnate," engaged in defense production work for the U.S. Army and provided samples of armor, armored glass, and armored vests. As early as 1936, "Magnate" described to the NKVD his work on miniature "bugging" equipment that could be concealed in a briefcase. "The results are very good," the station reported to Moscow in January 1937. "We hope to use this apparatus for our work here. We'll send you by the next [diplomatic] post a complete set of blueprints and details. If we are interested in this type of briefcase, we can organize its production in our country. . . ."[24]

The creative "Magnate" also promoted other devices of comparable or even greater interest to his Soviet contacts because of their value to dictatorships, as reported in the same memorandum: "Now 'Magnate' is working on a stationary eavesdropping apparatus for hotels, cells for imprisonment pending trial, etc. . . . Such a device consists of a central station connected by wire with microphones placed in different rooms. An officer on duty can listen to a conversation in any room. If needed, conversations can be simultaneously recorded."[25]

Sources working for Eastman Kodak provided the NKVD's New York station with secret information concerning production of photographic and motion picture film as well as drawings of the latest optical devices being used by the company.[26] Some exchanges transcended espionage and became virtual business agreements. Thus one source, code-named "Frenchman" and known as an inventor of radio equipment, brokered a deal that was negotiated between the NKVD and an interested Soviet ministry to sell plans for a new model teletype. The ministry offered $6,000, but in the end, "Frenchman" struck a deal with the New York station to sell the equipment for only $4,000! The station chief offered the ministry other bargains from this same source: a model of "theater television" (then in its infancy) for which the ministry in question had offered $30,000 but which "Frenchman" would sell to the station for only $9,000, and "television for planes" marked down from $15,000 to $6–7,000. The transactions may not have been concluded.[27]

One invaluable source of information to the Soviets in 1935—on American companies and businessmen involved in illegal economic activities with Nazi Germany—was an American woman code-named "Zero," who worked for a special U.S. Senate committee headed by Gerald Nye, then investigating the American munitions industry. "Zero" passed to her Soviet contact, code-named "Green," secret reports from the U.S. commercial attaché in Berlin and from several consular officials. These reports concerned American companies filling German military orders and memoranda from the U.S. military attaché in Berlin that described German army and industrial efforts.[28] Reporting to Moscow on these documents, Peter Gutzeit praised "Zero's" value: "They also touch upon the war-chemical industry, the division in spheres of influence among the largest international weapons manufacturers, methods of bribery, connections with intelligence services, purely war-technical matters on different kinds of weapons and etc. Plus, they expose ways and methods of the Dupont Company's intelligence service's activities against the USSR."[29]

Because the Nye Committee often subpoenaed classified documents from State, War, Navy, and other governmental departments in connection with its work, "Zero" was an important source for Soviet intelligence. When the committee completed its work, the NKVD tried to arrange for "Zero" to join the State Department. But the effort proved unsuccessful, Gutzeit reported, in part because State tried not to employ Jews.*[30]

The 1936–39 Great Purge years in the Soviet Union disrupted scientific and technical espionage efforts, along with all other types of intelligence work, in the United States. Thus, one valuable Soviet agent, recruited by the GPU in Germany and married to an American woman, who emigrated with his wife to the United States, could not be used by the New York station because his brother had been arrested as a spy in Moscow.[31]

Steady nerves are a minimal requirement for successful espionage. Soviet operatives in the United States discovered in the 1930s that their most reliable American sources were not those who demanded payment for the theft of specific information or documents, but those individuals driven by an ideological belief in communism and the Soviet experiment. Paid informants worked mainly for U.S. defense-related industries, while many of the "believers" rose steadily through the ranks of the Roosevelt Administration's bureaucracy. Ideological reliability and access to top-secret scientific information, however, converged at times, most notably during the Second World War. Then, a small number of devoted Communist scientists, engineers, and technicians—despite enormous security barriers—gathered information for

---

* Another Soviet source on the Nye Committee, Alger Hiss, proved more successful in obtaining a State Department post in 1936. See pp. 40–41.

Soviet operatives on the making of the atomic bomb in the program to which Moscow assigned the code-name "Enormoz."*

THE PURSUIT OF
TROTSKYISTS AND MONARCHISTS

At the same time, during the thirties, that Soviet intelligence sought scientific and military secrets in the United States, it also devoted significant time and attention to monitoring, and occasionally trying to infiltrate, groups supporting Leon Trotsky (whose followers called themselves "Trotskyists" while pro-Stalin detractors preferred the supposedly more pejorative "Trotskyites"). "The American Trotskyite organization is the strongest in membership and financing among all the Trotskyite groupings," NKVD Major Pavel Fitin reported in September 1939 to then–Commissar of Internal Affairs Lavrenty Beria.[32] During the 1930s, Stalin's obsessive fear of Trotskyist moles in the ranks of the Soviet government saturated communications between Moscow and its field agents, some of whom sought contact with key foreign followers of Trotsky, such as their American leader James Cannon. "Our idea is to watch the Trotskyites through the Socialist Party since we do not have trustworthy agents inside the Trotskyist organization," Moscow told its New York station in the spring of 1937.[33]

Among those recruited to spy on Cannon was Louis Budenz, the editor of *Labor Age*, a small socialist magazine, who a decade later would describe his involvement in Soviet espionage to the FBI and congressional committees. Other socialist sources also reported on Trotskyist activities during these years to NKVD operatives in New York and San Francisco. One, code-named "Actor," even managed to gain access to Trotsky's inner circle and visit Trotsky in Mexico.[34] American agents played a vital role in Stalin's plans to eliminate his arch rival, which eventually succeeded when Trotsky was assassinated.

Old enemies often prove the most enduring and emotionally essential. Thus, Soviet intelligence, while assiduously probing the ranks of Trotskyists, also spent considerable time and energy focused on a ragtag residue of pro-monarchist groups, "Whites," who plotted among themselves the unlikely restoration of the Russian monarchy. Writing from

* Discussed in Chapter 9.

New York in August 1935, Peter Gutzeit tried to explain to a Moscow superior the problems involved in "concrete cultivations" of the "Whites" in America—small, fragmented bands compared to organizations in Europe. Such groups, he wrote, "lacked backbone" and funding, though he would try to add to the two agents already infiltrated into their ranks. Nor had his efforts proved more successful, Gutzeit acknowledged, among Ukrainian separatists in the United States.[35] Although his Moscow correspondent wrote back with requests for more information on some specific leaders, in reality Stalin and his nervous cohort—paraphrasing FDR's inaugural phrase—had "nothing to fear but fear itself" from pro-monarchist enclaves in the United States.

Of more serious concern to Soviet intelligence during this period were the energetic activities of pro-German and pro-Nazi organizations. Reports to Moscow described in detail a number of these groups and their effect upon powerful Americans such as the newspaper publisher William Randolph Hearst, whose antagonism toward the USSR was credited by Soviet intelligence to German influence. "It would be of considerable interest for us to acquire compromising material on Hearst concerning his connection (especially financial) with the Nazis," Moscow instructed its American stations. "It is desirable to acquire an internal source at Hearst's [organization] standing close to the head of this concern."[36] At least one such agent in the newspaper world (though not working for a Hearst paper), a *New York Post* reporter codenamed "Blin," volunteered information about the publisher, allegedly provided by a Hearst journalist.[37] But like so much else in operatives' reports on political surveillance during the 1930s, there was no apparent follow-up.

How seriously Moscow Center believed German influence to be a major threat to Soviet interests in the United States was evident in directions given to its American stations, such as this September 1935 description of goals:

a. exposure of the Nazis' work directed against our interests with respect both to worsening our relations with your country and intelligence work directed against our institutions in your country and on our territory;

b. exposure of Nazi agents in the state institutions of your country, first of all in the State Department and intelligence organizations;

c. exposure of Nazis' work against the fraternal organization of your country [the Communist Party of the United States].

Soviet strategy focused on directing public attention to Nazi anti-Semitism and, as a result, generating in Jewish organizations opposition to the Nazis' U.S. support groups.[38]

PENETRATING THE
U.S. GOVERNMENT—EARLY PROBES

The main assignment for Moscow's American stations after diplomatic recognition in 1933 was neither the pursuit of scientific and economic data nor the monitoring of deviant bands of "Whites" or Trotskyists. Far more urgent was the collection of information related to U.S. foreign policy, especially in Europe and the Far East, and gathering American government intelligence data concerning German and Japanese actions that affected the USSR's security.

Launching this new intelligence initiative exposed an urgent and immediate problem for Moscow in early–New Deal Washington: a virtual absence of useful sources. "At present we don't have any agents," began one possibly overstated April 1934 memorandum from the New York station regarding possible contacts in Washington: "It is necessary to start this work with a blank slate. In previous years' archives, we have found some people who were connected to our work, but because of a long break in our activities, the connection with them was lost."[39] By then, however, Moscow had begun to pursue its intelligence-gathering work directly from Washington in addition to its New York–based activities. (The San Francisco station remained primarily a base for gathering information on Japan, as elaborate recruitment instructions given to Soviet agents based in that city in 1934 appear not to have yielded results.)

Soviet intelligence's 1934 directives concerning operations in the United States remained sensitive to the constraints of diplomatic recognition:

> As a basis for our work in the USA we assume the principle of combining legal and illegal work. All the activities on finding useful and interesting people for us are carried out through legal possibilities. . . . Recruitment and working with an agent must be transferred completely to illegals. This dictates the need to have at the station's disposal minimally two illegal recruiters who would carry out the recruitments. [Presently] the station doesn't have people of this sort except for "Brit."[40]

"Brit" would not long remain the sole "illegal" working on recruitment for the NKVD. He was a transitional figure from the mainly economic focus of Soviet intelligence in America during the 1920s to the growing strategic and global political use of its American "listening post" during the thirties.

Originally, "Brit," whose real name was I. V. Volodarsky and whom the FBI knew as Armand Lavis Feldman, was sent to the United States to establish an oil analysis business. Later, he took part in a 1937 scheme by Moscow to purchase ships that could sail under the American flag in European waters, allowing Soviet intelligence another source of contact in the event of war.*[41]

The most effective Soviet operative in the earliest years of the Roosevelt Administration was Valentin Markin, code-named "Davis." Although he was based in New York City, he increasingly focused on an expanding number of Washington sources. It was Markin who established the procedures of that period for receiving newly arrived "illegals" from the Soviet Union. Their initial instructions appear simple in retrospect. In 1934, all Soviet "illegals" reaching New York stayed at the Hotel Taft in the heart of midtown Manhattan. Markin, the station chief, would locate the new arrival at the hotel and approach him with "Greetings from Fanny." If the response was, "Thank you. How is she?," work could begin.[42]

Markin had been one of the few talented professional Soviet intelligence operatives in the United States prior to diplomatic recognition, even managing to recruit agents within the State Department. But his superiors in Moscow questioned whether he could supervise a rapidly expanding set of Washington networks. Thus, in March 1934, one cable to Markin asked "whether you will be able to ensure the service of your clientele with your small apparatus according to the principles of our profession."[43]

Markin's major responsibility was to acquire information about U.S. foreign policy. Soviet intelligence's belief in America's critical global importance probably exceeded even that of the Roosevelt Administration at this time, as seen in these 1934 instructions from Moscow:

> In world politics, the U.S. is the determining factor. There are no problems, even those "purely" European, in whose solution America does not take part because of its economic and financial

---

* Volodarsky would later break with the NKVD and cooperate with the FBI.

strength. It plays a special role in the solution of the Far Eastern problem. That is why America must be well informed in European and Far Eastern matters, and its intelligence service is likely to play an active role. This situation raises the following extremely important problems for our intelligence in the U.S. (especially illegal): It is necessary that the agents we now have or intend to recruit provide us with documents and verified materials clarifying the U.S. position in the matters mentioned above and, especially, the U.S. position on the Far Eastern problem.

Therefore the station's task, besides getting materials from [State Department employees] "Willie" and "Daniel," reports by ambassadors . . . mainly [on] the situation in the countries where those ambassadors are stationed, is to develop means of getting materials reflecting the U.S. position on international questions, especially Japan, such as:

a. directives by the American government to its ambassadors; [and] b. information from navy attachés coming to Washington, especially on Japan and Germany.[44]

These areas of interest for Soviet intelligence would remain constant throughout the decade—from 1934, when its major sources of information at State were supposedly those individuals code-named "Willie" and "Daniel," to the years that followed, when new Moscow operatives would develop their own sources within the Department, including Noel Field, Laurence Duggan, and Alger Hiss.* "Willie" and "Daniel," whose real names were not contained in the Soviet files that discussed their work, were both paid informants. "Daniel" received $500 a month and, according to an exchange between NKVD administrators about "Willie's" stipend, "we propose to pay him $15,000 per year in order to take from him the maximum he can give."[45] In return, "Willie" provided Valentin Markin with numerous ambassadorial, consular, and military attaché reports from Europe and the Far East. "Daniel," who allegedly worked in the same section of State as "Willie," managed to filch transcripts of recorded conversations Secretary of State Cordell Hull and his assistants had with foreign ambassadors. Moscow considered the information "precious," its highest compliment, and instructed Markin to nurture the pair: "These agents ensure considerable acquisition of materials from the State Department. Therefore, we consider inexpedient any further penetration into

* See also Chapters 1 and 4.

the State Department either by legal or illegal operatives. The task is to develop the agents we already have."[46]

Unfortunately for Markin and his superiors, the agent handling "Willie" and "Daniel" was a freelance journalist code-named "Leo," who turned out to be a confidence man, deceiving Soviet intelligence in order to collect monthly stipends. After analyzing material delivered by "Leo" supposedly from "Daniel" and an agent code-named "Albert," Markin reluctantly concluded that virtually all the information and documents involved had actually come from only one source: "Willie." Neither Valentin Markin nor his assistant had ever met "Daniel" or "Albert," and this was reported to Moscow on November 27, 1934: "We assume there is no 'Daniel' or 'Albert' . . . and that [they] were created fictitiously by 'Leo' to increase his remuneration."[47] Moscow agreed and stopped paying both "Daniel's" $500 monthly stipend and "Albert's" $400.[48] Despite this creative concoction of nonexistent agents, however, Soviet intelligence continued to rely on "Leo" for several more years as a paid agent handling the genuine "Willie," though it did not inform him about others at State subsequently recruited.

But Markin's network was not limited to the State Department. In New York, where he continued to live, the station chief had at least four additional major sources, including one, code-named "James," who had served earlier as German consul in the city and was linked to German intelligence. Markin considered "James" a unique source of information about German activities in Europe and America. Two journalists provided economic information, and several others (including a New York City police officer) were included in this amalgam of agents. Among Markin's agent-recruiters was Hedda Gumperz, who, along with her writer-husband, Paul Massing, was actively involved in attracting to covert activity various New Deal officials such as Laurence Duggan and Noel Field.[49]

One later-legendary figure in Soviet intelligence circles entered the United States for the first time in 1934 as one of Valentin Markin's Taft Hotel "illegals." Itzhak Akhmerov, whom Whittaker Chambers later knew under the code-name "Bill," was code-named "Yung" by Markin in 1934. Akhmerov arrived in New York on April 23, 1934, and quickly began tasks for the network while pursuing English language studies at Columbia University.

The KGB archives contain a 1954 lecture delivered by a then-retired Akhmerov to young intelligence officers on the process of blending into an American identity. He noted the ease with which this could be achieved during the 1930s (and perhaps even today) by carefully restricting the number of one's relationships: "Switching from the status of a foreign student to the status of an American in such a large city as New York was not difficult."[50] Akhmerov found love and companionship in his new assignment when, several years later, he met and married Helen Lowry, the niece of American Communist Party leader Earl Browder. Lowry, code-named "Nelly," worked alongside her husband, serving as a courier between "legal" and "illegal" stations while maintaining a Washington residence where Akhmerov met his sources. Lowry secretly took Soviet citizenship and moved to Moscow with Akhmerov in 1939, remaining an NKVD agent.[51]

Only months after Akhmerov's arrival in the United States, in August 1934, Valentin Markin's death in a car accident provoked consternation within Soviet intelligence ranks. Fearful that American counterintelligence agents might stumble upon its covert work, Moscow ordered "illegals" such as Akhmerov to halt their activity and to destroy all documents in their possession.[52] Perhaps most troublesome was the fact that Markin's American partner in the business firm the Soviet operative had used as a cover was privy to his espionage. The partner also knew both Akhmerov and Markin's assistant, a Soviet operative code-named "King."[53] Markin's partner (according to a cable from "King" to Moscow on the situation) "dreams of going to our country" and tried unsuccessfully to persuade Markin's mistress, also an American, to settle in the Soviet Union. Nor did the cleanup problems stop there. Markin kept money in a bank safety-deposit box, the cable continued, and also stored there "his notes, written in Russian."[54]

While "King" and Akhmerov dealt with the aftermath of Valentin Markin's untimely death, they were suddenly confronted with a far more serious threat to the security of their fledgling Washington operation. Akhmerov described the situation in an October 26, 1934, memorandum to Moscow:

> Meeting "Leo" in the center [at the State Department] two weeks ago, "Willie" said that B. [U.S. Ambassador to the Soviet Union William Bullitt] from your city [Moscow] communicated here to the center that the contents of his reports was known in your city. "Willie" was terribly embarrassed and anxious. "Willie" was ill nervously for a couple of days. The assistant to the Secretary of this firm [Secretary Hull's assistant] questioned . . . "Willie" about the possible leak of these reports here in the center. The assistant to the Secretary charged "Willie" with checking the employees and investigating the department headed by "Willie."

"Willie" says [thinks] that a corresponding investigation of this case is being carried out by firms of our type.

We ask you to observe maximum caution in sending reports from B. to offices neighboring yours. The cunning of B., his abilities, sociable disposition, and contacts with high-ranking persons in your city give him an opportunity to touch many people. An indirect hint in a conversation may be enough. . . ."[55]

Although no response from Moscow to Akhmerov's cable appeared in the NKVD records, within weeks Markin's assistant, "King," had been assigned to another country.[56] A new station chief, a Soviet operative named Boris Bazarov, code-named "Nord," arrived from Moscow in December 1934 with the following priority assignments:

1. to acquire data about the activities of the U.S. State Department (incoming and outgoing documents on important countries);
2. to organize acquisition of information on the War and Navy Departments as well as on the aviation ministry [sic] . . . ;
3. to acquire scientific-technical documentation about production by the Dupont Company.[57]

By that time, a number of radical New Deal officials were being recruited for Soviet espionage in Washington, some by Harold Ware, an American official in the Agriculture Department. Although Ware's group had been operating without connections to Valentin Markin's agents, one agent recruiter, Whittaker Chambers, briefly served as a link between the two networks.

Meanwhile, the new NKVD station chief in New York, Bazarov, had his hands full reorganizing Markin's tightly centralized group of sources; his courier, Chambers, knew all the various agents. "We have a situation in which a failure at one point in the organization will cause a failure of the entire organization," Moscow informed Bazarov, a problem that would recur in future years among Soviet intelligence's American networks.[58] Nor was Moscow pleased with the information being provided by "James," the German operative, whom it ordered cut adrift.[59] Bazarov sought to reorganize his unit's work, cooperating closely with Gutzeit's "legal" station and others (for example, in the recruitment of a U.S. Congressman, described elsewhere in these pages). At least one of Bazarov's assigned agents was later denounced by Moscow as a Trotskyist and "people's enemy,"[60] charges that would await Bazarov himself upon his return to the Soviet Union several years later.[61]

Although plagued by these signs of internal dissension, by mercenary American sources, and by bad luck—such as Valentin Markin's untimely death—within a year or two after diplomatic recognition, Soviet intelligence had built a solid foundation for its U.S. networks. Its most productive American agents in the years to come would be drawn primarily from the ranks of adventurous antifascists and doctrinaire Communists, often with the overt assistance of American Communist Party leadership.

· HISS, CHAMBERS, AND THE WARE GROUP ·

Competition was keen among Soviet operatives in 1934 to establish an agent beachhead within the Roosevelt Administration. One of the most effective early efforts was spearheaded by Joszef Peter, a Hungarian-born spymaster who worked closely with Earl Browder and the Communist Party of the United States (CPUSA) as well as with the Comintern's intelligence units. Peter (also known as "J. Peters" and a variety of other underground pseudonyms)* shifted Whittaker Chambers ("Karl") in August 1934 from his previous duties in New York City to a new assignment in Washington, where he began working as a courier between Peter and Harold Ware's group of covert sources:

> I understood that most of the members of this group were employed in "New Deal Agencies" [Chambers later recalled]. According to what Peters [Joszef Peter] told me, it was his "dream" to penetrate the "old line agencies," such as the Navy, State, Interior, etc. I was to learn the setup and the personnel of the present apparatus [Ware's recruits] and attempt to build a parallel apparatus . . . using certain members of the Ware Group at first and then branching out. Consequently, about the end [of summer] or

---

* Joszef Peter was deported to Hungary in 1949 after extensive questioning by the FBI about his underground involvement. He subsequently became a leading official of the Hungarian Communist Party and government. When Allen Weinstein interviewed the aged Peter in Budapest in 1975, Weinstein asked him whether he had ever thought of returning to the United States. "Once," Peter responded, laughing. "The fellows in the party wanted to throw me an eightieth birthday dinner. I went to the American Consulate and began filling out the application for a visa. Then I came to a question on the form about whether I had ever used an alias and, if so, to list all aliases. I put down the form and walked out."

in the fall of 1934, I made my first trip to Washington, D.C., where I met Harold Ware by prearrangement.[62]

Chambers later identified as members of the group a small coven of New Deal officials, most then working for the Agricultural Adjustment Agency (AAA), among them—in addition to Harold Ware and Alger Hiss—John Abt, Henry Collins, John Herrmann, Victor Perlo, Lee Pressman, Nathaniel Weyl, and Nathan Witt.* Most had abandoned positions in the private sector to become New Dealers in Washington. (After breaking with communism, several members of the group, including Pressman though not Alger Hiss, would acknowledge their earlier Communist Party membership, recalling that their activities included collecting CPUSA dues while discussing Marxist theory and current issues.) Gradually, in 1934, various participants, including Hiss, added the theft of government documents to their agenda, materials that Chambers would convey to Joszef Peter and other Soviet operatives in New York.[63]

One non-Communist witness to these activities, writer Josephine Herbst, who was married at the time to Ware Group member John Herrmann, later provided confirmation, as did Chambers and another former member, Nathaniel Weyl, of its activities. Interviewed in 1949, Josephine Herbst described her husband as "a member of a group headed by Mr. Harold Ware . . . of people holding small and unimportant positions in various branches of the Government and . . . organized for the purpose of collecting information for the use primarily of the Communist Party in New York City." Those involved, Herbst recalled, "took great pride in their sense of conspiracy," and the CPUSA's "ultimate purpose . . . in setting up 'cells' of this kind . . . was to provide for an organization capable of using influence and obtaining information in the event of a world or national crisis. . . . On one occasion, I saw in my apartment certain documents that had been taken from Government offices by members of the 'cell' . . . for transmission to New York."[64]

---

* On Alger Hiss, see also Chapters 1, 4, and 12. On Victor Perlo and his later "group," see Chapter 10. The Ware Group itself disbanded in 1935 after Harold Ware died in an automobile accident. Most of its members remained actively involved as Communist sources within the government but in other venues, a number closely linked to the CPUSA. Among many other sources on the Ware Group, see Earl Latham's balanced assessment in *The Communist Controversy in Washington* (New York: Atheneum paperback, 1969).

Chambers was introduced by John Herrmann to Herbst "simply as Karl" in the summer of 1934—"a heavy, tall, thickset man with a heavy opaque face, thick skin and mournful eyes . . . not too carefully groomed . . . kindly, but rather melancholy"—and she was unaware of Chambers's relationship to Soviet intelligence beyond the Ware Group's links to the CPUSA. Sharing a common interest in literature and writing, Herbst and Chambers became friends: "[H]e spoke to me of his difficulties and he told me that his wife and child lived in New Jersey. . . . He always seemed to be in anxiety and fear and always on the run. . . . [H]e was a courier and . . . his job was to make contacts high within the United States government."[65]

Josephine Herbst also confirmed that Alger Hiss became a person of considerable interest to "Karl" at this time. She recalled, as did Chambers and (at times) Hiss, that the two men first met in August 1934 shortly after Chambers began his work as a Soviet courier in Washington: " 'Karl' told me of such a meeting . . . everything I know about [Alger and Priscilla Hiss] was told to me by 'Karl,' Harold Ware or someone else," presumably John Herrmann. The reason that Chambers and Herrmann considered Hiss valuable, Herbst recalled, was obvious: "Chambers and John [Herrmann] . . . regarded Hiss as an important prospect to solicit for the purpose of getting papers. This was a task that was to be handled by Chambers because it was his function to make contacts with more important people in the Government service."[66]

What made Hiss distinctive among the Ware Group's dozen or more members was the fact that, in July 1934, he left the AAA to assume a new position on the legal staff of the Nye Committee, a special congressional investigating body established under the leadership of Senator Gerald Nye to probe the impact of foreign and domestic munitions makers on U.S. policy during and after the First World War. Employees at the AAA had access only to materials within that agency's limited domestic mandate. However, the Nye Committee—where Chambers and Hiss met barely a month after the latter began his work there—received a voluminous mass of past and current classified documents from the State, War, and Navy Departments (among other sources) dealing with munitions and foreign policy questions of major interest to the Soviet Union. Josephine Herbst later recalled, as did Chambers, that the latter, to take advantage of Hiss's new responsibilities, had discussed recruiting Hiss away from the Ware Group to become the first member of a new "parallel apparatus" of Soviet agents within the American government. Moscow acknowledged receiving deliveries of documents from a source or sources within the Nye Committee, one of whom was Alger Hiss, who began at this time his half-decade relationship with the Communist writer-courier-agent handler whom he knew as "Karl."[*67]

SOURCE AND COURIER:
THE HISS-CHAMBERS RELATIONSHIP

Hiss and Chambers worked together as Soviet source and courier from late 1934 until the latter's defection from the underground in 1938, and despite extraordinary differences in background, careers, and interests, they (and their wives) developed a personal bond. Alger Hiss was born into a prominent Baltimore family, disrupted at an early age by his father's suicide. Even as a young man, Hiss impressed others as intelligent, handsome, and extremely well mannered. He excelled both as an undergraduate at Johns Hopkins University and in his studies at Harvard Law School, where he became a protégé of Professor (and later Supreme Court Justice) Felix Frankfurter. Through Frankfurter, Hiss obtained a coveted clerkship with the Court's aging eminence Justice Oliver Wendell Holmes. By then, Hiss had married a New York writer and art historian, Priscilla Fansler, who later assisted in his Soviet underground work by retyping State Department documents for transmission. Alger Hiss worked for several years after his clerkship at a prominent New York law firm before heading to Washington and a post with the AAA in 1933, and both he and Priscilla were also active members of various radical groups. Because of this background, the Hisses later mixed easily with New Dealers of their own generation and with older, more influential figures in the Roosevelt Administration.[68]

Prior to meeting Alger Hiss, Whittaker Chambers's life had been much less charmed and far more turbulent. He, too, had lacked a stable paternal relationship—his father was a minor journalist who was frequently absent from home and, when there, frequently drunk. From his earliest schooldays, Chambers displayed an unusual ability as a writer and linguist, and while attending Columbia College during the 1920s, he cultivated a circle of friends largely focused on literary and

---

* For the complete story of the Hiss-Chambers relationship and its aftermath from the 1930s to the present, see Allen Weinstein, *Perjury: The Hiss-Chambers Case*, rev. ed. (New York: Random House, 1997) and Sam Tanenhaus, *Whittaker Chambers: A Biography* (New York: Random House, 1997).

artistic careers. But Chambers dropped out of college to lead a bohemian existence in and around New York City for several years until he gravitated toward membership in the CPUSA during the mid-1920s. There, he found a niche as a journalist, writing first for the *Daily Worker* and then for the *New Masses*, and marrying Esther Shemitz, another young radical and an aspiring artist.

In the spring of 1932, Chambers was recruited for "secret work" by a leading party official, Max Bedacht, a member of the CPUSA's Central Committee, who instructed him, with Chambers's acquiescence, to leave the *New Masses*'s staff, where Chambers had become a well-known "proletarian writer" and translator* and to disappear from other "open" Communist circles. Bedacht led Chambers to a meeting with an old friend from the *Daily Worker*, John Loomis Sherman, who was already involved in covert activities. Sherman, in turn, introduced Chambers that same day to Valentin Markin ("Herbert"), a Russian operative with whom he worked as an agent until Markin's death in August 1934. The subsequent disbanding of Markin's network led Joszef Peter that same month to identify a replacement assignment for Chambers as a Washington–to–New York courier.[69]

After their initial meeting, Hiss and Chambers, source and courier, developed a measure of rapport not unlike the personal link between Laurence Duggan and Itzhak Akhmerov. During the summer of 1935, for example, Chambers ("Karl" to the Hisses) lived for several months in an apartment rented by Hiss, and on other occasions, Esther and Whittaker Chambers and their infant son stayed with the Hisses while looking for their own apartment. At one point, Hiss even transferred to Chambers title to an old automobile he was no longer using, and several years later made Chambers a loan to buy another car.

Both Hiss and Chambers would later recall their various meetings, sometimes including wives, although the two men differed in recalling their number and meaning.† Chambers even purchased in Westminster, Maryland, farm property where he lived for the remainder of his life—the same property on which Hiss had previously placed, and then withdrawn, a deposit! Overwhelming evidence supports Chambers's

---

* Chambers's translations included the American edition of Felix Salten's children's classic *Bambi*, which appeared in 1928.

† When confronted in 1948 with Chambers's description of his involvement in Soviet espionage, Hiss asserted, despite a considerable body of evidence, that he had known Chambers only briefly during the mid-1930s, not as a collaborator in Communist espionage but innocently as a freelance journalist.

account of a deepening friendship and intimacy between the two families grounded in Alger Hiss's involvement in the Communist underground. Had they known of this blatant indifference to normal, cautious rules of tradecraft related to meetings between couriers and sources, Chambers's Soviet overseers would have been appalled at the strong personal friendship.[70]

The cross-cutting relationship among distinct Soviet intelligence units in the United States was illustrated vividly by Whittaker Chambers's six-year journey (1932–38) through the Communist underground. Chambers, recruited initially by CPUSA official Max Bedacht, first worked for New York's GPU station chief Valentin Markin. But he also maintained close contact with another Soviet "illegal" in New York, military intelligence (GRU) station chief Alexander Ulanovski ("Ulrich"), who returned to the Soviet Union in 1934, the year Markin died.* Then, in August 1934, Joszef Peter, who maintained close links to both the Comintern and CPUSA networks, brought Chambers to Washington. There he began an association with Harold Ware's group, which, in the New Deal's politically relaxed environment, operated as both a Marxist study group and a transmission belt for stolen government documents.[71]

When the group disbanded after Ware's death the following year, its members scattered among various party cells. Chambers continued to receive pilfered material from Hiss and other Washington sources, delivering it in 1935–36 to at least two different individuals: Joszef Peter (CPUSA and Comintern) and Itzhak Akhmerov (NKVD), whom Chambers knew as "Bill." Peter even suggested at one point, according to Chambers, that American Communist agents such as himself *sell* documents to Soviet operatives, using the funds to finance CPUSA activities, a suggestion Akhmerov promptly rejected.[72]

In 1936, Chambers changed units a final time when he began working primarily for the newly arrived head of Soviet military intelligence (GRU) in the United States, Colonel Boris Bykov, with whom Chambers would deal until his defection two years later. By then, Alger Hiss had concluded a rapid, upwardly mobile career climb from the AAA (1933) to the Nye Committee (1934) to a brief (1935–36) stint at the Justice Department (thus his underground code name "Lawyer") and, in

---

* When Allen Weinstein interviewed her in Israel in 1977, Ulanovski's widow, Nadya Ulanovskaya, confirmed Chambers's account of Soviet intelligence operations in the United States during the 1931–34 period. Weinstein, *Perjury*, pp. 105–10.

the fall of 1936, to a new post as aide to Assistant Secretary of State Francis B. Sayre. While still at Justice, Hiss unknowingly crossed Soviet intelligence's jurisdictional lines and attempted to recruit for his GRU unit a friend and colleague, Noel Field, who was already involved with Hedda Gumperz in "secret work" for the NKVD, generating a flow of embarrassed explanatory cable traffic by Gumperz, Akhmerov, and other Soviet operatives.* Shortly after Hiss's arrival at State in 1936, Bykov instructed Chambers to purchase Bokhara rugs for Hiss, Harry Dexter White, and two other government sources as tokens of appreciation from Moscow, the type of tangible gift Akhmerov had declined to make to Laurence Duggan when urged to do so. Meanwhile, Chambers and his wife continued their social relationship with the Hisses, and Alger Hiss, after arriving at State, began to convey classified documents and information to "Karl" on subjects of interest to Soviet intelligence.[73]

DEFECTION

In late 1937, Chambers began planning to abandon his work as a GRU courier and defect. For several months, he held back from Bykov a number of State Department items he had received from Hiss—specifically four handwritten notes, sixty-five crowded, single-spaced pages of retyped cables, and three rolls of microfilm—as (in his phrase) "life preservers," to be used to warn his Communist associates not to seek retribution lest he reveal the material to American authorities. The Hiss materials Chambers retained included a mass of important information related to major European and Far Eastern developments of obvious concern and interest to Moscow.[†] Hiss knew nothing of "Karl's" plans, obviously, nor did another of Chambers's major government sources, Treasury Department official Harry Dexter White, from

---

* See Chapter 1 for a complete account of this episode.

† For an extended analysis of the contents of Chambers's documentary cache, see Weinstein, *Perjury*, pp. 204–35. Prior to release of the VENONA documents in 1995–96 and publication of this book, the documents saved by Whittaker Chambers represented the most extensive tangible evidence of Soviet espionage within the U.S. government during the Stalin era outside of Soviet intelligence archives. Since military intelligence (GRU) archives were not available for this or any other book, we have been able to further clarify Alger Hiss's role as a Soviet agent only through his occasional appearance in NKVD/NKGB archives as cited in Chapters 1, 4, and 12.

whom Chambers had received (and kept) four pages of handwritten notes on important Treasury and State Department business. Finally, Chambers squirreled away two rolls of microfilmed documents from the Navy Bureau of Aeronautics, courtesy of yet another source.[74]

Whittaker Chambers defected on or about April 10, 1938, when he and his family left their Baltimore apartment to go into hiding in a Daytona Beach, Florida, bungalow. He and his wife, Esther, took turns on nighttime guard duty, fearing pursuit, and during the days Chambers worked on a commissioned translation he had obtained through a sympathetic publisher.

Although Chambers's defection may have been partly provoked by disaffection from Communist dogma and Soviet practice, survival, as his letters to friends at the time and their recollections confirm, was uppermost in his mind. In July 1937, Chambers had been instructed by his GRU superiors to travel to Moscow, supposedly to brief military intelligence officials. Since the previous year, rumors were widespread among agents about the purges underway within the USSR, including both the NKVD and GRU. Chambers decided, as did several leading Soviet operatives in the United States at the time, to stall and disregard the summons to return to certain arrest and (minimally) imprisonment.

During these months, he watched his friend and fellow agent John Sherman prepare and execute *his* defection, which appears to have served as Chambers's model. Beginning in December 1937, "Karl" began holding back his "life preservers" while also approaching several trusted anti-Stalinist friends (including art critic Meyer Schapiro and writer Robert Cantwell) to ask their help in his flight. American newspapers had begun reporting the defection or disappearance of other Soviet operatives, and in mid-April 1938, Chambers and his family left Baltimore and quietly moved to Daytona Beach without informing family, friends—or his underground associates.[75]

In the months that followed Chambers's disappearance, several family members and friends whom the defector contacted told him of visits from Communists acting on behalf of Joszef Peter and Boris Bykov and seeking his whereabouts. Bykov himself came to see Chambers's literary agent, Maxim Lieber, urging Lieber "to go and find Chambers." While in hiding, fear gave way to reflection, and what had begun for Chambers as an attempt to escape Stalinist retribution now became a review of—and rejection of—his commitment to communism.

In the early fall, Chambers transferred his "life preserver" documents for safekeeping to his wife's nephew in Brooklyn, with instructions to turn the package over to U.S. government authorities in the event of his death. He even appeared at an October 1938 gathering in New York of former anti-Stalinist radical friends and acquaintances — among them the critic Lionel Trilling and philosopher Sidney Hook — but since the group did not know of his break with communism, and many believed him to be an active Soviet agent, an abashed Chambers departed quickly. One leading Comintern agent, Otto Katz, known for his role in tracking down and assisting in the murder of key Soviet intelligence defectors in Europe, visited several of Chambers's friends seeking information on his whereabouts, further confirming the latter's fear of reprisal. After learning about Katz's inquiries, Chambers wrote Meyer Schapiro that he had been in touch with his former underground colleagues, warning them against continuing their pursuit:

> I wrote them through Washington that [Katz's] hunt amused me. . . . I sent them some photographic copies of handwritten matters the appearance of which would seriously embarrass them. . . . I said that at the first sign of monkey-business on their part, I would seek protection *bei einem amerikanischen Festungsgefaengnis, hostet was das persoenlich mag, denn wir haben eine Krise der Verzweiflung erreicht* [in an American prison, whatever the personal cost, given the crisis of despair involved].[76]

In December 1938, Chambers visited his friend journalist Herbert Solow, an anti-Stalinist, who had been urging Chambers without success to tell his full story to U.S. government officials or, at least, to write about it. In a memo written later that day, Solow noted of Chambers: "He also feels hesitant about breaking his story open because he does not wish to cause trouble to some agent whom he regards as a sincere and devoted person." During the Christmas season, however, Chambers paid a visit to that friend and his wife, Alger and Priscilla Hiss, with results that apparently ended his reticence over full public disclosure. "Happy New Year, and how!" he wrote Solow the following month. "Remember I told you I didn't have stomach for [disclosure] when I last saw you. Since then I've seen two old friends: do you know that everything is going right along the way I left it? These encounters gave me back the necessary iron."[77]

That same month, Chambers wrote Meyer Schapiro describing in more detail his meeting with the Hisses:

> We were very close indeed. Recently the wife told me that my occasional comments (the only form of letting off steam I dared

risk) on the Soviet Union were "mental masturbation"—the rank obscenity of cultured women! I was more shocked to hear her use such an expression than at the charge. Further, she said she had just read over the minutes of the [Moscow purge] Trials and anybody who could doubt they were guilty . . . The husband told me that the world is tottering on the verge of proletarian revolution. . . . Well, that's the type I meant.

Chambers also paid visits during this period to three other government sources for whom he had served as courier—Harry Dexter White, A. George Silverman, and Henry Julian Wadleigh—also apparently not persuading any of them to sever relations with Soviet intelligence.[*][78]

In 1939, Chambers wrote and tried, with Solow's assistance, to sell several articles on the Communist underground in America and his work in it. He was not successful. That year, Solow introduced him to another anti-Communist journalist, Isaac Don Levine. He, in turn, brought Chambers to meet Walter Krivitsky, a high-ranking Soviet intelligence officer who had defected in Western Europe and was now, also fearful of retribution, living in hiding near Washington. The two men talked through the night about their respective underground experiences and became close friends.[†][79]

In April 1939, a year after he ceased work as a courier, Chambers began a new life as a staff writer for *Time*. His friend Robert Cantwell, who worked for the magazine, had been describing the talented defector's break with communism to *Time* editor T. S. Matthews, who met Chambers and offered him a position. For the next few months, Chambers settled into his new routine. After the Nazi-Soviet Pact was signed on August 23, 1939, however, Isaac Don Levine visited him with news that Krivitsky had begun informing U.S. and British authorities about Soviet agents within the two governments. Levine urged Chambers to step forward also and to expose the sources whom he had known in the government. Fearing his own arrest on espionage charges, however, Chambers agreed to do so on condition that he meet personally with President Roosevelt and receive a guarantee of immunity from prose-

---

* After the Hiss-Chambers case broke in 1948, Chambers described to the FBI and other investigators his visit to the Hisses. At a pretrial deposition for a slander suit filed against him by Hiss, he recalled of this last encounter: "Mrs. Hiss was extremely unfriendly and referred to my doubts about Communism as mental masturbation." Wadleigh also confirmed his unexpected visit from Chambers. (Weinstein, *Perjury*, p. 234n.)

† On Krivitsky's activities in the United States, see Chapter 7.

cution. Levine took this proposal to FDR's appointments secretary, Marvin McIntyre, who suggested instead that the defector meet with the President's chief adviser on internal security matters, Assistant Secretary of State Adolf A. Berle, Jr., a proposal Levine persuaded the reluctant Chambers to accept.

The three men—Levine, Chambers, and Berle—met at the latter's home on the evening of September 2. Levine introduced Chambers only as "Mr. X," a former courier for Soviet intelligence. After their conversation ended, Berle drafted extensive notes of Chambers's statements, having assured his visitors that the memorandum would be sent directly to Roosevelt.[80]

Berle titled his memo "Underground Espionage Agent," and Levine, returning to his hotel, outlined his own recollections of those whom Chambers had named. Both Berle's memo and Levine's list included (quoting Levine): "[Laurence] Duggan, Hiss [Alger's brother, Donald, whose first name Levine had forgotten], Alger Hiss, [Noel] Field, [Julian] Wadley [sic] . . . Nat Witt, [Lee] Pressman, Treasury-Frank Coe (A. Gross), Mr. [Harry Dexter] White . . . John Abt . . . Peters [Joszef Peter], Lockwood Curry [Lauchlin Currie]." Berle's more carefully drafted notes proceeded name by name, department by department, referring specifically and repeatedly to "underground" spying rather than simply secret Communist associations. One long passage describes "Peters" (Joszef Peter) as "responsible for Washington Sector" and "after 1929—head of CP Underground." Noel Field is described, correctly, as one of Hedda Gumperz's contacts and both Field and Duggan as Communists, although "Duggan's relationship was casual."[81]

Chambers described a far more than "casual" involvement in the case of Alger Hiss, however, as Berle's memorandum noted:

Alger Hiss
Ass't. to Sayre—CP—37
Member of the Underground Com.—Active . . .

Although in the years that followed, Berle and his staff, based on Chambers's information, tried and eventually succeeded in pressuring Laurence Duggan into leaving the State Department, no similar persuasion was used with Alger Hiss for reasons that remain obscure. Berle delayed checking on the accuracy of his visitor's allegations against Hiss until 1941, when the latter's friend Dean Acheson, himself a leading official at State, and Felix Frankfurter both assured Berle that "Mr. X's" allegations were groundless.[82]

Alger Hiss continued to rise in importance at the State Department, untroubled by the charges that would effectively sidetrack his friend Laurence Duggan's career, while Whittaker Chambers's talents brought him promotions and growing influence as a writer and then editor at *Time*. The two former co-conspirators and friends, source and courier respectively of confidential State Department documents, did not meet again for almost a decade after their unsatisfactory Christmas 1938 encounter. When they finally did, it would be as historic and implacable adversaries.

CHAPTER 3

❖

Love and Loyalties, I: The Case of Martha Dodd

C ONSIDER THIS IMPLAUSIBLE PLOT for a spy novel: President Franklin Roosevelt sends to Hitler's Germany as U.S. Ambassador in 1933 an old friend, a well-known historian and vocal opponent of the Nazi regime. The Ambassador's daughter—young, beautiful, bored, and bitterly anti-Nazi—begins a love affair with a handsome Soviet diplomat in Berlin.

The Ambassador's daughter then volunteers her services to Soviet intelligence. These include access to secret embassy and State Department business, friendships with President Roosevelt and First Lady Eleanor Roosevelt as well as with a number of other highly placed Americans, and entry into German and American power elites. Because of her devotion to the Soviet diplomat and to communism, our would-be Mata Hari even launches love affairs with leading Nazis and other notables. She pleads for official Soviet permission to marry her reluctant lover but never learns that his entire intimate relationship with her has been guided by Moscow intelligence officials.

The Ambassador's daughter returns to the United States at the conclusion of her father's service in Germany. She continues to spy for the Soviets, however, even after her lover's departure for Moscow. Knowledge of his execution during the purges of the late 1930s is kept from her by NKVD operatives in America. Although still in love with the diplomat, she marries a wealthy American Communist whom she involves in her espionage activities. In this, they are joined by yet another Communist family member, her brother, whose long-shot race for Congress is encouraged and funded by Soviet intelligence.

During the 1950s, with Cold War tensions at their height, the Ambassador's daughter and her husband seek sanctuary in the Communist bloc from an indictment brought by a Red-hunting congressional committee. Unable to adjust to the post-Stalin Soviet Union, however, the couple live out their lives in Prague.

Much of this story was alleged or suspected by FBI counterintelligence agents and by McCarthy-era House and Senate investigators. But the remarkable tale of Martha Dodd, the daughter of U.S. Ambassador to Germany William Dodd, has emerged fully only from her Soviet intelligence file in Moscow.

Surviving NKVD records do not describe the initial contacts between Dodd and her diplomat-lover Boris Vinogradov. But their romance had matured sufficiently by late March 1934 for Moscow to dispatch the following set of instructions to its Berlin station chief:

> Let Boris Vinogradov know that we want to use him for the realization of an affair we are interested in. . . . According to our data, the mood of his acquaintance (Martha Dodd) is quite ripe for finally drawing her into our work. Therefore we ask Vinogradov to write her a warm friendly letter [and] to invite her to a meeting in Paris where . . . they will carry out necessary measures to draw Martha into our work.[1]

The lovers met in Paris and, that summer, again in Moscow where Martha traveled as a tourist.[2] They saw each other regularly after that in Berlin. "Currently the case with the American (Martha Dodd) is proceeding in the following way," Vinogradov wrote to Moscow on June 5, 1935: "Now she is in Berlin, and I received a letter from her in which she writes that she still loves me and dreams of marrying me. It is possible to work with her only with help from [our] 'good relations.'"[3]

Dissatisfied with Vinogradov's progress in preparing Dodd for agent work, the NKVD recalled the diplomat to Moscow shortly thereafter and assigned as Dodd's contact a Berlin correspondent for the newspaper *Izvestia*, Comrade Bukhartsev. At a diplomatic reception he introduced himself to Martha Dodd, who was given the code name "Liza." According to "Emir" (Bukhartsev's code name), she pledged to cooperate in passing along information.[4] An internal NKVD memorandum in Moscow written during this period described Dodd's commitment to the cause:

Martha argues that she is a convinced partisan of the Communist Party and the USSR. With the State Department's knowledge, Martha helps her father in his diplomatic work and is aware of all his [ambassadorial] affairs. The entire Dodd family hates National Socialists [Nazis]. Martha has interesting connections that she uses in getting information for her father. She has intimate relations with some of her acquaintances. . . . Martha claims that the main interest of her life is to assist secretly the revolutionary cause. She is prepared to use her position for work in this direction, provided that the possibility of failure and of discrediting her father can be eliminated. She claimed that a former official of the Soviet Embassy in Berlin—Boris Vinogradov—has had intimate relations with her.[5]

Under Bukhartsev's supervision, Martha Dodd plunged into secret work, even relating to her Soviet contact (among other things) Ambassador Dodd's private conversations. Meanwhile, her absent lover, Boris Vinogradov, had been reassigned to diplomatic duties in Bucharest. Martha's devotion and future expectations, mingled with acknowledgment of a more recent love affair, emerged in this October 1936 letter to Vinogradov:

Boris, this week it was a year since I saw you last. On the 8th I gave you a farewell kiss at the railway station, and since then we haven't seen one another. But I never, not for a minute, forgot you and everything you gave me in my life. This week, every night I thought about you—every night, and about that night we had such a stupid and mean quarrel—do you forgive me? I was scared and in a wild condition that night because I knew that I wouldn't see you for so long. I strongly wanted you to stay with me that night and forever, and I knew that I would never be able to have you. What have you been doing all this time? Have you been thinking about me and asking yourself how my personal life has gone?

From various sources I know that soon you will go home. Will you go via Berlin? Write me and let me know your plans. I would like to see you once more.

On December 8 I will be at home all night. Won't you call me, won't you talk to me from Bucharest—I want so much to hear your voice again—and on the 8th it will be the anniversary of our folly. We should blame our cowardice for this absence. Please, call me that night.

You may have heard about me indirectly. I have lived and thought many things since I saw you last time. You must know about it.

Armand is still here—but you must know that he means nothing to me now—as long as you are still alive—nobody can mean anything to me as long as you are alive.[6]

Martha's active personal life did not prevent her from focusing attention on her new career as a Soviet agent, as Bukhartsev reported to Moscow in January 1936:

For the last 2–3 weeks, I met with [Dodd] several times. At the first meeting, she told me about Bullitt's [U.S. Ambassador to France William Bullitt] swinish behavior during his sojourn in Berlin. According to her, Bullitt severely scolded the USSR in the American Embassy, arguing that in the next few months the Japanese would capture Vladivostok and the Russians would do nothing against it. . . . All of this exasperated the American Ambassador Dodd, who reported [the talks in a] letter to Washington. . . .

During previous meetings [Martha Dodd] frankly expressed her willingness to help the Soviet Embassy with her information. Now she is studying hard the theory of communism [and] "Matters of Leninism" by Stalin. Her teacher is [Arvid] Harnack* to whom she goes often. According to her, she now has to hide her Communist convictions due to her father's official status. This year her father will retire, and then she will be able to conduct Communist activities more openly.

However, this circumstance does not prevent her from maintaining rather intimate relations with Louis-Ferdinand, the Crown Prince's son. According to [Dodd], this is a perfect disguise, because those who earlier treated her suspiciously because of her open relations with Vinogradov now consider her previous passion "hearty" rather than "political."[7]

Martha continued to mingle her roles as courtesan, agent, and student of communism in her relationship with Bukhartsev. Thus she reported to the Russian in March 1936 the German industrialist Krupp's conversation with the American Consul in Cologne while, at the same

---

* Harnack, recruited in Berlin in August 1935, later headed the important Soviet espionage ring *Rote Kapelle* (Red Orchestra) in Nazi Germany during World War II.

time, requesting some English-language volumes of Lenin's works.[8] That September, Bukhartsev was recalled to Moscow. He was replaced as her Berlin contact by another Soviet operative, one Gnedin (code-named "Pioneer"). Subsequently, the NKVD files note that Martha Dodd was informed of Bukhartsev's execution in February 1937 as "a Gestapo agent."[9]

One of the NKVD's more prudish Moscow officials, after reading Dodd's October 1936 love letter to Vinogradov, noted on the document: "This amorality must be stopped."[10] In late October 1936, the NKVD's Berlin station reported Martha Dodd's willingness to follow all directives from Soviet intelligence, agreeing even to remain in Berlin as an agent after her father's departure the following year.[11]

Like other Western Communist agents, however, Dodd knew of the purges under way in the Soviet Union but was confused over their meaning and extent. Had Vinogradov fallen victim to repression? Finally, she heard from him. The KGB archives have preserved this January 29, 1937, letter from Martha to the Soviet diplomat, responding to his letter from Poland, his latest assignment:

> Honey, I'm so glad to get news from you and to know that you are finally in Warsaw. . . . You can't imagine, honey, how often you were with me, how I have been constantly thinking about you, worrying about you and craving to see you, how I adjusted to the inevitable when I heard the first news* and how I was glad to know the truth. I want to see you so much, honey. Couldn't I come before the end of the month? I would like to come on February 6, I think . . . and to stay for about a week. It is extremely important for me to see you and I promise to do it as soon as possible. I would like to stay in a small hotel not far from you, and I want nobody to know I'm there because I don't want to be entertained. I only want to see you as much as possible incognito. Probably, we'll be able to leave from Warsaw to the countryside for one or two days. I will come alone. After all, my parents quite agree that I do what I want. I am 28 and very independent![12]

Reverting to her agent's role, Dodd then requested NKVD permission to travel to Moscow via Warsaw for several days to discuss her future work for Soviet intelligence, whether in Germany or the United States.[13] Boris Vinogradov was then the USSR's chargé d'affaires in

---

* A report of Vinogradov's arrest, later denied.

Poland, and on March 9, 1937, after the couple's romantic interlude in the Polish capital, he briefed his Soviet intelligence supervisors:

> Today [Martha Dodd] left for Moscow. Since her father will retire sooner or later, she wants to work in her motherland. She established a connection with Browder [Earl Browder, the leader of the American Communist Party and an active Soviet agent] who invited her to work for him. She also established a connection (through her brother) with "The World Committee of Struggle for Peace" in Geneva and became close friends with Comintern workers Otto Katz and Dolliway. An authoritative comrade [in Moscow] must talk to her and convince her to stay in Europe and work only for us.[14]

But Dodd had a more personal agenda uppermost in her mind when she arrived in the Soviet Union. On March 14, 1937, she wrote a "Statement to the Soviet Government": "I, Martha Dodd, U.S. citizen, have known Boris Vinogradov for three years in Berlin and other places, and we have agreed to ask official permission to marry."[15]

The NKVD's top leadership, however, had other ideas. In Moscow, Martha met with Abram Slutsky, then head of its foreign department, who (on March 28) reported their discussion to Nikolay Yezhov, People's Commissar for Internal Affairs: "Some time ago, Martha Dodd, daughter of the American Ambassador in Germany, was recruited by us. We used her short-term trip to the USSR for detailed negotiations with her and established that she has very valuable possibilities and may be widely used by us."[16]

The value of Dodd's "possibilities" emerged in an extraordinary memorandum for NKVD leadership that she prepared at Slutsky's request, describing "her social status, her father's status, and prospects of her further work for us." Few such narratives by Western agents have surfaced from Soviet intelligence archives and none that address with such detail and candor the matters contained in Martha Dodd's statement:

> It goes without saying that my services of any kind and at any time are proposed to the party for use at its discretion.
>
> Currently, I have access mainly to the personal, confidential correspondence of my father with the U.S. State Department and the U.S. President.
>
> My source of information on military and naval issues, as well as on aviation, is exclusively personal contact with our embassy's

staff. I lost almost any connection with the Germans except perhaps for casual, high-society meetings which yield almost nothing.

I still have a connection to the diplomatic corps but, on the whole, it doesn't yield great results. I have established very close connections to journalists.

Germans, foreign diplomats, and our own personnel treat us suspiciously, unfriendly, and (as far as the Germans are concerned) insultingly. Is the information which I get from my father, who is hated in Germany and who occupies an isolated position among foreign diplomats and therefore has no access to any secret information, important enough for me to remain in Germany? Couldn't I conduct more valuable work in America or in some European organization such as the International Conference for Peace . . . ?

In America, I am suspected of nothing, except for the Germans, and I have countless valuable connections in all circles. In other words, is my potential work valuable enough to stay in Germany even for the [remaining] term of my father's sojourn there?

I have done everything possible to make my father remain in Germany. I'm still going to do everything I can in this direction. However, I'm afraid he will retire this summer or fall. He was of great benefit to the Roosevelt administration, contributing an anti-Nazi view. In any case, this was with regard to [Secretary of State Cordell] Hull and Roosevelt. Most State Department officials work with the Nazis, for example, Dunn, chief of the European department; Phillips, currently in Rome; Bullitt; and others. My father tried to prevent trade agreements [with Germany]; he refused to cooperate with bankers, businessmen, etc.

Recently he cabled to Hull and Roosevelt concerning a supposed loan to Germany which is supported by Bullitt and Blum [Leon Blum, Prime Minister of France], Davis, Phillips and England. . . . Except for Roosevelt and Hull, the State Department, representatives of American business circles, and the Germans all wish to remove my father. He personally wants to leave. Shouldn't he arrange his resignation with a provocation once he decides the question of timing? Shouldn't he provoke the Germans to make them demand his recall or create a scandal, after which he could speak openly in America both orally and in the press. . . . To resign and to publish a protest? He could be convinced to do it if it had significance for the USSR.

Roosevelt will be giving diplomatic posts to many capitalists who financed him.* . . . Having little experience with respect to European politics, Roosevelt will appoint . . . people or groups who will be dangerous now and in time of war.

Nevertheless, my father has great influence on Hull and Roosevelt, who are inclined to be slightly anti-Fascist, and thus could influence a new appointment without [Hull and Roosevelt] suspecting the underlying reasons for my father's behavior, who would be an advocate of my instructions.

Have you got anybody in mind who would be at least liberal and democratic in this post [Dodd's replacement in Germany]? . . . If there is information concerning our candidates, it would be important to know whose candidacy to the post [of U.S. Ambassador] in Germany the USSR would like to promote. If this man has at least a slight chance, I will persuade my father to promote his candidacy.[17]

Dodd's memo then reviewed her options for future service to Soviet intelligence. She offered to come to the Soviet Union, remain in Europe, travel to the Far East under cover as a journalist, or return to the United States, leaving the decision up to Abram Slutsky and his NKVD superiors in Moscow.

They, in turn, considered Dodd so significant an agent that they bucked the decision on how best to use her directly to Stalin. "TOP SECRET. Only personally. To the Secretary of the Central Committee of the All-Union Communist Party, Comrade Stalin," began Commissar Yezhov's March 29, 1937, memorandum. "The 7th department of the . . . NKVD recruited Martha Dodd, daughter of the American Ambassador in Berlin, who came in March 1937 to Moscow for business negotiations. She described in her report her social status, her father's status, and prospects of her further work for us. Forwarding a copy of the latter, I ask instructions about Martha Dodd's use."[18] Stalin's response, if he ever made one, did not survive in the NKVD records. Nevertheless, steps taken immediately after Dodd's visit to Moscow indicate her Soviet hosts' recognition of the care and sensitivity with which they should manage this valuable but emotionally volatile young American.

A memo in Dodd's file written shortly after her departure from Moscow instructed her handlers to route all correspondence between

---

* Dodd then mentions various "capitalists" rumored for diplomatic assignments.

Martha and Boris Vinogradov through the NKVD, which would intercept her love letters and compose his replies. The couple was also instructed to stop using ordinary postal services to send letters and to end all telephone contact. Martha would have been pleased with one portion of the memo: "In principle there is no objection (on our part) to Vinogradov's marriage to 'Liza.' However, this question will be resolved much later. For the present, in the interests of business, 'Liza' ceases even meetings with Vinogradov for six months. . . ."[19]

Nor did the NKVD wish the flamboyant Martha to maintain "any connections with members of Communist parties as well as with antifascist people and organizations. The connection will be maintained only with us." Furthermore, she was ordered to "take every measure to prolong Ambassador Dodd's sojourn in Berlin as much as possible." In one respect, Martha's memorandum had the desired impact in Moscow, since the NKVD respondent approved her suggestion that Ambassador Dodd's departure be accompanied by a public confrontation with the German government "in order to create strained relations between the American and German governments." Moreover, if the Ambassador left Germany, the instructions continued, his daughter should choose and recommend to Moscow the name of a potential successor while Moscow would conduct its own search for this person.

Most important, perhaps, there followed this NKVD directive for the remaining months of Ambassador Dodd's tenure: "In the nearest future [Martha] checks Ambassador Dodd's reports to Roosevelt in the archive and communicates to us short summaries of the contents, whose numbers we gave to her. She continues providing us with materials from the American Embassy, trying mainly to get data about Germany, Japan, and Poland."[20] Her NKVD mentors then reported giving her "200 American dollars, 10 rubles, and gifts bought for 500 rubles."

Soviet intelligence also kept Martha's erstwhile lover, Boris Vinogradov, busy during this period with several tasks. He referred to Dodd in a March 21 memo to his superiors as "Juliet #2," indicating that Vinogradov, as the Russian "Romeo," also provided simultaneous solace to an unidentified "Juliet #1":

With Juliet #2 everything was all right, and I think that you, having sanctioned her arrival in Moscow, did a good thing. But I don't quite understand why you have focused so much on our wedding. I asked you to point out to her that it is impossible in general and, anyway, won't happen in the next several years. You spoke more optimistically on this issue and ordered a delay of only 6 months or a year. We keep our promises.

I assured her in Warsaw before the trip to Moscow that, if she was told "yes," so it would be, as she was dealing with very authoritative people.

If "no," it would mean "no." Six months will pass quickly, and who knows? She may produce a bill that neither you nor I is going to pay. Isn't it better to soften slightly the explicitness of your promises if you really gave them to her? You can point to the interests of business and the necessity of *konspiratsia* [maintaining the security of covert operations].[21]

Plainly, Vinogradov, although delighted to pursue his dalliance with Martha Dodd, either feared being ordered by the NKVD to live an unwanted permanent relationship or had been instructed to maintain Martha's hopes while other Soviet operatives used her services as an agent.

He returned to the problem in subsequent correspondence with his superiors as in this November 5, 1937, report: "[Martha Dodd] again writes me in a letter about marriage. When she was leaving for Moscow, I wrote you asking that you not give this type of promise. Nevertheless, such a promise was given to her, and now she expects its fulfillment. Her dream is to be my wife, at least virtually, and that I will come to work in America and she would help me."[22]

Martha may not have told Boris in her letter that Ambassador Dodd had scheduled his departure from Berlin the following month. Determined to wed Vinogradov, she traveled once more to Warsaw shortly after sending her last letter, an encounter duly reported to Moscow in Vinogradov's November 12 memo:[23]

The meeting with [Martha] went off well. She was in a good mood. On December 15, she leaves for New York where a meeting with her is fixed [with NKVD operatives in that city].

[She] is still busy with [our] marriage plans and waits for the fulfillment of our promise despite her parents' warning that nothing would come of it.

Not unknown to you, journalist Louis Fischer proposed to her. She did not accept since she hopes to marry me. But if we tell her that I will by no means and never marry her, she will accept Fischer's proposal.

I think that she shouldn't be left in ignorance with regard to the real situation, for if we deceive her, she may become embittered and lose faith in us. Now she agrees to work for us even if it turns out that I won't marry her.

I proposed giving money to [Dodd], but she turned me down.[24]

After their brief encounter in Warsaw, Martha Dodd never saw Boris Vinogradov again. She returned to the United States with Ambassador Dodd the following month, where the NKVD's leading "illegal," Itzhak Akhmerov, received the following directive:

We inform you that our source "Liza"—Miss Martha Dodd, daughter of the former American Ambassador in Germany Dodd—is currently in your city.

You should contact her after receiving a special cable. Her address: Irving Place, New York City. You should come to her early in the morning between 8 and 9 A.M. and say: "I want to give you regards from Bob Norman."[25]

After Martha Dodd's departure, Vinogradov evidently was no longer of any use to the NKVD, and he returned to Moscow where he was arrested and denounced as "a people's enemy."[26] But NKVD officials feared informing Martha of his fate.

In New York, another NKVD operative, "Igor," contacted Martha on June 15, 1938. "What happened to Vinogradov? Is he arrested?" she demanded to know, according to "Igor's" memo to Moscow. He replied that Vinogradov was working in Moscow, but Martha complained inaccurately that she had not heard from him for more than a year. Since Vinogradov had promised to marry her as soon as he received permission from his superiors, she awaited word. After consulting with the Soviet Embassy's Counselor, Konstantin Umansky, who had told her he didn't think Vinogradov could marry her, Martha abruptly made other, more achievable plans, as this report to Moscow indicated:

At present she has a fiancé. . . . If Vinogradov reiterates his promise she will wait for him and reject the other man. Her fiancé is [Alfred] Stern, 40 years old, Jew, a man with an independent material status [who] stayed in Germany a couple of years ago and helped the Communist Party financially. . . . She doesn't think her marriage would prevent her from working with us, though she doesn't understand completely what she should do. . . .[27]

"Igor" advised Martha to pursue contacts with officials at the State Department, which she had been doing while her father was in Germany. That September, she passed to "Igor" a letter from Claude Bowers, the U.S. Ambassador in Spain, which created great enthusiasm among her NKVD contacts because it showed that Martha was still engaged in work for them despite her shifting personal scene.[28]

Prior to his execution, Vinogradov was forced to compose a letter to his lover, pretending that nothing in his life had changed except for a new Moscow posting. Martha responded on July 9, 1938, with the extraordinary news that, during the intervening half-year since her return to America, although protesting her continued passionate love for the Russian, she had fallen in love *again* and been married!

> Boris, dear! Finally I got your letter. You work in the press office, don't you? Are you happy? Did you find a girl you can love instead of me?
>
> Did you hear that my mother died in late May totally unexpectedly? You can imagine how tragic it was for me. Surely, you know better than anybody else how we loved each other and how close we were in everything.
>
> The three of us spent time together perfectly, and I remember how sweet she was to both of us when you were in Berlin.
>
> Mother knew very well how deep our love was and understood all the meaning that you had and will have in my life. She knew that I loved nobody before and thought that I would never love again but hoped that I would be happy anyway.
>
> You haven't had time yet to know that I really got married. On June 16, I married an American whom I love very much. I wanted to tell you a lot, but I will wait until our meeting. We are supposed to be in the USSR in late August or early September this year. I hope you'll be there or will let me know where I can meet you.
>
> You know, honey, that for me, you meant more in my life than anybody else. You also know that, if I am needed, I will be ready to come when called.
>
> Let me know your plan if you get another post. I look into the future and see you in Russia again. Your Martha.[29]

By the time news of Martha Dodd's wedding reached NKVD headquarters in Moscow, Boris Vinogradov had joined the millions executed in Stalin's purges. As for Mrs. Martha Dodd Stern, the NKVD's New York station reported to Moscow on December 1, 1938: "Since 'Liza' became the wife of a millionaire, her everyday life has changed considerably. She lives in a rich apartment on 57th Street, has two servants, a driver, and a personal secretary. She is very keen on her plan to go to Moscow as the wife of the American Ambassador." Although Alfred Stern was prepared to contribute $50,000 to the Democratic Party if promised the post, the cable continued, "his chances are still very weak."[30]

The Soviets nevertheless considered Martha's prospects in the American government—as the wealthy daughter of a highly regarded American statesman—far more promising. One January 1942 NKVD cable from Moscow to its New York station described her potential:

> A gifted, clever and educated woman, she requires constant control over her behavior. . . . Let [Dodd] move in the circles interesting to us rather than in circles close to the Trust [the Soviet Consulate where she had inquired concerning Vinogradov]. . . . It is necessary to continue activating her activities as a successful journalist. She should also be guided to approach and [deepen her relationship with] the President's wife, Eleanor, through different social organizations, committees, and societies. Here, the special interest of the Roosevelts in China and everything connected with it must be used. [Dodd] can play on this factor. Let her approach Eleanor through the committee on help to China. . . .[31]

Although Martha Dodd enjoyed, because of her father, Ambassador Dodd, a social friendship with the President and First Lady, her Soviet handlers' expectations of "Liza's" potential as an agent were not realized during the war years.

Still unaware of Vinogradov's fate, Martha wrote Konstantin Umansky asking for help in acquiring an entry visa to visit her former lover in Moscow. Umansky informed Moscow that he had declined Dodd's request but had told her of Vinogradov's arrest: "We try to convince [Martha] that her trip to the USSR is not expedient from the perspective of our work," a reference to her budding involvement with Soviet intelligence efforts in the United States. "[But] she continues insisting and demanding cogent motives [for our position]. She and her husband should be refused permission to enter the USSR."[32]

By this time, most of the Soviet operatives who had dealt with Martha Dodd, including Vinogradov, had been either imprisoned or executed. Their replacements in the NKVD at times seemed more concerned with Martha's morality than with her usefulness: "She considers herself a Communist and claims to accept the party's program," ran one such skeptical Soviet dispatch. "In reality, 'Liza' is a typical representative of American bohemia, a sexually decayed woman ready to sleep with any handsome man."[33]

One hapless NKVD agent in New York, an American technical specialist named Franklin Zelman (code-named "Chap") was assigned the task of listening to Martha's complaints about the continued denial of a Soviet visa. Instructed to question her closely about her acquaintances in Germany (in an interview only months after the German invasion of the Soviet Union had begun), Zelman reported to Moscow a September 24, 1941, discussion with Dodd about her affair with Vinogradov.

When last in Moscow, Martha had written, at her lover's request, two letters to Stalin, described in Zelman's memorandum as "Uncle Joe," which indicated that, by then, Vinogradov feared for his future and sought an American escape with Martha: "Vinogradov told Martha to describe her life and contacts to Stalin; that marriage with Vinogradov shouldn't be considered impossible since they would be a good couple in the United States." At least that was Martha Dodd's version of the situation; it may have contained more wishful thinking than truth, given Vinogradov's constant evasion of marriage when they were together.

Zelman's memo goes on to record a dialogue with Dodd that might have been transcribed verbatim from the pages of a "true confessions" magazine:

MARTHA: I have a weakness for the Russians.
I: Why for the Russians?
MARTHA: I don't know. There is something in them. Maybe
          it's because I have such a passionate nature. I react
          easily.
I: Sometimes we have to discipline ourselves . . . not to
          let feelings interfere with our relationships.
MARTHA: Why? What's wrong with it?
I: It may be demoralizing. The work may suffer. Rela-
          tions suffer because they become too intimate. Lovers
          chatter too much, especially in bed.
MARTHA: Yes, maybe so.[34]

By this time it was evident even from Zelman's reports to superiors that Martha had made yet another conquest. His queries had plainly "become too intimate," as in this report on their October 1, 1941, meeting:

Bluntly but frankly, I asked [Martha] if her sexual relations with her husband were satisfactory. She, of course, asked "Why?" . . . I explained that I was interested because she had twice remarked that she would divorce her husband if she stood in . . . the way of his political development. I suggested that one does not talk of divorce quite so casually unless one wanted a divorce. Martha explained: She loved her husband very much. Their relationship was quite satisfactory in every way. She loved him, not the wild love she felt for Boris Vinogradov, but still a satisfactory love.

Having once started, Martha, as in the past, talked quite freely. . . . Martha's life in Berlin can be summed up in one word — "sleep." Seemingly, she spent most of her time in bed. In addition to the Russian or Russians, she had slept with a full-blown fascist — General Ernest Udet, second in command (after Goering) of the German air force; Louis Ferdinand, grandson of the Kaiser; and some guy at the French Embassy in Berlin. (A real internationalist!)[35]

This conversation took place, Zelman's memo continued, during a heavy drinking session with Dodd while scanning her diary, which fascinated him: "Perhaps I should look over the diary for other 'contacts.' Surely there must be other countries represented in this International Brigade — including Scandinavia."

Why, Zelman asked, had Martha slept with General Udet? Her response was that "she learned much from him, [and] Vinogradov had not been in Berlin" at the time. When she told him about the liaison, "he did not object."

Martha then raised the obvious question with her NKVD interlocutor: "She asked me if it was now a rule that people in our work were not to have a sexual life." Of course not, Zelman responded, presumably thinking by then of his own possible relationship with this attractive woman:

We are interested in personal morals only when they reach the political plane. There followed a discussion of when and when not morals were to be considered political. . . . I lectured on middle-class morals, proletarian morals, when sex is permissible in our kind of work, when not, we discussed hormones and sheep ovarian extract's influence on humans, etc. I lectured on more than I knew.

Martha's response was that of a deferential pupil to a patient teacher: "I should have been told these things in Berlin. Nobody taught me anything there." She promised "not to have a sexual affair in the Soviet

Union" if told not to, bringing the conversation around again to her desire for a visa. The conversation ended with this instructive colloquy: "Martha made the remark that all men were vulnerable somewhere. Does this mean, I asked her, that you feel that you could sleep with almost any man if you chose to? 'Yes,' she said, and then: 'It might be advantageous at times.' " Her possible intimate—Franklin Zelman—concluded his memo to Moscow with, "This Martha meant in terms of political work."[36]

Frustrated by both Soviet and American official impediments in her quest for a return visit to Moscow while still holding out hope that Vinogradov was alive, Martha turned her energies to assisting the NKVD station in identifying potential recruits from among her numerous friends in Europe and the United States. In a December 26, 1941, letter to an NKVD contact, for example, she recommended various associates who should be approached as possible agents, including her husband, millionaire Alfred Stern.[37]

"In regard to my husband," who was then seeking a U.S. diplomatic post, she wrote her Soviet contacts on February 5, 1942, ". . . I think it would be a great mistake if he were not obtained for our work."[38] By then, under Martha's tutelage, Stern had become an active and visible member of the Communist Party and Communist-front organizations, so his suitability for secret intelligence work was questioned by her Soviet contacts. Still, she pressed the point with growing vehemence. "I must again insist that my husband be taken into our work," she wrote Vassily Zarubin, the NKGB's New York station chief, that same month. "If he is not seen, I must resign, since he is exposing both of us" because of his open fidelity to Communist causes. Apparently, Stern was not yet aware of his wife's work with the NKGB, a fact that greatly troubled Dodd: "If he did know what I was doing and would be doing the same work, he would be a highly disciplined person and of infinite value to us."[39]

By the following month, Martha's persistence had been rewarded with Soviet approval. After "a long weekend in the country" with her husband, she gained his agreement to join in her covert efforts. Alfred Stern, Martha wrote the station, "wanted to do something immediately. . . . He felt he had many contacts that would be valuable in this sort of work, if we were given time to develop them."[40]

Despite continuing discussions with Martha over the scope of his potential activities on behalf of Soviet intelligence and of hers, conversations she chronicled at length for her patient associates at the NKGB station, Alfred Stern's career in espionage was limited mainly to his role in organizing a music publishing house (code-named "Chord") to serve as a cover for Soviet "illegals" working in the United States and other countries. Stern's partners in the effort were New York NKGB station chief Vassily Zarubin, who supported the venture but did not contribute funds to it, and a flamboyant minor Hollywood producer, Boris Morros (code-named "Frost" and, later, "John"), who, while still working for the NKGB, was recruited as a "double agent" by the FBI. The business quickly lost money and, in any case, Zarubin's Moscow NKGB superiors may have wondered why otherwise-sensible station chiefs would spend time on such strange shadow enterprises. (Morros would assert in 1957 that he and Alfred Stern had fallen out because Stern detested the title of a popular song, "Chattanooga Choo Choo," later a hit record, which the publishing house had considered acquiring!)*[41]

Beyond Martha Dodd's occasional help as a "spotter," identifying potential agents from among her circles of radical friends, and Alfred Stern's cheerful willingness to invest and lose personal funds in an NKGB cover business, Moscow now found little of value in Stern (known as "the Red millionaire") and his socially active spouse. Martha combined NKVD service with work as a journalist and author, publishing in 1939 a European memoir, *Through Embassy Eyes*. The memoir focused mainly on Germany but was also filled with euphoric commentary on the Soviet Union, observations made during her trip around the country with Boris Vinogradov (though discreetly omitting any mention of him). Martha also co-edited with her brother William, another convert to communism, a popular 1941 book entitled *Ambassador Dodd's Diary, 1933–1938*, a vigorous account of the Ambassador's difficult years as an anti-Nazi Jeffersonian Democrat confronting the ugly realities of life in Hitler's Germany.

By that time, William Dodd (code-named first "Boy" and then "President") had also become deeply engaged in the covert family business of cooperating with Soviet intelligence. According to NKVD records, William began his efforts, as his sister had, while in Berlin, passing along modest tidbits of embassy scuttlebutt in 1936 and 1937.[42] Back in the United States, in 1938, William Dodd decided to run for Congress as a Democrat, and Peter Gutzeit promptly advised Moscow: "We think that now, before he is elected (it will be difficult afterwards),

---

* See Chapter 6 for a fuller account of "Chord" and the Morros-Stern partnership.

it is necessary to recruit him and help him with money for his election campaign. He may not be elected, but that is a risk we must take."[43]

As a result, William was recruited by his sister, Martha, that same year and received from the New York NKVD station both an unsolicited $1,000 contribution to his congressional campaign and a new code name, "President."[44] Although Dodd lost his bid, he remained an active source in the years that followed, providing the Soviets with information gathered from his discussions with leading Washington Congressmen, Senators, and government officials.[45] He also passed along documents from his father's private correspondence. Among William's contacts was a Justice Department employee named Helen Fuller, who conveyed to him in 1937 allegations about FBI Director J. Edgar Hoover, the accuracy of which was confirmed for the most part in later years:

> Hoover is keeping files on almost all major political figures: Congressmen, Senators and businessmen. He gathers compromising material on everybody and uses it for blackmail. In the course of the latest hearings on financing the FBI, Hoover blackmailed those Congressmen who tried to stand against [full funding]. . . . He used against some of them even cases of casual sex. . . . We settled with [William] that he would try to get closer to [Helen Fuller] in order to get regular information from her.[46]

After being turned down for a post at the Interior Department, William Dodd decided to purchase a small weekly newspaper in Virginia. He lacked funding, and, again, Moscow came to his rescue. "We think it necessary to give him 3–4 thousand dollars for the mentioned purpose," the NKVD station wrote its superiors.[47] William received $3,500 to purchase the *Blue Ridge Herald*. He asked the Soviets for another $5,000, though it is unclear whether they provided the money, however pleased they were with their direct influence on this modest and minor publication: "The direction of the newspaper will depend completely on us," the station informed Moscow in December 1939, hoping to exploit not the paper's own limited influence but its "direct connection with liberal Washington journalists."[48]

Like his sister, Martha, however, William Dodd remained a disappointment to the NKVD; promise again far exceeded performance as a Soviet agent. Thus, in January 1942, Moscow wrote Vassily Zarubin about these underachieving siblings: "For the last two years, we have been making unsuccessful attempts to use [William Dodd] in different areas of work. Now the most urgent task in the further use of these probationers is to split them and to use separately what represents considerable difficulty and requires major educational work on your side."[49]

The following year, William Dodd was investigated by the FBI for Communist activities and, therefore, compromised as an agent.[50] The NKGB lost all further interest in him, though not in Martha Dodd, who did not yet have a public reputation as a "Red."[51] By 1945, William had taken a post with the TASS news agency's New York office, run at that time by the NKGB station chief. After Martha complained to Soviet operatives that her brother's work at TASS was interfering with her and Alfred Stern's ability to pursue covert activities, and despite William's protests, he was fired by TASS in July 1945 and cut off from further contact with Soviet intelligence.[52]

With the death of Franklin Roosevelt, the end of World War II, and the rapid postwar collapse of America's wartime alliance with the Soviet Union, Communist enthusiasts such as Martha Dodd, Alfred Stern, and William Dodd confronted a decidedly chillier political climate in New York and Washington. After the defection in late 1945 of key NKGB agent and courier Elizabeth Bentley, Soviet intelligence agents in the United States were instructed to halt operations while awaiting the FBI's counterintelligence assault on those with whom Bentley had worked.* There were to be no meetings by NKGB operatives with the Sterns and other Soviet agents for two years.

In January 1948, "progressive" writers—a number of them Communists, including Martha Dodd and Alfred Stern—met with a Soviet propagandist named Valentin Sorokin to discuss issues such as the emerging third-party drive by former Vice President Henry Wallace, who preached a conciliatory policy toward the Soviet Union. Martha proposed to Sorokin that she and Alfred resume underground work and suggested a later meeting using code names and other precautions, persuaded that the FBI was monitoring their calls.[53]

When informed by Sorokin of Martha's proposal, Alexander Panyushkin, who then played a bizarre dual role as Soviet Ambassador to the United States and NKGB station chief in Washington, asked Moscow for instructions.[54] The response urged Sorokin to study Dodd carefully, determine her views on the Soviet Union, and consider her potential as a talent-spotter.[55]

Officials in Moscow apparently were still intrigued with the notion of Martha—if not Alfred—resuming efforts on behalf of Soviet intelli-

* See Chapter 5 for a discussion of Bentley's defection.

gence, as indicated by this 1948 memorandum: " 'Liza' didn't provoke suspicions either in her political or social activities as well as in her work with us. It is necessary to keep in mind that during the period of her work with us, she maintained intimate relations with some of our operatives. Besides our operatives, she lived in Berlin with some Germans and French diplomats. . . . She was passing us political information in Berlin."[56]

Sorokin met the Sterns again on March 18, 1948, in New York and sparred with the couple, who were concerned lest he prove to be not a genuine Soviet agent but an impostor from American counterintelligence. Their conversation focused on the Wallace campaign. Martha and Alfred, apparently unaware of the various Communist links to Wallace's staff and advisers, urged that the Soviet Union become actively involved in supporting the campaign. Subsequent meetings with the couple fell flat since neither of the Sterns trusted Sorokin, though they continued private talks with the Soviet official.[57]

By then Ambassador/station chief Panyushkin reported to Moscow in August 1948 that (according to Martha Dodd Stern) Henry Wallace had asked her to be his speechwriter, a dubious assertion. Dodd asked, again via Sorokin, for the Soviets to provide her with basic points she could use in her draft speeches.[58] NKGB authorities in Moscow responded two days later that they opposed her working for Wallace.[59] Specifically, the cable stated, they objected to Martha Dodd's maintaining open relationships with U.S. Communist Party officials and similar representatives of Eastern European Communist governments in New York. Moreover, Moscow found her to be a "blabbing, not serious nor a conspiratorial enough" person.

Why, they wondered, did Dodd insist that both she and her husband resume their roles as Soviet agents? Considering its concerns regarding FBI counterintelligence activities at the time, the NKGB felt it wise to keep the enthusiastic Sterns at a distance. Martha's insistence that Moscow resume the secret activities of "our group," therefore, was obviously an unwanted risk for Soviet intelligence.[60] The couple was passed from Sorokin's responsibility in 1949 to that of a New York agent code-named "Kostrov," who approached the Sterns asking them to acquire political information from various pro-Soviet public figures. The assignment remained unfulfilled because Martha was ill at the time and Alfred deeply involved in radical Vito Marcantonio's unsuccessful race for New York mayor.[61] After that, contacts between the NKGB and the Sterns were halted.

By the time they resumed six years later, in March 1955, the Sterns had fled U.S. government investigation to take up residence in Mexico.[62] After several attempts to correspond with friends in Moscow—including one letter from Martha to a journalist-friend asking him to find out what had happened to Boris Vinogradov after his arrest—Soviet intelligence instructed its Mexico station to establish contact with the couple to determine whether they were still of any value as agents.[63]

Since Martha and Alfred had already received several subpoenas to testify in cases involving alleged espionage then underway in the United States, the couple was in no position to resume active work as agents. At a June 18, 1956, meeting, the Sterns told "Ostap," the Mexico City KGB station chief, that they wanted to live in the Soviet Union but, if that was not possible, in Czechoslovakia, China, or the German Democratic Republic. They claimed to have a million dollars in a Mexican bank that they were transferring to Switzerland. (Their lawyer, Paul O'Dwyer, had informed them that Jack Soble, a government witness and former Soviet agent, had told the FBI about the publishing firm Stern had developed with Boris Morros to assist Soviet "illegals."[64]) On July 20, 1956, naturalized with Paraguayan citizenship and passports in exchange for a $10,000 bribe to an Paraguayan Embassy official in Mexico (the American government having canceled their U.S. passports), the couple left for Amsterdam. There, a Czech official met them and handed over airline tickets to Prague.[65]

The Sterns learned in 1957 that they had been fined in the U.S. courts for refusing to testify before a congressional investigating committee, which had heard their old colleague and friend Boris Morros state flatly that Martha and Alfred were Soviet agents.[66] They tried one final time to gain Soviet citizenship, offering their Mexican home and several paintings to the USSR.[67] The Soviets, however, preferred that the Sterns remain in Czechoslovakia, though the KGB did dispatch a Colonel Korneev to Prague to discuss their application for Soviet citizenship, which was turned down.[68]

There the matter remained until August 12, 1957, when Boris Morros, the Sterns' vocal nemesis, testified that he had served for the past twelve years as a double agent under FBI as well as Soviet instruction.[69] Within days, on August 28, the KGB recommended to the Central Committee of the Communist Party that Martha and Alfred Stern be allowed to settle in the USSR.[70] The Sterns arrived in Moscow the following month, at the same time an American court found them guilty in absentia of espionage on behalf of the Soviet Union.[71]

The post-Stalin "thaw" in Soviet life encouraged under Nikita Khrushchev's leadership was in full swing. The Sterns declined a KGB request to denounce Boris Morros's testimony as false.[72] They concluded, also, that their inability to speak Russian (and possibly their unwillingness to live under direct KGB supervision) made it difficult for them to remain in the Soviet Union. Seeking counsel from others who had defected to the East, they requested but were denied a meeting with Guy Burgess and Donald Maclean, the British agents who had fled for sanctuary to Moscow years earlier.[73] In October 1957, the Sterns formally asked for asylum in Czechoslovakia, where they proposed starting new careers, Martha as an editor of English-language books and Alfred in the export-import field.[74] The following January the couple returned to Prague.[75]

But an October 1975 memo from a KGB official in Prague noted that the Sterns had lived in Fidel Castro's Cuba from 1963 to 1970 and returned to Czechoslovakia only that summer. Apparently, even Havana, the newest of "New Jerusalems" for a couple perpetually suffused with Communist idealism, did not measure up to their hopes. During the 1970s, monitored by the KGB, American lawyers for Martha and Alfred began negotiating with the FBI for their return to America without prosecution or imprisonment for espionage.[76] The KGB did not object to their departure, according to an October 14, 1975, memo: "Data that the Sterns have about the activities of Soviet intelligence are obsolete and mainly known to the adversary from the traitor 'John's' [Boris Morros's] testimonies."[77]

The negotiations proved unsuccessful, however, and Martha Dodd and Alfred Stern spent their remaining years in the Democratic Socialist Republic of Czechoslovakia—unable to adjust to life in the Soviet Union, to which they had devoted their adult lives, and wanted in their native country as convicted and escaped traitors.

CHAPTER 4

❖

Communist Romantics, II: The Exuberant Michael Straight

M OSCOW'S INITIAL INTEREST in Martha Dodd during the 1930s stemmed in part from the fact that she was acquainted with President Roosevelt, Mrs. Roosevelt, and other prominent Americans. But if Soviet intelligence had awarded a prize at the time to its best-connected American recruit, the winner would not have been Dodd but Michael Straight, a wealthy young convert to communism cultivated for secret work while studying at Cambridge University. Straight's parents had begun their friendship with the Roosevelts at the time they founded the *New Republic* magazine earlier in the century. The President and First Lady retained a keen interest in young Straight's career and future, which they would display upon his return from England to the United States.

Moscow's file on Straight was opened in January 1937 with a memorandum from NKVD "illegal" London station chief Theodore Mally (code-named "Man"). Mally was responsible for cultivating at Cambridge a flock of talented young recruits willing to engage in covert activities on behalf of the Soviet Union, among them Donald Maclean, Guy Burgess, Harold "Kim" Philby, Anthony Blunt—and Michael Straight. "[I] draw your attention to Michael Straight . . . son of an American millionaire, devoted and ardent compatriot," Mally wrote Moscow. He proposed recruiting Straight and, "after this, he may be used either here or in America. But I have not decided this question yet. Let us study him further for the moment."[1]

Mally assigned Guy Burgess the task of approaching Straight, since Burgess had known the American in "open" Communist Party activities at Cambridge over the previous two years. Burgess promptly sent this assessment to Mally, the first of two that eventually entered Straight's NKVD file:

> Michael, whom I have known for several years, . . . is one of the leaders (as a person he is not an organizer) of the [Communist] party at Cambridge. He is the party's spokesman and also a first-class economist. He is an extremely devoted member of the party. . . . Taking into account his family connections, future fortune and capabilities, one must suppose he has a great future, not in the field of politics but in the industrial and trading world. . . . [O]ne may reckon he could work on secret work. He is sufficiently devoted for it, though it will be extremely difficult for him to part with his friends and his current activities. . . .[2]

Burgess had no idea how difficult, since Straight's unabashed Communist involvements (Mally noted in a February 16 memo to Moscow) were not only "well known in Cambridge . . . [but] in London," where Michael was "a friend of [Harry] Pollitt's," the leader of the British Communist Party. Straight also had been providing the *Daily Worker*, the Communist newspaper, "with a sum of about 1,500 pounds a year" for the past several years.

Straight's "status in the party and his social connections are very significant," Burgess's memo observed. "The question was whether to begin to act, when and how." It was not every day that the NKVD found as a potential recruit someone whose father was prominently linked to American banking interests and whose mother, then still part owner of the influential *New Republic*, was "on very friendly terms with the Roosevelts." Other relatives of Michael, Burgess noted, were comparably well connected, including some in the American aviation industry, which remained of utmost concern to the Soviet Union.[3]

Burgess instructed Anthony Blunt to persuade Straight to resign from the British Communist Party and to sever all links with Communist organizations in order to clear the way for intelligence work. By then, Burgess had concocted the code name "Nigel" for Straight. Blunt, in turn, undertook a series of successful talks on the matter with Straight. "I would not have instructed A.B. to set to work without consulting you beforehand," Burgess informed Mally, "if only [Straight's] departure from open work had not been so complicated and we had not had to use immediately a helpful circumstance, the death of John Cornford."[4] Cornford, another Cambridge Communist and Straight's closest friend, had been killed in action during the Spanish Civil War. His death left Michael distraught and prepared the ground for his recruitment by Soviet intelligence.

Using Blunt as intermediary, Mally and his conspiratorial cohort convinced Straight to begin the process of detaching himself from Cambridge and organizing his return to the United States. Presumably encouraged by his NKVD associates, Straight began to express publicly his admiration for FDR and the New Deal. In late March, he left for a brief vacation in the United States, still uncertain as to whether he had been accepted for an agent's role there. Meanwhile, Mally obtained Harry Pollitt's approval for shifting Straight from open to covert Communist activity, since Pollitt believed Straight could continue to subsidize his newspaper even in his new role.[5]

When he returned to England the following month, Straight provided Mally with a report on his contacts, employment prospects, and operational potential. In seeking a job, Michael had gone directly to the top, discussing his interests with Franklin and Eleanor Roosevelt. The First Lady suggested that Michael take an agricultural credit post in the Administration, which he rejected as useless to his Soviet friends. He preferred Treasury or the Federal Reserve Board: "In those places," Michael wrote Mally, "possibilities are great because of the influence on Roosevelt. . . . Treasury has great significance. Its head is Henry Morgenthau, who knows my parents well."[6]

Straight proposed another daring and very attractive option: an appointment as one of FDR's personal secretaries through his social links to the President ("My parents know Roosevelt well."). But the commander-in-chief had another slot in mind for his young friend at a central planning group called the National Resources Board: "Roosevelt himself picked out this job for me as the most important among those I could get and where I could be close to him."

Straight's memo also noted that Harry Hopkins, the President's closest aide, Secretary of Agriculture Henry Wallace, and Henry Morgenthau were among his more influential New Deal connections: "It means I can easily find any job." Straight had a sardonic response for Mally concerning his efforts to counter the impression among those American friends who knew him best that he had become a Communist:

All my relatives treat me negatively, since they think I was in Spain. Now I try to dispel this impression by the following means:

a. I use brilliantine and keep my nails clean;

b. by ardent speeches against the Reds in some places; in other places, I present myself as a radical.

His annual income, Straight noted, was then $50,000, a huge sum at the time, and would increase shortly to $75,000.[7]

By this time, Mally and the NKVD had come to a conclusion about Straight, outlined in Mally's June 9, 1937, memo to Moscow shortly before Michael's graduation from Cambridge. He "is to return to the U.S. where, at our instruction, he will join the National Resources Board. He leaves in July." Mally believed Straight an "unripe man" politically, requiring ideological bolstering. Moreover, he doubted that Moscow's available operative on the East Coast, Itzhak Akhmerov, was "fit for this job."[8]

To prepare Straight for his covert responsibilities, therefore, Mally and the London station arranged for another talented Soviet "illegal," Arnold Deutsch (code-named "Stephan"), to meet with the American recruit several times in June and July. Deutsch, accustomed to the British manners and character of the other agents in the Cambridge network, was singularly unimpressed with Straight and shared his impressions with Moscow:

> He differs very much from those people we dealt with before. He is a typical American, a man of wide-ranging enterprise who thinks he can do everything himself. . . . He is full of enthusiasm, well-read, very intelligent, and a perfect student. He wants to do much for us and, of course, has all possibilities for this . . . but he also gives the impression of being a dilettante, a young guy who has everything he wants, more money than he can spend, and therefore in part who has a restless conscience. . . . I think, under experienced guidance, he could achieve a lot. However, he needs to be educated and to have control over his personal life. It is precisely contact with people in his future profession which may turn out dangerously for him. So far, he has been an active member of the party and constantly surrounded by his friends.[9]

It was Straight's exuberance that most troubled Deutsch, who provided Moscow with an additional report of their final meeting in early August: "Tomorrow he is leaving for America. . . . He has very little experience and sometimes behaves like a child in his romanticism. He thinks he is working for the Comintern, and he must be left in this delusion for a while."[10]

Straight had not forgotten his commitment to the *Daily Worker* and gave Deutsch 500 British pounds for the newspaper, a sum he proposed transferring every three months through NKVD contacts in America. Thus, even after being recruited for Soviet intelligence work, far from breaking with all of his "open" party efforts, Michael proposed maintaining at least one of his earlier radical obligations, a symptom of the "romanticism" about which Deutsch complained—yet tolerated: "In my opinion, it is very important to take this money from him, since in his eyes, it speaks to his contact with the party which is [still] very important for him." Within a month of reaching the United States, Michael had been contacted by Akhmerov but in a botched manner that suggested the confusion that lay ahead. Deutsch told Straight before his departure that he would be sent a letter at his mother's apartment stating: "Dear Friend. I just arrived and would like to see you next week. Yours, Anthony." His visitor would state that he came from Anthony, who sends his greetings, to which Straight would respond: "Is he still at Cambridge?"[11] Unfortunately, a second note written by Straight and given to Deutsch to pass back to Straight through Akhmerov, to confirm the new courier's legitimacy, never reached the New York station.

On September 11, 1937, Moscow sent Itzhak Akhmerov instructions to contact Straight and described him as someone who under "experienced guidance will lead us to sources of exceptional importance and value."[12] Although given the contact passwords, his NKVD superiors forgot to give their Soviet operative the expected letter, which seemed to unnerve Straight who kept asking for it.[13] Akhmerov also sensed some ideological hesitation on the American's part, which Moscow believed was a reflection of links to certain Trotskyist friends. Nevertheless, his superiors reminded Akhmerov that nurturing Straight as an agent was his "main task."[14]

Although in time Akhmerov (whom Straight knew as "Michael Green") came to believe that the two had "struck up a friendship" and that Straight "listens readily and follows all my advice," he complained that Michael Straight's non-Communist liberal friends also continued to affect his views: "His milieu at the *New Republic* exerts a not-very-healthy influence on him. A liberal like Roger Baldwin, outwardly a friend of the USSR but in his soul and in fact its enemy with great sympathy for Trotsky, . . . cannot help but exert a negative influence on him."

Straight's wealth and cheerful self-confidence made him a most unusual Soviet source. For one thing, he continued his practice, begun in England, of *offering* money to his Communist associates rather than *asking* for some. Akhmerov informed Moscow about a conversation on this subject during the fall of 1937:

> [Straight] claimed that he has $10,000–12,000 in spare money and does not know what to do with it. He asked whether I need money; he could give it to me. This is his spare pocket money. I said that I do not need money personally; let him keep it or put it in a bank. As for his previous regular donations, I will take them and pass them along accordingly.* At another meeting, he gave me $2,000 as his quarterly Party fee and claimed he would be giving more in future.[15]

Moscow conveyed the $2,000 to the Comintern Executive Committee for the British Communist Party[16] and instructed Akhmerov: "With [Straight], return to the discussion about his pocket money (the $12,000). Receive this money from him and send it to us."[17] The episode afforded a unique illustration of the classic Marxist precept: "From each according to his means."

After several months spent leisurely adjusting himself to the American scene, Michael Straight resumed his remarkable job search. Akhmerov reported to Moscow in mid-November that Straight did not want to join the State Department and thereby risk assignment to some distant post. Rather, he sought a career in business or finance and was considering going to work for General Motors in Detroit for a few months. Akhmerov approved this plan but was overruled by his NKVD superiors, who insisted that the Soviet operative persuade Straight to work for State.[18]

In a January 25, 1938, memorandum to Moscow, Akhmerov reported success:

> [Straight] managed to join the State Department, where he works as an assistant to the Department's counselor on international economic problems. . . . Now he has been assigned to write a paper on international armaments. From [NKVD agent] "11's" department, he receives reports on this issue by Ambassadors and, when the paper is finished, promises to give us a copy. Reading the Ambassadors' reports, he will remember the important items and pass them to me at our meetings. I send his first notes from the reports he read.

---

* Presumably a reference to the funds Straight continued to provide for the British *Daily Worker*.

With Michael Straight now working at the State Department, a problem emerged. How was he to be kept from socializing with other Soviet agents in the department, among them Laurence Duggan and Alger Hiss? Akhmerov reported in his January 25 memorandum that Roger Baldwin had already introduced Straight to Laurence Duggan and recommended Straight as a fellow "progressive." Akhmerov told Straight to keep Duggan at a distance lest his own career be damaged.[19]

Straight's continued involvement in "open" Communist activities after his return to America compounded the problem. Thus, Akhmerov warned on February 18, 1938, that "local workers of the brother [party] have begun cultivating [Straight] in order to draw him into [their] work. [Sol] Adler from Treasury met with him. [Straight] declined the offer, claiming that he has nothing to do with this movement." Rather, Straight informed Adler that he was "a liberal with progressive ideas and nothing more."[20]

To end such complications, the NKVD's top officials in Moscow decided to instruct Earl Browder personally to avoid any CPUSA contact with Straight.[21] Closer to home, Akhmerov lectured Michael on the dangers of even casual encounters with known Communists: "All the time, I explain to [Straight] that by no means should he let people recognize that he is a compatriot. I recommend that he settle down in society as a liberal with some progressive ideas within the framework of the American Democratic Party. It is important for his career."[22]

Meanwhile, Moscow had become impatient for more important "deliverables" from Straight than he had yet provided, informing Akhmerov on March 26 that since Michael "may be a very valuable source, he must be taken care of and, most important, EDUCATED, made our man, have his brains rebuilt in our manner." Specifically,

Teach him to collect the material we are interested in. As [Straight] does not deliver genuine materials [documents] yet, but only his notes, he must put the date, the number of the document he describes, as well as from where the documents come (author) and where it is sent. Lacking this data, the value of his agent information is lost . . . work on his material as well as on him. . . . Besides, [Straight's] material sent with this mail is old. What has he got on his desk? Only last year's material?[23]

Unfortunately for the NKVD, Straight's work on international economic issues did not generate much classified material, and Moscow urged Akhmerov to press Straight to transfer, if possible, to the European Bureau in whose work it was more urgently interested. Also,

Akhmerov's superiors wanted Straight engaged in "talent-spotting" among his colleagues for other potential recruits.[24] But Michael continued to disappoint Moscow: "Ascertain with regret that thus far no success has been achieved in developing [Straight's] work," Akhmerov reported on May 24. "Meet with him every week. Talk for hours about the work and political topics but, so far, no results. I hoped to send his report on armaments, but unexpectedly he fell ill and failed to finish it." Straight was evidently troubled by the demand that he filch classified documents for his Soviet friends, pleading that he no longer received ambassadorial reports and that most of what he did read came from published sources.[25] Nevertheless, in June, he finally delivered his armaments report to Akhmerov, and, the following month, the Russian noted that Straight had passed on a report from the American consul in London about British war reserves of raw materials.[26]

During this same period, however, Moscow's earlier request that Straight serve as a "talent-spotter" threatened not only his own exposure but that of the Soviets' two most valuable agents in the State Department. In early spring, Michael had provided Akhmerov with a list of "progressives" at State, among them Laurence Duggan, whom Straight had heard was "very close to us ideologically."[27] At the time, he knew nothing about Duggan's link to the NKVD.

In June, however, Straight met another politically sympathetic State Department colleague who had been recruited years earlier by Soviet military intelligence (GRU)—Alger Hiss. Akhmerov described the situation in a June 28, 1938, memorandum to Moscow:

> According to the conditions of work, [Straight] established contact with Hiss.* [Straight] mentioned him to me earlier, indicating that he was an interesting person who occupied a responsible position, etc. He also said that ideologically Hiss was a very progressive man. I didn't show my interest in him, but, on the other hand, I can't tell him to stop seeing Hiss. If I tell him that, he might guess that Hiss belongs to our family. There is another danger: *bratskiy* [American Communist Party's underground agents] or Neighbors' [Soviet Military Intelligence] resident (I am not quite sure who Hiss is connected to) may ask Hiss to start working on [Straight's] recruitment.

---

* Evidently lacking knowledge of Alger Hiss's code name or even with which other branch of Soviet intelligence he was connected, Akhmerov referred directly to "Hiss" in this dispatch, an unusual practice in Soviet tradecraft at the time.

Apparently, Straight's own involvement in Soviet espionage was not known to Hiss, who, two years earlier, had displayed keen interest in recruiting Noel Field and possibly other department colleagues. Akhmerov's memo continued:

> I am sure that [Straight] would refuse to cooperate with them if they try to recruit him,* but in this case [Straight] would find out Hiss's nature.... I am writing about all this as a possibility that you should take into consideration and, if you have an opportunity, influence the Neighbors' resident if he starts to recruit [Straight] through Hiss....[28]

The following month, on July 31, 1938, Akhmerov clarified his understanding of Alger Hiss's role in the Soviet underground in this memorandum to Moscow:

> "Storm" [code name then used by Joszef Peter, *a.k.a.* "J. Peter," head of the U.S. Communist Party's own underground network] let out a secret during one of our conversations. Hiss used to be a member of *bratskiy* organization [the Ware Group period from 1934 to 1936] who had been routed into [the State Department] and sent to the Neighbors [GRU] later. He [Peter] told me about it when I was hunting for Hiss. In one of our discussions, "Nikolai" told me that it was possible that at the time [1935–36] the Neighbors were not connected with Hiss, most likely because of some organizational difficulties.[29]

Alger Hiss was presumably cautioned by his own controllers in Soviet military intelligence to avoid association with Straight, and Straight's personal NKVD file does not mention further contact with his State Department colleague, who had already been long involved in Soviet intelligence work.

Once it became clear to Akhmerov's superiors in Moscow that Michael Straight's limited access at State precluded him from obtaining valuable troves of secret documents and information, their focus shifted to advancing Straight's career as an agent in place. Thus, when Akhmerov reported that Thomas Corcoran, a key Roosevelt aide, had asked Straight to become his secretary, a post from which he might more easily transfer to the President's secretariat, Moscow was in-

---

* A reference to Soviet military intelligence, the branch with which Alger Hiss was associated.

trigued. Nevertheless, Straight was urged to remain at State unless an opportunity arose to work directly in the White House for FDR.[30]

The NKVD was evidently prepared to be patient with this extremely well-connected operative, cautioning Akhmerov: "[Straight] is a big agent in perspective, and burning him . . . is not our intention. It is better not to receive this or that nonurgent material or to communicate its approximate contents than to expose to needless risk our work and the relations between our countries. You must always keep this in mind."[31]

Moscow's interest was in maintaining a long-term relationship with the wealthy acolyte. Thus, after Straight received a letter that month from "Anthony" in London (presumably Anthony Blunt) requesting funds for Spanish refugees, Akhmerov cautioned Moscow that such contacts jeopardized Michael's reputation in Washington as a non-Communist "progressive." "If you have a chance," Akhmerov asked, "take all measures to make the brother workers in London [British Comintern agents], particularly Anthony, forget about [Straight]."[32] At that time, significantly, Michael Straight still believed that Akhmerov ("Michael Green") was an agent of the Comintern, the international Communist movement, and not the Soviet NKVD, a distinction important to many of the USSR's most energetic Western agents drawn to the cause by their antifascist beliefs.[33]

For that reason, the signing of the Nazi-Soviet Pact on August 23, 1939, was a watershed event in Straight's life as it was for other Western intellectuals who had been devoted to world communism and the Soviet Union. Although Akhmerov was successful in persuading other American sources in his networks to accept this bewildering shift in Soviet policy, he informed Moscow on September 8 that Straight "openly expressed his disappointment at the Soviet Union [and] sharply criticized Soviet policy as well as the policy of the American Communist Party." * [34]

Straight angrily rejected the various American Communist *apologias* for the Pact in discussions with Akhmerov over the next month. Despite the latter's disingenuous memorandum to Moscow on October 25, 1939, asserting that he had "managed to . . . put [Straight] on the right path; now he agrees with all my arguments," Akhmerov earlier admitted that Straight "had not been coming to meetings for a month." Michael Straight's infatuation with international communism was

---

* Straight's eloquent memoir described this sense of disillusionment. Michael Straight, *After Long Silence*, pp. 143–44.

drawing to a close, doubtless accelerated by his recent marriage. Straight confided to Akhmerov, as had Laurence Duggan at virtually the same time, his constant fear of exposure: "he was not afraid of prison, etc., but he did not want to damage the future of his bride."[35]

Straight's newfound personal happiness, combined with political discontent over Moscow's policy shift, led to his break with Soviet intelligence. Itzhak Akhmerov's departure for the Soviet Union in late 1939 completed the separation process. Although the NKVD then assigned Straight to "Igor," an operative of Washington's "legal" station, he no longer delivered information or material from State and avoided contact with his designated controller.[36]

When another Soviet agent from the NKVD's "legal" station in New York met with Straight on July 15, 1941, Michael informed him that he was then working at the *New Republic* magazine. He had resigned from State, he explained, because of boredom with his work and because he had failed to receive an expected posting to the U.S. Embassy in London.[37] Decades later, in his memoirs, Straight credited his departure to an unwillingness "to be a Soviet agent in the Department of State" and called it "a welcome escape . . . an escape from the trap that had held me captive."[38] All of these factors probably figured in Michael Straight's decision to abandon an increasingly uncomfortable role as a source of information for Soviet intelligence as they did in Laurence Duggan's comparable disengagement.

The NKVD made one final effort to regain Straight's cooperation when Itzhak Akhmerov returned to the United States in 1942 for a second tour of duty. After restoring contact, "Michael Green" urged Straight to use his still-close association with the Roosevelts and other key Washington figures on behalf of the Soviet Union, a request that Straight firmly rejected. Describing the encounter in a June 3, 1942, memorandum to Moscow, Vassily Zarubin, the station chief in New York at the time, called Straight:

> ideologically demoralized: his anti-Soviet statements prove it. For instance, he claims that in the war against Germany, the USSR defends narrow national interests and that the world Communist movement has no meaning for the USSR. In his view, one should render assistance to the Soviet Union only as long as the war which the USSR wages is advantageous for England and the U.S.[39]

It was another Soviet master-operative, Yuri Modin, one of the "Cambridge group's" controllers, who later described the end of the association:

In 1942 [Straight] decided to make a clean break. He relayed this decision to his handler [Akhmerov], though at the same time, he gave his word to keep secret the small amount of work he had done for the Russians. [Akhmerov] did not object.

We never spoke to Straight again, and he kept his side of the bargain scrupulously. He never uttered a word to anyone about Burgess or Blunt. In my opinion, he was scared of them. He must have believed that if he denounced Blunt and his friends they would find some way to exact revenge. Only after Burgess's death in 1963 did Michael Straight confess. . . . His thirty-year silence was motivated above all by his fear of the KGB. . . .[40]

Straight (according to his NKVD file) did meet once or twice with Burgess after his break and once with Burgess and Blunt in London in May 1946, where Straight had journeyed to visit his ailing mother. Michael Straight told his former Cambridge friends, the pair responsible for his original recruitment, what he had told Itzhak Akhmerov in 1942. He had broken all links to Soviet espionage because, although remaining an American liberal, he had abandoned belief in the progressive nature of communism or the Soviet Union.[41] Franklin and Eleanor Roosevelt's former protégé, Michael Straight, now considered those convictions to have been tragically naive and false.*

---

*In recent correspondence with Allen Weinstein, Michael Straight acknowledged that "the Soviet intelligence files on myself" quoted in this chapter "confirm and substantiate the story published in my own autobiography, *After Long Silence*." Straight took issue, however, with reports to Moscow in the Soviet archives about him supposedly sent by Soviet operatives Theodore Maly and Andre Deutsch. Straight states that he had met Maly only once, briefly, and had never met Deutsch. He believes that many of the statements and actions described in the cables probably came from his letters to Anthony Blunt, and "that Blunt gave my letters to Deutsch . . . [who] then forwarded Blunt's appraisals, reports of meetings, and comments as his own." Similarly with Maly, according to Straight, he believes that excerpts from his letters to Blunt "were forwarded to Moscow by Maly *as if they had been written by him*." Nevertheless, Straight concludes, whether via Blunt or directly from the Soviet operatives, "the appraisal of my character and state of mind is sophisticated, accurate, and very perceptive." (Michael Straight to Allen Weinstein, January 25, March 8, and April 26, 1999.)

CHAPTER 5

❖

Love and Loyalties, II:
Elizabeth Bentley
and Jacob Golos

THE AFFAIR was an unlikely one from the start: Jacob Golos, a fifty-year-old Russian Jew who coordinated an underground Communist network involving dozens of Washington and New York sources, and his lover, Elizabeth Bentley, an old-family American and a Vassar graduate, two decades younger, and Golos's most trusted courier. Their liaison lasted from 1938 until Golos died on November 25, 1943. Within two years of his death, Bentley had shifted her allegiance from the Soviets to the FBI. Her defection compelled Soviet intelligence immediately to shut down virtually all of its underground operations in the United States.

Both before and after Golos's death, the tale of Elizabeth Bentley ("Miss Wise," a code name later changed to "Myrna") and Jacob Golos (code-named "Sound") also involved dozens of other Soviet agents and their American sources in the United States, including Earl Browder, the leader of the American Communist Party. Under the code name "Helmsman," Browder, too, was deeply enmeshed in "secret work" during these years.

To protect the identity of their American sources and control them personally, in one of the most unusual efforts of its kind by leading Soviet operatives, Golos struggled prior to his death (and Bentley thereafter) to prevent other Soviet intelligence operatives from meeting directly with the American agents in government and industry whom they had cultivated. As a result, many of those who cooperated with Soviet intelligence, ideologically committed Communists, often believed (or professed to believe) that the information and documents they provided were actually sent via Golos to the American Communist Party or the Comintern, and not directly to the NKVD in Moscow.

JACOB GOLOS

Golos's background was summarized by a 1939 Comintern memo requested by the NKVD: "Golos, Jacob—member of the CPUS [Communist Party of the United States]. Born April 30, 1890, in Russia. Jewish. U.S. citizen. Worker. Lower education. Knows English and Russian."[1] By that time, he had already developed the habit of working simultaneously with several distinct Soviet intelligence components.

Other NKVD documents provided further details of Golos's background. He spent two years in Siberia after his arrest in 1907 for operating a clandestine Bolshevik printing house. Golos escaped first to Japan, then to China, and in 1910 arrived in America.[2] Several years later, he became an early organizer of the U.S. Communist Party and a member of its "Russian bureau." After holding a series of posts within the party during the 1920s, Golos returned to the USSR in 1926.[3] The then-secretary of the U.S. Communist Party, Jay Lovestone, formally requested his transfer back in 1928 because "Comrade Golos has considerable influence among Russian laboring masses in the United States,"[4] a request probably encouraged by Golos himself.

By 1930, Jacob Golos had begun a new career in Soviet intelligence work as a GPU operative in New York, devoted at first largely to acquiring American and other passports for the U.S. Communist Party and the Comintern. Such passports were critical to assuring easy international movement by "illegals" and others. His major contact in the United States (after 1933) was a consular official and Soviet operative in New York, Gaik Ovakimyan. Through bribes, Golos developed a network of foreign consular officials and U.S. passport agency workers who supplied him not only with passports but also naturalization documents and birth certificates belonging to persons who had died or had permanently left the United States.[5]

Golos also continued to maintain links during the mid-1930s with "open" Communist Party organizers. This was unavoidable because his primary cover involved management of a Comintern-owned business called World Tourist, essentially a full-service travel agency for party members and other "progressives" planning trips to the Soviet Union.

Golos, long-married, arranged in 1935 for his wife and son to return to Moscow, supposedly to allow his son to attend a Soviet school.[6] In an autobiography written in 1944 at the request of the NKVD, after Golos's death, Elizabeth Bentley explained her lover's tangled personal life. Although, according to Bentley, Golos had asked her to marry him,

> [h]e explained to me that he was in a very complicated situation. At the beginning of the 1920s, he was asked to declare as his wife a woman from his party cell who needed a passport to enter and leave the [United States]. He didn't marry her formally but slept with her. She, in turn, against his wish, gave birth to a son. . . . He said that to get a divorce he needed to return home [to the Soviet Union] in order not to disclose the entire affair. Therefore, he asked me to live with him and wait to marry until everything was arranged.[7]

Golos's most important visit to Moscow occurred in November 1937, when Peter Gutzeit took him to meet Abram Slutsky, then the Soviet intelligence chief. Slutsky told Golos that, in addition to his main task of locating useable passports, he should begin to recruit Communist sailors in American ports, to be used as international couriers for the NKVD.[8]

By this time, Golos had expanded his passport production contacts to Canada. (One NKVD file noted in 1938 that a Soviet operative named "Norma," who became both mistress and courier for Donald Maclean in London that year, received her passport in Toronto with Golos's assistance!)[9] World Tourist, meanwhile, had taken on a new assignment. In addition to expediting politically correct tourists to the Soviet Union along with Comintern agents or CP officials, it also produced documents needed by American volunteers traveling to Spain to fight in the Communist-dominated International Brigades. So extensive were his activities and those of World Tourist that an NKVD agent in the Justice Department turned over FBI reports in spring 1937 that identified Golos as someone under Bureau scrutiny as "a Comintern agent" known to have organized travel by American volunteers into the Spanish Civil War zone. World Tourist became a genuine moneymaker for Communist causes during the late 1930s.[10] By that time, Golos also had become primary assistant to a leading NKVD "illegal" in New York named Rabinovich (code-named "Harry"), who noted in a report to Moscow on 1938–39 activities that he had met with Golos some 500 to 600 times during this period, often two or three times a day.[11]

The Justice Department began a formal investigation of Golos and his company in 1939, which resulted in his arrest and trial on various violations of America's espionage and neutrality laws. The USSR's People's Commissar for Internal Affairs, Lavrenty Beria, was sufficiently concerned over the episode that he forwarded a report to the Soviet Union's leadership troika—Stalin, Molotov, and Voroshilov—on March 5, 1940, the same day the NKVD's station chief in New York wrote to Moscow: "[Today] trial hearings are starting on the case of 'World Tourist' . . . accused of military espionage on behalf of foreign states and of violating the registration law. At one time, this office was being used by the Comintern to transfer money for the American Communist Party. Golos (manager of World Tourist), Brodsky (lawyer for the Communist Party), and others were summoned to trial."[12]

Ten days later, after negotiations between attorneys for the government and the defendants, Golos plea-bargained to a lesser charge and was sentenced to four to twelve months probation and a $1,000 fine.[13] Bentley noted in her December 1944 NKGB* "autobiography" that the guilty plea incensed Golos because it stemmed from a deal by his attorney with prosecutors that if one of the Communist organizations (his) pleaded guilty the others would be left alone. A leadership meeting of the U.S. Communist Party, in which Golos did not take part, decided that he should undertake the possible jail-time assignment. An angry Golos agreed but complained "that it was the worst thing that ever happened to him—pleading guilty at a bourgeois trial."[14]

ELIZABETH BENTLEY
AND JACOB GOLOS

By 1940, Golos and Bentley had lived together for two years, an arrangement Bentley described candidly in her December 1944 NKGB memoir:

> In addition to a strong physical attraction to [Golos] as well as a strong feeling of camaraderie—since we had common ideas and worked for one cause—I admired him as a hero, since for me he was the best kind of revolutionary.
>
> For the first years of our relationship, [he] deliberately trained me a great deal, stating that I was like a soldier at the front and I must work hard and produce good results. He claimed that, be-

---

* As the NKVD had become by this time, later changed to the KGB.

cause of his love for me, he wanted to be proud of me and my work. He supported me in moments of fatigue and disappointment.[15]

Elizabeth Bentley took seriously Moscow's request for a complete account of her life and background. She described the family genealogy, which began allegedly with ancestors who had arrived on the *Mayflower*. Her mother's forebears had fought in the Revolutionary War, according to Bentley, and one of them—Roger Sherman—even signed the Declaration of Independence as a Connecticut delegate.[16] In short, she was, as NKGB station chief Gaik Ovakimyan informed Moscow, "a genuine American Aryan."[17] Because of the anti-Semitism still prevalent in American government and society at the time, Soviet intelligence considered non-Jewish agents in the United States such as Elizabeth Bentley especially useful.

Born on January 1, 1908, in New Milford, Connecticut, she recalled a lonely childhood spent, primarily, reading books and comparatively isolated teenage years, since "my mother didn't allow me to be friendly with girls of my age who drank, smoked and visited nightclubs."[18] After attending and graduating from Vassar College, Bentley studied at Columbia University (1932–33) and briefly in Italy. Although drawn to the theater, she held a variety of jobs after graduation as a saleswoman, librarian, teacher, and secretary.[19]

Bentley also provided the NKGB with an intimate glimpse into her love life. Thus, in college, "I was shy and a virgin," and her first "very youthful" romance was in 1929 with a British engineer as they sailed for Europe on the same ship. Two years later, she lived with a much older Hungarian officer in Italy. Before meeting Golos in 1938, she had two other affairs, one with an Iraqi student at Columbia and another with a Greek worker and fellow member of the New York City Communist cell she had joined in January 1935.[20] Another educated and free-spirited woman, Juliette Stuart Poyntz, steered the footloose Bentley toward deeper engagement with the party ("Friends began calling me 'Red' when, in fact, I knew nothing about either socialism or communism").[21]

Poyntz, a party member and underground agent, tried to persuade Bentley to travel to Italy as a new recruit, according to Bentley's 1944 memoir, stating that she would have to sleep with men to gain information. Bentley refused, and after discussing the matter with Communist Party officials at Columbia, Poyntz was told to keep away from the new recruit.

A confrontation followed. Poyntz, according to Bentley, came to her apartment a few days later, called her a Trotskyist, and threatened to kill her.[22] That was the last time Bentley saw Poyntz, whom Soviet intelligence archives describe as a member of a "special operations" group working in the United States beginning in the early 1930s under the supervision of one Jacob Serebryansky. Poyntz disappeared in New York in June 1937 under mysterious circumstances and was never seen again.[23] At the time, veteran NKVD, GRU, and Comintern agents were finding it increasingly difficult to escape the vengeance of Stalin's virtually indiscriminate purges. Most of Poyntz's friends and some Soviet agents—Whittaker Chambers among them—assumed, correctly or not, that she had been murdered at Moscow's instructions. By then, 1938, another Communist Party official had introduced Elizabeth Bentley to Jacob Golos, and the couple remained inseparable from that first encounter until Golos's death five years later.

The years of the Great Purge in the Soviet Union, 1936–39, provoked Moscow's suspicious scrutiny of many Soviet intelligence operatives abroad, including Golos. Because of his long-standing Communist involvement, both open and secret, begun before the Bolshevik Revolution, Golos's independent habits were well known within his circle of associates. Some thought him too casual to manage a growing network of agents and sources in both New York and Washington. Others believed his obvious visibility to American counterintelligence after his conviction a matter of grave concern. Still others accused him of being a Trotskyist.

Moscow began trying as early as the fall of 1939 to bring the maverick Golos back to the Soviet Union: "It is too late [for him] to run away, but possible," Gaik Ovakimyan cautioned his NKVD superiors on October 21, 1939.[24] His "disappearance will inflict damage on the compatriots." Supported by Earl Browder, Golos opposed returning at that moment. (In any case, after Golos's conviction, several attempts on his part to obtain an American passport for a Moscow trip were rejected by American authorities.)[25] Throughout the late 1930s, Peter Gutzeit and other NKVD operatives in the United States had to defend Golos periodically against allegations of Trotskyist sympathies. Even after Gutzeit himself was recalled to Moscow in 1938 and arrested as "a people's enemy," he persisted at his Lubyanka interrogation in supporting Golos's loyalty as an operative: "[He] never provoked any suspicions or doubts."[26]

For two years, the NKVD debated whether to recall, arrest, or execute Jacob Golos, based less on concrete evidence of disloyalty than on the pervasive paranoia in Moscow at the time. Several arrested anti-Bolshevik agents (one, a scientist named Ilya Durmashkin, who "confessed" before his execution to having worked over three decades as a spy in turn for the Czarist Okhrana, the Mensheviks, the Trotskyists, and the Nazis!) implicated Golos in one or another of these alleged conspiracies, sometimes several. In September 1939, for example, an NKVD official in Moscow filed a memo with his superiors stating categorically that "[Golos] may by no means remain in the list of agents in the U.S. Since he knows a great deal about the station's work, I would consider it expedient to bring him to the Soviet Union and arrest him."[27]

That same month, Major Pavel Fitin of State Security wrote Lavrenty Beria proposing the recall from America of two "illegals" suspected of being "people's enemies" who, in addition to relationships with other executed former NKVD agents, had been "exposed to the agent [Golos], who is strongly suspected of Trotskyite activities."[28] As late as July 1940, yet another Moscow NKVD memo stated that there was "every ground to assert that Durmashkin's statements about [Golos] are corroborated." The memo implicated Golos in relationships with "persons who turned out to be Trotskyites, English and German spies": "On the grounds of all this material, it is necessary to isolate [Golos] urgently from all affairs at the [New York] station and to recall him immediately to the Soviet Union. Further, [Golos's] sojourn in the U.S. endangers all of our work due to an absolutely inadmissible situation that, in fact, he knows more than the station chief."[29]

Moscow's madness over "people's enemies" in its American ranks did not stop with Golos, since "the station chief" mentioned in this memo, Gaik Ovakimyan, was under similar suspicion. And his recall to Moscow was ordered in 1939. Like Golos, however, Ovakimyan stayed alive by remaining in New York.[30]

Although shielded in America from Moscow's vengeance, Golos's colleagues discussed a more immediate danger to their personal security posed by his very presence. The start of the Second World War led to increased activity by U.S. counterintelligence organizations, including the FBI. The Bureau already kept Golos under constant surveillance after his conviction. Nevertheless, with Earl Browder's consent, in 1940, Golos added important Washington bureaucrats in the Roosevelt government to his numerous agents and sources. These included "Pal" (code name for Nathan Gregory Silvermaster, who coordinated a group of Communist agents in important Administration posts), "Richard" (Harry Dexter White), and others.[31] The NKVD's New York station considered Silvermaster's network, whose oversight Golos acquired in 1940, a major source of political information in Washington during the war.*

One New York–based agent, Pavel Pastelnyak ("Luka"), wrote Moscow in April 1940 complaining about Golos's presence and that of another agent who was also under FBI surveillance:

> If something happens to them, much of what has been created will be reduced to ashes. Some operatives believe that [Golos] has become a virtual station chief in the U.S. He provides people for different kinds of services and missions in every field of our work. [Yet Golos] . . . is on the books of American [counter]intelligence as a major NKVD agent. . . . [Therefore] his presence in the station becomes dangerous for business. . . .[32]

In fact, Golos was being monitored by at least one individual at the time, a Soviet agent by the name of "Armand Lavis Feldman," a pseudonym for I. V. Volodarsky, who also reported to the FBI. Feldman reported on both Golos and Ovakimyan to the Bureau.[†] The NKGB discovered this only in 1945, when another of its sources, Judith Coplon ("Sima"), then working at the Justice Department, acquired Volodarsky's file from the New York FBI office. The dossier showed FBI knowledge of meetings between Golos and Ovakimyan in 1941 where envelopes were exchanged and also identified Elizabeth Bentley as Golos's courier.[33]

The prewar purges within the USSR's intelligence community and virtually every other area of Soviet life had receded by this time, as Stalin and his associates sought to rally a demoralized citizenry against the invading Nazi armies. Moscow no longer considered Golos to be a "people's enemy," nor were his superiors overly sensitive to the problem of FBI monitoring. What ensued instead was a struggle between Golos and several professional Russian agents, recent Soviet arrivals, for control of Golos's vast network of sources. Golos considered the new arrivals "operational youngsters," culturally unprepared to work with his covert American contacts, some of whom he had been cultivating since the mid-1930s.

Bentley's 1944 NKGB memoir described the physical and emotional strains involved in this process:

---

* Chapter 8 describes the Silvermaster Group's activities.
† "Feldman's" activities are also discussed in Chapter 2, p. 33.

At the beginning of spring 1941, [Golos] and I began working with a large number of people from the U.S. Communist Party, and I received my first people in Washington. [Golos] instructed me to treat them as Communists, gather dues, and educate them, in addition to receiving information from them. [Golos] also insisted that I should make copies of their materials since he wanted to keep them in order to show [Earl Browder] when the latter leaves jail. Before that, I never made copies.

Plainly, Browder's imprisonment had led to the urgent transfer to Golos's oversight of underground contacts the American Communist leader had previously personally supervised. The strain of this additional work and responsibility took its toll on Golos, according to Bentley, who called the period from spring 1941 to spring 1942 a "very unfavorable" year for her lover: "His heart attack was progressing, . . . [Browder] was in prison, and [Golos] couldn't get along with CP functionaries downtown."[34]

Germany's attack on the Soviet Union in June 1941 led to a general acceleration of effort throughout its American intelligence networks. Frustrated with his NKVD colleagues, Golos began to talk about leaving the United States to fight alongside his son in the Soviet army. Although Browder was released from prison in the spring of 1942 and Golos's relationships with the Communist Party appeared to improve as a result, "his heart condition worsened [according to Bentley], and his physical and mental decline began."

At this time, Jacob Golos began quarreling fiercely and constantly with various Russian operatives with whom he worked. He told Bentley that "they were young and inexperienced, didn't work hard, and were not careful. He told me all the time that [Browder] was his only friend, the only man who understood him." Golos's complaints intensified along with his physical suffering during these months: "He told me," Bentley later wrote, "that Russians didn't understand Americans, that they treated him badly, and that he was the only man in the organization who was able to deal with Americans."[35]

The final straw for Golos was an instruction from his Soviet superiors in New York and Washington to turn over to their direct control various American sources whose information and documents he had been receiving. He traveled to Washington to protest directly, but unsuccessfully, to NKVD station chief Vassily Zarubin. Golos's world was collapsing around him, since even Bentley obeyed instructions other than his own. Zarubin had instructed Bentley to turn Golos's Washington network over to the control of recently arrived Soviet operative Itzhak Akhmerov. As a result, Golos "got completely upset. He complained that, not limiting themselves to taking his best people from him, they were also taking his assistant and that was the last straw. When I began delivering materials to [Akhmerov, Golos] warned me that Russians were rude people and that I should be firm dealing with them if I wanted to get along."

During his last months, Bentley recalled in 1944, Golos's "only bright moment seemed his friendship with [Browder]. When [Browder] passed him a new group [of sources, Golos] said to me bitterly: 'He is the only man who trusts me.' . . . He said that if something happened to him, I should go on working in his place. Then, he said bitterly that he didn't know what would happen to me when he was dead—that I was completely unprepared for working with 'rude Russians.' "[36]

What Golos chose to ignore in his final years was that, especially since his arrest and conviction, he himself was the most vulnerable link in the NKGB's U.S. operations. Golos posed to any American he contacted the threat of identification by FBI surveillance and possible exposure.

His May 1, 1943, letter to an old friend, Pavel Fitin, at NKGB headquarters in Moscow was a last "official" effort to protect his elaborate American franchise against a home office takeover. Describing "numerous" counterintelligence inquiries in progress throughout the U.S. government against "all liberal and progressive people," Golos pointed to all of the various problems he confronted in attempting to manage his intelligence work. Despite the obstacles, he asserted that "we are producing quite a lot" and promised even better results in future.[37] Perhaps in an attempt to placate the still-useful Golos, on November 24, 1943, Fitin recommended that he receive the Order of the Red Star in recognition of his work over many years as "a talent-spotter, personal data gatherer, group controller and recruiter, who drew a number of valuable sources to our work."[38]

The following day, November 25, Golos and Bentley met for lunch at the London Terrace restaurant in New York and later went to Bentley's apartment. A tired Golos slumped into an armchair to take a nap. Several minutes later, Bentley heard him cough heavily and then stop breathing. By the time an ambulance arrived, he was dead. Police questioned Bentley for six hours before releasing her.[39] Golos's Moscow superiors, when informed of his death, decided not to award his medal posthumously.[40]

"I think Golos's great misfortune," Bentley speculated the following year, "was that he worked mainly as an individualist from the first days we met." Other than accusing him of having been a "people's enemy," Bentley could have made a no more damning accusation against a Soviet operative. She continued:

> On the basis of his experience both at home and in this country, he reckoned that he was the only one who knew how to behave in various situations. This concerned both his firm [World Tourist] and his work for the organization. He ran the firm as a one-man business neither giving power to others nor preparing them for it. He also acted this way in the organization's affairs, the major part of whose work he did himself. He was very secretive and told very little to others about his moves. Only when he fell ill did he provide me, out of pure necessity, with many details. This is how I now evaluate [Golos]. I don't know; maybe I am wrong. Until recently, I was not able to assess him without bias, partly because of my love for him and partly because I knew little about his activities in our organization and the CP.[41]

One 1945 NKGB report on Golos's work concluded that he should never have remained a visible functionary of the American Communist Party while also engaged in espionage; it drew U.S. counterintelligence attention to him. Nor, without knowing more about his agents and operating methods, should Golos have been allowed to become "the main pillar of our intelligence work in the U.S."[42]

ELIZABETH BENTLEY

Jacob Golos's death resulted in greater attention by Soviet operatives in New York and Washington to his mistress, who knew much more about his work than any of the Russians. Golos, Vassily Zarubin informed Moscow, had given him "the impression that [Bentley] was only a courier. As it turns out, she was his closest assistant from whom he had no secrets." Even Bentley acknowledged that typically Golos did not tell his closest colleagues—herself included—the names and personal data of his American agents and sources. Thus, initially he did not even report Bentley's involvement to Moscow, and she entered the NKVD's files only in 1939.[43] Later, because of the FBI's close monitoring of Golos, he delegated Bentley to serve as the contact for Silvermaster and other Washington sources from whom she collected materials once or twice a month.[44]

When questioned by Itzhak Akhmerov and his wife, Helen Lowry, on November 29 about Golos's death, Bentley blurted out one important piece of news. He had told her shortly before his demise that, if anything happened to him, she should destroy immediately a sealed envelope kept in his safety-deposit box. Following his instructions to the letter, the next day Bentley removed the envelope and destroyed it unopened. Akhmerov was skeptical of this in his report to Moscow: "She seems a very careful and accurate person. Strange that she destroyed [Golos's] envelope without opening it. . . . Personally, for me, this kind of psychology is incomprehensible."[45]

During their November 29 meeting, Bentley rejected Akhmerov's request that she introduce him to Silvermaster on the grounds that he and other members of Golos's network were afraid of direct contact with Russians. "Here," Akhmerov reported to Moscow, "undoubtedly she expressed [Golos's] psychology. . . . [Nevertheless,] she made a good impression on me. Intelligent, sober-minded, and a quiet woman . . . a sincere person. Surely the late [Golos's] psychology is inserted into her psychology also. I hope we'll get along with her in a spirit essential to [our work]."[46]

Although Bentley recognized that she (and Golos) were working with and for the NKGB, in order to gain control of his agents, she exploited the distinction, crucial to a number of cooperating sources, between delivering material to Americans such as herself and Browder, on the one hand, and working directly for the Soviet Union. (For years, even Browder's close relationship to Soviet espionage had not been shared with Bentley.) For months following Golos's death, Bentley conducted a skillful campaign, occasionally helped by Browder, to prevent the various Soviet operatives from gaining control of Golos's networks.*

At times, Elizabeth Bentley appeared to have inherited her late lover's intensely negative attitude toward the NKGB operatives with whom she worked. For example, although she agreed to arrange a

---

* Two partially deciphered December 11, 1943, cables from New York station to Moscow attest to Soviet intelligence's interest in Elizabeth Bentley immediately following Golos's death. "[Bentley] has twice seen [Earl Browder], who . . . [undeciphered] more precise picture. We will advise the results." The deciphered portions of the second December 11 cable read as follows: "On 6th December [Bentley] advised that . . . [undeciphered] . . . continue work." Nos. 1139–40, VENONA files.

Washington meeting between Nathan Gregory Silvermaster and Akhmerov in March 1944, the following month she raised a variety of objections to the Soviet operative's request that Silvermaster come to New York for a second talk. Instead, she informed Akhmerov—nominally her superior within Soviet intelligence—that Silvermaster would be unable to travel to New York until the end of summer, a delay the Russian found unacceptable. He appealed to Moscow once again to persuade Browder to transfer Silvermaster's group entirely to his control, given Bentley's potentially dangerous habit of meeting with as many as a half dozen or more sources, sometimes in small groups, on each trip to Washington.[47]

Pressure on Earl Browder by Akhmerov and New York station chief Zarubin, reflecting Moscow's instructions, led Browder to instruct Bentley on June 6 that, in future, Silvermaster would deal directly with Akhmerov.[48] Browder recognized, however, that with such transfers of agents from Bentley to direct Soviet control, his authority declined along with hers. Basically, after Jacob Golos's death, the NKGB's New York station tried to compartmentalize his network as quickly as possible while transferring agent management from Bentley to more professional Soviet operatives.

If Earl Browder could give up old sources, he could also replace them with newer ones. Thus, he instructed Bentley in April 1944 to contact another group of American Communist agents working in U.S. government posts in Washington, a network that included Victor Perlo ("Raid"), Charles Kramer ("Mole" or "Lot"), and others who wished to pass information to Soviet intelligence. Browder intended that Bentley act only as a courier with the group, whose efforts had been neglected by various Soviet operatives. However, she held a number of longer meetings with its members before complaints about her intrusiveness again came from the NKGB stations in Washington and New York.[*49]

---

* The Perlo Group is discussed in Chapter 10. On Earl Browder's instructions to Elizabeth Bentley to meet with Victor Perlo and other agents in his group, see also the following 1944 VENONA cable: "On 27th April [Bentley] reported as follows: 'After [Jacob Golos's] death, [Earl Browder] ... [undeciphered] ... on [Browder's] instructions, [Golos] [undeciphered] ... [Silvermaster] used to meet [Browder] before meeting me. In future if [Browder] permits my meeting with [Silvermaster]. ... Even [Golos] used not to meet [Silvermaster] more often than once in six months.' Possibly she is making this up and exaggerating. At least ... [undeciphered] exclusive control of the [agents] and expressed ... fear

Although Akhmerov and other Soviet agents liked Elizabeth Bentley personally, the NKGB professionals were still concerned that she was more knowledgeable than they were about Soviet intelligence operations in the United States:

> She is a rather complicated and controversial character [Akhmerov wrote Moscow]. . . . she knows perfectly well that she is working for us. She, as a rule, carries out my instructions gladly and reports everything about our people to me. However, her behavior changes when I ask her to organize a meeting with [Silvermaster] for me or to connect some of the [American] probationers with our operative. She becomes an absolutely different person and . . . claims that she is not our operative, that she works for [Browder]. . . . Sometimes, by her remarks, I can feel that at heart, she doesn't like us [i.e., Russians]. She is inclined to distinguish us from compatriots [i.e., American Communists] and bitterly notices only our professional interest in different questions. She says that all of us [personally] care little about Americans, that the USSR is the only country we love and work for. I tried to explain that she is mistaken. . . .[50]

Akhmerov tried to defend the "dual loyalties" of Soviet agents such as Silvermaster and Perlo, but the native-born Bentley contemptuously dismissed both as more Russian than American. After the death of her Russian-born lover, in short, cultural tensions reinforced Elizabeth Bentley's growing alienation from Soviet espionage.

Although the gentle Akhmerov, always fascinated with American folkways, continued to trust Bentley—"I think she is undoubtedly one hundred percent our woman . . . [and] with a tactful attitude, friendly treatment, and firm businesslike relations, it is possible to correct her behavior,"[51] he wrote Moscow that spring—Pavel Fitin at NKGB headquarters was less certain: "It is necessary to take into consideration

---

[that] we will contact them direct. It is essential that [Zarubin] or I should see [Browder] and come to an agreement: that the whole group and [Bentley] [undeciphered]. . . . I recommend [asking] . . . [undeciphered]. . . . For more than a year [Zarubin] and I tried to get in touch with PERLO and FLATO. For some reason or other [Browder] did not come to the meeting and has just decided to put [Bentley] in touch with the whole group. If we work with this group it will be necessary to remove her and [undeciphered]. . . ." Itzhak Akhmerov to Moscow, April 29, 1944, No. 588, VENONA files.

[her] unbalanced state and inconstancy (today, she says one thing; tomorrow another)."[52]

Eventually Akhmerov grew concerned over what he called Bentley's "morbid feelings" toward, and "bad and morbid remarks" about, her Soviet colleagues and their country. But he assured Moscow on June 25 that Bentley had changed her tune: "Now she tells me that her life is connected with us, that she doesn't have any other interests besides her work, and that she loves our country more than anything else . . . her entire life for the past years has been devoted to our work . . . and her life will lose its meaning without this work . . . except for us, she has nobody she can share her feelings and thoughts with. . . ."*

After having failed to prevent Akhmerov's takeover of many of her Washington sources, Bentley now reversed course and insisted "she wanted to be connected to a Soviet operative rather than to an American Communist" such as Browder, gaining Akhmerov's agreement to link her to one of "our senior operatives." Bentley even told her Russian supervisor that she wished to become a Soviet citizen and became for the moment "completely obedient."[53]

At that point, Akhmerov briefly abandoned his responsibilities as a spymaster for the role of matchmaker, informing Moscow:

> I would like to resolve [Bentley's] personal problem. As I wrote you, she is a rather attractive person. The major part of her personal time is devoted to our work. She is alone in her personal life. . . . If I could, I would give her in marriage to one of our operatives. If there is no one [here], why not send somebody from home? Send him as a Polish or Baltic refugee to South America or Canada. We'll arrange the rest. It will bring great happiness . . . for our operative.

Nor did Akhmerov lack specifications for the role: "He must be 35–45 years old, single. Think this proposal over. Maybe, you will approve the idea." An apparently interested Pavel Fitin in Moscow responded: "The question of a husband for her must be thought over."[54]

---

* See also a July 11, 1944, cable on the situation from New York station to Moscow: "By post No. 5 of 7th July there was sent to you a detailed communication of [Akhmerov's] about [Bentley]. Here are the contents: [Bentley] is very much taking to heart the fact of [Akhmerov's] direct contact with [Silvermaster], evidently supposing that we do not trust her. [She is] offended at [Browder] for having consented to our liaison." No. 973, VENONA files.

Although some NKGB operatives by this time had become enamored of Elizabeth Bentley, both personally and professionally, her old protector Earl Browder now urged her separation from Soviet intelligence work. Browder was primarily concerned that Bentley's continued activity in managing not only World Tourist but yet another firm begun by Golos, the U.S. Shipping Corporation (which mailed packages to the Soviet Union), would bring increased FBI surveillance upon himself, Bentley, and all of their associates. Either she should continue working for Soviet intelligence, Browder argued, and sever her links to the companies, or she should focus on the "business" role alone, abandoning her work as an underground courier.*[55]

Earl Browder's complaint about Elizabeth Bentley backfired, leading to growing Soviet distrust of Browder, not Bentley. She encouraged this process by reporting to the NKGB in October 1944—falsely perhaps—that Browder had changed his view of Soviet intelligence and now called Bentley's work "dirty blackmail," urging American Communists to keep their distance from Russian operatives. Moreover, according to Bentley, Browder had complained that although he had rendered great assistance to Soviet intelligence, the USSR's operatives had done nothing for him.[56] Whether or not linked to this latest turn in Bentley's loyalties, Washington station chief Anatoly Gorsky informed her in November that she had been decorated with the Order of the Red Star. In response to the news, Gorsky informed Moscow, "she expressed cordial gratitude and assured me that she would work indefatigably to justify the reward."[57]

By the following month, however, Bentley's emotional restlessness resurfaced dramatically. In a meeting with Gorsky where they exchanged Christmas presents, Bentley informed her Russian colleague that he reminded her of Jacob Golos. It was difficult for a young and lonely woman to live without a man, she told him, noting that she thought more and more often about having a family. A flustered Gorsky, plainly hoping to avoid entanglement, immediately cabled Moscow stating that it was urgent to find a husband for Bentley. He repeated the concern expressed by Akhmerov six months earlier: "Think over the issue of [Bentley's] marriage," Gorsky told his superiors.[58]

---

* "The People's Commissariat of Foreign Trade has already asked the [Amtorg Trading Corporation] three times about the expediency of continuing the contract with [Bentley's] firm and at the same time proposes to recommend it to other firms." New York station to Moscow, December 21, 1944, No. 1802, VENONA files.

Complaints about Elizabeth Bentley's tradecraft had increased by then, especially her intermingling of public and secret activities. In December 1944, Moscow learned from other American agents that Bentley's associates in the U.S. Shipping Corporation knew of her intelligence work, that she failed to recognize other Soviet agents following her, and that she was dangerously careless in her work: "Sometimes [Bentley] used her apartment for meetings with agents, and some . . . have her home telephone number."[59] Because the members of her network knew one another, "the entire organization is in such a state now that, if somebody began even a very superficial investigation, the entire group with its direct connections would be unmasked immediately," one of her adversaries wrote the station.[60] Virtually all of the professional operatives who dealt with her had come by then to similar conclusions.

Such inattention to the crucial details of her responsibilities as a courier may have reflected the primacy of personal matters for Bentley during the spring of 1945. Elizabeth's NKGB associates discovered that she had found a new lover, an American named Peter Heller. At the same time, Bentley pursued a second liaison with a female acquaintance. "Some time ago," Anatoly Gorsky reported to Moscow on June 27, " 'Irma' [a woman employed at the U.S. Shipping Corporation] told us indignantly about [Bentley's] proposal that she become her lover . . . [and] establish an intimate liaison with her 'despite the fact that she already has a male lover.' "

In conversations with NKGB supervisors, Bentley continued to complain about her "lack of a male friend to satisfy her natural needs." When confronted with "Irma's" assertions, Bentley told Gorsky (in his words) the following story: "At the beginning of May this year at her hotel, she became acquainted with a man [Peter Heller] waiting for a room there. That very day, they had intimate relations, and she began seeing him from time to time. [Bentley] showered compliments on the man and claimed that he would be an ideal husband for her." Gorsky continued questioning her about Heller, and Bentley "told us a number of details about her lover which left no doubts that he was an agent of the 'Hut' [the FBI] or one of 'Arsenal's' [the U.S. War Department's] counterintelligence." Gorsky urged Bentley to halt the romance and take a vacation, which she apparently did, "but it is difficult to say to what degree she left her lover."[61]

Bentley's own description of Peter Heller confirmed Gorsky's worst fears. Heller described himself as a lawyer and National Guard reserve officer who worked as an investigator for the government, verifying the qualifications of people recommended for promotion in the U.S.

Army—in other words, a military intelligence operative. "Overall now," Gorsky informed Moscow, "[Bentley] is a serious and dangerous burden for us here. She should be taken home [to the Soviet Union], but how to do it, frankly speaking, I don't know since she won't go illegally."

Even Bentley had concluded by then that Heller had worked for the FBI at some point, telling her that he had taken part in investigations of Communists and knew the Russian language.[62] As the romance continued, so did planning by her NKGB colleagues for Bentley's imminent (if involuntary) departure from the United States. "Some time ago," Gorsky reported to Moscow on September 10, "we began preparing her for removal from New York to another city or country to continue work for us there." Gorsky suggested that Bentley relocate "in a country where entry visas for Americans are not needed—Canada, Mexico, Brazil, etc. She has refused to leave New York illegally."[63]

Bentley told Gorsky that she wanted only to return to work at the U.S. Shipping Corporation, which she had left earlier that year. But Gorsky still believed that she should be taken to the Soviet Union. (Wartime restrictions precluded any obvious "legal" means of removing Bentley to the USSR.) Moscow responded on September 14, again urging Gorsky to convince Bentley to end her affair with Heller, but cautioned against further discussion with her about leaving America: "She understands what this is all about."

By that time, the NKGB believed (correctly, as it turned out) that Bentley "is evidently being actively cultivated" by U.S. counterintelligence agents and therefore Gorsky should not meet with her as frequently. Despite the warning signs, Moscow's response to the situation remained surprisingly paternal, suggesting that Bentley be offered another position and, if necessary, financial help: "After she is back from vacation, use her only on new talent-spottings and recruitments. . . . It is important for us to load [Bentley] up so much that she has no time to think too much [and] no time to practice romance, etc. Try to avoid using her for contact with old agents known to her and valuable to us. It would be good to give her in marriage, even with the help of [known] Communists."[64]

The situation did not improve. Gorsky reported on September 27 that Bentley had returned from vacation and met with him "semi-drunk." She declined Gorsky's suggestion that they meet at a later time and stated that "if I broke up the meeting, we would never see her any more . . . [and] that she drank in order to tell in a drunken state that which she did not dare discuss sober."[65]

Bentley demanded that either Gorsky provide new financing for her troubled U.S. Shipping Corporation or she would break off relations with her Soviet contacts. She expressed a willingness to testify before the House Committee on Un-American Activities, which was then about to question Earl Browder. She spoke incoherently about never dealing with Russians again since "all of them are gangsters and care only about Russia" and said that "she had hated us for ten years." At one point, Bentley even told Gorsky that "some time ago Heller made her an indirect proposal to become an FBI agent. . . . She allegedly turned down the proposal." As for the American Communist Party, she called it "a gang of foreigners." Regarding her beloved Golos, "only death prevented him from taking a most important decision all the nation would know about," presumably meaning his defection and exposure of his Soviet network. She claimed that one Soviet operative—Akhmerov—"tried to rape me," and, referring to another one, "as soon as I see him, I will kill him." Gorsky ended the conversation as quickly as possible and fixed their next meeting for the beginning of November.

In evaluating the confrontation for Moscow, Gorsky concluded that Bentley, "although working with us for a long time, is an alien and hostile to us personally. Judging by her behavior, she hasn't betrayed us yet, but we can't rely upon her. Unfortunately, she knows too much about us." His conclusion: "Taking into account that [Bentley] won't go anywhere voluntarily and she may damage us here very seriously, only one remedy is left—the most drastic one—to get rid of her."[66]

Moscow responded to this proposal to kill Bentley with more cautious counsel in an October 11 letter from the NKGB's Vsevolod Merkulov to Gorsky, who had traced Bentley's erratic behavior to "oddities of her character, shattered nerves and [an] unsettled private life."[67] Merkulov discounted the idea that Bentley would soon betray her associates, although "undoubtedly, her threats to communicate information about our work to American authorities known to her are a real danger." He urged Gorsky not to wait until November to meet Bentley again but, instead, to arrange an immediate "friendly" meeting: calm her down, remind her of past services, and offer her "necessary financial help (up to $3,000)" to end her complaints about being mistreated at the U.S. Shipping Corporation.

Merkulov also wrote that for Bentley to inform U.S. authorities about her Soviet intelligence links "is not only disadvantageous but also dangerous . . . [and] will harm her personally and [other] Americans." In addition, "take all necessary precautions with regard to yourself and other agents known to [Bentley]." He proposed reducing "as much as possible" her involvement in further secret work while keeping her under Soviet influence, maintaining "an appearance of our complete confidence in her and friendly interest in her private life."

Gorsky followed each point in Merkulov's instructions and reported on October 29 that Bentley had arrived completely sober for their next meeting, apologizing for her previous behavior. Gorsky gave her $2,000 at the meeting. Bentley expressed concern over the recent defection of Louis Budenz, an American Communist journalist, who had known Golos and been involved in Soviet intelligence efforts. She explained that after Golos's death she had occasionally met with Budenz until October 1944. Budenz knew not only her name and place of business but also about her involvement in Soviet espionage. Bentley asked for advice if questioned by the FBI about Budenz's defection and received Gorsky's instructions on this. Nevertheless, Gorsky reported to Moscow his surprise that Budenz's defection and his knowledge of Bentley's complicity did not seem to make her nervous.[68] The reason for this would become clear to the Soviet operative later that month: Elizabeth Bentley had already begun cooperating with the FBI.

Gorsky next met Bentley on November 21, at a New York restaurant. The subject turned first to the disputed ownership of the shipping company: Did it belong to the NKGB or to the American Communist Party, one of whose leading functionaries had visited Bentley to discuss the problem? Bentley seemed to be asking leading questions of Gorsky involving the relationship between the NKGB and the American Communist Party (Gorsky denied any), the Budenz situation, and the fate of other agents. Gorsky, in turn, asked Bentley about her liaison with Peter Heller, whom she claimed not to have seen recently, after discovering that he had a wife and two children. Nothing was said about Heller's background as an investigator.

After a long and relaxed discussion, Bentley and Gorsky left the restaurant, agreeing to meet again the following January. A few minutes later, Gorsky realized that he was being followed by three men in a car. He broke away from them and fled into a nearby subway station. Since Gorsky was certain that he had arrived at the meeting without surveillance, he concluded that Bentley had been followed to the restaurant.[69]

DEFECTION

On his return to Washington the next day, Gorsky received a cable from Moscow citing reliable information that Elizabeth Bentley had defected, instructing NKGB operatives in the United States to take appropriate precautions and not to meet with her again.[70] The New York station chief, Vladimir Pravdin, received the same cable.[71] Moscow's informant was Harold "Kim" Philby (code-named "Söhnchen" at the time), who told the NKGB's London station about the defection on November 20.

Philby was then privy to a great deal of U.S. intelligence material because of his responsibilities within British intelligence. He described exchanges among American, British, and Canadian security chiefs over common measures to be taken in response to information provided by Igor Gouzenko, a Soviet code clerk who had defected earlier that year in Canada. J. Edgar Hoover, according to Philby, asked that joint measures be postponed since the FBI had not yet completed its scrutiny of the Soviet agent network in the United States. According to Philby's cable, Hoover informed William Stephenson, British station chief in the United States, about Bentley:

> In early November 1945, Elizabeth Terrill Bentley came to the FBI and reported about her work at Global Tourist corporation in New York. The owner of this agency until 1943 was Jacob Golos. This agency and "The United States Shipping Corporation" were being used by Soviet intelligence for espionage activities. Cultivation of Golos's network by the Federal Bureau of Investigation revealed that Golos's agents penetrated into government circles. The FBI assumes that the network is controlled by the NKVD. It succeeded in spotting 30 Soviet agents at present, whose names the FBI [has] not yet given Stephenson.[72]

Philby's devastating information concerning Bentley's defection could not be kept from the Soviet Union's leadership for long. On November 24, the NKGB's Vsevolod Merkulov sent a carefully designed report to Stalin, Molotov, and Beria. Its first part concerned information on the aftermath of Gouzenko's defection, which had been known previously.* The next section, however, traced the major consequence

---

* Gouzenko's defection on September 5, 1945, provoked intense concern by Soviet intelligence chiefs in Moscow over protecting their agent networks not only in Canada and the United States but in England. Several September 1945 cables from Moscow to the NKGB's London station describe the situation, including this September 18 instruction to one London-based operative: "As I am thinking of relieving you of the burden of meetings with the valuable agent network, thus ensuring that it is protected from compromise (this is because of . . . the disruption

in the United States of the Gouzenko episode—intensified FBI surveillance of Soviet citizens and American Communists suspected of intelligence involvement. The recent embarrassing defection of Louis Budenz, then editor of the *Daily Worker*, was duly noted along with his link to Golos's network from 1940 to 1943. As for Golos,

> he coordinated a large number of informers, members of the CPUSA, working in various American institutions. Golos, using this group, whose composition he kept secret from our U.S. station until 1943, passed us various [items of] secret information. In November 1943, Golos died, and the management of both his organization, World Tourist, and of Golos's information network passed to his closest assistant, Elizabeth Bentley.[73]

Merkulov's memo went on to describe Bentley as "from 1936 to 1938, agent of the Main Intelligence Directorate of the General Staff of the Red Army," the GRU, before being transferred "with [Browder's] permission" to Golos's operation as its courier.* After explaining the steps taken by operatives in the United States to shift to direct Soviet control Bentley's "large group of informers whose identities were unknown to us," Merkulov speculated that "Bentley's betrayal might have been caused by her fear of being unmasked by the renegade Budenz who . . . knew about [her] participation in Soviet intelligence work in the U.S."

Considering the dangers posed by Elizabeth Bentley's cooperation with the FBI, Merkulov informed Stalin and his associates that all station chiefs of the NKGB in America had been instructed "to cease immediately their connection with all persons known to Bentley in our work [and] to warn the agents about Bentley's betrayal. . . ." The Soviet operatives with whom Bentley had dealt were recalled to the Soviet Union.[74] Understandably, Merkulov neglected to inform Stalin about

---

in our work [in Canada] and the intensification of counter-measures against us which is being carried out in [Great Britain]), do you not consider that it would be advisable to transfer 'JOHNSON' to 'BORIS's' control [both names unidentified] and leave you only with 'STANLEY' ["Kim" Philby's new code name] and 'HICKS' [Guy Burgess]?" No. 47. See also Moscow to London station, September 17, 1945, No. 46; September 21, 1945 (2), Nos. 34, 43; VENONA files.

* Since no information corroborates Merkulov's assertion that Bentley—and Golos—had links to the GRU at any point, the statement may have been an attempt to share with "the neighbors" in military intelligence the responsibility (and blame) for Bentley's defection.

the November 21 meeting, stating instead that a late October meeting had been the last with Bentley. He also chose not to describe his response to Gorsky's suggestion earlier that fall that Bentley be removed to the Soviet Union because of the dangers of defection, a proposal with which Merkulov had disagreed.

Because of her extensive knowledge of the Soviet agent networks that she and Golos had coordinated, Elizabeth Bentley managed virtually overnight to freeze all active NKGB intelligence activity in the United States, a condition confirmed by Moscow's November 23 instructions to Anatoly Gorsky:

1. To cease connection with "Ruble," "Mole," "Izra," "Raid," "Sid," "Tan," "Page," "Gore," "Muse," "Hare," "Adam," "Arena," "X."*

2. To communicate to "X," "Mole," "Ruble," "Raid," and "Adam" under strict secrecy that halting all contact was caused by [Bentley's] betrayal. To warn them that, if American counterintelligence summoned them or took measures against them (interrogation, threats, arrest, etc.) they should deny their secret connections with [Bentley], stating that her testimony was a lie and provocation by the authorities. As counterintelligence may have arranged some meetings with [Bentley], they shouldn't deny simply being acquainted with her.

3. The aforementioned sources should cease all connections with their subsources; [but] they should not inform them about the real reason for halting contact. Mention, instead, intensified counterintelligence activity against Communists and progressive elements in the U.S.

4. Documents from American government institutions [and] other documents and notes which could compromise agents and their subsources should not have been kept at their homes. If they existed, they should be destroyed immediately. Personal meetings should be minimized.

The memorandum also instructed Soviet operatives to cease temporarily connection with other functioning agents, in addition to those

---

* The references are code names for the following Soviet agents: "Ruble" (Harold Glasser), "Mole" (Charles Kramer), "Izra" (Donald Wheeler), "Raid" (Victor Perlo), "Sid" (Allen Rosenberg), "Tan" (name omitted), "Page" (Lauchlin Currie), "Gore" (unknown), "Muse" (Helen Tenney), "Hare" (Maurice Halperin), "Adam" (Eva Getsov), and "X" (Joseph Katz).

mentioned specifically, and to provide those agents receiving salaries with their stipends for the next three to four months. Moreover, "all the files and notes in the station should be reviewed, and unnecessary ones should be destroyed personally by [Anatoly Gorsky]," who, the memo concluded, was asked "what measures could be taken with regard to [Bentley]?"[75]

Similar instructions were sent to the New York station chief Vladimir Pravdin ("Sergei") as well as to Itzhak Akhmerov, whose sources—"Art," "Berg," "Echo," and "Robert"—should also "have been informed about Bentley's betrayal."* Nathan Gregory Silvermaster (whose code name had been changed in 1944 from "Pal" to "Robert"), coordinated a number of other American informants within the government and was specifically instructed to "cease getting information from his subsources and minimize ordinary meetings with them without explaining the real reason." Bernard Schuster, also, was to be told the truth about Bentley's defection, which Moscow blamed on Budenz's earlier betrayal. Moreover, "[Schuster] should have let Earl Browder know about it."[76]

Both Akhmerov and Pravdin were ordered home once these instructions had been fulfilled. On November 26, Moscow sent Anatoly Gorsky, who had met frequently with Bentley, a cable ordering him back to the Soviet Union for "vacation leave."

Because his NKGB superiors assumed that FBI agents had photographed Gorsky's last meeting with Bentley, the November 26 cable stated also that Moscow's most important concern was to avoid exposing its British agent "Homer" (Donald Maclean), then stationed in Washington, to American counterintelligence: "All meetings with him should have stopped, and both password and conditions of a future meeting been arranged."[77]

From his London post, Philby continued to be an invaluable source of information on these North American matters. Thus he reported to Moscow on November 26 that, despite pressure from British intelligence, the Canadians had held back arresting Soviet agents in their country until the FBI completed its interrogation of Elizabeth Bentley.[78] Merkulov also conveyed to Stalin, Molotov, and Beria another Philby contribution, the draft text of the statement to be made by Canadian Prime Minister Mackenzie King at the time of these arrests.[79]

---

* "Art" (unknown), "Berg" (Alexander Koral), "Berg's" wife (Helen Koral), and "Echo" (Bernard Schuster).

The following day, Anatoly Gorsky responded to his superiors' request for a recommendation regarding Elizabeth Bentley. Although he urged her "liquidation," Gorsky could not think of an immediate method of killing her. Since Gorsky's memo described her daily routine in great detail, an NKGB operative may have been following her even before the FBI began doing so.

Gorsky discussed and rejected in his November 27 memo a variety of options: shooting Bentley (too noisy), arranging a car or subway accident (too risky), and faking a suicide (too chancy). In connection with the last option, Gorsky noted that he had selected agent "X" (Joseph Katz) for the task of eliminating Bentley. However, organizing a phony suicide would prove difficult because the intended victim was "a very strong, tall and healthy woman, and 'X' was not feeling well lately." In the end, Gorsky decided that a slow-acting poison should be administered to Bentley, something "X" could place on a pillow or handkerchief or in her food.[80] Again, as earlier that year, Vsevolod Merkulov exerted Moscow's restraint upon Gorsky's exuberant plans, cautioning in response to his "liquidation" letter: "No measures should be taken with regard to [Bentley]. It is arranged with Comrade Beria."[81] In short, the NKGB's leadership had its own plans for the latest defector.

Meanwhile, Philby continued to monitor the situation for Moscow from London as a one-man damage control unit. He evaluated Bentley's interviews with the FBI and even reported on December 4 the list of forty-one Soviet agents and their American sources whom Bentley had identified for the FBI.[82]

Somehow her designated executioner, Joseph Katz ("X") escaped mention on that list and left shortly thereafter for a new European assignment. Over the next several years, Elizabeth Bentley would testify before congressional committees and government agency security hearings regarding her relationships as a Communist agent and courier. NKGB leaders had not given up, however, on the idea of somehow eliminating this pivotal former participant in their American espionage networks. On August 16, 1947, Moscow asked the Paris NKGB station chief to meet with Joseph Katz to review the prospects for eliminating Bentley, fearful especially of her testimony in any court trials of American agents that might be held. The Paris station reported back on August 25 that Katz was prepared to undertake the assignment. Again, however, Moscow backed down and urged that the matter be studied further before a final decision was taken.[83]

The KGB archives mention an unsuccessful search for Elizabeth

Bentley's whereabouts as late as 1955.[84] By that time, however, Bentley had long abandoned her turbulent years as Jacob Golos's lover and courier for a more public afterlife of congressional hearing and trial witness, lecturer, and memoirist as America's notorious "Red Spy Queen."

CHAPTER 6

❖❖❖

Double Agent/
Hollywood Hustler:
The Case of
Boris Morros

IF A PRIZE had been awarded to Soviet intelligence's longest-serving American agent during the Stalin era, undoubtedly it would have gone to Boris Morros, a minor Hollywood producer-director and the owner of a failed record company, whose career began in 1934 and ended in the mid-1950s. Morros spent the last decade of his work for Soviet intelligence doubling as an agent for the Federal Bureau of Investigation. He gained notoriety in 1957, at the age of sixty-two, when he went public with "revelations" of Soviet espionage in appearances before congressional Red-hunting committees, media interviews, press conferences, and in a melodramatic memoir—*My Ten Years as a Counter-Spy*. He also served as chief prosecution witness that same year, helping to convict three associates on charges related to spying for the Soviet Union.

Morros became involved with Soviet intelligence almost by accident, after a May 1934 meeting at the Soviet Consulate in New York with Peter Gutzeit on a family matter. Morros had brought his father, then visiting the United States, to the consulate, and Gutzeit, in his cover role as diplomat, discussed items that the senior Morros was allowed to bring with him on returning to the USSR. Boris asked Gutzeit's assistant, an operative code-named "Ossip," to facilitate his father's return through Soviet diplomatic channels.[1]

Born in St. Petersburg in 1895, the younger Morros had immigrated to the United States while most of his family remained in Russia. He explained to Gutzeit that he was a movie director at Paramount Pictures in Hollywood, offering to assist Soviet organizations in the United States. But the creative Gutzeit envisioned a more important service for Morros to perform, describing it in a memo to Moscow: "During a conversation with [Morros], I got the impression that he might be used to place our operatives in Paramount offices situated in every country and big city."

Gutzeit assigned "Ossip" to sound Morros out on whether he would assist a Soviet operative in finding employment using an overseas Paramount office as a cover identity. "Ossip" found Morros favorably inclined, "pointing out that now we knew him well, that we trusted him, that we knew about his brothers—senior officials in the USSR. Apparently, he was flattered and claimed he was trustworthy."[2]

"Ossip" learned that Paramount was opening an office in Berlin and asked Morros to place an NKVD operative in that pivotal office: "[Morros] claimed absolutely calmly that . . . he was ready to arrange this when there was an opportunity . . . [and] that he would recommend this man as his good acquaintance. . . ." At a subsequent meeting on August 21, 1934, Morros informed "Ossip" that Paramount's Berlin office would be opened shortly. Through a company friend who managed its foreign department he would assist in placing an operative there on condition that the person not be Jewish, know some German, and "understand and know something" about the motion picture industry. Morros also asked to meet the designated agent before he traveled to Berlin.[3]

Using an American motion picture company as foreign cover for "illegals" corresponded with the priorities of Soviet espionage in and from the United States during this period. The United States was not the major target of NKVD attention but a listening post for gathering especially governmental and military information on threats to the USSR from Germany and Japan, paying close attention also to American foreign policy toward these countries. Gutzeit's Moscow superiors responded enthusiastically to the notion of infiltrating someone into Paramount's Berlin office: "We are attracted to the possibility of placing our illegals in capitalist firms [especially in Europe and the Far East]."[4] The Center assigned a leading operative to the Berlin post: Vassily Zarubin (then code-named "Katya"), accompanied by his wife and NKVD colleague, Elizabeth.

The Zarubins traveled to the United States to meet with Morros, and Gutzeit then cabled Moscow: "There is neither vacillation nor fear on [Morros's] part, though he knows and understands that this is not a usual service [performed for] a Soviet official. . . ."[5] Until Zarubin had taken up his post, the New York station chief rejected Moscow's request that he talk to Morros about placing additional agents elsewhere in Europe. Gutzeit cautioned his colleagues that they would have to begin to prepare carefully for such a new cover assignment:

> . . . [It] is necessary to teach the film industry to those comrades selected for this cover, so that placing [them] in the firm is not fictitious but real. The man working at the firm [Paramount] must know either the production, mechanical, or commercial part; otherwise, he will not make it. . . .
>
> I think this is a good form of preparation for our illegal cadre. The man will be well trained in production [and] find himself in a situation providing an opportunity . . . to know and study the language [and] make connections and acquaintances that he can count on later, which is very important for every illegal. . . . I would recommend using Paramount as a cover [also] for our Far Eastern operatives.[6]

Through Boris Morros's intervention, by autumn 1934, Vassily Zarubin was working at Paramount's Berlin office. Gutzeit's Moscow colleagues were extremely pleased with the development, cabling him on October 5: "We consider the matter with [Zarubin] settled. Now we are interested in the possibility of placing our operatives at Paramount, first of all in Harbin, China, and Japan. You are absolutely right that one shouldn't press too much on [Morros], for he may get scared. Anyway, he is a valuable acquisition who must be taken care of."[7]

Boris Morros had already begun the practice with Soviet intelligence, which he would continue in the two decades ahead, of exaggerating his position and relationships. He informed the New York station that he had been promoted to "director of the firm's entire production in Hollywood." Quick to seize upon this announcement, Gutzeit reported to Moscow that "we asked [Morros] about taking one or two people for training in his studios. He agrees, but . . . [at the moment] can't tell exactly how he will be able to achieve this in practice."[8] Although Morros (to whom the NKVD assigned the code name "Frost") continued to discuss the possibility of using Paramount Studios as a training program for Soviet "illegals," he never implemented the proposal. Instead, he spent much of the following year visiting his dying mother in the USSR, a trip organized by his new NKVD associates.[9]

Gutzeit and his colleagues reassessed their fascination with Boris

Morros after a New York station operative ("Archimedes") paid a surprise visit to Paramount Studios in December 1935. The agent had been sent to Hollywood to give Morros cash to be forwarded to Vassily Zarubin in Berlin and to conclude an arrangement for NKVD "apprentices" to be placed in other positions at Paramount.

,"Archimedes's" trip report, however, was discouraging. He tried to contact Morros at the studio for several days, only to be turned away by his secretary. Phone calls also proved futile. Finally, when he suggested an NKVD connection by telling Morros's secretary that he "had come from New York with regards from [Boris's] close relatives," Morros took the agent's call and agreed to a meeting: "By his tone of voice," "Archimedes" wrote Gutzeit, "I felt he was not very pleased about my arrival."[10]

Morros agreed to forward the funds to Zarubin. As for placing additional NKVD operatives at Paramount, he said that it would be difficult to respond immediately "since I don't know how to do it," promising an answer the following day. Meanwhile, in checking for a studio phone number, "Archimedes" discovered that Morros was simply "a director of the musical subdepartment of the firm's production department," not, as he had claimed, Paramount's top director. To avoid embarrassing Morros, the New York operative did not confront him on this deception.

At a subsequent meeting, Morros admitted to his actual subordinate role at Paramount and blamed that for his inability to place NKVD "apprentices" at the studio. He promised to meet in New York several months later to review the situation, but by then "Archimedes" had become thoroughly skeptical of the man's reliability. How would Morros use Paramount to send funds to Zarubin if he was only a minor functionary? Morros asked that the station warn him by letter nearly a week in advance before coming to see him again.[11]

Peter Gutzeit was livid when he received "Archimedes's" report, which (he wrote Moscow) "makes our relations with [Morros] absolutely clear. . . . [If] all his machinations since his return from the Soviet Union were not evidence of his desire to break with us, now it has become a fact. . . . Anyway, we are not going to leave him, and in 2–3 months will meet with him again and seek the contribution he promised."[12]

Another New York station operative ("Tan") met next with Morros in California, this time mainly to transfer additional funds to Vassily Zarubin in Berlin. After returning to New York, "Tan" reported his shock at discovering that Morros's secretary "is aware of all his negotiations with our people." Apparently, she knew of his involvement in Zarubin's placement with Paramount: "[Zarubin's] file . . . is kept by that secretary. She knows the name under which [Zarubin] is there. The file contains all the letters [from Morros] to [Zarubin] about money transfers, etc." When "Tan" berated him for working in this transparent manner, Morros responded: "The more open, the better."[13]

Despite his refusal to infiltrate Paramount's Hollywood studios with Soviet operatives, for the next several years Morros continued to serve as a liaison for money transfers and possibly other tasks related to Zarubin's important "cover" posting in Berlin. Those in the New York station critical or skeptical of his sincerity as an agent, including Peter Gutzeit, had returned to, and been purged in, the Soviet Union by 1938, while Morros retained one influential supporter then rising in NKVD ranks.

After his return to Moscow in June 1938, Vassily Zarubin wrote to his superiors about the Berlin assignment, defending Morros's important contribution to his work: "For all this time, [Morros] worked exceptionally carefully and fulfilled all of our operative's* instructions and directives to the smallest details, not once allowing a break in supplying money or in maintaining business correspondence, providing our operative with additional documents of his firm as we needed these."[14] Zarubin's memorandum, which blamed the New York station's handlers for not recognizing the value of Morros's relationships, laid the groundwork for greater future effort to cultivate him:

> [Morros] has a colossal circle of acquaintances and connections both in the U.S. and in Europe, but being out of touch with our guidance and excessively busy with his firm's work, he could not develop and give these connections to us.
>
> We never paid much or even sufficient attention to [Morros]. Since he has been living far from our centers of work, [NKVD operatives] met very rarely with him and were not concerned with his education.

Zarubin believed that, if cultivated appropriately, Morros

> may and must be used mainly as a man who can provide legalization to our people—or rather, supply them with documents confirming that this or that operative is involved in his firm's busi-

---

* Zarubin wrote about himself in the third person, a normal style in official NKVD correspondence.

ness. As the practice [in Berlin] showed, those documents are so good that they are quite sufficient for settling and receiving a residence permit under the most difficult conditions of our underground work.

Morros's role in sending funds to him in Germany supposedly from Paramount, Zarubin argued, demonstrated that he can further legitimize Soviet agents by providing them with sources of income. This could be done, Zarubin concluded, in "all the countries of the world," although it might be more difficult in particularly small nations. As for the United States, he still believed that Morros—if energized—could find work for "illegals" at Paramount and help others with entry visas.

Zarubin had persuaded himself that Morros was a prominent figure in his industry and in the United States. His memorandum asserted inaccurately that "in the movie business, [Morros] is a man with a world name." Nor, in the antifascist climate of the decade, did his reputation as a liberal openly sympathetic to the USSR hinder "his status in the firm and in society."

As for Morros's secretary handling his affairs with Soviet intelligence, Zarubin did not object but supported the practice "since it legalizes our people even more, because everything is being done not in secret but fully, or three-quarters, officially." The secretary in question had worked for Morros for ten years, was used mainly for administrative tasks, but had "never been let into the essence of the matter." The process did not disturb Zarubin, who had remained in Berlin from 1934 to 1938 living undetected as a Paramount employee, and his enthusiastic endorsement of Morros concluded: "Everything this man says or promises he always does. This is confirmed by having worked with him for almost four years."[15]

During an interrogation at Lubyanka Prison late that year, Peter Gutzeit—perhaps after Zarubin's memo had been read to him—provided a more restrained but still positive endorsement of the value of Boris Morros as an agent:

[He] considers himself a political friend of the USSR and is ready to render any help he can. He was never paid. Due to the character of his work, [Morros] could be used as a talent-spotter for recruiting people he knows in Hollywood, who could be useful in [our] work and for providing covers for our illegals working in other countries. . . . [He] has exceptionally wide connections among actors and movie people in Hollywood, but these were not used because in the West [western USA] the station had no constant base. Developing . . . [Morros's] connections may yield interesting results.[16]

Perhaps the only episode that might have changed Gutzeit's skeptical attitude toward Morros involved a Hungarian composer named George Sebastian, who lived in the USSR for a long time but settled in Hollywood in 1937. Morros provided the New York station with a report on the "dreadful stories about horrors in the USSR" that Sebastian told his movie industry friends. The report was much appreciated in Moscow (as indicated in a late-November 1937 cable) during the height of the purge hysteria, when the pursuit of "people's enemies," "Trotskyites," and "foreign spies" preoccupied Soviet authorities.

The NKVD's conclusion, in response to Morros's report—"We have grounds to believe that Sebastian is a German spy and has many connections in the Soviet Union"—did not bode well for Sebastian's longevity upon his scheduled return to the USSR (as it turned out, Sebastian was denied reentry).[17] Peter Gutzeit was executed the following year as an "enemy of the people" and, in 1940, Morros's brother Alexander was arrested and put to death "for taking part in a counterrevolutionary Trotskyite terrorist organization."[18] Even Morros's father was threatened with arrest in March 1940 on similar charges.[19]

But the hustler's luck held (as in the case of Zarubin's fortuitous return to Moscow and praise of Morros two years earlier), and his prestige within the NKVD suddenly was enhanced again due to a completely unforeseen occurrence. Stalin's closest associate in supervising the ongoing purge of Soviet life, Lavrenty Beria, informed his underlings in Soviet intelligence that he remembered having worked for the Cheka in Azerbaijan when (in his words) it "exported oil and imported sugar" through Boris Morros![*][20] What greater "legitimization" short of Stalin's own imprimatur could the Hollywood producer have received from the Soviet hierarchy?

Later that year, Moscow instructed the New York station chief, Gaik Ovakimyan, to contact Morros. The two met in New York on November 2, 1940, and Ovakimyan reported that "[Morros], as before, treats us well." Morros expressed his regret that the NKVD had been out of touch for the past two years and noted that, during this period, he had

* Although Beria most likely confused Morros with someone else, Boris Morros (who was told of Beria's comment by an NKVD operative in the United States) would boast in the years ahead about his friendship with the fearsome Beria.

launched an independent motion picture company in Los Angeles. The station proposed several ideas for activating Morros's immediate involvement in its work, which he rejected.[21]

Only after his friend and former associate, Vassily Zarubin (now code-named "Maxim"), arrived in the United States in December 1941 did Moscow develop plans for utilizing Morros's services that appealed to him. During a New York rendezvous, the two agreed that Morros would organize covers for two Soviet "illegals" in Switzerland. One would be assigned to negotiate the removal of a Swiss ban on a recent movie produced by Morros (*Flying Duo*), proscribed at the request of the French Embassy because the movie satirized the French Foreign Legion. Thus did Morros launch a pattern of promoting his own interests while assisting Soviet intelligence. The second "illegal" would be placed as a diamond trader with a Swiss friend of Morros's. In addition, he agreed to provide a Los Angeles cover identity for an "illegal" code-named "Nora" and, at Zarubin's request, to try and establish yet another cover identity for Itzhak Akhmerov upon his return to the United States.[22]

Morros, in turn, exacted from Zarubin and other NKVD officials their promise to assist his relatives who were now refugees from advancing German troops in the city of Omsk. At his request, Soviet intelligence arranged for better housing and food as well as a monthly stipend. Mendel Moroz, Boris's father, was issued a rare wartime exit permit, allowing him to come to the United States in September 1942.[23]

Later news of the Moroz family, learned from Zarubin, included word of the arrest and imprisonment (in 1943 and 1944) of Boris's two brothers, Yuli and Savely, on charges similar to those that had led to the execution of his brother Alexander in 1940. In both cases, the NKGB intervened. Yuli and Savely were released from prison to Red Army units; they subsequently became decorated soldiers.[24]

Concerned that the persistent harassment of his family members might affect Boris's attitude toward the Soviet Union, Vassily Zarubin monitored his friend closely: "I got the impression," Zarubin wrote Moscow, "that these affairs did not move [Morros]. He remained a man devoted to us. He may be relied on." True to form, Morros had other things on his mind.

"Some months ago," Zarubin reported in 1943, Morros "put forward to me a commercial proposal. . . ." Before passing along the proposal to Moscow, however, Zarubin had wanted to be certain of Morros's loyalty to the Soviet Union; now convinced, he strongly supported the idea.[25]

Using funds provided by the NKGB, Morros would establish a music publishing house in the United States—a business that could also serve as a cover for Soviet "illegals." Since Moscow could not provide funds for such a project at the time, Zarubin approached "the Red million-aire," Martha Dodd's husband, Alfred Stern ("Louis"). Zarubin's supe-riors in Moscow endorsed the project and assigned the code name "Chord."

Soviet intelligence's adventure in the American commercial music industry was launched at a September 1944 meeting of Morros and Stern brokered by Zarubin. The enterprise that unfolded resembled the classic film comedy *The Producers*, substituting for that movie's fa-mous song line ("Springtime for Hitler and Germany") a chorus of "Autumn for Stalin and Motherland." Zarubin described the venture's opening phase to Vsevolod Merkulov in Moscow: "At the first meet-ing . . . we discussed all the questions of principle. I repeated once more that [Stern] wouldn't have the right to interfere in ["Chord's"] operational and commercial essence. . . . Afterward, the lawyers drew up an agreement."[26]

The New York station chief became enmeshed in the project's "op-erational and commercial essence." Zarubin told Merkulov that plans for the company already underway, led by the energetic Boris Morros, included contests involving South American composers, with the winners and best works signed to contracts, and negotiations with well-known conductors Leopold Stokowski and (in Paris) Serge Kousse-vitzky for purchasing their works. Morros had already acquired record production equipment for a Los Angeles plant he intended to pur-chase. In addition, he had already begun to promote the new company to broadcasting networks, orchestras, and motion picture studios:* "In fact," Zarubin proudly informed his Moscow colleague, " 'Chord' has already begun practical activities. . . . Financially, it will be ready this winter for use as a cover but, if we needed [it] even earlier . . . , we could send people under 'Chord's' flag right now."[27]

Only one problem related to the new company's "commercial essence," Zarubin informed Merkulov, remained unresolved: "Our ju-

---

* "On one of his previous visits to Los Angeles [in the late 1930s or early 1940s], [composer Igor] Stravinsky had been escorted around the Paramount lot by music chief Boris Morross [sic], who was ardently campaigning for the studio to hire con-temporary composers for contemporary pictures." Gary Marmorstein, *Hollywood Rhapsody: Movie Music and its Makers, 1900–1975* (New York: Schirmer Books, 1997), p. 88; see also p. 109.

dicial rights and interests in 'Chord' are not insured. We can trust [Morros]. He will not run away with money, but [if he died], all rights to this business would fall into his heirs' hands. . . . [But] at the moment, we have no people to put into 'Chord' as joint owners."

Zarubin's detailed memorandum also alerted Moscow to Morros's new NKGB handler, Jack Soble ("Abraham"), who was assigned to oversee the Hollywood entrepreneur in the early spring of 1944. Zarubin's account states plainly how the station tried to develop careful cover stories (or "legends") for such relationships:

> [Soble's] wife [Myra Soble, another Soviet citizen and NKVD operative like her husband, Jack] wrote some music and sent it for [Morros's] approval. In reality, the music was written by [Morros], but in ["Chord's"] files there is special correspondence with [Soble's] wife. Hence, they cover their acquaintanceship further by alleging that on one of [Morros's] trips to [New York], [Soble] and his wife visited him to find out the fate of her work and, in that way, they met.

Nevertheless, Zarubin concluded, it would be risky to make Jack Soble a co-owner of "Chord" since he was a Soviet citizen. This could draw additional attention from the FBI, which, apparently, had already indicated its interest in Boris Morros.[28]

As station chief, Vassily Zarubin felt especially troubled by Morros's improbable account of recent possible FBI scrutiny, as reported to Moscow later that year:

> On [Morros's] last trip to [New York] last July [1944], he did not come to a rendezvous with [Soble] because he spotted a surveillance on him. In [his] words, the story of this surveillance is the following. [Morros] has friendly relations with "Captain's" deputy.* Flying out to us [on Wallace's trip to the USSR] and China, [Wallace] stopped off in San Francisco, phoned [Morros], and asked him to come see him. [Morros] went immediately and spent some hours with [Wallace] at his hotel. After returning to [Los Angeles] . . . , [Morros's] son noticed a car following them. . . . On his latest visit to [New York], [Morros] again spotted surveillance on him.

---

* "Captain" was an NKGB code name for President Roosevelt, and the "deputy" was probably a reference to Vice President Henry Wallace.

There may be several reasons for this surveillance. The competitors could have begun cultivating him in connection with his father's arrival from the USSR, but I am inclined to think—and [Morros] shares this opinion—that just meeting with [Wallace] was the reason for surveillance.

When [Morros] once came to [Alfred Stern's] apartment with a certain artist wearing glasses, upon leaving . . . [Stern] was warned by the doorman that his guests were being followed. The doorman had been approached by an [FBI] agent and asked where a short fat man and the other one in glasses had gone.[29]

Despite his professional experience, Zarubin had succumbed in this instance to a condition that normally affected only his junior colleagues. His judgment was impaired by personal devotion to an agent. Three and a half years as the American contact for Zarubin during his sojourn in Berlin, Morros's protestations of devotion to the Communist cause, and his nonstop name-dropping of prominent American figures as friends or acquaintances all captivated Zarubin. The station chief abandoned his normal vigilance and placed his trust in "the short fat man's" unlikely explanation of Bureau surveillance.

Zarubin left the United States in August 1944, and both Boris Morros and the "Chord" project continued without NKGB supervision or attention in the year that followed. Only in the spring of 1945 did Jack Soble resume contact with Morros in Los Angeles, spending ten days inspecting the troubled business. Alfred Stern joined them to review his $130,000 investment. The visit was duly reported to the New York station and, from there, to Moscow.[*30]

At one point, Morros and Stern argued vehemently about how Zarubin's original proposal to Stern had been altered: "The initial idea was to publish music, not to build a record [producing] plant." Morros then

---

* "[Akhmerov] sent a confidential memorandum from [Alfred Stern] that was handed over to [Akhmerov] through [Boris Morros's] wife. [Stern] is complaining about [Morros and] emphasizes that unless prompt drastic measures of reorganization are taken, the whole business is doomed to failure. To the memorandum are attached a series of corroborating documents. Advise whether to telegraph the contents of the memorandum in more detail and what instructions to give [Akhmerov]. Take into account that I am not abreast of the scheme." New York station to Moscow, December 27, 1944, No. 1824, VENONA files. An entire series of cables from New York to Moscow regarding Stern's complaints about the music company followed. See New York station to Moscow, January 3, 1945, Nos. 4–5; January 4, 1945, No. 11; and Nos. 18–19; VENONA files.

tried to explain the economics of the music industry, that the "popularization of any song or dance music is currently accomplished with recordings, not through music [publishing]." But Soble recognized (as did Stern) that Morros was attempting to subvert the raison d'être of the scheme:

> ... Boris, having fallen for music [Soble reported to Moscow], almost forgot about the main idea, i.e., that ... music is only a means of fulfilling our central goal, that is penetration [by providing "cover" identities to Soviet operatives] into a number of countries neighboring the U.S. Publishing music would require an insignificant financial investment, and we could open branches wherever we need.[31]

Morros opposed his visitors' suggestion that he resume the initial plan for a music *publishing* company, first making it successful in the United States before expanding abroad.

"Chord" was close to collapse at the time of Soble's 1945 inspection. Of Alfred Stern's $130,000 investment, only $6,500 remained in a New York bank account. Morros also claimed that he had put $62,000 of his own funds into the enterprise, and he had a simple if brazen solution to the cash-flow problem: Moscow should provide "an immediate investment of one hundred and fifty thousand dollars"!

Alfred Stern provided the NKGB with his own proposal for rescuing the business, which involved replacing Morros as the head of "Chord" with an "impartial administrator" who also worked for Soviet intelligence. Stern wanted nothing more to do with Boris Morros. Soble, on the other hand, was more directly critical of Vassily Zarubin for "having blindly entrusted Boris with such a huge fortune" (in 1997 dollars, Stern's $130,000 investment was the equivalent of over $1.2 million) and for having agreed to Morros's demand that, despite his investment, Stern not participate in managing the business.

Soble was also angered by Boris Morros's obsessive commercialism, and his irritation increased when Morros proposed that Moscow immediately invest $150,000 in his company. In addition, Boris wanted his $62,000 investment back because he needed money for a movie. "This is strange and incomprehensible," Soble's memo to Moscow observed, "because Boris considers himself a comrade, is deeply devoted to our cause, and allegedly believes strongly in the future success of the firm."[32]

Under the circumstances and despite Morros's schemes for promoting the company—for example, bringing conductor Leopold

Stokowski to Leningrad to perform and record Tchaikovsky's symphonies with that city's orchestra—Soble considered further investment in the company "an illusion." Nor was Soble impressed by another of Morros's alleged projects, a nine-record set of the Vatican Chorus performing in the United States, arranged through a niece of New York's politically influential Cardinal Francis Spellman.

In the end, Soble urged that the New York station remove Morros as manager of "Chord," that the record plant be sold, and that Alfred Stern's money be repaid from the proceeds. Especially troubling to Soble was Morros's operational carelessness in their contacts. He reported that on several occasions, Boris had held conversations with him in his Los Angeles apartment, which would have revealed to the FBI—if it had been listening—their real connection. Apparently, by that time, Morros had begun playing his double game: identifying for American counterintelligence a key Soviet operative such as Soble, while demanding additional funds from Moscow and continuing to interest the NKGB with his alleged influential contacts.

Beginning in 1945, when the supportive Vassily Zarubin was replaced as Morros's Soviet contact by a skeptical but less-sophisticated Jack Soble, Boris's name-dropping increased dramatically. And with the onset of his years of dual collaboration with Soviet intelligence and American counterintelligence, Boris exploited the NKGB's fascination with relationships (real or imagined) that he claimed to enjoy. Thus Morros described for Soble his link to Lavrenty Beria and asserted, also, that while Soviet Foreign Minister Molotov was in New York, Zarubin had brought them together for a forty-minute talk.[33]

After his trip to Hollywood, Soble was transferred to the NKGB's Washington station, then headed by Anatoly Gorsky. He, in turn, informed Moscow in early June 1945 of Soble's account of Boris's indiscreet behavior: ". . . [Morros] knows for what organization he works, does not mind boasting of it, and sometimes, absolutely out of place, mentions his acquaintance with Comrade Pavel [Lavrenty Beria]. . . . At the same time, he has wide connections, mainly in the artistic world. . . ."[34]

Moscow responded quickly and skeptically to Gorsky's memo. He was told to "conserve" Morros and to end any contact between Morros and Soble, who was instructed to refuse contact if Morros attempted it. But Alfred Stern, who had offered to invest another $250,000 in an NKGB-sponsored enterprise—but only if not connected to Morros—and his wife, Martha Dodd, were to remain under Soble's supervision. Moscow decided to accept Morros's promise to return $100,000 of the

"Chord" investment to Stern, with the remainder to be written off as a business loss.[35]

Boris Morros was not as easily sidelined as Moscow had hoped, however, according to a mid-December 1945 memorandum from Jack Soble. Morros had contacted him in New York with news of the record company and a provocative, even cheeky, offer for Soviet intelligence:

> He let me know that he had sold 75% of the record plant's shares . . . and that his son Richard . . . was [now] a partner in the firm.
>
> Personally, [Morros] had returned to the movie industry. He is preparing to release four films next year.
>
> If we want to work with him, he is ready to set up together with us a movie firm in the "Federal Film" system, which will produce these movies. $200,000 is needed for this. (Personally, I am sure that it can be done for an investment of $100,000.) This firm could open branches in any country for distributing these films, not drawing suspicion from authorities, since his name is sufficiently known both here and abroad. He has proposed me as a candidate for manager of the New York office since I know languages and foreign countries and come from a capitalist environment.
>
> He guarantees this business will be a success since movies are his craft. He is ready to give a guarantee that in due course money invested in this business will be returned with interest.
>
> He laid down two conditions: 1. Without [Stern] (he will not take him as a partner). 2. To give him an answer within a month. If there is no answer by the middle of January, he will consider himself free.[36]

One NKGB reader in Moscow underlined the last phrase of this memorandum in red with an exclamation point. Agents, such as Boris Morros, normally do not give an ultimatum to their superiors with such evident impudence. Further reflection might have led Soviet intelligence supervisors to ask themselves who approved Jack Soble's decision to disobey a clear instruction *not* to make contact with Boris Morros again, and, once having met, how Soble could present with such apparent enthusiasm this latest scheme (which, incidentally, included a post for Soble that seems to have interested him)? Morros's talent for salesmanship had once again affected the judgment of a Soviet operative.

As a double-agent, Morros reported to the FBI meetings such as his

December 16 encounter with Jack Soble, so there was little risk attached to his proposal. If Moscow agreed to become a partner and investor in his film company, the Bureau could only be impressed at his skill in building a credible relationship. If, on the other hand, Soviet intelligence refused his time-urgent demand, then Morros could simply back down from the ultimatum.

As things turned out, the 1945 defections of Elizabeth Bentley and Igor Gouzenko persuaded Moscow to temporarily halt virtually all its contacts with American agents and sources. Eighteen months passed before Boris Morros resumed his complicated dialogue with Jack Soble on espionage and motion picture production. By then, Soble had lost his sympathy toward Alfred Stern and had shed his contempt for Boris Morros, as this August 18, 1947, report indicated:

> One has to be an iron man to tolerate Alfred Stern in a commercial affair, especially in America, where risk, broad scope, and timeliness are the basic elements in any commercial enterprise. . . . [But] certainly, Boris Morros is a talented, energetic, and enterprising man. Undoubtedly, he can keep a secret and wants and is ready "to do business" with us. But his problem is . . . living in a Hollywood environment in conditions of luxury and abundance . . .
>
> Strong hands are needed to keep him within budgetary limits. Strict . . . and constant financial controls are necessary. But . . . he is an honest man and obeys our decisions. When I suggested that he return Alfred's money, without hesitation, he . . . liquidated [$100,000 of] this debt within three months.

Soble described Morros's continuing interest in "partnering" with Soviet intelligence to produce films, especially those that might target the postwar European audience. Soble again endorsed the alliance, pointing out that Morros's film *Carnegie Hall* was playing throughout the United States and Western Europe where "he met important political and public figures . . . provided with a personal letter from Cardinal Spellman, asking all the Catholic organizations to render him every assistance." Morros renewed his 1945 proposal through Soble, offering the NKGB a partnership in his new film company in exchange for $250,000. The eager Soble thought "he will agree to a lesser sum — $150,000."[37]

Apparently, it did not puzzle the credulous Jack Soble that while American grand juries, congressional investigating committees, and the FBI all pursued alleged Communists and pro-Communists in a bitterly anti-Soviet atmosphere, somehow a Russian-American producer and friend of the USSR, Boris Morros, appeared unaffected by the internal security probes then swirling through Hollywood, Washington, and most of the United States. Thus, when Morros renewed his offer of a film company partnership early in 1948, Soble wrote to Moscow in March:

> Boris is not under suspicion, although as you know, there is an incredible "purge" of Reds going on in Hollywood now. . . . He travels everywhere, is on friendly terms with Cardinal Spellman, meets with the biggest cinema stars, [and] has countless acquaintances all over the world, but . . . is doing nothing [with Soviet intelligence] . . . and will be doing nothing if we don't take him into our hands.[38]

Soble's superiors in Moscow were more cautious and, after the record company experience, lacked interest in the latest scheme for a joint venture film company. Meanwhile, Soble continued to meet Morros in Paris, New York, and Hollywood. A May 4 memorandum to Moscow reiterated Morros's offer "to work with us . . . on *direct and systematic* liaison" while insisting that "the changed situation in the U.S. doesn't allow 'boys' (literally), ignorant of the country, language, customs, etc., etc., to control him." Morros complained to Soble about having been visited at Paramount Studios years before by such inexperienced operatives demanding money and jeopardizing his security: "Not for this was I transferred from Soviet Russia thirty years ago," ran Boris's flamboyant, if fabled, assertion of veteran agentry duly transcribed by Soble, by this time Morros's devoted Boswell: "I was sent by Lavrenty Pavlovich [Beria], and I want at least to talk with the heads of Soviet power. If they don't want to work with me henceforth, let them say 'no,' but if they want to work, let it be in a systematic form with directions and instructions."

Soble urged Moscow to renew the connection with Morros and argued that his influential friends and acquaintances—Cardinal Spellman foremost among them—justified a new initiative. Almost as if the NKGB handler had become a Hollywood publicist, Soble filled pages with recitations of Morros's self-described achievements and relationships. Nor had Morros forgotten his earlier promise to control finances, recounted by Soble in the same memorandum:

> He proposes that I personally become a partner in his firm heading the administrative sector. . . . I am prepared to take this on but

only on condition [that] . . . we explain to Boris that he answers to me in financial matters. Without this control, he will waste money right and left . . . he must understand that this is working money, not his personally, that it is meant only for our cause.[39]

Soble insisted that an NKGB operative meet with Morros during a forthcoming trip to Europe because without such a meeting "he is lost to us."[40]

Morros (with a new code name, "John") continued to fascinate Moscow if only because of his apparent association with the influential Cardinal Spellman and other professed acquaintances. These included Milton Eisenhower (newly important in Washington because of his brother, the General) and a variety of other political and military figures who may or may not have ever really met the FBI-controlled Morros. He even claimed a friendship with former New York Governor and Republican presidential candidate Thomas E. Dewey, which allegedly developed when Morros and a music teacher friend tried to help Dewey correct a lisp that affected his radio speeches. Morros now also renewed his offer from Paramount days to provide, through his new film company, cover identities for Soviet operatives in the United States and Europe.[41]

While the impressionable Jack Soble continued to serve as Morros's unpaid NKGB press agent, alerting Moscow (for example) to the film producer's interviews with French actresses, Morros renewed his demand for a meeting with a high-ranking official of Soviet intelligence.[42] He offered to travel to Moscow under the guise of negotiating Soviet distribution of his new movie *Carnegie Hall*. The NKGB's station chief in Paris reported Soble's endorsement of the idea: "According to [Soble], such an open trip to the Union will not draw suspicion, since he traveled around every European country for his music business. Besides, [Morros] refers to his close acquaintanceship with Prokofiev and Khachaturian." Reading this report, Peter Fedotov, then-head of Soviet intelligence, wrote on the document: "Comrade Korotkov. I do not fully believe in [Morros's] unselfishness in terms of cooperating with us. Nevertheless, he is not a man to be rebuffed."[43] Colonel Alexander Korotkov was in charge of the NKGB "illegals" department and decided to clarify Boris Morros's intentions himself.

An additional report from Soble relayed Morros's assertion that he had become acquainted with the wife of General Lucius Clay, then in command of the American occupation zone in Germany. A mid-July 1948 dispatch from Moscow to the Paris station demanded additional details on the relationship. Morros, in turn, promised to send the information in September, when he would meet with the Clays while shooting his new film in Berlin.[44]

But Korotkov decided not to wait that long. Through Jack Soble, he arranged a meeting in Bern, Switzerland, traveling in August as a diplomatic courier to the Soviet delegation at a United Nations conference then in progress.[45] Korotkov questioned Morros about his background, past work for Soviet intelligence, and future interest in such involvement, terminating the discussion without any future assignment though agreeing to meet again.

Korotkov's report on the meeting mentioned Morros's alleged links to Spellman, Dewey, and other dignitaries such as California's Governor Earl Warren, noting Boris's various offers: "If we are interested, he can use Spellman's recommendations to arrange an audience with the Pope, be a guest of the Spanish Foreign Minister, whom he met during his recent trip to Spain, where he was also introduced to Franco, [and] he can go to Berlin and be [General] Clay's guest. . . ."

Morros raised directly with Korotkov his proposal that the NKGB join him as partner in a company to produce and distribute films (mainly musicals) for movie theaters and (a new suggestion) television. ("This idea of his," Korotkov noted, "to transmit films this way [for television] is not done yet but, undoubtedly, it will find a very favorable . . . reception in America.") Morros now upped the ante to $300,000, half to be returned within six months. Korotkov asked Morros, in turn, to clarify his request to be "dismissed" from NKGB service if Soviet intelligence had no interest in the film project. Responding with "evident disappointment and confusion," Morros stated that he was still "ready, of course, to carry out our instructions without it, but he wouldn't have the same opportunities and freedom of action."

Soble lobbied Korotkov the following day, urging acceptance of the film partnership. But the NKGB official's report to Moscow recommended against approving the proposal while holding out the possibility of future involvement. Korotkov urged that, instead, Morros be used to gather information about his various high-level friends and acquaintances, even proposing to cover his expenses while continuing to check "all the obscure episodes in his biography." Most important, "his work for us in the past doesn't give grounds for considering him closely connected to our intelligence service, the more so since he has never done for us anything directed against the U.S."[46]

Moscow attributed its caution regarding Boris Morros to the Russian-American entrepreneur's evident passion for collecting Soviet money and not American secrets.[47] Korotkov never even bothered to ask Morros why he expressed so little anxiety about meeting a Soviet operative despite the growing pursuit of alleged "subversives" within his own industry. Korotkov pursued his discussion with Morros on August 27. At this meeting, Morros accused Vassily Zarubin, once his friend and former NKVD handler, of breaking his promise that Soviet intelligence "would cover the entire world with a network of commercial enterprises that would be used as covers" for operatives. Korotkov remained skeptical.[48]

Jack Soble, however, was torn between obligation as a Soviet operative to oversee Morros and enthusiasm for a new (and more lucrative) role as partner in Boris's proposed film company. He sent long and emotionally engaged memos to Moscow about his discussions with Morros. Never was a Soviet handler more fascinated with his source. In the end, though, Soble supported Korotkov's strategy and urged Morros to cooperate and to set aside, for the moment, his dream of an NKGB-backed motion picture company.

Morros persisted in tantalizing Soble (and Moscow) with his alleged contacts, this time shortly after the Bern meetings with Korotkov. He described to Soble a September meeting with the Pope (arranged, naturally, by Cardinal Spellman) and another longer meeting with leading Vatican aide Count Enrico Galeazi. Morros offered Soble, who duly reported to Moscow, an almost-verbatim account of his purported half-hour talk with the Pope, mainly about Russian literature![49]

Despite this ecclesiastical first—an account of a papal meeting transcribed for the NKGB files—and despite Morros's aggressive campaign for acceptance, he remained for Soviet intelligence an exotic figure, forever pursuing personal financial gain. Not surprisingly, after the president of the Motion Picture Association, Eric Johnston, visited Moscow in the fall of 1948 to sign a distribution agreement for American films, potentially worth $5 million, Morros complained of Soviet neglect to Jack Soble. In a report to Moscow, Soble parodied his friend Boris: "Why can the reactionary Johnston visit Moscow, talk to Comrade Molotov, and sell films to the USSR? Why can't [Morros] do it with his film *Carnegie Hall*?"[50]

But Morros would surpass even his papal-visit story the following February with his account of an alleged visit to the White House, supposedly invited to dinner by President Truman's aspiring singer-daughter, Margaret, who (according to Morros) hoped for a part in one of his future films or television programs. "At the dinner," Jack Soble recounted in society column style, "her mother (Madame Truman) was present and, later, Truman himself came. The basic topic at the dinner was music, films, and television." But then, Soble's memo recorded possibly the most politically relevant information—if real—ever conveyed by Morros to Soviet intelligence:

> . . . after the parents left, Margaret . . . told [Morros] about an important conference in which Truman, [Vice President] Barkley, [Secretary of State] Acheson, [Charles] Bohlen, Bernard Baruch, and Eisenhower took part (this information Margaret got from her mother).
>
> At this conference, Eisenhower and Bernard Baruch, whose opinions the President takes very much into consideration, insisted that Truman free himself from the tutelage of reactionary-inclined generals and reactionary Wall Street businessmen, and staff his cabinet with people willing to talk to the Soviet Union in "an honest commercial language." Eisenhower, banging his fist on the table, called . . . General Clay . . . "a protégé of German Fascists."[51]

Soble's report then had Truman and the conferees discussing names of possible future ambassadors and agreeing to meet more frequently to discuss world economic issues—the importance of "markets and world trade"—a point stressed especially by Bernard Baruch. Margaret, Morros went on, lamented her father's heavy burden, "to organize peace between nations in a period of history when communism has grown into such a gigantic force. [She railed against] American reaction, racist persecutions . . . against blacks in the U.S., the avidity of big landlords, Wall Street machinations, the Un-American Activities Committee, and those 'black reactionary forces' in the U.S. against whom her 'poor father' had to struggle." At this point, according to Morros, the conversation ended, and he promised to keep Margaret in mind for future musical film productions.

This improbable discussion reflected either the FBI's view of what might make Boris Morros more credible to Soviet intelligence or Morros's own invention to increase NKGB interest in him as an agent—or both. Soble's memo went on to report other alleged recent conversations of Boris's with Vice President Alben Barkley (also portrayed falsely as pro-Soviet), Averill Harriman ("who commissioned [Boris] to make a documentary about the Marshall Plan in Europe"), and a range of other Supreme Court Justices, cabinet members, leading Senators and Congressmen, Generals and Admirals.

At a time when Soviet intelligence anywhere in the United States had few if any cooperating sources, influential or otherwise, Boris Morros presented himself to Moscow as an apparently successful interlocutor with America's power elite: "[Morros] mentions all these previously named persons," Soble wrote, "wishing to know your instructions on which of them to concentrate more of his attention." The memorandum did not stint, either, in conveying Morros's fervent hope that the NKGB would see *Carnegie Hall* at a European showing and arrange for him to visit Moscow, both to negotiate the film's Soviet release and to pursue his earlier dream of an NKGB-Morros film partnership.[52]

The attractive bait dangled before Moscow brought instructions that the producer be assigned to gather detailed information on the "private life, commercial and official connections, financial situation, backstage person, commercial and official activities of . . . the Trumans, Cardinal Spellman, General Eisenhower, [Earl] Warren, and [Averill] Harriman." Even more important for Morros, Moscow instructed Soble to obtain from him "a concrete and detailed proposal on organizing, filming and distributing Soviet composers' music through a television network in the U.S."[53]

In September 1949, the NKGB arranged for Morros to meet with the Soviet Ambassador to France and to show two of his films, *Carnegie Hall* and *Manhattan Fairy Tales*, at the embassy.[54] Meanwhile, Soble reported on yet another deal being organized by Morros in Paris for a film production arrangement with Sergey Rachmaninoff's son-in-law and urged NKGB support.[55] Morros's new scheme apparently involved persuading Soviet intelligence that its propaganda goals could be advanced by using Russian and Soviet musical classics in American films and television. Boris prepared a long memo for the NKGB analyzing in detail the value of this approach, stressing especially the importance of television—then a new medium—in spreading Moscow's message.[56]

This proposal persuaded Peter Fedotov, head of the intelligence service, to arrange for Morros's long-hoped-for trip to Moscow, nominally invited by officials in charge of Soviet film but covertly by the Central Committee of the Communist Party of the USSR. Though Soviet officials were intrigued by the energetic American's proposals, they remained cautious until he had clarified the practical issues involved in co-production.[57] Moreover, Fedotov and his colleagues intended to question Morros closely about his efforts to gain information on U.S. government leaders.[58]

In January 1950, Boris Morros reached Moscow, officially the guest of SOVEXPORTFILM, previewing *Carnegie Hall* finally and, on January 20, meeting with the NKGB's Alexander Korotkov, who criticized Morros's fitful efforts to send useful data on the various leaders he had been assigned to monitor.[59] Morros pleaded inexperience at such agent tasks. Korotkov in turn asked especially that Morros use his friendship with Cardinal Spellman and his relationship with Margaret Truman to place illegal Soviet operatives in "cover" positions.[60] As a token of his commitment, Morros delivered a detailed memo about Cardinal Spellman filled with insiders' political gossip concerning Spellman's highest-level political contacts and most intimate personal ones.[61]

In the days ahead, Boris Morros met with several other NKGB operatives, whose growing skepticism concerning their American informant was barely concealed. Thus, on February 4, one raised the delicate question of "whether he had been given tasks of an intelligence character by Comrade Beria," as Morros had alleged. The report of the meeting noted that Boris "felt quite uncomfortable and didn't give an intelligible answer. . . . [I]t was clear to me that [he] had not been given any special tasks and that he reported it to us earlier for the purpose of raising his authority in our eyes."[62] Yet Morros continued to name influential Americans from whom he could gain information; former President Herbert Hoover now joined the small army of influential Morros relationships, along with the previously mentioned Dewey and Warren![63]

Morros left Moscow with the NKGB's renewed interest. Fedotov and his colleagues provided him with a detailed assignment regarding the specific data it wanted on President Truman, Cardinal Spellman, Secretary of State Dean Acheson, and a range of other influential Americans.[64] Alexander Korotkov was especially fascinated with Spellman's role in encouraging the Vatican's anti-Soviet activities, including training Russian-speaking Roman Catholic priests for potential use in a religious underground within the USSR—efforts that apparently loomed larger in Kremlin fantasies than in papal policy.[65]

As for Boris Morros, he returned home believing that the government overseers of the Soviet film industry would soon conclude profitable deals for him to distribute their movies in the United States while also co-producing musical films for American television. Apparently, the Deputy Chairman of the Council of Ministers, Kliment Voroshilov, had agreed to the proposal, awaiting only the approval of Stalin, the country's premiere moviegoer.[66] Alexander Panyushkin, the USSR's Ambassador and station chief in Washington, was asked to provide detailed information about Morros's firm and its financial prospects as well as the viability of the agreement, given the current anti-Soviet mood in the United States.[67]

The Ambassador's response undoubtedly cooled Soviet support for the deal:

> Comrade Panyushkin reports that the firm, "Federal Films," owned by B. Morros, belongs to "independent cinema companies." The firm doesn't have its own means of producing [or distributing] films. The firm produced only *Carnegie Hall*, released in 1947, an average American film distributed through United Artists.
>
> Comrade Panyushkin believes there is no need to produce special musical films for the U.S. since, if our own film industry can release more musicals, such pictures can be shown in the U.S.[68]

Panyushkin considered it "inexpedient to grant one man a monopoly for distributing Soviet films in the U.S. and Europe" and dismissed the notion that the USSR needed Morros's services at all: "In the current political conditions in the U.S., he would be unable to do more [than existing Soviet film distributors]."

At that point, Morros bid for U.S. rights to a single Russian film, *Child of the Danube*, appealing directly to top NKGB figures such as Alexander Korotkov and Vsevolod Merkulov.[69] But on August 10, 1950, the station chief in Vienna, "Ostap," whom Morros had cultivated, was instructed to tell him that he had yet to fulfill the intelligence-gathering promises he had made while in Moscow.[70] Boris responded a week later, avowing another highest-level American associate.

Morros claimed an allegedly "close friend" from his years at Paramount had recently been appointed chairman of the U.S. Atomic Energy Commission. Boris offered to seek information from the man in addition to the others previously discussed in Moscow.[71] He also offered to recruit his son to work for Soviet intelligence.[72] The NKGB in Moscow discussed this proposal with Leonid Kvasnikov,* still a leading scientific intelligence operative, who believed that if the offer was genuine, Boris Morros, Jr., should be placed at the General Electric Company's plant then studying the feasibility of atomic-powered battleships.[73]

Commercial to his core, however, Boris Morros had not offered his son's services for nothing, but in exchange for the rights to distribute

---

* For Kvasnikov's leading role as New York station chief dealing with atomic espionage during the war years, see Chapter 9.

Child of the Danube! This ploy proved too outrageous even for the most gullible NKGB officials in Moscow. The intelligence service's head, Sergei Savchenko, responded angrily to a cable from the Vienna station outlining the proposal: "These speculators deceive us, extort money from us, and don't want to work. One must put an end to this situation."[74]

By the following month, Moscow had calmed down and wrote Vienna that Morros's offer to place an NKGB agent or his own son on the AEC staff "deserves serious attention" once it had been judged a "real" possibility. The memorandum also asked that Morros provide detailed information on the chairman.[75] Apparently, it never occurred to Soviet intelligence that Boris Morros was once again merely tempting it, this time with the outlandish suggestion that his son, an untrained amateur, could play an agent's role close to America's overseer of atomic energy. Adding to the incredible nature of this idea is the fact that it came at the height of the Second Red Scare. When Morros made his offer concerning the chairman of the AEC, Klaus Fuchs and Harry Gold were already in prison, and David Greenglass and the Rosenbergs were under arrest. Yet in an ongoing exchange of memoranda with operatives who met with Boris Morros, Moscow treated seriously the bizarre notion that his show-business son, politics unknown, could be transformed overnight into a inside source of American atomic secrets. Raising the ante still further, Morros now dangled the name of physicist J. Robert Oppenheimer for his Soviet associates.[76]

By the following year, Morros had backed away from his suggestion that his son could enter a high-security post for the Atomic Energy Commission—an idea even his FBI handlers undoubtedly believed to exceed the bounds of credibility. Sergei Savchenko wrote in a cable concerning this issue: "As usual, [he] interested us but then did nothing."[77] Going on the attack against complaints from his Soviet contacts that he had produced no valuable information, Morros demanded "more concrete tasks" as well as the long-sought liaison with a new Soviet operative in the United States (obviously of interest to his FBI handlers), which Moscow continued to reject in an April 14, 1951, set of instructions to New York.[78] By this time, the NKGB was interested only in his tidbits of inside information, not in using the unreliable Morros as a source of cover identities for "illegals." This memorandum also reiterated Moscow's refusal to provide the $50,000 requested earlier for Morros's television production venture.[79]

Moscow's impatience produced results. At Morros's next meeting with "Ostap" in Vienna, he delivered written accounts of alleged meetings with Cardinal Spellman, Herbert Hoover, and others. This transcription of the Cardinal's supposed table talk did not differ markedly from the public record of this deeply conservative, anti-Communist cleric.[80] But the quotations from Herbert Hoover's alleged comments might have been transcribed from a "B-movie" script: "That idiot (throughout the evening Hoover never once called [President] Truman by name) is not selling America. He's simply betraying it. The biggest criminal is the idiot's brains—[Dean] Acheson. . . . From top to bottom, the State Department is filled with pederasts and quasi-Reds."[81]

Moscow did not think much of Morros's memos but encouraged him to continue providing accounts of such meetings with dignitaries.[82] Morros also reported that his government friend, even while serving as head of the AEC, had agreed to become "chief consultant" to his television company![83]

By then, Soviet intelligence's interest in Morros finally appeared to be waning. In December 1951, Sergei Savchenko and his colleagues decided to recall Boris's pliable handler Jack Soble to Moscow, after deciding that this veteran operative's effort had become "pointless and doesn't correspond to the interests of our work since it does not yield practical results."[84] An operative code-named "Yakov" met with Boris Morros in Vienna on January 23, 1952—this time to question him about Soble, whom Morros had not encountered for some time.

Morros, of course, came prepared with still another business proposal, and although Moscow privately rejected the new proposal, "Yakov" was encouraged to string the American along in hopes of gaining useful information on Jack Soble. Apparently, Soble, in an effort to disengage from Soviet espionage or out of fear, had informed Moscow in August 1950 that "he was being cultivated," presumably by Western counterintelligence agents. Soble asked to be left alone in the months ahead, and Moscow's curiosity was aroused.

The NKGB now proposed that "Yakov" persuade Boris Morros, who had been a double agent now for six years and had exposed Soble to the FBI, to renew contact with his former NKGB liaison.[85] Morros had begun meeting with Soble in New York and Paris, conveying Moscow's instructions and letters from Alexander Korotkov that demanded Soble's return to the USSR.[86] But Jack Soble had other plans.

Ironically, it was the fiercely anti-Communist head of the State Department's Passport Bureau, Ruth Shipley, who helped to persuade Soble to leave France and return to the United States. According to

Morros, Shipley's assistant was an old friend of Boris's wife, and she and the Soviet operative met to discuss renewing Soble's passport. Shipley informed her visitor "that she didn't consider his occupation in Paris so important and remarkable [to allow a five-year passport renewal if he continued living there], gave him a lecture on American patriotism, [and] slightly rebuked him for leaving the U.S. and moving to France several months after becoming a U.S. citizen. . . ." Shipley recommended that Soble sell his small factory in Paris and move with his family back to America.

Amazingly, no negative reference appeared in Soble's file, according to Morros, who persuaded Shipley's assistant to check out the dossier: "She let me know there was nothing political, no 'Red' suspicions about him."[87] Meanwhile, Moscow continued its complaints about Soble's lack of responsiveness. His French factory had been started when (according to a September 1951 Moscow cable) "the intelligence service invested $57,000" in the enterprise. The NKGB now demanded its money back, but Soble refused to return to France and opened a factory in New York, apparently fearful of Soviet vengeance for having "defected" to a career in business.[88]

Recognizing that the uncommunicative Soble was "on alert," Moscow decided to kidnap him. It would tempt him back to Europe under the guise of negotiating his future, where it would secretly "carry out his kidnap and removal to the USSR." Moscow directed that this "principal task" be achieved by any possible means. But Boris Morros was not to be trusted as an accomplice in this scheme, at least according to a November 11, 1952, memo from Moscow, which noted: "We finally were convinced that he is not interested in our work; he tries to maintain liaison with us only for his selfish ends, seeking to arrange his business affairs with our help."

By then, the NKGB had finally realized that Morros's demand for a Soviet contact other than Soble may have had an ulterior purpose: "[W]e don't trust [Morros] and don't intend to use him in our affairs, especially in connection with [Soble's] case." Savchenko and his colleagues suspected that Morros was simply fishing for information to pass along to his old friend but, nonetheless, instructed a New York NKGB operative code-named "Old" to meet only with Morros. Moscow had finally taken a decision that could only have pleased Morros's FBI controllers, who had urged this course for years—direct contact with its double agent.[89]

The assignment was not an enviable one: The NKGB operative in New York, at a time of maximum American counterintelligence activity, was to contact an American agent of questionable loyalty (Morros) to determine the location of Soble, a reluctant Soviet operative in hiding. A January 7, 1953, meeting was arranged, but Morros never showed up. He was actually in Vienna at the time, where he told that station's operative, "Yakov," of meeting Soble in New York. Soble had professed amazement at Moscow's concern over his loyalty, but he declined the trip to Europe because he believed that American counterintelligence agents were following him and, besides, his U.S. passport had expired. Soble claimed to have met with a Soviet operative in Switzerland the previous year to straighten out relations, but Moscow denied such a meeting had occurred. Morros gave Soviet intelligence his friend's New York address.[90]

Whatever the truth of these accounts, one of the ironies of the situation was that an FBI double agent was now the only channel between NKGB headquarters in Moscow and an "illegal" station chief in New York. Jack Soble was certainly aware by the summer of 1953 that his life was in danger from Soviet intelligence. His anxieties increased later that summer when Martha Dodd—whom, along with her husband, Alfred Stern, Soble had supervised—made headlines as a possible target of Senator Joseph McCarthy's Red-hunting probe. Soble fretted, according to Morros's account to Moscow, that Dodd could identify and name him and had "become cowardly."[91] In mid-December, however, Morros wrote Moscow that the McCarthy committee had begun to investigate Soble's activities in France but had failed to discover any incriminating evidence.[92]

The NKGB had by then become hopelessly confused over the divided loyalties of both Soble and Morros: "Examine these letters," Alexander Korotkov observed of Morros's latest communications. "The [Service's] aim is the same—how to get these rascals."[93] But Moscow's judgment in the matter was so clouded by anger at Soble's adamant refusal to climb into its European net that it avoided focusing on the greater betrayal by that "rascal" Boris Morros.

Morros had begun trying to persuade his Soviet contacts that he could oversee the small number of alleged U.S. government sources whom Soble had previously handled. He also reinforced Moscow's suspicion of his former friend by describing him as leading a prosperous life, thus contradicting Soble's complaints about his financial difficulties in letters to Korotkov.[94] The NKGB's Vienna station followed up on June 1 with a report to Moscow that supported Morros's efforts to supplant Soble as an agent handler: "In [Morros's] words, he would like to get exact instructions regarding [Soble's] further work. In particular, he expressed a wish that, if needed, he could take all of [Soble's] people as he thought he was beyond suspicion. . . ."

Morros lobbied his Soviet friends, when it was clear that Soble would not return to Europe for the meeting, to allow him to replace Soble in handling the latter's other American sources.[95] A July 1954 report from a Moscow operative, V. Pavlov, to the then-head of the intelligence service, Alexander Panyushkin, displayed more confidence in Morros than in Soble but argued that only if the producer assumed Soble's $50,000 debt to the NKGB—"pay-per-spy," in short—should he be assigned the latter's sources.[96]

But the indefatigable Morros had an even more audacious proposal for Moscow in the wings. He wrote the NKGB in Vienna on June 18, 1954, proposing that he "organize a trip for ten of the most popular figures in the United States to live permanently in [the Soviet Union] with their families—ten literary, scientific, and artistic world figures." The group would include comedian Charlie Chaplin, already being hounded by American authorities for his radical political views, singer Paul Robeson (a committed Communist), Ira Gershwin, and seven others: "I have already talked with Chaplin," Morros noted.[97]

By reminding Moscow of his links to famous Americans, Morros sidetracked for the moment the NKGB's suspicions regarding his loyalties. Thus, in fall 1954, Moscow dispatched N. Aksenov ("Semyon") to Vienna especially to work with Morros, not to recruit his musical or artistic friends for residence in the Soviet Union but on an even more extraordinary mission, as Aksenov's instructions indicated: "Can [Morros] meet with 'Chester' [J. Robert Oppenheimer] and find out his opinion in principle about leaving for the Soviet Union? Won't [Morros] propose other similar candidates among scientific workers and his plans for their use on the spot or [their] removal to the USSR?"[98] The NKGB had been speculating since 1945 (without evidence) that Oppenheimer, under pressure from U.S. Administration security officers and congressional investigators, might be preparing to leave for the Soviet Union to assist in atomic research.

At their first meeting, on November 5, 1954, Aksenov did not discuss the Oppenheimer issue but asked Morros about Jack Soble. According to Morros, Soble had lost his American citizenship and moved to Canada, where he was engaged in business. Again, Boris asked to be assigned an NKGB liaison in America and also for some "large concrete task."[99] A few days later, prodded by Moscow, Aksenov steered the conversation to the AEC chairman and nuclear scientists. He reported that Morros (presumably coached by the FBI) was "receptive."

Boris soon shifted the discussion to yet another commercial proposal, this time a new firm he was organizing in Liechtenstein where, he assured his NKGB contact, citizenship for several Soviet operatives could be acquired for a price! When brought back to the subject of Oppenheimer, Morros claimed to be "acquainted with" him. Asked if he could arrange to bring him to the USSR, Morros "said that in about three months he would give us ... a detailed plan ... , and he was going to consider [this] his principal task." Aksenov also urged him to seek others for similar emigration, and Boris agreed to do so.[100] Then, Morros again asked NKGB permission to shift the remaining agents in Soble's group to his control. Aksenov demurred, expressing a wish to hear from Soble himself on the matter. Back to business, Morros then requested permission to stage Sergey Prokofiev's opera *War and Peace* in the United States, a proposal to which Soviet authorities subsequently agreed.[101]

Despite all evidence to the contrary, a March 30, 1955, dispatch from the Vienna KGB station suggests that Moscow retained its faith in Morros's loyalty and credibility. Morros had described at a meeting with the Vienna station chief his contacts with several of Soble's other sources, pursuing his earlier request to be assigned oversight of these individuals. The Vienna station scheduled a follow-up meeting with Boris Morros for April 6, 1955, and asked for instructions from Moscow.[102] But Morros didn't appear at this or any subsequent meetings with KGB operatives.

Boris Morros was in Munich in January 1957 when the FBI cabled him a one-word coded message—"CINERAMA"—apparently a warning that he was in imminent danger. Morros left immediately for New York. Based on his testimony to a federal grand jury, Jack Soble, Myra Soble, and Jacob Alben, another confederate, were indicted for espionage and subsequently convicted. Morros wrote a melodramatic memoir, *My Ten Years as a Counter-Spy*, and almost immediately began negotiating film rights for the story of his career as a double agent.

The producer's long involvement in the entertainment industry had nurtured a talent for public relations and self-promotion that he evidenced during the late 1950s while marketing his experiences as both a Soviet and American agent. "I hated everything the Communists stood for," he explained to interested journalists, "[and] had to play a role more difficult than any of my actors played in movies which I shot in Hollywood."[103]

Perhaps. But Boris Morros managed, even before he began his association with the FBI, to make his connection with Moscow not only manageable but profitable. Continuously searching for a featured role that never materialized, both as a covert agent and as a businessman, Morros was the longest-serving and possibly most flamboyant American ever involved with Soviet intelligence. He died on January 8, 1963.

CHAPTER 7

❖

"Crook":
A Soviet Agent
in Congress

THE MOST DEVOTED and reliable American sources recruited by Soviet intelligence during the 1930s were more often than not radical ideologues, performing "secret work" because of their commitment to the triumph of communism over both fascism and capitalism. They worked for little or no pay. Some of them—for example, Michael Straight and members of Washington's Ware Group—even paid dues and contributed funds to the Communist Party. One notable exception to this band of believers was a Soviet agent whose career in national government was in the legislative and not executive branch, U.S. Congressman Samuel Dickstein.

A Lithuanian Jew born in 1885, Dickstein immigrated to the United States with his parents when he was six. His family settled in one of Manhattan's Lower East Side tenements, a neighborhood Dickstein would later represent in Congress. The elder Dickstein became cantor of the Orthodox Norfolk Street synagogue. After receiving a law degree from New York Law School in 1906, Samuel Dickstein served as a Deputy State Attorney General and then became a member of the New York City Board of Aldermen in 1917. Two years later, he was elected Assemblyman in the New York State Legislature and in 1923 won a Democratic seat in the U.S. House of Representatives, where he would serve eleven terms over the next two decades.[1]

Dickstein's congressional focus throughout his career concerned immigration issues, since he represented a largely foreign-born constituency. During the mid-1930s, however, Dickstein's major interest turned to investigating the network of pro-Nazi and fascist groups in the United States at a time when Jewish persecution in Hitler's Germany had become a prime concern of American Jews. In 1934, Dickstein drafted and gained House support for a resolution appointing a special committee to probe Nazi and other subversive activities in the United States. He was appointed its vice chairman. The committee chairman, John McCormack of Massachusetts, later became Speaker of the House. The McCormack-Dickstein Committee concentrated in its brief—1934–35—history on exposing American Nazis and their supporters, though it also took extensive testimony on the international Communist movement. Perhaps the most important of its recommendations to be enacted was a pioneering law that required registration of foreign agents.[2]

The liberal Dickstein introduced several subsequent resolutions to create a continuing committee to investigate so-called un-American activities. When the coalition of Republicans and southern Democrats that controlled the House after the 1936 election finally authorized a successor to McCormack-Dickstein in May 1938 by a 191 to 41 vote, however, his colleagues awarded the chairmanship to conservative Democrat Martin Dies of Texas. Dickstein did not manage even to gain a seat on the new committee. Despite this setback, "no cause took more of [Dickstein's] energies or his passion," Walter Goodman, the committee's leading scholar wrote, "than the creation of a committee to investigate subversive activities. If any man deserves the title of Father of the Committee, it is Representative Dickstein. He earned the distinction by relentlessly trying [to create such a committee] from 1933 to 1938 and had the rest of his life to regret it."[3]

We can only speculate on the factors that tempted Samuel Dickstein to launch a covert arrangement with Soviet intelligence. The first contact came on July 8, 1937, when an Austrian "illegal" agent for the Soviets, seeking help to become an American citizen, came to the New York law offices shared by the Congressman and his brother.[4] Samuel Dickstein informed the agent, code-named "Buby," that the 1937 quota for Austrian immigrants was only 1,413, but that he could obtain visas for the visitor and his wife in Montreal where the U.S. Consul was a friend. He asked "Buby" for $3,000 to be given to "Canadian authorities" as a guarantee that he would not become a public burden there, with the money to be returned at some unspecified future time. He assured his visitor that he had "settled dozens like you" who went on to become U.S. citizens.[5]

"Buby" returned the following day "after having discussed the matter in the New York NKVD station," bringing only $1,000, which Dickstein agreed to accept but charged the Austrian an additional $200 for the service: "Others take huge money for these things and become millionaires," he told "Buby," according to the NKVD memo on the meeting, "and I, Samuel Dickstein, am a poor man."[6] Writing later about this initial contact, the NKVD's New York station chief Gaik Ovakimyan took a less sympathetic view of the matter, describing Dickstein to Moscow as "heading a criminal gang that was involved in shady businesses, selling passports, illegal smuggling of people, [and] getting the citizenship. . . ."[7]

Dickstein visited Soviet Ambassador to the United States Alexander Troyanovsky in Washington in December 1937, after which the following report was sent to Moscow: "Congressman Dickstein—Chairman of the House committee on Nazi activities in the U.S.— . . . came to the Ambassador and let him know that while investigating Nazi activities in the U.S., his agents unmasked their liaison with Russian Fascists living in the U.S." Complaining that "Congress didn't allocate credits for investigation of activities by [Russian Fascist leader] Vonsyatsky's group," Dickstein, who professed "a friendly attitude toward the Soviet Union," offered to pass to the Ambassador information on the Vonsyatsky group that his own investigators would cultivate and for which "he would need 5–6 thousand dollars."[8]

Both Troyanovsky and the NKVD's Washington agents, although interested, were initially skeptical of Dickstein's proposal. Nonetheless, they received personal instructions from Nikolay Yezhov, then People's Commissar for Internal Affairs, to proceed.[9] The NKVD station still managed to make clear its own view of the new recruit by assigning Dickstein the code name "Crook." Troyanovsky met with the Congressman several months later—on April 20, 1938—and assigned his personal secretary ("Igor") to conduct subsequent business, which appears to have begun with two meetings that week.

Although Dickstein and his Soviet handler agreed to exchange secret information for money, they disagreed vehemently on price. This argument over fees would continue throughout the Congressman's relationship with the NKVD. "Igor" rejected the initial materials provided by "Crook" as "widely known" and, therefore, without value.[10] Dickstein demanded $2,500 a month for his work but was initially offered only $500. Igor raised the monetary ante in order to nurture the relationship, hoping that "in a certain period of time" Dickstein could be asked "questions more urgent for us."[11]

On May 9, 1938, shortly after the House of Representatives had approved creation of a Committee on Un-American Activities (HUAC), Dickstein informed "Igor" that he hoped to gain membership in the body in order to probe fascist organizations, whether German or Russian, on behalf of his new paymasters. That day, also, Dickstein agreed to a compromise monthly payment of $1,250 in exchange for his assistance, which, he reiterated, came only "out of sympathy toward the Soviet Union."[12]

Later that month, on May 18, "Igor" and Dickstein agreed on details of the relationship, which the embassy conveyed to Moscow in this cable:

1. [Dickstein] will get for us documentary materials about fascist work—both from the government organs and private intelligence organizations he is connected with.
2. [Dickstein] agreed to provide us with supplemental data answering our questions following from these materials.
3. [Dickstein] agreed to guide actively the committee's attention to those facts of fascist and White Guard activities we would point [out] to him.
4. [Dickstein] gets $1,250 from us every month. The first monthly pay was given to him that very day and a corresponding receipt was given by him. . . .[13]

Peter Gutzeit wrote a long memo to his Moscow superiors on May 25 justifying this delicate and unusual relationship on the grounds that Dickstein could provide extremely useful material regarding American "fascists" of all descriptions, a category that, for Stalin's agents, included not only Russian monarchists, Nazis, Ukrainian nationalists, and Japanese operatives but, also, supporters of Leon Trotsky. Gutzeit, however, remained cautious about his congressional catch:

We are fully aware whom we are dealing with. "Crook" is completely justifying his code name. This is an unscrupulous type, greedy for money, consented to work because of money, a very cunning swindler. . . . Therefore it is difficult for us to guarantee the fulfillment of the planned program even in the part which he proposed to us himself.

The NKVD station chief pledged to monitor closely Dickstein's promise and his actual performance.[14]

When the House leadership failed to appoint Dickstein to HUAC the following month, his value declined considerably in the view of his NKVD handlers. As a result, they informed Moscow, "he won't be able to carry out measures planned by us together with him." This cable cited as one example Dickstein's inability to obtain grand jury interrogations of suspected German agents.[15] Nevertheless, according to a June 1939 memo to Moscow from then-NKVD station chief Gaik Ovakimyan, the documents that the Congressman did hand over after he began working for the Soviets included, in addition to Dies Committee transcripts and lists of American Nazis, "materials on the war budget for 1940, records of conferences of the budget subcommission, reports of the war minister, chief of staff and etc."[16]

On the whole, however, the information Dickstein conveyed to "Igor" in June 1938, according to his Russian contacts, did not justify his monthly payments. This led to several fierce arguments with the Congressman: "He blazed up very much, claimed that if we didn't give him money he would break with us . . . that he is employing people and he must pay them, that he demands nothing for himself."

The dialogue between "Igor" and Dickstein reached comparative shopper's status in a June 23 discussion at the latter's New York office, when he again threatened to break off the relationship because too much was expected of him while the Soviets still mistrusted his efforts:

> . . . if there was no trust, it was impossible to work. For illustration he told that for some years he had worked for Poland and everything was OK. He was paid money without any questions. A couple of years ago he worked for the English [and] was paid good money without any questions. Everything was delicate and on the sly. Our case is only trouble. . . . Apparently, he really managed to fool the Poles and the English—i.e., to promise something substantial and to limit himself to rubbish.[17]

Dickstein's audacious assertion that his Soviet deal was merely the third in a series of apparently lucrative agreements with foreign intelligence agencies made little impression upon the Soviet operative, who reminded the Congressman that his other arrangements involved only money while with the NKVD "he is guided by ideological considerations, by [the] necessity of struggling against [a] common enemy—fascism." The two men then bickered about Dickstein's understandable concern over signing receipts for money received. Again, his Soviet handler rejected any compromise. Finally the two agreed to meet at Dickstein's Washington office the following week, on June 27.

After this meeting, Peter Gutzeit reported to Moscow on issues that went well beyond future dealings with the Congressman. He outlined a more general strategy for NKVD operations in the United States to maximize Soviet political influence. Even granting Dickstein's tendency to exaggerate the importance of information he was providing, Gutzeit urged his superiors nonetheless to consider not only spending the $15,000 or more annually to maintain Dickstein on the payroll (with receipts) but also "probably . . . to throw him a round sum for the reelection campaign."

His rationale for this arrangement might well have been written by certain foreign intelligence operatives in America during the 1990s:

> In this connection we put forward a general matter of a necessity to have several people of ours among Congressmen and even Senators if we decided to penetrate seriously and actively into the politics of this country. It is necessary to decide this question on principle as very big money will be needed for this purpose. . . . Helping during the elections with money means to define relations with a future Congressman or Senator, possibly, for some years. It doesn't mean that they should be obligatorily recruited by all traditional rules (some could be recruited), but it does mean that we create a group of our people in the legislative bodies, define their political positions, and insert [them] there to actively influence [events].[18]

Gutzeit's Moscow superiors approved his proposal and even expanded it to include funding American journalists as well as politicians. They instructed the Soviet agent to begin immediate work on the plan. Gutzeit responded to Moscow with this blunt August 2, 1938, memorandum:

> The realization of the scheme following from the tasks formulated by you in your latest letter will demand, as it has been already said, huge means. Amounts of these means can't be compared with the expenditures we currently have.
>
> Financing of Congressmen's election campaigns, paying journalists, maintenance of newspapers—all this means expenditures that are impossible to tally beforehand. For instance, expenditures on Congressmen may vary in different cases. It is impossible to say beforehand for what sum we'll manage to buy the pens of popular journalists. It is very difficult to define even approximately the sum necessary for buying newspapers. Besides, the character of all this work is such that it is impossible to know beforehand the limits of expenditures and impossible to say beforehand whether we need one journalist or ten, whether we need one newspaper or two, etc.

Therefore, I frankly claim that I find much difficulty in defining even an approximate estimate of forthcoming expenditures. Proceeding from considerations stated above, I can't say whether these expenditures will be $500,000 or $1,000,000 per year.

The decision of this question must be up to you. It is necessary to [decide] how much will be allocated on this work for our country [the United States]. And then, proceeding from this sum, we'll build all our calculations. Or according to this decision, we'll get the expenditures right depending on practical necessities. Surely, in all cases, the expenditures will be carried out with the Center's permission.

It should be taken into account that, if you wish, expenditures for buying a newspaper can be returned without difficulty, though definitely with some losses. It doesn't represent any major difficulty, either, to protect ourselves from any surprises on the part of the so-called newspapers' owners. Controlling shareholdings of these newspapers can be easily reregistered to a Soviet citizen and kept in the [Soviet] Union.

Congressmen's work must be appraised according to their activity in the directions you pointed out to us (antifascist activities, anti-Japanese position, anti-isolationist, [and] favoring rapprochement with us). We shouldn't demand more from the Congressmen.

We are going to pay journalists for their positive stands also on the same questions. Certainly, it doesn't rule out using this one or that one among them outside the framework of this scheme.[19]

No response to Gutzeit's detailed memo could be found in the NKVD files, and the station chief's subsequent recall to the Soviet Union marked the end of this grandiose scheme.

As for continuing to use Congressman Samuel Dickstein's services, Moscow responded to Gutzeit's earlier inquiry by sounding a note of extreme caution. Further dealings with the Congressman, a July 15 cable noted, represented a "danger" because "this type . . . is not simply a crook but a mercenary of many intelligence services."[20]

Meanwhile, Dickstein carried on his modest efforts for the NKVD. In response to Peter Gutzeit's request in September 1938, the Congressman publicly denounced the Dies Committee's focus on Communist groups and their allies. Dickstein also provided his Soviet associates with the names of several informants within the ranks of fascist organizations in the United States whom he argued could provide useful information. He even turned over transcripts of alleged tape-recorded hotel room conversations between American Nazi leader Fritz Kuhn and his mistress, the latter a Dickstein snitch. By then, the New York Democrat had begun to speak out in favor of terminating the Dies Committee.[21]

NKVD operations in America had been hurt at this time by arrests in Moscow of key intelligence agents during Stalin's purges. One of those imprisoned and later executed after answering a summons home was Peter Gutzeit, who cautioned his interrogators in Lubyanka Prison that Samuel Dickstein's professed antifascism was a sham justification for his continued work with the NKVD: "Money brought him to cooperation with the USSR."[22]

The NKVD decided to make one last effort to persuade the Congressman to be of greater use to them. One of its leading officials, Zinovy Passov, took the unusual step of writing Dickstein a long letter on April 14, 1939, reviewing their sixteen months of "joint activities in exposing fascism." The Soviets even agreed to provide Dickstein his payments without demanding receipts. They asked him generally to provide "information about all the important political questions regarding your country and its relations with other countries," while also identifying others who "could be of use to us." Passov asked also that Dickstein seek to penetrate U.S. intelligence agencies to obtain information "about our enemies."[23]

After four months, Dickstein replied evasively, noting mainly that he was on the job already and that any attempt to obtain intelligence information would require additional funds from the Soviets.[24] He raised the question of this payment again when the NKVD station in Washington reinforced Passov's letter with a specific request that Dickstein penetrate the FBI for information on Soviet, German, and Italian citizens resident in the United States. Although the Congressman claimed that he had an FBI source willing to assist, his Soviet handlers counterproposed, offering only $300–$400 for "concrete stuff plus a receipt." That ended the discussion.[25]

By the time Dickstein's response reached Moscow, Passov, too, had been arrested. An internal NKVD memorandum expressed regrets that some of the Congressman's Soviet handlers had turned out to be "people's enemies."[26]

No matter. Purge trials or not, Dickstein countered as usual with a request for additional tens of thousands of dollars, supposedly to pay a lawyer to defend Moscow's interests before a commission that had been established in July 1939 to address issues of American financial claims against the Soviets. Again the NKVD declined to fund his proposed services.[27]

Not until late 1939 did the Soviets contact Dickstein, this time in connection with the appearance before the Dies Committee in executive session of a major Soviet defector, Walter Krivitsky (code-named "Enemy"), who in 1941 would be found dead in a Washington hotel room. His handlers asked Dickstein to provide them, as apparently he had on earlier occasions, with transcripts of Krivitsky's testimony to Dies and his colleagues. What the Soviets received instead was a short memo purportedly summarizing Krivitsky's testimony, which the Congressman (who was not present for the interrogation) described as helpful to the Soviet Union because Krivitsky had presented no concrete evidence of espionage on its part in the United States.

The NKVD agents, however, found Dickstein's memo suspicious when they recognized that portions of it strongly resembled news accounts and Krivitsky's public speeches: "We treated ["Crook's"] report very distrustfully," the Washington station reported on November 5, 1939.[28]

Nor was Dickstein successful in responding to another urgent petition from his Soviet handlers to arrange for Krivitsky's deportation from the United States. The request had come directly from NKVD officials in Moscow in July 1939.[29] Despite Dickstein's efforts to question U.S. immigration authorities concerning Krivitsky's visa, the Dies Committee was able to forestall the defector's deportation.[30]

Nor did Dickstein's accounts of his alleged discussions with leading State Department officials impress his NKVD handlers. A January 1940 memo to Moscow from the New York station concluded that Dickstein's *only* possible future use was in giving speeches in Congress under NKVD direction, receiving for each from $500 to $1,000.[31]

As it turned out, one of Dickstein's first speeches to follow that suggestion was given on January 16, 1940, in support of increased appropriations for J. Edgar Hoover's FBI, which had begun modest if ineffectual counterintelligence efforts directed against Soviet agents in the United States.[32] The NKVD arrived at the inescapable conclusion that, even as a designated speaker, Samuel Dickstein was simply not worth the effort and money that had been spent in cultivating him. "According to all data," observed a February 27, 1940, report to Moscow, "this source can't be a useful organizer who could gather around him a group of liberal Congressmen to exercise our influence and, alone, he doesn't represent any interest. On the other hand, [Dickstein] refuses to give documentary materials and refused to switch to per-piece pay [i.e., for speeches] and we are not going to pay thousands for idleness. Therefore, we decided to break with [Dickstein]."[33] By then, Soviet intelligence operatives had paid over $12,000 to Samuel Dickstein for his various services, a sum equivalent in 1997 dollars to more than $133,000.

Although his NKVD overseers had long since decided that Samuel Dickstein was "a complete racketeer and a blackmailer"[34] (in the words of Gaik Ovakimyan's June 1939 memo to Moscow), that characterization fails to acknowledge also the genuine antifascist sentiment typical of Americans in that generation who cooperated with the Soviets. That dollop of antifascism doubtless reinforced Dickstein's evident and over-riding concern for the money involved.

Possibly the keenest insight into the potential uses of such influential "agents in place" in the United States came from Peter Gutzeit, who, before returning to Moscow, sent his superiors a memorandum in June 1938 regarding "our work here [in America] in the field of big politics." Gutzeit had been in the country for five years, unusually long for Soviet intelligence chiefs in that decade. He recognized the amounts other major countries, but not the Soviet Union, were spending in the United States "on propaganda" to influence American policies, public opinion, and the press "as well as [on] bribing political figures in the government, Senate, and Congress. . . . We are shocked [that Dickstein worked for the Poles and English as well as for the Soviets], but here it is normal."

Gutzeit's memo did not advocate bribing key figures (as in Dickstein's case) or stealing documents, but rather spending significant funds to shape the attitudes of sympathetic political and public sectors toward Soviet interests. In an assessment decades ahead of his time, Gutzeit tried to persuade his superiors in Moscow that such efforts would help to produce within the Roosevelt Administration, Congress, and the American public "a certain number of people (ours) who by their speeches and all their work would influence U.S. policy."[35]

As for Samuel Dickstein, his brief adventure in the spy trade left no visible mark on his public career at the time. Other than his efforts first to help create and then to oppose the House Committee on Un-American Activities, the veteran Dickstein was best known for his expertise while serving as chairman of the House Committee on Immigration and Naturalization. He ran successfully for the New York State Supreme Court in 1945 and served as a justice from 1946 until his death on April 22, 1954.[36]

But even long after Dickstein and the Soviets had parted company, he managed to rankle them. In a famous incident in 1948, Dickstein, while serving as a judge, ordered Soviet officials to produce in court a

Russian citizen and schoolteacher of diplomatic children who was being held against her will in the USSR Consulate in New York. Hours later, Mrs. Oksana Kasenkina, who had refused a Moscow order to return home, made a daring and successful "leap to freedom," as media throughout the world described her bruising jump from an upper-floor window ledge at the consulate into the courtyard below. It was Soviet Consul-General Jacob Lomakin's disobedience of Dickstein's court order, however, that outraged the once-friendly former-Congressman-turned-jurist. "I will compel him to obey," Samuel Dickstein exclaimed. "I am not going to let him ignore the law."[37]

The irony of Dickstein's declaration would not have been lost on any Soviet intelligence official in Moscow whose case file included an earlier encounter with "Crook."

PART TWO

◈

The
Third Front:
Soviet
Espionage in
the Second
World War

CHAPTER 8

❖❖❖

Harvest Time, I: The Silvermaster Network in Wartime Washington

RETURN OF THE OPERATIVES

T HE 1936–39 PURGE YEARS in the Soviet Union affected every institution in the country, including its intelligence service. A number of foreign operatives from the NKVD and the GRU were summoned home to face arrest, interrogation, torture, and often death. Stalin and his inner circle were especially suspicious of those who had served in Western countries where anti-Soviet, Trotskyist, and even czarist influences found free expression. Operatives who defected from intelligence assignments abroad, such as Ignatz Reiss and possibly Walter Krivitsky, were tracked down when possible and murdered. Others—among them Elizabeth Bentley, Whittaker Chambers, and Alexander Orlov—through careful preparation managed to escape retribution after leaving their covert assignments.

Several key NKVD figures were recalled from the United States in 1938 to face imprisonment and execution, including New York station chief Peter Gutzeit.[1] In 1939 and 1940, another seven Russian agents in the United States were summoned home.[2] As a result—although Soviet intelligence had cultivated a broad network of American sources within the government and in other key posts by the late 1930s—there were virtually no NKVD (or GRU) operatives left to supervise their work. This led to a significant break in contact between handlers and sources from 1938 to 1941, lamented in later NKVD memoranda:

In spite of the fact that among older agents in our American station there were a number used by us in political and diplomatic work, and many agents from European stations have come to the U.S. because of the war (forced to leave occupied territories), we didn't have the ability to use . . . the presence of a large network of [Soviet] agents to organize proper work in this field . . . operatives who could direct the activities of the above-mentioned agents. . . . Unfortunately, the American station for the past several years has suffered an acute crisis in operatives. . . . Thus, [despite] breakthroughs in the most important sectors of our intelligence work, we were obliged to put on conservation [to halt all contact with] a large number of agents and . . . to carry out work on a minimal scale.[3]

Nor, because of poor training and limited background, could the few existing Soviet intelligence operatives in the United States from 1939 to 1941 meet the NKVD's primary goal of acquiring American agents close to the White House and President Roosevelt:

Difficulties in this work [ran one candid internal assessment] rest on the lack of corresponding cadre in our station, qualified workers [NKVD-trained Soviet operatives] capable of ensuring the handling of prominent and respectable agents surrounding Roosevelt or such persons as [Harry] Hopkins. Therefore, qualified intelligence officers with high culture and horizon, experienced in politics, knowing English and conditions in the U.S., must be sent to the station for political and diplomatic work. The success of our work in such an important sector depends on it to a considerable degree.[4]

Gaik Ovakimyan wrote Moscow in September 1938 asking for funds to maintain two very nervous "illegals," code-named "Yuz" and "Smith," despite "the uncertain situation"; fearing recall, "Smith" had suffered a heart attack.[5] However, because of the continuous purges, no one at NKVD headquarters had been there even a few years earlier. Moscow instructed Ovakimyan to recall the two operatives "since [they were] not known to anybody in the section and were sent abroad for the mission by enemies" already purged from the Service.[6] Only Ovakimyan's subsequent arrest by the FBI rescued him from accepting a similarly perilous summons home.[7]

The NKVD made one attempt in 1941 to bolster its thin red line of operatives in the United States. One of its Moscow department chiefs,

Pavel Fitin, wrote Lavrenty Beria asking approval to set up a new "illegal" station in New York and to send as station chief Arnold Deutsch ("Stephan"), who had been working effectively in Great Britain, where he recruited (among others) Harold "Kim" Philby. The New York "illegal" station, in addition to the effort at reestablishing relationships with sources, was given two additional assignments: "Organizing new recruitments especially in defense industries and in [government] ministries that are impossible to penetrate through the legal station; . . . [and] organizing recruitment of agents for transfer to Europe."[8] But Deutsch never reached the United States. His ship was sunk in the mid-Atlantic by a German submarine.

After Deutsch's death, designating the new "illegal" station chief was made more urgent by Germany's June 1941 attack on the Soviet Union. The NKVD assigned Itzhak Akhmerov (now code-named "Mer"), who returned to the United States in December 1941 with his wife, Helen Lowry ("Nelly"), Earl Browder's niece. The couple settled in New York, where Akhmerov developed a cover identity as both an accountant and a partner (with another NKVD agent) in a furrier's shop.[9] Such small businesses were favorite cover enterprises for Soviet "illegals," producing a credible public identity or "legend" while also serving as a source of revenue. (A famous KGB tale in later decades concerns one such successful factory entrepreneur-operative who returned home after years spent abroad. Invited to speak about his business experiences to an audience of workers at a Moscow factory, after briefly inspecting the plant, the "illegal" began his speech by announcing: "If this were my company, I would fire all of you immediately!")

So fascinated had Itzhak Akhmerov become with American business that he easily might have been that speaker. Soon after reaching New York and assuming his nominal role as a furrier, he expanded the shop and increased its profits. Emboldened by his success, Akhmerov proposed to his Moscow superiors that he be allowed "with a small [amount of] capital . . . to establish connections with a solid banking firm on Wall Street" or to invest in the stock market, pointing out to his undoubtedly puzzled Soviet colleagues that "there are about 13 million [stock] shareholders in the U.S." Akhmerov claimed that his wealthy American source, Michael Straight, had offered to help him organize a new "cover" identity as an international banker! Alternatively, Akhmerov wrote Moscow, he wished to open a "small fashionable fur shop" in the high-rent district on Madison Avenue in midtown Manhattan with his wife running the business. Despite the operative's accurate description of the status and benefits involved—"In the U.S., the more one is involved in . . . trade and business affairs, the more respected he is and better social status he has. Here, a semi-literate merchant looks down on a professor."—his superiors firmly rejected this most-un-Bolshevik plan of action.[10]

Getting down to real business, Akhmerov spent a great deal of time in the months after his return to America trying unsuccessfully to revive earlier cooperation from sources he had known in Washington during the 1930s. Despite both Laurence Duggan's and Michael Straight's willingness to accept personal relationships with Akhmerov (whom Straight knew as "Michael Green"), Straight would not resume his earlier work for Soviet intelligence, and Duggan cooperated only fitfully.* Nor did Akhmerov's attempt in 1942 to recruit for his network several active NKGB sources in government posts—including Victor Perlo ("Eck") and Charles Kramer ("Lot")—prove successful. Their agent group reported directly to Jacob Golos in the New York NKGB station.[11]

Hoping to explain his singular lack of success as a returning "illegal," Akhmerov described for Moscow in August 1942 the wartime constraints on meeting potential sources:

> Conditions for such meetings in Washington become very complicated. It is almost impossible to talk about business matters in restaurants . . . [which] are always overcrowded, and every delicate conversation draws the attention of surrounding people. To sit whispering scares the interlocutor. Counterintelligence here has become very flexible and far-sighted. Recently, the FBI issued an order to fire all the Washington waiters who are not American citizens. Hundreds of policemen and FBI cars are circulating around the city.[12]

Although Akhmerov may have exaggerated the extent of counterintelligence activity, plainly the additional dangers of exposure helped to persuade both Duggan and Straight to remain cautious in their contacts with him. Akhmerov turned to business for one of his few 1942 initiatives, recruiting an American Communist Party member ("Bark") to open a "night café-restaurant for officials and political figures" in Washington. The enterprise opened but quickly closed without explanation in the report received by Moscow.[13]

---

* Akhmerov's efforts are described in Chapters 1 and 4.

SILVERMASTER AND FRIENDS

Akhmerov's luck improved (and his workload increased) in November 1943, after Jacob Golos's death and the NKGB's decision to transfer, over Elizabeth Bentley's objections, a significant group of Washington sources directly to Akhmerov's control, especially a network of government officials run by economist Nathan Gregory Silvermaster. In January 1942, long before Golos's death, NKGB leadership believed that the group's importance to Soviet intelligence collection required stricter individual oversight by a professional, not Golos's practice of casually mingling "open" U.S. Communist Party associates and covert Washington sources.

"It is necessary to break the group into separate links," Moscow had instructed Golos in January 1942, "with a view toward its most effective use and guidance as well as ensuring *konspiratsia* [observing the rules of agent security] and removing complexity from the entire system." Initially, Moscow proposed a modest reorganization of Golos's operations, allowing him to continue working with Silvermaster, who, in turn, would maintain control of *his* various sources. One of these was Treasury official Harry Dexter White (code-named "Lawyer" at the time), whom Moscow understandably considered "one of the most valuable probationers [agents]." In time, the NKGB leadership would want White transferred to Akhmerov's direct supervision. Meanwhile, the January 1942 instructions continued, Silvermaster should also maintain contact with at least one other close associate in the network, William Ludwig Ullman ("Polo"), while both continued their recruitment of an even more important figure, White House adviser Lauchlin Currie ("Page").[14]

Assisted by Elizabeth Bentley, Golos viewed his work as a cooperative effort with CPUSA head Earl Browder. He rejected efforts at direct supervision by Soviet NKGB "illegals" such as Akhmerov. Often this plethora of overseers led to confusion among Golos's sources concerning whether their material went to the American Communist Party, the Comintern, the NKGB in Moscow—or all three.

Through Earl Browder, Jacob Golos's contact with Nathan Gregory Silvermaster had begun in 1940, possibly even earlier. Silvermaster spoke Russian, which made him a popular figure among Soviet operatives. Born in Odessa in 1899, Silvermaster and his family had reached the United States in 1914. After spending his postcollege years from 1920 to 1935 as an active Communist on the West Coast, he came to

Washington to work at various New Deal agencies before settling at Treasury. He had met Earl Browder and served as his courier during the 1934 "general strike" in San Francisco. It was through Browder that Silvermaster was introduced to Golos and the Soviets' East Coast intelligence network. Silvermaster's wife, Helen, a distant relative of the famous czarist Prime Minister Count Witte, shared her husband's enthusiasm for assisting the NKVD.

Because of his relationship with Golos, in 1941–42, Silvermaster became the coordinator of several other Soviet sources—economists like himself—within the wartime U.S. government: Frank Coe ("Pick"), William Ludwig Ullman ("Polo"), and David Silverman ("Eleron").[15] Others would follow, including Treasury's Harry Dexter White, who had been involved during the 1930s with the GRU network for which Whittaker Chambers had been a courier.* "According to our information," Moscow cabled New York station chief Vassily Zarubin in November 1942, "at one time [White] was a probationer of the neighbors," confirming his earlier role. Moscow advised "singling out a special 'illegal' to work with him," considering White's special importance.[16]

The "Silvermaster Group," as it was called by American counterintelligence experts once it was exposed, was actually an untidy assemblage of agents and sources with little "group" identity. Thus, one member—Frank Coe—complained frequently to handlers that his agent work was hindering his "official" career. Another—Solomon Adler ("Sax")—had actually left Washington for duties in China, though Moscow still counted him in Silvermaster's conspiratorial cohort.[17] Even Harry Dexter White, a veteran Soviet source, was a reluctant recruit: agitated constantly over the possibility of exposure, concerned with career advancement within Treasury, and generally (in Zarubin's words) "a very nervous and cowardly person."[18]

Despite the organizational disarray, Silvermaster and his associates produced for the NKVD the most valuable information then being generated from its American stations. Immediately after Germany's invasion of the Soviet Union in June 1941, for example, Silvermaster delivered to Golos and other Soviet operatives documents from the U.S. military attaché's office in London and elsewhere containing recent data on the German armed forces and its deployment in Germany and various occupied countries.[19] He also turned over information on U.S. military-industrial plans and on the views held by leading American

* See Chapter 2 for Chambers's relationship with White and others during this period.

policymakers concerning developments on the Soviet-German front, much of which presumably reached Silvermaster (a mid-level bureaucrat) from his more highly placed friend Harry Dexter White. Accurate or otherwise, such opinions held great interest for Stalin and his closest colleagues.

Often the information conveyed was especially timely and came directly from the top. Thus, on August 5, 1941, the New York station learned from Silvermaster that at a July 31 luncheon, Navy Secretary Frank Knox had offered to bet that the Germans would capture Moscow, Leningrad, Kiev, and Odessa within a month. Treasury Secretary Henry Morgenthau took the bet and shared this news with Silvermaster and other key staff members.[20] Moscow concluded that Morgenthau sympathized with the USSR's plight and could help influence FDR's aid policies.[21] Presidential adviser Harry Hopkins's confidential report to Roosevelt on his summer 1941 trip to Moscow also reached the NKVD, probably via another FDR counselor, Lauchlin Currie, by that time a colleague in Silvermaster's network.[22] That fall, even before Averill Harriman left for Moscow to lead the U.S. delegation to a trilateral conference on Anglo-American financial assistance to the USSR, Soviet intelligence had received a briefing on the Roosevelt cabinet's discussion of this issue.[23]

Despite the vital material from Silvermaster and his group, NKGB leadership in Moscow continued to complain about its lack of focus on questions of priority interest to the Soviet Union. "Left to their own resources," ran one June 1942 dispatch to Vassily Zarubin, the American agents "often give either out-of-date or completely unfit materials. . . . [Silvermaster's] materials represent in essence an incidental motley collection of information [ranging] from those which we sent in part to the Instance [the Soviet leadership] to those which have no value."*[24]

This same cable outlined the type of information Moscow sought, such as whether the American government was implementing its latest pacts with the USSR, including the Lend-Lease agreement, and who, if anyone, opposed such support. Had preparations begun to open a second front in Europe and, if so, "when and in what place"? More-

---

* The VENONA intercepts contain a number of reports based on classified U.S. government and military documents turned over by Silvermaster and his associates. See, for example, New York station to Moscow, May 21, 1943, Nos. 732, 735; May 25, 1942, Nos. 746–48; May 28, 1943, Nos. 794–99; June 9, 1943, No. 888; June 22, 1943, No. 977; June 29–30, 1943, Nos. 1017, 1022; July 3, 1943, Nos. 1061–63; July 20, 1943, Nos. 1176–78; July 21, 1943, No. 1189.

over, who favored and who opposed the second front? "What questions did Churchill discuss with Roosevelt . . . at their last meeting in June? What are the divergences between the English and Americans on the main matters of the war?" Turning to postwar Europe, the NKGB wanted to know how America's "leading circles" felt about the "frontiers of our country" and about "reestablishment of the independence of small countries bordering with us." This extensive list of priorities concluded with queries about the extent of "fifth column" sabotage in the United States—by which the NKGB meant the work of isolationist and pro-Nazi groups—and about the actions of U.S. counterintelligence against Soviet operatives.[25]

Nor did Soviet intelligence's hunger for secret information from the United States stop there. During the 1930s, neither the NKVD nor the GRU had displayed much interest in (or knowledge of) the close connections between America's domestic politics and its foreign policy. All that changed, however, after Hitler's armies began slicing through the USSR in June 1941. A precise understanding of U.S. intentions and perspectives—such as Silvermaster's August 5, 1941, account of the cabinet luncheon discussion—became a priority for Stalin and his colleagues, who turned to their intelligence networks in America, as this April 6, 1942, dispatch from Moscow indicated:

> We are interested in the [U.S.] government's plans for the country's foreign and domestic policy, all machinations, backstage negotiations, intrigues, all that is done before this or that decision of the government becomes known to everybody. . . . The task is to penetrate into those places where policy is born and developed, where discussions and debates take place, where policy is completed.[26]

The NKGB leadership's practical instruction accompanying this general mandate was to coordinate regular receipt of crucial secret information from all major sources within the government—the State Department and other cabinet ministries as well as the OSS, FBI, and other intelligence or counterintelligence bodies—but especially the White House. Moscow believed, correctly, that where possible, Roosevelt avoided using official government channels for fear of leaking information and losing control of policy. Thus, the April 6, 1942, memorandum concluded that "penetrating the surroundings of Roosevelt himself is the goal that we seek in our everyday work."[27] In practice, this meant seeking access to a small circle of the President's closest friends and associates such as Harry Hopkins and Treasury Secretary

Henry Morgenthau (hence the crucial importance of sources such as Lauchlin Currie and Harry Dexter White).

The activities of Silvermaster and his associates were disrupted for a time in the spring of 1942 by four separate investigations of the economist's links to the Communist Party. Silvermaster informed Jacob Golos at a March 26 meeting that the House Committee on Un-American Activities had listed him among a hundred government officials suspected of being Communists, in Silvermaster's case because of his activities in California during the mid-thirties. At this time, the FBI also began to probe the same information, contacting a number of friends (including Harry Dexter White) who promptly informed Silvermaster.[28] Shortly thereafter, a separate extensive investigation by the Civil Service Commission could not confirm Silvermaster's Communist associations nor could an Office of Naval Intelligence inquiry.[29]

Moscow ordered a two-month break in acquiring materials from Silvermaster and his group while these inquiries were in progress, assigning Elizabeth Bentley to maintain contact with the agent himself.[30] A number of the letters exchanged between Silvermaster and his U.S. government superiors (most of whom believed his disavowals of Communist links) were later sent by Golos to Moscow. The Treasury official's interrogators did not ask whether he had committed espionage or had links to any Soviet intelligence organization.[31]

At the insistence of Naval Intelligence, however, Silvermaster was discharged from the Treasury Department in June 1942 only to be hired soon afterward by the Farm Security Administration.[32] Since Silvermaster met his various sources away from their places of employment, his change in venue did not noticeably interfere with his ability to continue collecting government documents and information for Jacob Golos. Nor did a renewed probe of Silvermaster the following year by the Justice Department interfere with normal covert business.

This time, his friend and fellow-agent Lauchlin Currie used his White House post to help quash the inquiry, as Zarubin reported to Moscow in October 1943:

> Recently [Silvermaster] told us that [Currie] made every effort to liquidate his case: when [Silvermaster's] case was given for examination to the committee [presumably White House security personnel] . . . attached to "Captain" [the President], [Currie] managed to persuade the majority of members of this committee

to favor repealing this investigation. . . . [He] believes that the investigation will be stopped.*[33]

Zarubin, Akhmerov, and the other Russian operatives at the NKGB's New York station were persuaded that their major problem with Silvermaster and his group was not exposure by American counterintelligence but Jacob Golos's deficiencies as a supervisor. At this time, the NKGB still did not know the real names of various members of the group nor many details of Golos's oversight. They contented themselves with receiving the information but brooded about their lack of control over the process. Thus, Zarubin complained to Moscow in October 1942 that although "[Silvermaster] and his people" were productive sources, much more could be done with the group: "We already receive from them, especially from [Silvermaster], valuable materials. . . . One could satisfy one's self with it. However, if . . . one can count on them as a serious base now and in future, they must be taught our work, included in our network, and attached to us. The connection of [Golos] with [Silvermaster] will not ensure this, since he is against such an approach."[34]

Akhmerov's takeover was confirmed at a December 19, 1943, meeting between Earl Browder and Elizabeth Zarubina, wife of the NKGB's New York station chief and herself an experienced agent handler.[35] When Akhmerov finally met Silvermaster on March 15, 1944, his initial impression was highly favorable (as reported in a March 20 dispatch to Moscow). Silvermaster was "a man sincerely devoted to the party and the Soviet Union . . . politically literate, knows Marxism, a deeply Russian man . . . known in Washington as a progressive liberal . . . [and] understands perfectly that he works for us."[36]

Silvermaster's major government sources also remained faithful. William Ludwig Ullman had been in Silvermaster's CPUSA cell and lived in his apartment. Ullman collected information and, according to KGB records, also photographed documents for transmission to the Soviets.[37] Frank Coe also provided valuable material but believed that his data went to Earl Browder rather than directly to Soviet intelligence. David Silverman, another clandestine CPUSA member, was a third source, cautious and never asking to whom Silvermaster gave his

* "[Jacob Golos] has reported that the [FBI] has resumed investigation of the case of [Nathan Gregory Silvermaster]. A few days ago, two representatives of the [FBI] visited [Lauchlin Currie] and began to [ask] about [Silvermaster], in particular is he a [Communist Party member]. [Currie] apparently replied that he knows [Silvermaster] . . . [undeciphered]. . . ." New York station to Moscow, September 1, 1943, No. 1431, VENONA files.

material. Silvermaster's wife, Helen, code-named "Dora," assisted her husband's secret efforts. Finally, Treasury Department official Harry Dexter White remained an ongoing source of information, documents, and policy assistance, using his friend Silvermaster as a conduit to Soviet intelligence throughout the war years.*[38]

Moscow instructed Akhmerov to organize more regular deliveries of information, instruct the group's members in tradecraft, and shift several to direct contact with other Soviet operatives, thereby "compartmentalizing" the group.[39] More effective training was obviously essential: Over half the photographed documents in one batch submitted by Ullman in the summer of 1944, for example, were unreadable.[40]

Untimely translation was another source of complaint from Moscow. Pavel Fitin's memorandum to Vsevolod Merkulov in July 1944 expressed his displeasure about the belated arrival of certain materials from Silvermaster and his colleagues but also confirmed their first-rate quality:

> The New York station is systematically delaying the processing of acquired documentary and agent materials; in particular, materials from [Silvermaster's] group. Consequently, much important data . . . comes to us with a long delay, thereby losing its value to some extent.
>
> For example, by Post #2, which we received on May 25 this year, the station sent, among other materials, [the following documents, which had been received by the station in February or March]:
>
> 1. draft of a four-page agreement between the U.S. and England about lend-lease;
> 2. a 41-page Treasury Department memorandum on postwar financial and trade relations between the USSR and the U.S.;
> 3. a three-page draft memorandum composed by [Harry Dexter] White for [Secretary Henry] Morgenthau about

---

* Information also came regularly from FDR's close aide Lauchlin Currie ("Page"), as in this important June 1944 cable: "According to [Currie's] information, [Roosevelt's] reluctance to recognize [General DeGaulle's] government is explained by the fact that he is striving to compel the French to take a more liberal position with respect to the colonies. [Currie] expresses his certainty that [Roosevelt] considers the USSR's conditions for the Polish-Soviet border to be acceptable. . . ." New York station to Moscow, June 24, 1944, No. 900, VENONA files.

amendments to the Soviet-American agreement on lend-lease and about granting a loan to the Soviet Union for reconstructing the national economy, etc.

Timely receipt by us of these materials could turn out to be very useful for the Instance [Stalin and Soviet leaders] and, particularly, for our delegation to the international currency-financial conference that is now taking place in the U.S. [the crucial Dumbarton Oaks Conference in Washington on postwar monetary policies].

Also, a 12-page secret document of the Foreign Economic Administration about the future of Germany. . . . This material would be of major interest to our leading government organizations, representatives in the European Consultative Commission.

[We recognize the] considerable overload for station operatives because of agent work.[41]

Fitin then asked Merkulov's consent to transfer a Soviet operative, code-named "Julia," from Los Angeles to the New York station to assist in expediting document processing and transfer.

The Silvermasters' troubled marital relations also disrupted the group's cohesion, although, at first, without noticeable impact on its remarkable delivery of top secret U.S. government data. Akhmerov informed Moscow that Helen Silvermaster and William Ludwig Ullman (who lived in the couple's apartment) had become lovers, apparently with her husband's consent, a ménage à trois known to other members of the group. "Surely these unhealthy relations between them cannot help but influence their behavior and work with us negatively," Akhmerov complained to his superiors. He suggested (correctly) that Silvermaster's leadership of the group had been jeopardized.[42] Nevertheless, Akhmerov assured Silvermaster, while confronting the pressures of security investigations, that if fired he would receive a monthly stipend from Moscow.[43] At one point in 1944, the NKGB even offered to put a $6,000 down payment on a farm the Silvermasters were thinking of purchasing as a base of operation in the event he became unemployed.[*44]

Adding to the station's troubles at this time was a confirmed report during the summer of 1944 that the FBI had installed wiretaps in every

---

* In the end, after several cables from Akhmerov detailing Silvermaster's request for such a loan, Moscow agreed to provide half the amount: "[Akhmerov] has handed three thousand dollars to [Silvermaster], who was very satisfied as a

Soviet organization in the United States, through which they had learned the code names of a number of NKGB sources. Moscow ordered an immediate and massive change in code names, generating great confusion in its American networks. Thus, "Mer" (Akhmerov) became "Albert"; his wife "Nelly" (Helen Lowry) "Elsa"; "Pal" (Silvermaster) "Robert"; "Polo" (Ullman) "Pilot"; and "Lawyer" (Harry Dexter White) "Richard," later changed to "Reed." [*][45]

On balance, however, Moscow was extremely pleased with the work done by Akhmerov and others at the New York station in gaining such valuable materials from the Silvermaster network and praised them for having begun to professionalize Golos's "clumsy and disorganized" group of American agents. Compartmentalization, however, remained a problem for Akhmerov. Silvermaster continued to resist strenuously any attempt to reduce his influence over his sources, including his wife's lover. [†][46]

Nonetheless, Akhmerov's labors earned him a Red Banner decoration in 1944, while his wife, Helen, received the lesser Red Star honor. Silvermaster, too, was decorated. However, his award, in keeping with custom, was shown to him by Akhmerov but returned to the station lest it be discovered. [47] The medals were well earned from Moscow's perspective. Pavel Fitin reported to Vsevolod Merkulov in August 1944 that, since the beginning of the year, Silvermaster's group had placed in NKGB hands 386 important U.S. government documents on a wide range of issues. [48]

Throughout this period, despite the enormous value of the information delivered by his sources, Silvermaster's behavior continued to pose difficulties and even dangers for Soviet intelligence. Akhmerov characterized him "as a man wholly devoted to us but exceptionally self-

---

result." New York station to Moscow, December 20, 1944, No. 1798, VENONA files.

[*] To compound the confusion, during the mid-1930s, Alger Hiss, who reported, while a Ware Group member, to Joszef Peter's Comintern network and then to the GRU, was also assigned the code name "Lawyer" for a time. See Chapters 1 and 2.

[†] "It is possible that [Silvermaster] thought we wanted to take away some of his people counting on getting better results and concluded from this that we were not altogether satisfied with his achievements. . . . [Silvermaster] reacted very unfavorably saying that before [Akhmerov's] time somebody else tried to part him and [Ullman]. . . ." New York station to Moscow, January 4, 1945, Nos. 12–15, VENONA files, a long cable devoted to the difficulties within Silvermaster's group.

willed, stubborn, confident of his superiority over all others and behaving with respect to other [agents] as a dictator or 'fuhrer.' " He provided his superiors with documentation of this character sketch, including a dubious story, told to him by Silvermaster, about a meeting with the confidential secretary to Treasury Secretary Henry Morgenthau (whom the NKGB dubbed "Nabob," and the secretary "Mora"). This woman, according to Silvermaster, had had an earlier affair with Morgenthau that produced a then-teenaged daughter. Impressed by Silvermaster's ideas and background, "Mora" urged the Secretary to offer him a counselor's post in the Department. Although he claimed that Morgenthau proceeded to do so, when Silvermaster urged Harry Dexter White to support his candidacy, White objected and pointed out that the obligatory FBI investigation would threaten his own future and that of Henry Morgenthau. A shouting match ensued, with Silvermaster complaining that White objected only because of personal jealousy. The new position never materialized.[49]

Deeply troubled by this irascible independent streak, Akhmerov's supervisor, New York station chief Vladimir Pravdin, complained that he remained too passive when Silvermaster, the group's nominal head "over organizational and operational matters[,] presented him with a fait accompli." Akhmerov responded bluntly to Pravdin's demand that he discipline Silvermaster more effectively: "The main thing is the results. For twenty-five years, we couldn't get information about the politics of this country. Now [Silvermaster] is carrying out enormous work and giving our government a complete picture of [American] politics on all questions." Pravdin's reaction was conciliatory: "Without belittling [Silvermaster's] work, we tried to prove . . . that this work could be much more valuable if it is organized properly."[50]

In this exchange, an older tradition of Soviet espionage involving ideologically committed local Communist agents collided directly with the increasingly professionalized imperatives of the USSR's wartime intelligence service. Itzhak Akhmerov, like Jacob Golos and Gaik Ovakimyan before him, demanded concrete results in the form of vital secret government information from his often sensitive and troubled sources. To achieve this goal, Akhmerov did not object even to assuming a deferential, subordinate role when dealing with arrogant sources such as Silvermaster. During the 1940s, however, the new NKGB sought both greater respect for professional tradecraft (*konspiratsia*) from its operatives and their sources as well as subordination of often-individualistic agents such as Silvermaster to Moscow's discipline.

The Akhmerov-Silvermaster relationship suffered also from the fact that the latter did not know that his contact was a Soviet intelligence officer. He believed that Akhmerov, who spoke fluent English, was a U.S. citizen and a Communist businessman code-named "Bill" who, like himself, cooperated voluntarily with the NKGB—in short, an equal and not a superior. In the spring of 1945, Akhmerov even refused a suggestion from Pravdin, who worked under a cover identity as the Soviet Information Bureau head, that he reveal his true identity to Silvermaster.[51]

By this time, Silvermaster's obnoxious personal style had thoroughly alienated Harry Dexter White and David Silverman, both of whom declined to supply him with further information. Because of "his hot temper [and] sharpness," Pravdin cabled Moscow, only William Ludwig Ullman and a pair of new married recruits—Bella Gold ("Acorn") in Commerce and Sonya Gold ("Zhenya") at Treasury—continued to supply data to Silvermaster. Contributing to the latter's difficulties throughout the 1944–45 period was a chronic and intensifying asthmatic condition.[*][52]

Whatever the reasons, from Moscow's perspective the disarray of the Silvermaster Group could not have occurred at a worse time. A new and potentially more hostile American President, Harry S Truman, had entered the White House after the mid-April 1945 death of Franklin Roosevelt. The need for accurate intelligence on Truman's perspectives and those of his closest advisers regarding a postwar settlement became the Soviet leadership's most urgent preoccupation, as Moscow wrote to Pravdin on June 1:

Currently, studying Truman's surroundings has exceptional importance. This is one of the main tasks of the station. Determine the relations between Morgenthau and Truman, whether he influences Truman, etc. Also, try to use [Harry Dexter White] to cultivate (through his connections) leaders of the State Department and other government institutions. . . . Charge [Silvermaster], besides leading the group, with explaining [former Vice

* Beginning in the fall of 1944, a number of cables to Moscow from Soviet operatives in the United States such as Akhmerov dealt with the internal strife within the Silvermaster Group, for the most part inconclusively. See, for example, New York station to Moscow, August 31, 1944, No. 1243; October 1, 1944, Nos. 1388–89; and January 4, 1945, Nos. 12–15; VENONA files. See also Moscow to New York station, March 20, 1945, No. 253, VENONA files.

President Henry] Wallace and his relations with Truman. . . . Besides studying political, social, and military figures of interest to us, you must direct the [agents] to study Truman himself, his intentions, politics, etc . . . [based] on conversations with high-ranking officials, etc.*[53]

After Truman replaced Roosevelt, the attitude toward the Soviet Union emanating from the White House and major federal government departments quickly became distinctly less friendly. Lauchlin Currie was forced to leave his post as presidential adviser and Harry Dexter White, under threat of imminent dismissal, prepared to shift from Treasury to a job at the World Bank.[54] Silvermaster tried to talk White, with whom he had apparently patched up relations, into remaining at Treasury.[55] By the fall of 1945, however, it was clear that Truman's new Secretary of the Treasury, Fred Vinson, did not share Morgenthau's confidence in White's abilities: "Although [Vinson] outwardly treats him in a friendly manner," Pravdin wrote Moscow on October 29, "[White] is convinced that the question of his dismissal is a matter of weeks or months. [Vinson] . . . never consults him, etc." White had concluded, correctly, that he had no alternatives left for employment in the Truman Administration and that maintaining his credibility required prompt departure for one of the recently created international financial institutions such as the World Bank.†[56]

---

* Several key members of Silvermaster's group apparently served as sources of inside information on U.S. policy at the founding conference of the United Nations in San Francisco that April: "Tell [Akhmerov] to make arrangements with [Silvermaster] about maintaining contact with [White] and [Ullman] in [San Francisco]." New York station to Moscow, April 6, 1945, No. 328, VENONA files. White proved a voluble informant for the Soviets at San Francisco. One May 4 cable transmitted "the contents of a prolonged conversation" with him while a May 13 dispatch described in detail White's account of the Conference's issues, procedures, and cloakroom conversations. San Francisco station to Moscow, May 4, 1945, No. 230, and May 13, 1945, No. 259, VENONA files.

† Even while Roosevelt was President, White was extremely nervous about his personal contacts with Soviet operatives. At a July 31, 1944, meeting with a Moscow operative named Koltsov, White declared himself "ready for any self-sacrifice; he himself does not think about his personal security, but a compromise would lead to a political scandal . . . and [the discredit] of all supporters of the new course. Therefore he would have to be very cautious." Although White agreed to meet again in mid-August, he "proposes infrequent conversations lasting up to half an hour while driving in his automobile" rather than meeting at his apartment. New York station to Moscow, August 4–5, 1944, Nos. 1119–21, VENONA files.

At this moment of declining prospects for Nathan Gregory Silvermaster's previously productive group, Pravdin finally succeeded in achieving Moscow's technical goal of compartmentalizing the various sources. Akhmerov arranged a meeting for his station chief with Silvermaster on September 2 that lasted for nine hours. Later, Pravdin described for Moscow the American's "antagonism to all our measures" as a reflection of "petty-bourgeois proprietary ideology that, together with purely American anarchism, is one of the most typical features of a very large number of local compatriots."[57]

Pravdin traced Silvermaster's often-hysterical arguments with members of his group to the emotional impact of his worsening asthmatic condition. (Akhmerov reported that Silvermaster had been subject to fainting spells. He had even stopped breathing on one occasion, and these near-death moments apparently generated his dramatic mood swings in dealing with members of the network.) Silvermaster, in turn, pleased to be meeting finally a bona fide Soviet operative such as Pravdin (Akhmerov had still not revealed his identity), complained that except for Ullman, who still shared bed and board with the Silvermasters, "nobody among the other [agents] wanted to work." Frank Coe failed to carry out promised assignments to acquire information and was now "hiding from him." David Silverman "without consulting him" had taken a better-paying post in the private sector. Even Harry White "doesn't pass information or documents," believing that his major role for the Soviet Union now was "to give advice on major political and economic matters."[58] By then, Pravdin had begun meeting Harry Dexter White directly, keeping this fact from Silvermaster, who would have objected vehemently.[59]

Confronted with total disarray, Pravdin tried to salvage at least one of Silvermaster's previous contacts, instructing Akhmerov to organize a meeting (which took place on October 1) with David Silverman, who complained that neither he nor his colleagues in the group understood why Silvermaster had been chosen as their leader: "they had been working for us much longer than [he had]." A "group," as such, did not really exist any longer, Silverman pointed out, and he demanded that Pravdin organize a new and more effective network, with a different leader, before he would resume work. Such participatory management of a Soviet espionage cohort was hardly what Pravdin had sought from the meeting.[60]

The station chief's immediate response to the collapse of Silvermaster's network in the more hostile climate of Truman's Washington was petty but understandable. He complained to Moscow about his colleague Akhmerov, urging that he be sent "back home to work in the central apparatus" because of his supposed failure to display "a proper understanding of our work."[61] The request was granted. In December 1945, Itzhak and Helen Akhmerov returned to the Soviet Union, leaving behind a greater record of achievement than that of other Soviet operatives in the United States. Although he failed to persuade Laurence Duggan and Michael Straight to resume agents' roles, Akhmerov nurtured the volatile Nathan Gregory Silvermaster and his comparably temperamental band of sources while they delivered a remarkably rich harvest of wartime documents and information to Moscow.

Shortly before Akhmerov's return to Russia, he told Silvermaster that Elizabeth Bentley had defected, another reason for the Russian's hasty departure. Although Bentley knew and might expose her former associate, Silvermaster responded calmly: "He said all this was very sad and serious, but he was not scared or excited at all." He refused to believe that Bentley would cooperate with the FBI and name co-conspirators, given her own prominent role. Nevertheless, preparing for the worst, Silvermaster and Akhmerov discussed what his responses would be to counterintelligence agents who might question him about his covert activities: "Naturally [he] will deny completely any allegations about his connection and cooperation with us," Akhmerov reported. Still, Silvermaster expected to lose his current government position once a probe began and speculated about moving to the Soviet Union or some other country to continue his work.

Akhmerov, in turn, told the American that he might not be meeting with him again and arranged contact procedures for a future operative's meeting. Because of Bentley's defection, the two men agreed for the present "to stop our work totally."[62] When Soviet agents next located Silvermaster in July 1947, he was living in New Jersey with a Russian friend.[63] By then, both FBI and congressional probes had begun based on Bentley's identification of Silvermaster as a Soviet agent. Periodic attempts by Soviet operatives in New York and Washington to monitor Silvermaster's activities in the years that followed—his career as an espionage agent having concluded in 1945—produced one NKGB report that he and his faithful housemate, William Ludwig Ullman, had become by 1951 prosperous home builders on the New Jersey shore.[64]

As for Akhmerov, during the late 1940s and early 1950s, he finally achieved (at least publicly) his earlier dream. While working as a KGB "illegal" in Switzerland, he chose a cover identity as a successful American businessman! Later, the Akhmerovs returned to Moscow. There, Helen taught English to young Soviet "illegal" operatives while Itzhak instructed them in tradecraft's most difficult lesson: leading a humane life amid the unpredictable hurly-burly of secret work, sometimes in a thoroughly individualistic society such as the United States.[65]

CHAPTER 9

❖

Atomic Espionage: From Fuchs to the Rosenbergs

O N NOVEMBER 24, 1941, the NKVD's New York station chief Pavel Pastelnyak (code-named "Luka") cabled Moscow that three American scientists—one the well-known physicist Harold Urey—had left for London to work on "an explosive of enormous force." According to information collected by the station, the scientists were studying the possible harnessing of an explosive force that would allow a bomb dropped from a plane to spread its impact over more than two hundred miles.[1] Moscow instructed its London station to verify this report through a source in British intelligence, John Cairncross ("List"), and speculated that the New York cable referred to Uranium-235.[2] The London station chief, Anatoly Gorsky ("Vadim"), reported that Pastelnyak was wrong. Urey and his colleagues had already left England and returned to America. He could discover nothing about the purpose of their visit.[3]

In this muddled and unsatisfactory manner, Soviet intelligence began what would become its obsessive pursuit of information about "Enormoz," the apposite code name it assigned to nuclear research and production in the United States, England, and Canada.

THE XY LINE

In 1941 and 1942, at a time when German armies approached the gates of Moscow and other major cities in the USSR, atomic research was only one of several Western defense industries of interest to Soviet agents. In early April 1941, NKVD leadership divided its operatives into separate "political" and "scientific-technical" fields rather than mixing assignments, and one of the new breed of Soviet "scientific-technical" agents was Semyon Semyonov ("Twen").[4] He had come to America in January 1938 for advanced studies at MIT, where, two years later, he received a graduate degree. "I did not regard studying [there] as a goal per se," Semyonov wrote in a November 1944 report to Moscow, "but as a way of preparing for intelligence work, learning the country [and] the language and increasing [my] general technical knowledge."[5]

Semyonov would prove one of Moscow's most effective operatives during the war years. "Short, with a duck nose and big eyes which, while he was talking to somebody, [revolved] like parabolic antennas," Alexander Feklissov ("Kalistrat") later wrote, "he was quick [at] getting along with people . . . and could easily be taken for a middle-level American businessman."[6]

More experienced operatives at the NKVD's New York station such as Gaik Ovakimyan privately complained about the unruly manners displayed by Semyonov and others in a small group of Soviet student-spies shifted during the late 1930s and early 1940s to scientific and technical assignments, known as "XY line" work (three others, code-named "Lavr," "Kurt," and "Glan," are mentioned in the Moscow records). "Unfortunately," Ovakimyan wrote in one letter to a Moscow colleague who evidently had been involved in training the new agents, "I have to report that you spoiled the guys and didn't orient them correctly on some matters. Most of them don't like working properly (I mean, for the moment, studying), [and] their academic preparation turned out rather weak. Besides, there is no Bolshevik modesty. . . . Surely, these people are unripe and conceited."[7]

Similar complaints about scientific arrogance, conceit, and unwillingness to submit to discipline were reported during this same period by General Leslie Groves about the *American* scientists transported from university careers to work on the U.S. wartime atomic energy program.

Soviet scientific and technical espionage in the United States halted briefly on May 5, 1941, when Gaik Ovakimyan was arrested. By mid-

June, however, Soviet agents had reestablished their American contacts and resumed acquiring material.[8] One August memo reported restoring contact with an entrepreneur-chemist ("Talent") who offered to work with the station to establish companies that could patent products and inventions of use to the USSR.[9] In the end, Moscow declined the offer.

One of "Talent's" subsources, "Tal-1," however, had already opened such a firm. Concerned about security, Moscow cautioned its New York station in June 1942:

> In the report of a stranger—Julius Rosenberg—about the firm of "Tal-1," received through [Jacob Golos], it is said that "Tal-1" introduced "Talent" as one of the backers who had contact with Mikhael Kaganovich [then the Soviet's People's Commissar for the aviation industry]. Thus, with creation of his very first firm, "Talent" became known as an agent of the Soviet Union to people who were not connected with us.[10]

Golos had evidently reported a warning by his source, Julius Rosenberg, at that time still "a stranger" to the NKGB in Moscow. Rosenberg's secret work on behalf of the USSR was then coordinated by Golos, but he would not remain "a stranger" in the years that followed.

The German invasion of the Soviet Union in June 1941 had led to accelerated efforts by "XY line" agents and sources to supply Moscow with information on advanced nonatomic American defense production. Thus, on November 5, 1941, the station forwarded to Moscow plans "about [an] anti-tank weapon which is called here a 'Molotov cocktail,' " provided to Jacob Golos by the same Communist physician (Dr. Emil Connison) who had been told of Harold Urey's secret visit to London.[11] Semyonov received from a chemist-bacteriologist ("Cherny" or "Black") secret data on penicillin, then in an experimental stage.[12] One valuable source in the aviation industry, Jones Orin York ("Needle"), who had cooperated with the NKVD in California and New York in the 1930s,* reappeared in New England to provide highly valuable material until his courier was identified by American counterintelligence agents and broke off contact.[13]

The New York station noted this increased surveillance in a revealing late-July 1942 memorandum to Moscow:

> Since the beginning of the war in Europe, but especially after December 7, 1941, when America actively entered the world war,

---

* See Chapter 2 for a discussion of York's covert work during the 1930s.

conditions of work on the "XY line" have changed radically in comparison with prewar times. This change is shown mainly in the following factors:

1. As always in wartime, patriotic feelings have grown . . . greatly. We have to take this factor into account not only while cultivating new candidates . . . but also in working with older agents.

2. One highly important factor is the considerable increase in counterintelligence and police activity. This involves increased vigilance of average Americans as a result of propaganda by the press, cinema, and radio against the activities of foreign agents. . . . Workers and employees . . . in defense enterprises are being screened meticulously by the FBI and counterintelligence organizations.

3. Possibilities for traveling around the country are considerably more complicated. Surveillance has increased so much that travel to such cities [with military installations] as San Diego, Los Angeles, Norfolk, etc. without an official reason is totally excluded . . . [and] all passengers are screened thoroughly.[14]

Another problem for Soviet intelligence in America during the war years was a perpetual shortage of ready cash. Even during the thirties, a number of "XY line" sources in defense industries, unlike Washington's ideologically committed agents, worked on a strictly "cash-and-carry" basis. The situation did not change during the war. When Moscow instructed Semyonov to see if a chemist ("Solidny" or "Solid"), who had received $350 monthly in the late 1930s and now had joined U.S. government service, would help the USSR without pay, the chemist's answer came back "no"—as Semyonov reported to Moscow in a February 1943 letter.[15] After resuming cash payments to "Solid," however, Semyonov received valuable data concerning Japanese chemical plants and chemical production in Germany and in German-occupied countries, all duly recorded in the NKGB files.[16]

But even the "XY line" had its doctrinaire Communists, as Semyonov discovered when he tried to offer another source, Alfred Slack ("Al"), a $150 bonus for a particularly useful bit of work. Slack declined, suggesting instead that the funds be sent to the USSR to help finance the highly publicized "Joseph Stalin tank column." Semyonov followed the suggestion and asked that Moscow provide a receipt for Slack's records![17]

Slack was one of a group of sources within the Eastman Kodak Company, where he procured important data on the chemical composition and production details of photo and movie film. Slack had been associated with Soviet intelligence since 1938 and was regarded as a valuable agent,[18] run directly by station chief Gaik Ovakimyan ("Guennady"), whom Slack knew as "George."[19] In August 1941, after Ovakimyan's arrest, Slack was assigned a new controller—a fellow-chemist and fellow-American named Harry Gold.

ENTER HARRY GOLD
AND JULIUS ROSENBERG

Harry Gold began his long career in Soviet intelligence, like so many other American Communist sympathizers, in the mid-1930s. Initially, he provided economic information from his manufacturing company to an agent ("Black") in New York. "Black" described Gold's background in an August 1935 report, calling him "absolutely trustworthy."[20] In an account of his life written later for the NKVD, Gold wrote: "I was born on December 18, 1910, in Bern, Switzerland. My mother moved to Switzerland from France, where she had to move from Russia because of her revolutionary activities there. My father fled from Russia in 1903 to escape being drafted into military service."[21] Gold's family came to the United States when he was an infant. His profile was typical of many Soviet intelligence recruits in the United States during the 1930s, from Russian or Eastern European immigrant parents and boasting a radical family tradition.

Gold's initial assignment—he had earned a degree in chemistry and was working at a sugar by-product processing plant in Pennsylvania—barely foreshadowed his later importance to the Soviets: He filched a dry-ice process that prevented ice cream from melting![22] Because of Gold's dedication and technical skill, which increased after the Soviets paid for his graduate studies, he was given more important assignments as a courier.[23]

Throughout Gold's early years as a Soviet courier, he dealt with sources at various sensitive locations.[24] Acting as Alfred Slack's contact beginning in 1941 was an important task for Gold, since Slack not only provided his own data but served as a "talent-spotter" for other sources.[25] Gold was also assigned another contact, a chemical engineer named Abraham Brothman ("Constructor").[26] By the spring of 1942, Harry Gold had become someone Moscow considered a "very valuable worker" for Soviet intelligence, running his own small agent group.[27]

Gold had become too busy and too useful as a courier to hold down his day job as a chemist. In the summer of 1942, the station began paying him $100 monthly to supplement his income. Semyon Semyonov now met with Gold once or twice weekly to coordinate his tasks as a courier for Slack, Brothman, and other sources.[28] In June 1943, Gold was assigned the additional job of running an operation code-named "Sulpho," aimed at acquiring materials on biological warfare.[29] Moscow noted its interest in the operation in a memo to the New York station on July 1, 1943: "At this decisive stage of the war, acquiring information about the preparations and intentions of the enemy (the Axis countries and its vassals), as well as details about the achievements of the Country [the United States] and the Island [Great Britain] in both their means of defense and possible means of assault, should receive special importance."[30]

The number of scientific and technical agents controlled by Semyon Semyonov and his colleagues had increased dramatically by 1943. In a report to Moscow on May Day that year, New York's station reported managing twenty-eight agents on the "XY line," twenty-one controlled directly by Semyonov. Eleven sources dealt with various problems of chemistry and bacteriology, six with radio equipment, and five with aviation issues, including one code-named "Gnome" who focused on jet-propelled aircraft research.[31]

Several sources were provided by an American Communist Party cell supervised by Jacob Golos in 1941 through a party functionary, Bernard Schuster ("Echo").[32] Golos informed his sources that they were supplying information for CPUSA leaders, a comforting fiction for the more nervous among them. In fact, without identifying his agents by name, Golos delivered their material directly to Soviet NKVD operatives. But Moscow's files show that the leader of this party cell—a radio engineer ("Antenna") who collected both information and party dues from four colleagues, Communists and engineers like himself—understood that the materials were going to the Soviet Union. "Antenna" (a code name later changed to "Liberal") was Julius Rosenberg.[33]

Because Golos had virtually no scientific or technical knowledge, though he was controlling dozens of sources providing information in these fields, it was difficult for him to supervise Rosenberg's group. Therefore, even before Jacob Golos's death in 1943, station chief Vassily Zarubin reassigned Julius Rosenberg and his colleagues to Semyon

Semyonov's control.[34] Semyonov described the process in a November 1944 report:

> In 1942, I learned that [Golos] was working with a group of local compatriots in the field of technical intelligence. From the [Moscow] Center's letters, one could conclude that nothing was known about the group and that it was providing desultory materials rated low in importance. Having fragmentary data about this group, nevertheless, I determined that it had great potential possibilities in the field of radio-engineering and aviation. Therefore, I brought the station chief's [Zarubin's] attention to the matter of giving me [Rosenberg] with his group, which was done despite a certain resistance on [Golos's] part. In the person of [Julius Rosenberg], I found a young party member willing to render technical help to our country using channels of the fraternal organization [CPUSA]. He was absolutely unripe in matters of working as an agent, our demands regarding the type of materials we acquire, and elementary rules of *konspiratsia*. His group worked on the principles of a Communist party group, and [Rosenberg] ran it as a party organizer.[35]

Semyonov was pleased with his training of Rosenberg and his colleagues, and the New York NKGB station reported to Moscow in fall 1942 that "the group has begun working in a more organized and purposeful way and has given us a number of valuable materials. [Rosenberg] is content with [his] transfer to direct connection with us."[36]

In 1942, Semyonov focused Julius Rosenberg and his colleagues on "XY line" interests in radio engineering and aviation. At about the same time—March 27, 1942—however, Moscow sent to the New York station possibly its first atomic-related assignment: "Currently, they are working extremely hard in England, Germany, and the U.S. on the problem of extracting Uranium-235 and its use as an explosive to produce bombs of enormous destructive force. Therefore, the problem seems close to practical solution. We need to take up this problem with all seriousness."[37]

Soviet operatives in the United States had begun to collect information on scientists at Columbia University, MIT, and other research centers already at work on atomic energy. Several early attempts to recruit scientists involved in this research had led nowhere, as Soviet agents desperately sought ways to tap into the complex research program then underway in the United States, Canada, and the United Kingdom designed to produce an atomic bomb.

THE "RADIO-ACTIVE"
BOMB: EARLY WARNINGS

A chance meeting in March 1942 between an agent of the NKGB's New York station, Franklin Zelman ("Chap"), and a Communist acquaintance, Columbia University chemistry professor Clarence Hiskey, produced tantalizing gossip about the atomic research project. Zelman visited the academic seeking a recommendation for postdoctoral research, and after a brief talk, Hiskey accompanied Zelman to the subway.[38] As they walked, Hiskey described a hypothetical situation, which the Soviet agent immediately reported to his superiors: " 'Imagine [Hiskey began] a bomb dropped in the center of this city which would destroy the entire city.' I scoffed at that ... [which] seemed to make him angry, with the result that he said more than he intended to say. 'There is such a bomb,' he stated very emphatically. 'I'm working on it.' "

But Zelman was skeptical and asked "if it was a 'death ray' or gas," to which Hiskey replied that "it was a radio-active bomb":

Talking very rapidly now, he told me plenty:
The essential points are as follows.

1. That the Germans were far ahead on this bomb.
2. That his [researchers], together with a number of leading chemists and physicists, were working with desperate haste.
3. The radio-active bomb had not been perfected in their laboratory, but considerable progress has been made.
4. The Germans may be advanced sufficiently to be ready to use it.[39]

In fact, however, much of Hiskey's "inside" information was inaccurate: The Germans were not close to being "ready to use" any superbomb, nor were his American colleagues making "considerable progress" at this early stage.

Hiskey also confided to Zelman that "scientists in the Columbia research lab have advanced far enough to be planning to try it out in some vast desert area ... , [and] a great fear exists among those who know of the bomb that it might truly destroy millions of people at a crack." By then, Hiskey expressed his regret at having "told me about this and swore me to silence. I said that I hoped the Soviets knew about this. He said he hoped so, too."[40]

Vassily Zarubin cabled the report to Moscow, expressing his intention to try and recruit Hiskey through his association with Zelman.[41] Moscow responded on April 15, 1942, presumably after consulting with Soviet scientific experts on atomic energy, such as the NKGB's Leonid Kvasnikov, with a detailed outline of its research needs:

The report . . . from Hiskey on the matter of major American work on Uranium-235 is correct, though strongly exaggerated regarding achievements. They work intensively on the matter in England, Germany, and the U.S.

The problem of using uranium energy for military purposes is of great interest for us. We need the following data on the matter:

1. Isolation of the main source of uranium energy—Uranium-235 from uranium. Achievements of the Americans on this matter. Laboratory and factory methods of isolation. Industrial equipment for the isolation process.
2. At what stage of development is current research on the use of uranium energy in bombs?
3. By whom and where is work carried out on elaborating the uranium bomb's shell?
4. The way to produce the uranium bomb's explosion—i.e., fusion.
5. Methods and protective measures from uranium radioactivity in the process of production.
6. What is known about the Germans' work on the uranium bomb, and what are their advantages in comparison with American work, as Hiskey says?
7. What is known about [the] factory production of laboratory work on the uranium bomb?[42]

Like other atomic scientists at the time, Leonid Kvasnikov had become interested in the 1930s in the theoretical prospects for creating an atomic weapon. By autumn 1940, Moscow had instructed several stations abroad—though not in the United States—to identify local scientific centers working on the military use of nuclear energy and to acquire information about them. Another Soviet agent, Vladimir Barkovsky, assigned to acquire atomic secrets in Great Britain during the early 1940s, recently told Alexander Vassiliev that the first reliable information about work in this field was received by the NKVD's London station in autumn 1941. At that time, Soviet operatives acquired information on a meeting of the British Uranium Committee and a subsequent session of the Joint Chiefs of Staff Committee where nuclear issues were discussed.

In March 1942, Lavrenty Beria agreed to present Stalin with a proposal from the NKGB's scientific and technical officials to create a special scientific advisory body at the State Defense Committee to coordinate work on atomic energy in the USSR. This led to the Kremlin's decision two months later to establish a special wing ("Laboratory #2") of the Academy of Sciences as the central body to work on developing an atomic weapon, which began under Igor Kurchatov's direction in the spring of 1943.

Meanwhile, information on research in the West trickled in slowly from various sources, including Clarence Hiskey, who continued to meet with Zelman socially. Hiskey proposed that Zelman apply for a job on his research project before realizing that the obligatory FBI background check would expose Zelman's Communist background and spill over into a possible inquiry into Hiskey's own radical associations. Even if Zelman managed to obtain a position involving atomic research, Hiskey told him, he "would not see the results. Only the leading personnel get to see the results."[43]

NKGB officials in Moscow became increasingly concerned with their lack of knowledge regarding the American atomic research program. "We attach great importance to the problem of Uranium-235 (we call it 'ENORMOZ')," began one November 26, 1942, cable. "[Although we are] having some rather good opportunities to cultivate agents working on the problem in the U.S., we haven't yet begun such cultivation." At the same time, however, some sources had been indiscreet. The unidentified agent-scientist code-named "Talent," for example, who reported on efforts to meet "with a number of people working on the problem of 'Enormoz,' " had apparently been especially brazen in his inquiries of Harold Urey and other American scientists. Therefore, the NKGB instructed its American operatives and (in a November 28 cable to London) its British agents, then led by Anatoly Gorsky, to redouble their efforts to acquire atomic research information but, at the same time, to avoid exposure through dangerous initiatives.[44]

AN ENGLISHMAN NAMED "ERIC"

The most useful Soviet source on "Enormoz" in 1943 was in England, not the United States. A young Communist physicist code-named "Eric" provided Vladimir Barkovsky with detailed reports on research dealing with the military use of nuclear energy. "Eric" also had access to American data that reached England as a result of scientific cooperation between the two countries. "In the field of their work," "Eric" informed the Soviet operative, "the Americans are far ahead . . . and the information ["Eric"] passes to us reflects American achievements in this field along with English ones."[45]

Moscow was furious at the New York station's inability to provide similarly knowledgeable sources. A July 1, 1943, cable complained that, at a time when over five hundred people were already involved in "Enormoz" with many millions being spent on the project and with "research grandiose in scale and depth being carried out near to you, the prolonged pace of agent cultivation in the U.S. is particularly intolerable."[46]

The NKGB had learned that much of the British research staff and equipment by then had been transferred to Canada, making it even more urgent to obtain reliable inside sources since "contact in work between the English and the Americans will be even closer." Later that month, on July 27, Vassily Zarubin received from Moscow a list of the major research groups the NKGB wished to penetrate, names compiled mainly on the basis of information received from "Eric" in England:

1. A group of Professor A. [Arthur] Compton's, who headed the project in the Research Committee of National Defense . . . ;
2. the Columbia group, first of all, Professors Dunning and Urey;
3. the Chicago group;
4. the California group;
5. the Kellogg firm.[47]

Zelman's efforts to recruit Clarence Hiskey (now code-named "Ramzai")[48] also persisted. In October 1943, Zarubin cabled Moscow about Hiskey's latest information: "Recently to direct [work] on the problem of 'Enormoz,' a committee was set up consisting of five directors: a mechanic, a physicist, a chemist ('Ramzai'), and a biologist, headed by the president of MIT with its Center at the University of Chicago, where works and equipment are being moved from Columbia University. . . . 'Ramzai' is leaving for Chicago, where he [was] granted the right to select workers." Unfortunately, Zarubin continued, strenuous counterintelligence efforts were directed toward preventing both German and Soviet agents from penetrating the research site.[49]

NKGB Intelligence Service Director Pavel Fitin complained in an August 11, 1943, memorandum to his superior, the USSR's head of state security, Vsevolod Merkulov, about the existing duplication of effort between his agency and Soviet military intelligence (the GRU). Both tried to recruit agents linked to the atomic energy program in America and England. Fitin called "the state of agent cultivation on this problem and its prospects . . . unsatisfactory, especially in the U.S."[50] (Three months later, all "Enormoz" agents within the GRU were transferred to NKGB supervision to help coordinate information on the project more effectively.)

Elaborate plans were developed by various Soviet operatives and station chiefs—Grigory Heifetz in San Francisco, Zarubin, Semyonov, and others—to recruit at least one leading American scientist involved in the program: Hiskey, Enrico Fermi, J. Robert Oppenheimer, and others were mentioned as prospects. Extensive preparations—also unrealized—were made to study "the progress of construction of an 'Enormoz' plant in the vicinity of Knoxville, Tennessee [the Oak Ridge facility], and to acquire data on the technological process . . . in 'Camp Y' in the Santa Fe, New Mexico, area [Los Alamos]."[51] But material concerning research at these facilities, at the University of Chicago, and elsewhere continued to reach Moscow most dependably in 1943 and into 1944 from Barkovsky's British source, "Eric," who recycled information he culled from documents provided by U.S. researchers.[52]

THE ELUSIVE OPPENHEIMER

The hunt for a major cooperative American scientist willing to share with Soviet intelligence secrets of the atomic bomb project continued throughout the war, and "Enormoz's" scientific coordinator, J. Robert Oppenheimer, became a primary if elusive target of the pursuit through various Communist friends and associates. Oppenheimer had been involved in a range of radical causes prior to the Second World War, and NKGB memoranda in 1942 and 1943 urged that he be "cultivated" by American operatives since its military intelligence "neighbors" were rumored to have already made contact with him.[53]

In the end, the rumors proved unfounded. Even after the NKGB, under Pavel Fitin, won the bureaucratic turf battle to consolidate under its auspices all Western agents engaged in atomic research, the effort to recruit Oppenheimer proved difficult, if for no other reason than the security cordon that surrounded him.

A report sent to Vselovod Merkulov in Moscow in February 1944 about Oppenheimer (who was assigned the code name "Chester") documented both the NKGB's hopes and frustration concerning the physicist:

"Chester"—Oppenheimer, Robert, born in 1906, American Jew, *secret member of the compatriot organization [the American Communist Party]*,* professor at the University of California, works on "Enormoz" in the field of rapid neutrons, directed the construction of the California cyclotron. In connection with the special significance and importance of his work, [he] is allegedly under special guard in consequence of which the compatriot section [the Communist cell to which Oppenheimer had belonged prior to beginning his work on the project] received from its center an instruction to cease relations with "Chester" to avoid compromising him.

[Oppenheimer] represents a very large interest for us. *His membership in the compatriot organization** and friendly attitude toward our country provide grounds for counting on a positive result of his cultivation.

According to data we have, [Oppenheimer] has been cultivated by the "neighbors" [GRU] since June 1942. In case [Oppenheimer] is recruited by them, it is necessary to have him passed to us. If the recruitment is not realized, we must get from the "neighbors" all materials on [Oppenheimer] and begin his active cultivation through channels we have . . . [including Oppenheimer's] brother, "Ray" [Frank Oppenheimer], also a professor at the University of California and a member of the compatriot organization but politically closer to us than [Robert Oppenheimer].[54]

The assertion in the memo to Merkulov and in other NKGB documents that Robert Oppenheimer was a "secret member" of the American Communist Party cannot be independently corroborated. If true, it would explain the high hopes Soviet intelligence had throughout the war and thereafter for his eventual recruitment. The fact that station chief Grigory Heifetz was recalled to Moscow in 1944 because of his failure to bring any of "Enormoz's" scientists into the fold suggests, however, that Oppenheimer never agreed to become a source of information for the Soviets, as some recent writers have asserted.[55]

In 1945, an NKGB informant on Senator Harley Kilgore's staff, Charles Kramer ("Mole"), met with Oppenheimer several times in Washington, also without evident result. In Kramer's report to Washington station chief Anatoly Gorsky (conveyed to Moscow on October

* Italics added.

19, 1945), on his discussions with Kilgore, Oppenheimer emerges as a visionary seeking international agreement on atomic energy matters, and not as a potential agent. Atomic secrets should be "disclosed," he told Kilgore and Kramer, "only when there is political cooperation among the countries." Naturally, he hoped that the United States would pursue such cooperation for atomic energy's peaceful uses, but Kramer's report described the scientist as a "liberal" and not a covert Communist. Nor did Gorsky, in sending Kramer's report to Moscow, describe Oppenheimer as a source.[56]

Although Oppenheimer eluded Soviet efforts to recruit him, the NKGB was more successful with another leading physicist among the scientists working on "Enormoz," initially in Great Britain. In November 1943, however, this important agent was one of a group of researchers transferred to America as the project moved toward conclusion. Soon finding himself enmeshed in an often-unsatisfactory relationship with his newly assigned courier, Harry Gold, the German-born physicist and covert Communist Klaus Fuchs ("Rest"), a Soviet agent since 1941, reached the United States.

ENTER KLAUS FUCHS

The NKGB's London station first noticed Fuchs on a list of people working on "Enormoz" in 1943 and cabled Moscow to check him out in "the neighbors'" files,[57] an inquiry to which the GRU responded in late November of that year:

Klaus Fuchs has been our source since August 1941,* when he was recruited through the recommendation of Urgen Kuchinsky [a leading economist and exiled German Communist resident in Great Britain]. In connection with the laboratory's transfer to America, Fuchs's departure is expected, too. I should inform you

* Remarkably, the probable earliest Soviet cable dealing with Klaus Fuchs's recruitment as an agent emerged, deciphered, in the VENONA files in 1996. An August 10, 1941, cable from the GRU's London station "to DIRECTOR," Moscow (No. 2227) states: "On 8th August BARCH [Soviet operative Simon Davidovich Kremer] had a meeting with [a former acquaintance], Doctor KLAUS FUCHS, who . . ." [undeciphered except for references to "all the material will be sent to CANADA for industrial production," "Professor HEISENBERG" (the German atomic scientist), and "1000 tons of dynamite"]. In context, the cable probably refers to the atomic energy project ("Enormoz").

that measures to organize a liaison with Fuchs in America have been taken by us, and more detailed data will be conveyed in the course of passing Fuchs to you.[58]

A subsequent memorandum noted that the GRU had received materials from Fuchs twice in September 1941 and five times in 1943.[59] "While working with us," the January 21, 1944, memo noted, "Fuchs passed us a number of theoretical calculations on atomic fission and creation of the uranium bomb. . . . [His] materials were appraised highly." Nor did Fuchs spy for money, the GRU reported; he was a devout Communist "whose only financial reward consisted of occasional 'gifts.' "[60]

Fuchs's arrival in America was a boon to the New York NKGB station's frustrated quest for information on "Enormoz." A Moscow memorandum had defined the station's responsibility: "[Fuchs] is an important figure with significant prospects and experience in agent's work acquired over two years spent working with the neighbors. After determining at early meetings his status in the country and possibilities, you may move immediately to the practical work of acquiring information and materials."[61]

The elaborate procedure for Fuchs's meetings worked out by GRU operatives in London provoked understandable criticism from the NKGB in Moscow. Beginning in January 1944, Fuchs was instructed to come on the first and third Saturdays of every month at 4 P.M. to the entrance of the Henry Street settlement on New York's Lower East Side and to stand there holding a green book and tennis ball in his hands. He would await a man wearing gloves, who would also be holding a third glove. The contact would ask directions to Chinatown, and Fuchs would respond: "I think Chinatown is closed at 5 P.M." Although too late to be changed, Moscow thought the arrangement ridiculous: "Periodic appearances at the appointed days while waiting at the same place for a man, [holding] unusual objects such as those described, could easily draw everyone's attention."

The backup procedure was simpler. If Fuchs did not appear before April 1, his courier Harry would travel to Cambridge, Massachusetts, to visit Fuchs's sister, whom Moscow described as an American Communist Party member, to try and locate the man. Again, the passwords evoked a mediocre spy movie: Gold: "I bring you regards from Max." Sister: "Oh, I heard he had twins." Gold: "Yes, seven days ago."[62]

The NKGB had chosen Gold, an experienced group handler, as Fuchs's contact on the grounds that it was safer than having him meet directly with a Russian operative, but Semyon Semyonov was ultimately responsible for the Fuchs relationship.[63] First contact between Gold and Fuchs came on February 5, after which Gold filed this report:

> The following developed about K. [Klaus]: He obviously has worked with our people before and he is fully aware of what he is doing. . . . He is a mathematical physicist . . . most likely a very brilliant man to have such a position at his age (he looks about 30).
>
> We took a long walk after dinner and he explained the "factory" [code name for "Enormoz" used between Gold and Fuchs] setup: He is a member of a British mission to the U.S. working under the direct control of the U.S. Army. . . .
>
> The work involves mainly separating the isotopes of "factory" and is being done thusly: The electronic method has been developed at Berkeley, California, and is being carried out at a place known only as "Camp Y" — K. believes it is in New Mexico. . . . Simultaneously, the diffusion method is being tried here in the East. . . . Should the diffusion method prove successful, it will be used as a preliminary step in the separation, with the final work being done by the electronic method. They hope to have the electronic method ready early in 1945 and the diffusion method in July 1945, but K. says the latter estimate is optimistic. All production will be done in the U.S.; only preparatory work is being carried on in England. K. says that the work is being done in "watertight" compartments, but that he will furnish us with everything in his and [Rudolph] Peierles's divisions and as much of the other as possible; Peierles is K.'s superior, but they have divided the work between them.
>
> The two countries had worked together before 1940, and then there was a lapse until 1942. Even now, K. says there is much being withheld from the British. Even Niels Bohr, who is now in the country incognito as Nicholas Baker, has not been told everything.
>
> We made careful arrangements for meeting next in two weeks, when K. will have information for us.*[64]

* "On 5 February, a meeting took place between [Harry Gold] and [Klaus Fuchs]. Beforehand [Gold] was given a detailed briefing by us. [Fuchs] greeted him pleasantly but was rather cautious at first . . . with discussion [Gold] satisfied himself that [Fuchs] was aware of whom he was working with. [Fuchs] arrived in the [United States] in September [1943] as a member of the [British] mission on

After Gold's second meeting with Fuchs on February 25, the station reported to Moscow that Fuchs had turned over material dealing with his personal work on "Enormoz."[65] At a third rendezvous on March 11, he delivered fifty additional pages,[66] and Gold's report to Semyonov discussed his exchange with Fuchs about the material previously delivered:

> He asked me how his first stuff had been received, and I said quite satisfactorily but with one drawback: references to the first material, bearing on a general description of the process, were missing, and we especially needed a detailed schema of the entire plant. Clearly, he didn't like this much. His main objection, evidently, was that he had already carried out this job on the other side [in Great Britain], and those who receive these materials must know how to connect them to the scheme. Besides, he thinks it would be dangerous for him if such explanations were found, since his work here is not linked to this sort of material. Nevertheless, he agreed to give us what we need as soon as possible.

On March 28, Fuchs complained to Gold that "his work here is deliberately being curbed by the Americans, who continue to neglect cooperation and do not provide information." As a result, he might return to England by July or be sent to "Camp Y" in New Mexico. If Fuchs went back, "he would be able to give us more complete general information but without details."[*][67]

The meetings continued into May, with Fuchs providing Gold both information on "Enormoz" and gossip concerning those working on it, especially what the scientist perceived as an ongoing Anglo-American competition to dominate the project.[68]

ENORMOZ. According to him, the work on ENORMOZ in the [United States] is being carried out under the direct control of the [United States] Army. . . . The whole operation amounts to the working out of the process for the separation of isotopes of ENORMOZ. The work is proceeding in two directions: the electron method by Lawrence . . . [seventy-one groups unrecoverable] separation of isotopes by the combined method, using the diffusion method for preliminary and the electron method for final separation." Kvasnikov to Fitin, February 9, 1944, No. 195, VENONA files.

* "[Fuchs] advises that the work of the Commission of [the British] in the United States is not meeting with success in view of the unwillingness of workers of the United States to share secrets with the [British]. It will be proposed to [Fuchs] that he should either return to [England] or work at the special laboratory-camp. . . ." New York station to Moscow, May 8, 1944, No. 645, VENONA files.

Harry Gold was transferred in mid-1944 from Semyon Semyonov's oversight to that of Anatoly Yatskov ("Alexsey") because "Semyonov was being followed closely by the FBI and thus compelled to miss a number of meetings with his many agents."[69] Returning to Moscow, Semyonov described in a November 1944 memorandum the difficulties of evading U.S. counterintelligence. He complained that "a considerable intensification of counterintelligence work [is directed] against us. In particular, this is reflected in extremely intense surveillance of the consulates, the embassy, and trade organizations. Cases of systematic surveillance of Soviet citizens are also known."[70] Semyonov never returned to the United States; according to Alexander Feklissov's memoirs, Semyonov was removed from Soviet intelligence during an anti-Semitic purge in the years prior to Stalin's death.[71]

Although Gold and Fuchs continued to meet throughout late spring and early summer 1944, Moscow's annoyance at the casual nature of their contacts reached Yatskov in this July 28 memorandum:

> At one time, when we instructed [Gold] to establish contact with [Fuchs], we drew special attention to the need for detailed accounts of [Fuchs's] work. After establishing his liaison with [Fuchs], we receive his information with every mail, but we do not have a single report from [Gold] about his work with [Fuchs] or about [Fuchs] himself. Missing also are precise data about where [Fuchs] works, his address, how and where meetings take place, [Gold's] impressions of [Fuchs], etc. Nor do we have the conditions of meeting [Fuchs] adopted by himself and [Gold in case of] sudden loss. . . . [This, too,] is unknown.[72]

In this curious mixture of informality and secrecy, Harry Gold followed closely the style of an earlier Soviet associate, Jacob Golos. But with "Enormoz," the stakes were significantly higher.

Moscow's fear of losing contact with Klaus Fuchs was realized the following month when he failed to show up for a scheduled August 5 meeting with Gold. At their next scheduled rendezvous, it was Harry Gold, who also served as courier to Alfred Slack and Abraham Brothman, who did not appear. Gold was reprimanded for this breach. When Fuchs failed to appear for a third scheduled meeting, Gold turned to their backup plan and traveled to Cambridge to meet with Fuchs's sister, who was out of town. A neighbor confirmed for Gold, however, that Fuchs had paid a farewell visit to his sister before departing for England.*[73]

---

* "In July, when it became known that [Klaus Fuchs] might be leaving for [England], instructions were given to [Anatoly Yatskov], and by the latter to [Harry

Moscow's anger over the abrupt loss of Klaus Fuchs's services focused on the single meeting that Gold had missed. But even before Fuchs's disappearance, complaints had reached the New York station (for example, in this June 30, 1944, memorandum) concerning its supposed ineffectiveness in producing valuable sources on atomic research: "For all the period of our work on 'Enormoz,' despite our constant reminders about realizing one or another operation and many concrete reminders—where to work, on which questions—except for 'Fogel,' we have nothing. [Fuchs] doesn't count since he was passed to you in finished form. We cannot consent further to such a situation."[74] Losing Fuchs without prior warning merely compounded Moscow's irritation.

"PERSIAN" AND "PERSEUS"

Who was the otherwise unidentified "Fogel" (a code name later changed to "Persian"), the remaining hope of New York's NKGB station to run its own agent within the "Enormoz" program?* He was a young U.S. engineer and Communist Party member whose father was a close friend of Earl Browder's.[75] Seeking employment that would benefit the party during the war, he consulted a CP member who, in turn, talked to Semyon Semyonov. Semyonov urged "Fogel" to apply for a job at the Kellogg Construction Company, which was a major object of NKGB interest because of its work on "Enormoz."

"Fogel" found a job with a Kellogg subcontractor, Kellex, and began to deliver information on the plant structure and equipment being

---

Gold] to arrange a password for a meeting with [Fuchs] in case he was leaving. On August 5 [Fuchs] did not appear at the meeting and [Gold] missed the next meeting, pleading pressure of work. [Fuchs] was not at the following control meeting. When he checked on [Fuchs's] apartment, [Gold] was informed that [Fuchs] had left for [England]. In order to recheck, I sent [Gold] to [Fuchs's] sister. . . ." New York station to Pavel Fitin, Moscow, August 29, 1944, No. 1233, VENONA files.

* During the 1990s, the Russian Foreign Intelligence Service (SVR) created the code name "Perseus," which resembles "Persian," in an apparent effort to confuse those who worked on the NSA/CIA's "VENONA" deciphering project. An aged and carefully briefed Morris Cohen informed American and Russian journalists that he had handled an unknown atomic masterspy named "Perseus." The truth of the NKGB's relationship to "Persian" was more mundane. Although the SVR's motives remain unclear, it seems to have hoped that Western scholars would credit the still-undetected "Perseus" with mysterious and still-revealed Soviet

used in the "Enormoz" project's New York facilities.*[76] " 'Fogel' knows that he is working for the USSR," Semyonov reported in November 1944. "From the very beginning of his activities, he proved to be an able, resourceful agent."[77] Moreover, despite the increase in U.S. counterintelligence activities, Semyonov noted that "the agent situation for developing work on technical intelligence in America [is] more favorable than at the beginning of the war."

Several factors, Semyonov concluded, accounted for this change in intelligence climate. These included support for the Soviet Union as an ally "among a wide strata of American engineer-technical workers," the ability of "progressive elements" to gain employment in sensitive war industries that could not be penetrated prior to the war, and the growth of new industries involved in military production with "little experience of counterintelligence work or of protecting secret drawings, specifications, and documents." As for "Enormoz," specifically, "the agent situation is [even] more favorable because the circle of scientists, engineers, and technicians admitted to this work grows daily, making [American] counterintelligence work more complicated."[78]

That "complication" did not apply to Semyonov himself, who experienced active FBI surveillance in the spring of 1944. For that reason, he had transferred both "Fogel" and Julius Rosenberg to the supervision of another Soviet operative, Alexander Feklissov ("Kalistrat").[79]

Feklissov arrived in New York on February 27, 1941,[80] and went to work at the Soviet Consulate in New York as his cover.[81] Assigned to develop radio contact between the NKVD station and Moscow, Feklissov set up his equipment in the consulate's upper floor where, with the help of a technically skilled American agent, "Condenser,"[†] he built a new radio transmitter. Earl Browder had originally recruited "Condenser" in 1939, and he had spent some weeks in Moscow learning aspects of tradecraft. The Feklissov transmitters were discovered by American authorities, or so Soviet intelligence believed, in 1943, and Feklissov was transferred to "XY line" activities, including "Enormoz."[82]

---

espionage triumphs. The best account of this disinformation effort can be found in Joseph Albright and Marcia Kunstel, *BOMBSHELL: The Secret Story of America's Unknown Atomic Spy Conspiracy* (New York: Times Books, 1996), Chapter 28, "The Perseus Myth," pp. 267–77.

* "By the same post were dispatched two secret plans of the layout of the ENORMOZ plant received from FOGEL." New York station to Moscow, June 16, 1944, No. 854, VENONA files.

† His real name, like "Fogel's," is unknown.

"Fogel's" cultivation, meanwhile, slowed considerably because, despite the new agent's enthusiasm, his work brought him only to the periphery of what (by then) was referred to, among the involved U.S. government officials, as "the Manhattan Project." "In August [1944], we didn't receive any materials from 'Fogel,'" the station reported to Moscow the following month. "He informs us that his enterprises are moving indecisively forward. The construction of 'Enormoz's' experimental plant is proceeding slowly as if by its own momentum. They say this happens because great changes and alterations in the plant's initial construction are expected."[83]

Once again, as in the case of other American sources (for example, Laurence Duggan), a troubling combination of family pressures and fear of exposure dampened "Fogel's" enthusiasm for continuing "secret work." Thus, the NKGB's New York station learned in February 1945 that "Persian" ("Fogel's" new code name) had declined his company's invitation to transfer to an "atomic" camp (presumably Los Alamos) as a construction engineer. When pressed by Feklissov to change his mind, "Persian" offered as many excuses as a student with an unfinished homework assignment: No one had told him what his work would be at the camp. There was no housing for his family there, and "Persian" had a wife, a small child, and a comfortable apartment. He had begun a new business with another Communist and invested $20,000, which would be lost if he left.

Frustrated by the self-absorption of American agents such as "Persian" in declining an assignment of such critical importance to the Soviet Union, Moscow instructed Feklissov and his colleagues to impress upon their reluctant recruit his obligation to "our common cause." They also promised a sizable cash payment if he left a relative in charge of his business and traveled West.[84]

But nothing would budge the obstinate "Persian." When Anatoly Yatskov met with him on March 11, 1945, a new problem was his wife's illness. Also, his company had not renewed its earlier proposal that he work in the "atomic" camp. "Persian" feared that suddenly volunteering to go would invite suspicion, since most of his cohorts tried to avoid transfer. Although "Persian" sought to console his Soviet supervisors by continuing to deliver material throughout the spring, only in May did he provide some drawings and plans directly linked to "Enormoz."[85] By that time, the station had turned elsewhere in its pursuit of a reliable source inside one of the major "atomic" camps.

One mysterious but helpful episode related to atomic espionage had occurred the previous year. Although never explained, it brought an unexpected intelligence bonanza to the USSR. In the summer of 1944, a stranger delivered a package containing top secret materials on the atomic project to the Soviet Consulate in New York. Rather than being pleased with this unexpected turn of events, however, Moscow was furious, rebuking the station in this August 28 memorandum:

> The receipt of material on "Enormoz" from a source unknown to you, first of all, reflects your unsatisfactory work on this subject, with available possibilities neither being discovered nor used by you, letting the cultivation of this primary problem drift.
>
> The tranquillity or indifference with which you reported to us about this material and the circumstances of its receipt . . . surprised us very much. If somebody dared to make such a risky move, to bring this most secret document to the Plant [the Soviet Consulate], how could you . . . not take every step to determine who the unknown person was?
>
> We attach great importance to this event: The stranger's material is exceptionally interesting, and our data, received from other sources, support its contents. Therefore, take every measure to locate this person. Report the results immediately.[86]

The Soviets' mysterious benefactor was never found. The "other sources" mentioned in the angry cable from Moscow referred mainly to Klaus Fuchs and to "Eric," whose deliveries of documentary material (the NKGB's London station reported in August 1944) had become even more valuable. One of "Eric's" colleagues had provided him with a key to the laboratory's library, where reports on the "Enormoz" project were kept:

> We decided to make a copy of the key for "Eric" [the cable to Moscow continued] and worked out liaison arrangements that gave us the possibility of contacting him three times a week without preliminary arrangements. . . . As a result, we managed to receive from "Eric" all the available American materials . . . and other interesting materials on "Enormoz." . . . ["Eric"] continues to decline the slightest hint at material reward. . . .[87]

Nor was "Eric" the only reason Moscow considered its resources in England more productive than those in the United States on atomic problems throughout the war years. Thus, Pavel Fitin reported to Vsevolod Merkulov in August 1945:

> Valuable information on "Enormoz" is coming from the London station. The first materials on "Enormoz" were received in late

1941 from our source "List" [John Cairncross], containing valuable and absolutely secret documents both on the substance of
the "Enormoz" problem and on measures by the British government to organize and develop work on the problem of atomic energy in our country. In connection with American and Canadian
work on "Enormoz," . . . materials describing the state and
progress of work in three countries—England, the U.S., and
Canada—are [all] coming from the London station.[88]

Still another agent, code-named "Tina," surfaced in London only in
May and June 1945. "Tina" was a secret member of the British Communist Party, recruited for intelligence work by the GPU in 1935. She
worked for the British Association on Non-Ferrous Metals and provided on several occasions in 1945 all of the up-to-date research for the
"Enormoz" project in the metallurgical field.*[89]

Until late 1944, as Pavel Fitin's gloomy November 5 report made
clear, American sources on atomic research remained disappointing:

Despite participation by a large number of scientific organizations and workers on . . . the problem of "Enormoz" in the U.S.,
mainly known to us by agent data, their cultivation develops
poorly. Therefore, the major part of data on the U.S. comes from
the station in England. On the basis of information from the London station, [Moscow] Center more than once sent to the New
York station a work orientation and sent a ready agent, too [Klaus
Fuchs]. The New York station didn't use those opportunities
completely. For the entire period of cultivating agents on "Enormoz," it drew only one agent—"Persian"—not having great possibilities.[90]

Frustrated in its lack of success in the United States, Moscow decided in October 1944 to establish a separate "XY line" NKGB station
in New York and assigned Leonid Kvasnikov ("Anton") as its head.[91]
Both Yatskov and Feklissov were among those operatives designated to
work under Kvasnikov's direction. Initially, the new station's head was

* Soviet intelligence's Moscow headquarters cabled the London station concerning "Tina's" work in mid-September 1945: "We agree with your proposal about
working with 'Tina.' At the next meeting tell her that her documentary material on
ENORMOZ is of great interest and represents a valuable contribution to the development of the work in this field . . . instruct her not to discuss her work with us
with her husband and not to say anything to him about the nature of the documentary material which is being obtained by her." September 16, 1945, No. 1413,
VENONA files.

not particularly pleased with either Yatskov's or Feklissov's work, as he reported to Moscow.[92] Nevertheless, the following month, all three and others involved in the pursuit of "Enormoz," including Harry Gold and Semyon Semyonov, received medals for their strenuous efforts if not yet for their achievements.[93]

ENTER THEODORE HALL

At that moment, however, several newly acquired American agents finally emerged. Kvasnikov's recently inaugurated station in New York informed Moscow on November 12, 1944, that an agent-journalist for the *Russian Voice* named Sergei Kurnakov ("Beck") received a report on Santa Fe's "Camp 2" from a young physicist who also provided the names of those who led the work on "Enormoz." Apparently, the physicist, Theodore Hall, had run into difficulty seeking a Soviet intelligence contact. Ted Hall ("Mlad") was a member of the Young Communist League, and it was through the mother of a mutual friend in the League, Saville Sax ("Star"), himself a party member, that Hall met Kurnakov.[94] The journalist's report to the NKGB described Hall vividly:

> Rather tall, slender, brown-haired, pale and a bit pimply-faced, dressed carelessly, boots appear not cleaned for a long time, slipped socks. His hair is parted and often falls on his forehead. His English is highly cultured and "rich." He answers quickly and very fluently, especially to scientific questions. Eyes are set closely together; evidently, neurasthenic. Perhaps because of premature mental development, he is witty and somewhat sarcastic but without a shadow of undue familiarity and cynicism. His main trait—a highly sensitive brain and quick responsiveness. In conversation, he is sharp and flexible as a sword. . . . He comes from a Jewish family, though doesn't look like a Jew. His father is a mere [sic] furrier; his mother is dead. . . . He is not in the army because, until now, young physicists in government jobs at a military installation were not being drafted. Now, he is to be drafted but has no doubts that he will be kept at the same place, only dressed in a military uniform and with a correspondingly lower salary.[95]

Kurnakov probed Hall's attitude toward the Soviet Union's various policy twists and a range of other safe subjects in an apparent attempt to discover why Hall had sought him out. Kurnakov's memorandum recounts the transition to more confidential subjects:

> As the conversation went on, [Hall's] nervousness grew . . . he began biting his nails. I took out a clipping from the *Times* with a story about the U.S. preparing "flying bombs" similar to the German ones, and said, "Perhaps you are disturbed by that?" Then he gave a deep sigh and said: "No, it's much worse."
>
> He told me that a new secret weapon represents an "atomic bomb" with a colossally destructive impact. I interrupted: "Do you understand what you are doing? Why do you think it is necessary to disclose U.S. secrets for the sake of the Soviet Union?" He answered: "There is no country except for the Soviet Union that could be entrusted with such a terrible thing. But, since we can't take it [away] from other countries, [we should] let the USSR know about its existence and be aware of the progress of experiments and construction. Then, at a peace conference, the USSR—on which my generation's fate depends—won't find itself in the position of a blackmailed power. . . . All the outstanding physicists of the U.S., England, Italy and Germany (immigrants), and Denmark are working on this thing." The list of physicists is on the last page of [Hall's] report.* "We know that both Germany and the USSR are working on a [bomb] whose action is based on fission of the atom of some elements (uranium and another element, which we call plutonium and which is the 94th element) [*sic*]. However, there are few doubts that the U.S. is ahead of the rest, since all of Europe's brains, except the Russians, are concentrated in this country, and billions are being spent. Besides, we have four (or more) cyclotrons, and in other countries, according to data we have, there are no more than two in any country."

Hall then provided Kurnakov with a summary explanation of the principles of the atomic bomb before handing over his report, where the matter was described in detail. "He proposed organizing meetings, if needed," Kurnakov's report continued, "to inform [us] about the progress of experiments, for he considers this most important: i.e., the principle itself is not important, since it is known to everyone, but the stage at which practical experiments on explosion and its control, the [bomb] shell's construction, etc., are important."[96]

---

* Hall gave Kurnakov a written report on his work and the entire project at this first meeting.

AMERICAN AGENTS, I

Laurence Duggan *(right)*, then-director of the State Department's Latin American section, is shown being presented an award by Undersecretary Edward Stettinius. Duggan provided information to Soviet intelligence during his years at State.

THROUGH EMBASSY EYES (HARCOURT, BRACE, 1939)

LIBRARY OF CONGRESS

Martha Dodd, daughter of the U.S. Ambassador to Germany, was a Soviet agent throughout the 1930s and 1940s, even recruiting her husband, wealthy businessman Alfred Stern (known as the "Red millionaire") for secret work. Dodd is pictured boarding a plane to fly to the Soviet Union.

Noel Field—working at State and for various international agencies—was another Soviet agent during the 1930s and World War II. He is pictured here with his wife, Herta.

AMERICAN AGENTS, II

Beginning with his involvement in the "Ware Group" of New Deal officials in 1934–35, Alger Hiss worked mainly for Soviet military intelligence networks for the next decade, while rising to prominence in the State Department.

Whittaker Chambers, among his other underground duties as an agent handler, became Hiss's courier and main link to Soviet intelligence until Chambers defected in 1938.

Elizabeth Bentley served as courier for Jacob Golos, her lover and a Soviet operative. Bentley defection in 1945 forced Moscow to halt most espionage activity in the United States for fear that, as an FBI informant, she endangered many Soviet operatives and American agents.

SOVIET OPERATIVES, I

Three of Moscow's most effective station chiefs in the United States during the 1930s were Boris Bazarov, Peter Gutzeit, and Gaik Ovakimyan.

Bazarov, pictured here in a rare candid shot reading *The New York Times*, had to untangle the embarrassing Hedda Gumperz–Noel Field–Alger Hiss encounter (Chapter 2).

The astute Gutzeit devised a never-implemented scheme for Soviet intelligence to buy influence among members of the U.S. Congress and media (Chapter 7).

Back in Moscow by then, Ovakimyan helped negotiate the wartime agreement between the OSS and NKGB (Chapter 11).

SOVIET OPERATIVES, II

The three wartime station chiefs pictured here—Itzhak Akhmerov, Jacob Golos, and Vassily Zarubin—all began their involvement with American agents during the preceding decade.

Akhmerov worked with Laurence Duggan and other Roosevelt Administration officials before and during World War II.

Golos sheltered his many agents and sources within the U.S. government from contact with other Soviet operatives until his death in 1943. Then Moscow ordered Elizabeth Bentley—Golos's chief aide—to turn agent supervision over to Akhmerov (Chapter 5).

In 1934, long before he reached the United States in late 1940 as station chief, Zarubin had been provided by Hollywood producer (and Soviet agent) Boris Morros with a "cover" post working for Paramount Pictures in Nazi Germany (Chapter 6).

AGENT-ENTREPRENEURS

Most Americans who spied for Moscow during the 1930s were antifascist admirers of the Soviet Union whose involvement in espionage had ideological roots. There were two notable exceptions, one a U.S. Congressman (Chapter 7) and the other a Hollywood producer (Chapter 6). Samuel Dickstein (*above*) and Boris Morros—although both antifascists—offered their services as Soviet agents with a price tag.

SOVIET ESPIONAGE
IN WARTIME WASHINGTON, I

Nathan Gregory Silvermaster coordinated one of the most active and successful networks of Soviet agents within the U.S. government in wartime Washington (Chapter 8). He is shown here being sworn in at a 1948 congressional hearing at which he called this accusation "false and fantastic."

Earl Browder, leader of the "open" Communist Party of the United States, was at the same time an active agent and agent handler for Moscow throughout the 1930s and World War II until his expulsion from the party at the war's end.

The single most valuable Soviet intelligence agent in the American capital during the closing years of the war was probably the British diplomat Donald Maclean, then posted to his embassy in Washington (Chapter 12).

SOVIET ESPIONAGE
IN WARTIME WASHINGTON, II

Three high-ranking Soviet agents in policy-making positions in the wartime Roosevelt Administration—Lauchlin Currie, Alger Hiss, and Harry Dexter White—all provided Moscow with crucial documents and information on a range of major U.S. actions and policies.

Currie, a chief aide to President Roosevelt, is pictured here *(center)* receiving a cigarette case upon retiring in 1945 as president of the federal government employees' association (Chapter 8).

Hiss *(second from right)*, who coordinated for the State Department American organization of the United Nations' inaugural meeting in San Francisco in April 1945, stands in this photo (taken at the meeting) between then–U.S. Secretary of State Edward Stettinius *(to his right)* and then–Soviet Ambassador to the United States, Andrei Gromyko (Chapter 12).

White remained a key Treasury Department official throughout the war, providing Soviet intelligence with valuable information on Roosevelt Administration policies.

THE SOVIET SNITCH

~~TOP SECRET~~
UNCLASSIFIED

Copy No 10
Copy to 7th Ctr St.
54-00

Mr. HOOVER,

       Exceptional circumstances impel us to inform you
of the activities of the so-called director of the Soviet
Intelligence in this country. This "Soviet" intelligence
officer genuinely occupies a very high post in the GPU (now NKVD),
enjoys to a vast extent the confidence of the Soviet Government,
but in fact, as we know very accurately, works for Japan himself,
while his wife (works) for Germany. Thus, under cover of the name
of the USSR, he is a dangerous enemy of the USSR and the U.S.A.
The vast organisation of permanent staff [KADROVYE] workers of
the NKVD under his command in the U.S.A. does not suspect that,
thanks to the treachery of their director, they are also
inflicting frightful harm on their own country. In this same
false position is also their whole network of agents, among
whom are many U.S. citizens, and finally BROWDER himself, who
has immediate contact with them. BROWDER passes on to him
very important information about the U.S.A., thinking that all
this goes to MOSCOW, but, as you see, it all goes to the
Japanese and Germans. ⧈ The "Director of the Soviet Intelligence"
here is ZUBILIN, Vasilij, 2nd secretary in the embassy of the
USSR, his real name is ZARUBIN, V., deputy head of the Foreign
Intelligence Directorate [UPRAVLENIE] of the NKVD. He personally
deals with getting agents into and out of the U.S.A. illegally,
organises secret radio-stations and manufactures forged documents.
His closest assistants are:

1. His wife, directs political intelligence here, has a vast
network of agents in almost all ministries including the State
Department. She sends false information to the NKVD and
everything of value passes on to the Germans through a certain
Boris MOROZ (HOLLYWOOD). Put her under observation and you will
very quickly uncover the whole of her network.

2. KLARIN, Pavel, vice-consul in NEW YORK. Has a vast network of agents among Russian émigrés, meets them almost openly,
brings agents into the U.S.A. illegally. Many of his agents
work in very high posts in American organisations, they are all
Russian.

3. KHEJFETS - vice-consul in SAN FRANCISCO, deals with
political and military intelligence on the West Coast of the U.S.A.
has a large network of agents in the ports and war factories,
collects very valuable strategic material, which is sent by
ZUBILIN to Japan. Has a radio station in the consulate.
He himself is a great coward, on arrest will quickly give away
all the agents to save himself and remain in this country.

4. KVASNIKOV, works as an engineer in AMTORG, is ZUBILIN's
assistant for technical intelligence, through SEMENOV - who also
works in AMTORG, is robbing the whole of the war industry of
America. SEMENOV has his agents in all the industrial towns
of the U.S.A., in all aviation and chemical war factories and
in big institutes. He works very brazenly and roughly, it would
be very easy to follow him up and catch him red handed. He would
just be glad to be arrested as he has long been seeking a reason
to remain in the U.S.A., hates the NKVD but is a frightful coward
and loves money. He will give all his agents away with pleasure
if he is promised an American passport. He is convinced that he
is working for the USSR, but all his materials are going via
Z. to Japan, if you tell him about this, he will help you find
the rest himself.

                                       [Continued overleaf]

UNCLASSIFIED BY _Spacegan_
ON _7-10-96_

UNCLASSIFIED

~~TOP SECRET~~

In August 1943, a disgruntled intelligence official at the Soviet Union's New York consulate
mailed a letter to FBI Director J. Edgar Hoover purporting to identify various Soviet operatives and American agents operating in this country. The FBI found it difficult to confirm the
information, which it translated from the original Russian.

CHANGING THE COVER NAMES

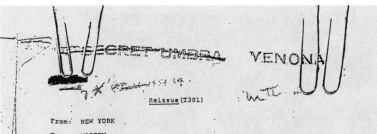

Reissue (T301)

From: NEW YORK

To: MOSCOW

No: 1251

2 September 1944

To VIKTOR[i].

In accordance with our telegram no. 403[a] we are advising you of the new cover-names: KAVALERIST - BEK[ii], DROZD - AKhMED[iii] KLEMENS - LI[iv], ABRAM - ChEKh[v], TYuL'PAN - KANT[vi], AIDA - KLO .[vii], RYBOLOV - [C% BLOK][viii], RELE - SERB[ix], ANTENNA - LIBERAL[x], GNOM - YaKOV[xi], SKAUT - METR[xii], TU.... - NIL[xiii], FOGEL' - PERS[xiv], ODESSIT - ROST[xv]. All these cover-names were selected [C% by you] with a view to economy of means. Among the new cover-names introduced by you there are disadvantageous ones which we propose to replace as follows: STELLA - ÉMILIYa[xvi] DONAL'D.- PILOT[xvii], LOJER - RICHARD[xviii], DUGLAS - IKS[xix], ShERVUD - KNYaZ'[xx], [1 group unrecovered]T-²ZONA[xxi], MIRANDA - ART[xxii], SEN'OR - BERG[xxiii]. All these cover-names are economical from the point of view of encoding. Please confirm. Continuation will follow later[b].

No. 700

MAJ[xxiv]

2 September

Notes: [a] NEW YORK's no. 744 of 25 May 1944. However, no. 744 has nothing to do with the subject of this message so must be an incorrect reference.

[b] See NEW YORK's no 1403 of 5 October 1944

Comments:

[i] VIKTOR: Lt. Gen. P.M. FITIN.

[ii] KAVALERIST - BEK: i.e. CAVALRYMAN - BECK, Sergej Niko-laevich KURNAKOV.

[iii] DROZD - AKhMED: i.e. THRUSH - AKhMED, unidentified.

[iv] KLEMENS - LI: i.e. CLEMENCE - LEE, unidentified.

[v] ABRAM - ChEKh: i.e. ABRAM - CZECH, Jack SOBLE.

[vi] TYuL'PAN - KANT: i.e. TULIP - KANT, Mark ZBOROWSKI.

[vii] AIDA - KLO: Esther Trebach RAND.

[viii] RYBOLOV - BLOK: i.e. OSPREY - BLOCK, unidentified. BLOK is repeated as GE. There is no other occurrence of eithe]

[ix] RELE - SERB: i.e. RELAY - SERB. RELE has been tenta-tively identified as Morton SOBELL. However, the only other reference to SERB is in NEW YORK's no. 50 of 11 January 1945 and would not appear to refer to SOBELL.

[x] ANTENNA - LIBERAL: Julius ROSENBERG.

[xi] GNOM - YaKOV: i.e. GNOME - YaKOV, William PERL (origin-ally MUTTERPERL).

VENONA

Concerned over reports of expanded FBI surveillance, Moscow instructed its station chiefs in the United States to provide new cover names identifying American agents and sources. The NKGB's New York station complied with the instruction in this September 2, 1944, memo-randum, deciphered in the VENONA program (Chapter 12).

THE OSS AND THE NKGB

With the Soviet Union and the United States cooperating as wartime allies, General William "Wild Bill" Donovan—head of the OSS—and his counterpart at the NKGB, General Pavel Fitin, agreed that their two services would share vital intelligence information.

FBI Director J. Edgar Hoover, more suspicious of Soviet intentions than Donovan, maneuvered successfully in Washington to quash the agreement (Chapter 11).

THE "ALES" MEMORANDUM: ALGER HISS IN MOSCOW

VENONA

MGB

From: WASHINGTON

To: MOSCOW

No: 1822

3ø March 1945

Further to our telegram No. 283[a]. As a result of "[D$ A.'s]"[i] chat with "ALES"[ii] the following has been ascertained:

1. ALES has been working with the NEIGHBORS[SOSEDI][iii] continuously since 1935.

2. For some years past he has been the leader of a small group of the NEIGHBORS' probationers[STAZhERY], for the most part consisting of his relations.

3. The group and ALES himself work on obtaining military information only. Materials on the "BANK"[iv] allegedly interest the NEIGHBORS very little and he does not produce them regularly.

4. All the last few years ALES has been working with "POL'"[v] who also meets other members of the group occasionally.

5. Recently ALES and his whole group were awarded Soviet decorations.

6. After the YaLTA Conference, when he had gone on to MOSCOW, a Soviet personage in a very responsible position (ALES gave to understand that it was Comrade VYShINSKIJ) allegedly got in touch with ALES and at the behest of the Military NEIGHBORS passed on to him their gratitude and so on.

No. 431   VADIM[vi]

Notes: [a] Not available.
Comments:
[i] A.: "A." seems the most likely garble here although "A." has not been confirmed elsewhere in the WASHINGTON traffic.
[ii] ALES: Probably Alger HISS.
[iii] SOSEDI: Members of another Soviet Intelligence organisation, here probably the GRU.
[iv] BANK: The U.S. State Department.
[v] POL': i.e. "PAUL," unidentified cover-name.
[vi] VADIM: Anatolij Borisovich GROMOV, MGB resident in WASHINGTON.

8 August 1969

VENONA

20?.

"PAL"

COURTESY NSA/CIA VENONA TRANSCRIPTS

This March 1945 cable from Soviet intelligence in Washington to Moscow described a leading American agent, code-named "ALES," whom VENONA project analysts determined was "probably Alger Hiss." Other Soviet cables at the time that mentioned "ALES" confirm the identification (Chapter 12).

ATOMIC ESPIONAGE AGENTS, I

Two of the Soviet Union's critical sources on the Western Allies' atomic energy program were both based at Los Alamos in 1944–45: Klaus Fuchs, *(left)* a distinguished German exile physicist working for the British government, and Theodore Hall, a young American scientist. Both were devoted communists and responsible for transmitting extremely valuable data on the atomic bomb project to Soviet operatives.

Harry Gold, a chemist, served as a courier for Fuchs and other Americans working for Moscow (Chapter 9).

ATOMIC ESPIONAGE AGENTS, II

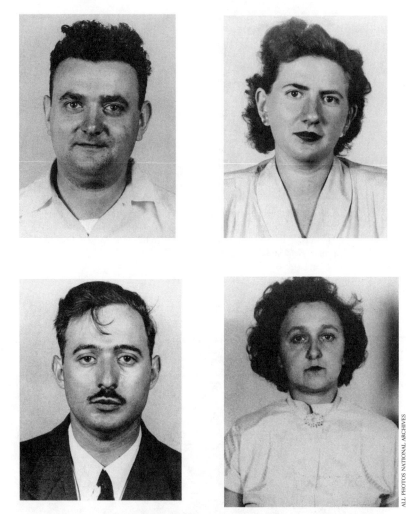

A young technical worker named David Greenglass *(top left)* was also at Los Alamos. Greenglass agreed, after discussions with his wife, Ruth *(top right)*, to provide Soviet intelligence with valuable data on the atomic bomb project. David's brother-in-law, Julius Rosenberg *(bottom left)*, was a veteran Soviet agent and agent handler who persuaded Ruth Greenglass to recruit her husband. Ethel Rosenberg's active involvement in espionage—if any—was minimal.

ATOMIC ESPIONAGE—THE SOVIET OPERATIVES

The Soviet intelligence operatives who focused on gathering information on the atomic bomb project in the United States and England were experienced and skillful. Two key operatives in this process were Leonid Kvasnikov *(left)* and Alexander Feklissov.

Four major former Soviet operatives involved in atomic espionage met for a recent group photo in the History Room at Yasenevo (Russian Foreign Intelligence Service headquarters), with the atomic bomb display in the background. From left to right: Anatoly Yatskov, Leonid Kvasnikov, Vladimir Barkovsky, and Alexander Feklissov.

HENRY WALLACE MEETS THE STATION CHIEF

ем.2   ✓   156

СОВ.СЕКРЕТНО

* РАССЕКРЕЧЕНО *
Служба внешней разведки РФ
10

Телеграммой № 1601 от 27.10.45 резидент НКГБ
СССР в г.Вашингтоне "Вадим" сообщил следующее:

"Некоторое время тому назад я был представлен
бывшему вице-президенту США, теперешнему министру
торговли Генри УОЛЛЕСУ. После этого я несколько раз
встречал его в официальной обстановке и обменивался
несколькими беглыми фразами.

На днях УОЛЛЕС позвонил мне лично и пригласил
к себе в министерство на завтрак. Согласовав этот
вопрос с заместителем посла, я принял приглашение,
и завтрак состоялся 24 октября с.г.

Вначале УОЛЛЕС поинтересовался вопросом о том,
какова будет наша реакция, если американские органи
зации пригласят группу видных советских ученых для
ознакомления с наукой в США (в ответ на недавнюю
поездку группы американских ученых для участия в раб
те юбилейной сессии Академии Наук). Уклонившись от
прямого ответа, я попросил УОЛЛЕСА несколько подроб-
нее развить его мысль. УОЛЛЕС сообщил, что вернувший
ся из СССР доктор Харлау ШЕПЛИ много рассказывал о
научном прогрессе в СССР, в особенности, за время

Оп 43/73.
156-

On October 24, 1945, President Truman's Secretary of Commerce, former Vice President Henry Wallace, sat down for a breakfast meeting that he requested with Anatoly Gorsky, the Soviet intelligence station chief in Washington. At this extraordinary session, Wallace urged Moscow to provide support for leading Americans such as himself who opposed the emerging postwar confrontation between the two countries. Gorsky described the talk in his report to Moscow several days later, the first page of which is reprinted here.

THE AUTHOR AND THE
POST–SOVIET INTELLIGENCE WORLD

Allen Weinstein *(left)* at an exclusive 1995 interview with Morris Cohen, a Soviet agent for over a quarter century in the United States and Europe, held at the Russian Foreign Intelligence Service's hospital in Moscow.

Allen Weinstein *(far left)* and three key Russian Foreign Intelligence Service officials were guests of former CIA director William Colby *(third from right)* in 1993 in the New York law office of the late General William Donovan. At the far right is a representative of the OSS's retired agents group.

Allen Weinstein *(center)* meets in 1995 with General Yuri Kobaladze *(left)*, head of the Russian Foreign Intelligence Service's (SVR) Public Affairs and Press Bureau, and General Vadim Kirpichenko, chairman of the SVR's senior consultants' group at the Press Bureau offices in Moscow.

The meeting took place in New York City while Hall was on leave from Los Alamos. Toward the end of their talk, the young physicist noted that it was time for him to return to Santa Fe. "I asked him (semi-jokingly)," Kurnakov observed in his report, "why he didn't fear that I would betray him. He answered, 'About half a million readers and everyone in the progressive movement knows you. If you can't be trusted, nobody can.' "* Hall asked Kurnakov to introduce him immediately to a Soviet operative, but the Russian remained cautious. Hall later handed Sax a copy of the report he had given to Kurnakov, with a request that his friend deliver it to the Soviet Consulate.

Sax turned the report over to Anatoly Yatskov on October 25, and the pair met the following day so that Yatskov could review the situation.[97] At that point, Yatskov asked for a report from Kurnakov, although he subsequently received instructions from Moscow to stop using the journalist and begin training Sax to serve as Hall's contact.[98] Ted Hall was told in November that he would be drafted but kept at the same work. Now, however, as a soldier, he could leave the camp only with special permission.[†][99]

Hall was not the only new Soviet recruit at New Mexico's "Camp 2" during the fall of 1944. In September, Julius Rosenberg (whose code name had been changed recently from "Antenna" to "Liberal"), by then a veteran NKGB agent previously supervised by Jacob Golos, ap-

---

* "[Kurnakov] visited Theodore Hall, 19 years old, the son of a furrier. He is a graduate of Harvard University. As a talented physicist he was taken on for government work. He was a [member of the Young Communist League]. . . . According to [Kurnakov's] account, Hall has an exceptionally keen mind and a broad outlook and is politically developed. At the present time H. is in charge of a group at 'CAMP-2' [Santa Fe]. He handed over to [Kurnakov] a report about the CAMP and named the key personnel employed on ENORMOZ. He decided to do this on the advice of his colleague Saville Sax, a [member of the Young Communist League] living in [New York City]. Sax's mother is a [Communist Party member] and works for Russian War Relief. With the aim of hastening a meeting with a competent person, [Hall] on the following day sent a copy of the report by [Sax] to the [Soviet Consulate]. [Yatskov] received S. [Hall] had to leave for CAMP-2 in two days' time. He was compelled to make a decision quickly. . . . [He] gave [Kurnakov] consent to feel out [Hall], to assure him that everything was in order and to arrange liaison with him. [Hall] left his photograph and came to an understanding with [Kurnakov] about a place for meeting him. . . . We consider it expedient to maintain liaison with [Sax] and not to bring in anybody else. . . . We shall send the details by post." New York station to Pavel Fitin, Moscow, November 12, 1944, No. 1585, VENONA files.

† Joseph Albright and Marcia Kunstel's *BOMBSHELL* provides a thorough and reliable account of Ted Hall's brief but important career as a Soviet source.

proached Feklissov and told him about his wife's brother and sister-in-law, both of whom had backgrounds in the American Communist Party. For several years, Rosenberg had been a trusted agent and supervisor of other agents (or "probationers" as the Soviets referred to their American sources), specializing in scientific and defense plant secrets. "We consider it necessary to organize the filming of [Julius Rosenberg's] probationers' materials by [Rosenberg] himself" at the apartment of a Soviet operative, the New York station informed Pavel Fitin in Moscow in a May 22, 1944, cable. By June, Moscow was told that photographing the Rosenberg group's material had shifted to the apartment of Leonid Kvasnikov ("Anton"), the Soviets' scientific-technical station chief in New York. Feklissov had good reason to be struck by Rosenberg's report that his brother-in-law, David Greenglass, had been drafted into the army and now worked at one of the major Santa Fe installations involved with "Enormoz."

ENTER THE GREENGLASSES

On September 21, 1944, the station requested Moscow's permission to recruit the Greenglasses, with David's wife, Ruth, to serve as a courier for information to be provided by her husband during authorized spousal visits to Santa Fe.*[100] The Center agreed on October 3, assigned code names to the couple — "Wasp" for Ruth and "Bumblebee" (later "Caliber") for David — and recommended that they be handled directly by Harry Gold.[101] The Greenglasses, Feklissov later would report in Moscow after returning in October 1946 from his long mission in America, "are young, intelligent, capable, and politically developed people, strongly believing in the cause of communism and wishing to do their best to help our country as much as possible. They are undoubtedly devoted to us."[102]

---

* "Lately the development of new people . . . [Julius Rosenberg] recommended the wife of his wife's brother, Ruth Greenglass. . . . She is 21 years old, an [American citizen], a [member of the Young Communist League] since 1942. . . . [Rosenberg] and his wife recommend her as an intelligent and clever girl. . . . [Ruth] learned that her husband was called up by the army but he was not sent to the front. He is a mechanical engineer and is now working at the ENORMOZ plant in Santa Fe, New Mexico." New York station to Pavel Fitin, Moscow, September 21, 1944, No. 1840, VENONA files.

When David Greenglass was told in November 1944 that he would receive a two-week vacation from his duties, he asked Ruth to join him in New Mexico the following month. Before she left New York, Julius Rosenberg led Ruth through a series of instructions on how to persuade her husband, who apparently had not yet been informed of the new secret role for which his brother-in-law had volunteered him, to provide materials on his work.[103] On December 5, Julius drafted a remarkable third-person account of the discussion, which Feklissov duly forwarded to Moscow:

> The following is a record of the conversation held by Julius, Ethel, and Ruth.
>
> First of all, Julius inquired of Ruth how she felt about the Soviet Union and how deep in general her Communist convictions went, whereupon she replied without hesitation that, to her, socialism was the sole hope of the world and the Soviet Union commanded her deepest admiration.
>
> Julius then wanted to know whether she would be willing to help the Soviet Union. She replied very simply and sincerely that it would be a privilege; when Ethel mentioned David, she assured us [Julius and Ethel] that [in] her judgment [this] was also David's understanding.*
>
> Julius then explained his connections with certain people interested in supplying the Soviet Union with urgently needed technical information it could not obtain through the regular channels and impressed upon her the tremendous importance of the project in which David is now at work. Therefore, she was to ask him the following kinds of questions:
>
> 1. How many people were now employed there?
> 2. What part of the project was already in operation, if any; were they encountering any difficulties and why; how were they resolving their problems?
> 3. How much of an area did the present setup cover?
> 4. How many buildings were there and their layout; were they going to build any more?
> 5. How well guarded was the place?

---

* "[Ruth Greenglass] has agreed to cooperate with us in drawing in [David Greenglass] with a view to ENORMOZ. On summons from [David] she is leaving on November 22 for the CAMP-2 area. [David] will have a week's meeting. Before [Ruth's] departure [Julius Rosenberg] will carry out two briefing meetings." Kvasnikov to Fitin, November 14, 1944, No. 1600, VENONA files.

Julius then instructed her that under no circumstances should they discuss any of these things inside a room or indeed anywhere except out-of-doors and under no circumstances to make any notes of any kind. She was simply to commit to memory as much as possible. Ethel here interposed to stress the need for the utmost care and caution in informing David of the work in which Julius was engaged and that, for his own safety, all other political discussion and activity on his part should be subdued.

At this point, we asked Ruth to repeat our instructions, which she did satisfactorily.[104]

The station informed Moscow separately on December 7 that "[Julius Rosenberg] held a conversation with [Ruth Greenglass] about her assistance to us. She agreed to carry out assignments that would come from [Rosenberg], and, as [Rosenberg] has done, expressed confidence that [David Greenglass] would agree to help." Julius Rosenberg, the station's memorandum continued, had met with Ruth Greenglass three times before her departure "and held a briefing corresponding to our instructions," the discussion described in the December 5 report.[105]

The recruitment of David Greenglass thus posed no special problems. When Ruth returned from New Mexico in mid-December, she informed Julius that David agreed that data concerning the atomic bomb should not be held secretly by the United States. He would begin immediately to assist the Soviet Union in acquiring information, while cautioning Ruth that security measures at Camp 2 were extremely strict.

Greenglass also told his wife that he would travel to New York in mid-January, and Rosenberg suggested to Ruth that a Soviet operative should contact him directly because he (Julius) was not familiar with the technical details of "Enormoz." Rosenberg then told Feklissov that he believed Greenglass would welcome such a meeting.*[106]

---

* "[Ruth Greenglass] has returned from a trip to see [David Greenglass]. [David] expressed his readiness to help in throwing light on the work being carried on at CAMP-2 and stated that he had already given thought to this question earlier. [David] said that the authorities of the Camp were openly taking all precautionary measures to prevent information about ENORMOZ falling into Russian hands. This is causing serious discontent among the progressive [workers]. . . . [I]n the middle of January, [David Greenglass] will be in [New York City]. [Julius Rosenberg], referring to his ignorance of the [atomic energy] problem, expresses the wish that our man should meet [David Greenglass] and interrogate him personally. He asserts that [Greenglass] would be very glad of such a meeting. Do you

True to his brother-in-law's word, when Greenglass returned to New York the following month, he brought with him materials on "Camp 2" and news that work there was far behind schedule; the documents and information he gave to Julius Rosenberg were, in turn, passed along to Soviet operatives. He confirmed the presence of J. Robert Oppenheimer and George Kistakowsky among the leading scientists at the camp. He noted at one point in his debriefing that a visiting army colonel at the facility had exclaimed: "If we work this slowly in future, the Germans and the Russians may be the first to use the bombs while we still don't have them."[107] The comment undoubtedly reinforced the views held by many Soviet operatives that Americans viewed the Soviet Union, despite wartime cooperation, as a potential adversary.

Prior to Greenglass's arrival in New York, Moscow had provided its station there with a list of questions for him:

1. Data on Camp 2: location, [machine] shops and their purpose, ways of communicating, power engineering, supplies, buildings, internal regulations?
2. Data about workers at Camp 2 known to [Greenglass]: names, posts, character of work, living conditions, etc. Indicate separately who belongs to the sector of progressive people whom [Greenglass] mentions?
3. Data about work at Los Alamos, 40 miles from Camp 2.[108]

In early January 1945, Julius Rosenberg and David Greenglass met for a discussion that preceded David's delivery of the new material. Feklissov provided Moscow with an account of the talk:

[Julius Rosenberg] and [David Greenglass] met at the flat of [Greenglass's] mother . . . [Rosenberg's] wife and [Greenglass] are sister and brother. After a conversation in which [Greenglass] confirmed his consent to pass us data about work in "Camp 2" known to him, [Rosenberg] discussed with him a list of questions [those previously described] to which it would be helpful to have answers . . . general questions clarifying the kind of work done there.

[Greenglass] has the rank of sergeant. He works in the camp as a mechanic, carrying out various instructions from his superiors.

---

consider such a meeting advisable? If not, I shall be obliged to draw up a questionnaire and pass it to [Rosenberg]. Report whether you have any questions of priority interest to us." Kvasnikov to Fitin, December 16, 1944, No. 1773, VENONA files.

The place where [Greenglass] works is a plant where various devices for measuring and studying the explosive power of various explosives in different forms (lenses) are being produced. Experimental explosions are being carried out in proving grounds ([Greenglass] calls them "sites"). To be admitted to a proving ground, one must have a special pass. [Greenglass] says that he noticed there were at least four proving grounds where they were sending various materials and things. . . . As far as we understand, research and selection of explosives for imparting a necessary speed to "Enormoz's" neutrons to get fission (explosion) are being executed in those proving grounds. It seems to us that [Greenglass] doesn't know all the details of the project. At the end of his report, he lists people whom he considers progressive and pro-Soviet.*[109]

Feklissov, Kvasnikov, Yatskov, and the other Soviet operatives in New York were delighted with David and Ruth Greenglass and not simply because of their willingness to cooperate. Just as important, the Greenglasses represented a turnkey, "ready-to-spy" agent group, a source and his courier, husband and wife. Moreover, Ruth intended to move to New Mexico, which would provide her with daily access to her husband's work. The station enthusiastically reported this news to Moscow:

In late February, as soon as she receives a railroad ticket, [Ruth Greenglass] will go to live in Albuquerque, where most wives of camp workers live. . . . She intends to live there for 6–7 months and then return to [New York] to give birth to a child. Before her departure, we will ask her to give us material and verbal passwords in case we need to restore contact with her. After . . . finding an apartment, she will give us her address in a letter to her mother-in-law. We assume that [Ruth's] stay in Albuquerque will allow us to study better the working procedures and people at the

---

* "[David Greenglass] has arrived in [New York City] on leave. He has confirmed his agreement to help us. In addition to the information passed to us through [Ruth Greenglass], he has given us a hand-written plan of the layout of CAMP-2 and facts known to him about the work and the personnel. The basic task of the camp is to make the mechanism which is to serve as the detonator. Experimental work is being carried out on the construction of a tube of this kind and experiments are being tried with explosive. . . ." Kvasnikov to Fitin, January 8, 1945, No. 28, VENONA files.

camp and, in case [David] has valuable data, she can come to [New York] to inform us.[110]

With the Greenglasses, Ted Hall and his friend Saville Sax, "Persian," and reports that Harry Gold had picked up Klaus Fuchs's trail, the New York "XY line" station began 1945 confident of its immediate and future potential.

Harry Gold's remaining link to the British physicist was through Fuchs's sister in Cambridge, Massachusetts, Mrs. Heineman, whose friendship Gold (now code-named "Arno") cultivated. Moscow even proposed bringing the woman* into their network, a notion promptly rejected by Leonid Kvasnikov. Nevertheless, when Gold visited her in Cambridge in early November 1944, she reported that her brother had phoned from Chicago. Fuchs was now stationed in New Mexico and promised to visit his sister for two weeks over Christmas.[111] At a subsequent December meeting with Mrs. Heineman, Gold gave her a small piece of paper with the telephone number of a Yatskov agent code-named "Guron" whom Fuchs should phone.[†112]

For whatever reason, Fuchs did not make contact over Christmas. It was only two months later that Yatskov learned from "Guron" of a stranger's call inviting someone named "Raymond" (the name by which Fuchs knew Gold) to visit him at his sister's home.[113] (At this time, Yatskov proposed—and Moscow rejected—the notion that the NKGB find a woman who could double as Fuchs's courier and lover!)[114]

Gold finally renewed his relationship with Fuchs on February 21, 1945, in Cambridge, initially under the guise of a good friend visiting both the physicist and his sister, even bringing gifts for her and her children. Fuchs explained that he had not received an expected leave at Christmas, hence the delay in reaching the Boston area. Later that day, Fuchs finally told his story, as reported by Harry Gold:

K. outlined the setup at the camp to me:

a. When he went there in August there were only 2500 to 3000 people. Now it has expanded to 45,000!

* Code-named "Ant" but whom Gold called "Mrs. D." in his memos to NKGB operatives.

† "On [Gold's] last visit to [Fuchs's] sister it became known that [Fuchs] has not left for [England] but is at [Los Alamos]. He flew to Chicago and telephoned his sister. He named the state where the camp is and promised to come on leave for Christmas. He is taking steps to establish liaison with [Gold] while he is on leave." New York station to Moscow, November 16, 1944, No. 1606, VENONA files.

b. The work being carried on is the actual production of "factory" bombs. Employed there are physicists, mathematicians, chemists, engineers—civil, mechanical, electrical, chemical—and many other types of technical help, as well as a U.S. Army Engineer Detachment.

c. They are progressing very well and are expected to go into full-scale production in about three months—but K. was hesitant about this date and said he would not like to be held to it.

d. The area is about 40 miles N.W. of Santa Fe and covers the grounds of Los Alamos Ranch, a former Ranch School. K. is allowed only one day a month off to go shopping in Santa Fe (as are all others), and we made a date for the first Saturday [there]. I am to get off at the bus station at Shelby and set my watch by the large clock on San Francisco. Then I am to meet him at 4 P.M. on the Castillo St. Bridge crossing the Santa Fe River. The waiting time is 10 minutes. If we do not meet, the same procedure is to be repeated month after month. Should a substitute have to come (though he would very much prefer me) he is to be identified as follows: The man will have a yellow pencil between two blue ones in his lapel and he will be carrying a copy of Bennett Cerf's *Try and Stop Me*. K. will say to him, "How is your brother Raymond?" and the answer will be "Not well, he has been in the hospital for two weeks." Final identification is to be by means of two [halves] of a paper torn in a jagged pattern, one of which K. has. K. was really prepared and gave me a bus schedule and a map of Santa Fe—he advises me not to go directly there but to a nearby city such as Albuquerque. He also gave me the material I submitted, and we parted at 3:30 P.M.

My attempt to give him money was unsuccessful—but I did not offend him as I led up to the subject very delicately. He says that he is making all he needs. K. does, however, want one thing: When we enter Kiel and Berlin in Germany, he wants the Gestapo headquarters there searched and his dossier (which is very complete) destroyed before it falls into other hands. This, I told him, we would try to do if at all possible.[115]

Fuchs also expressed to Harry Gold concern about protecting his father, who was then being held in a concentration camp in Germany "and may be in a territory occupied by the Red Army. In case [Fuchs's] father is found among prisoners in a concentration camp, we would have to pay special attention to him. Inform us about his liberation, so we can pass the news to [Fuchs]."[116] Moscow especially appreciated Fuchs's rejection of money payments—in this case, the $1,000 offered by Gold: "He wants to save the clean idealism of his relations with us and doesn't want to bring an element of material interest into them."[*][117]

What a difference a few months had made. After years of having been berated by Moscow for nonperformance on "Enormoz," Kvasnikov dispatched a February 1945 report outlining what he viewed as his station's successes in various fields of scientific and technical espionage:

> Currently the network of [agents] is mainly rather efficient and . . . highly qualified technically. [Most agents] are people with great technical erudition and knowledge of their business. Mainly there are engineers with a layer of scientific workers. [Most] . . . work with us not for selfish ends but on the basis of a friendly attitude toward our country on an ideological basis. There are many compatriots [members of the CPUSA] among our [agents]. . . .[118]

Despite this recent record of achievement, Kvasnikov and his colleagues expressed concern about the growing vigilance of American counterintelligence, directed (or so they believed) against Soviet operatives and agents.[119] Of particular concern to them was Julius Rosenberg, who had been fired from his plant because of Communist Party membership. Thus, Moscow wrote Kvasnikov on February 23, 1945:

> The latest events with [Julius Rosenberg], his having been fired, are highly serious and demand on our part, first, a correct assessment of what happened, and second, a decision about [Rosenberg's] role in future. Deciding the latter, we should proceed from the fact that, in him, we have a man devoted to us, whom we

---

* But Moscow had not yet received the report of Gold's February 23, 1945, meeting with Fuchs when it fired off this anxious February 27 inquiry to the New York station: "Advise forthwith: Exactly where and in what capacity [Fuchs] is working in [Los Alamos]; the object of his trip to CHICAGO [and] whom he met there; what he has been doing since August; why did he not have a discussion . . . [undeciphered] . . . [Gold] about [Fuchs's] arrival, how in detail their meeting went off; what materials were received [from Fuchs]." No. 183, VENONA files.

can trust completely, a man who by his practical activities for several years has shown how strong is his desire to help our country. Besides, in [Rosenberg] we have a capable agent who knows how to work with people and has solid experience in recruiting new agents.

One must suppose that, besides the motive stated when sacking [Rosenberg] of his belonging to the compatriots, the competitors [the FBI] may have other data compromising him, including information on his liaison with us. Proceeding precisely from this, we think that [Rosenberg] shouldn't start any legal actions to restore his job, leaving this matter to the trade-union, which must do what is being done for other members of the trade-union in this sort of case. There shouldn't be pressure from [Rosenberg] on this matter.

Though we don't have any documentary data, saying that the [FBI is] aware to an extent of his connection with us, we, nevertheless, must take into account the circumstances preceding [Rosenberg's] sacking—his extremely active work, especially in the first period working with us, and his certain haste in the work. We consider it necessary to take immediate measures to secure both [Rosenberg] and the agents with whom he was connected.

Before ceasing direct connection with [Rosenberg], it is necessary to explain to him the need to halt personal contact and to instruct him about the need to be careful, to look around himself. One should continue paying him maintenance. Warn him not to take any important decisions about his future work without our knowledge and consent. In our current relations with him, it must be explained that his fate is far from indifferent to us, that we value him as a worker, and that he, undoubtedly, may and must rely on assistance from our side.[120]

Moscow's NKGB leadership thus focused intensely on Julius Rosenberg's past, present, and future role in its American network. The same February 23, 1945, letter instructed the New York station to secure his safety without completely severing relations. On February 16, another Moscow memorandum had reached New York that detailed the measures to be taken. It ordered Rosenberg released from his duties as a group handler, directed that all his sources (including the Greenglasses, presumably) be transferred to other controllers, and instructed Alexander Feklissov to stop meeting Rosenberg. This cable also ordered future contact between Julius and Feklissov to be made through a courier. Moscow recommended Lona Cohen ("Leslie") for this role, herself an agent for the past three years and the wife of Morris Cohen ("Volunteer"), a long-term NKGB agent.[121]

Morris Cohen* had become a Communist as a young man during the early 1920s, he claimed, after listening to the journalist-revolutionary John Reed speak in his Lower East Side neighborhood. Cohen joined the Abraham Lincoln Battalion during the Spanish Civil War and was recruited for Soviet intelligence work in 1938 by Alexander Orlov, then an NKVD general but soon to become one of its leading defectors.

Upon returning to the United States from Spain, Cohen reported to Semyon Semyonov, who described him, in a report to Moscow, as "exceptionally honest, developed, politically literate, [and] ready to devote his life to our work."[122] Drafted into the U.S. Army in 1942, Cohen fought in Europe for the remainder of the war before returning to his duties for the NKGB. Meanwhile, his wife, Lona, also had been drawn into NKGB service, prior to Morris's departure for the army. She, too, Semyonov wrote Moscow, is "devoted to us . . . [and] may work as a courier. [She should] maintain a secret address. Subsequently, she must work as [her husband's] assistant."[123]

But Moscow's instructions regarding the reorganization of Julius Rosenberg's agent network required *immediate* use of Lona Cohen's services rather than waiting for Morris's return at war's end. In February 1945, Moscow told New York that "a number of instructive conversations about prudence and *konspiratsia* in our work should be held with [Lona]. She should also be taught a number of practical methods for checking oneself when going to and departing from a meeting."[124] By then, Anatoly Yatskov had begun preparing Lona Cohen for her new assignment.[125]

At this time, the New York station's preparations for future meetings continued on other fronts as well. The next scheduled contact between Klaus Fuchs and Harry Gold, fixed for the first Sunday in June 1945, suddenly involved Lona Cohen as well. But why? Why, Moscow asked its New York operatives, should Fuchs now have to send a prearranged letter to Lona's address in case of unexpected changes? Why not continue to use his sister as a contact? And why such a long period between meetings?[126]

Kvasnikov responded on March 2 with logical answers to these com-

---

* Allen Weinstein interviewed Morris Cohen in 1995 at his KGB hospital-nursing home in Moscow. He died in 1996.

plex questions. Fuchs himself had requested the "long breaks between meetings [held] in the 'Nature Reserve' region [apparently a reference to the New Mexico atomic "camps"] for security purposes and because, by that time, [he] will have at his disposal the results of work on preparing 'Enormoz' equipment for a test that is to be carried out in a different place [apparently a reference to the first atomic bomb detonated in the desert later that year]." As for using Lona Cohen's address instead of Mrs. Heineman's as they had done earlier, the Cambridge woman intended to divorce her husband—or so Kvasnikov had been told. Frequent trips by Gold to Cambridge at this time, therefore, could compromise Fuchs's sister.[127]

Nevertheless, Harry Gold and not Lona Cohen remained Klaus Fuchs's courier. He would also become, briefly, the NKGB liaison to David and Ruth Greenglass as well. Only Theodore Hall, among the group of sources being tapped by Soviet operatives in New Mexico, continued his link to the NKGB along less traditional lines, in this case through his young Communist friend Saville Sax. In March 1945, Hall wrote Sax asking him to come to Albuquerque.[128] But it was May before his friend was able to make the trip. Sax traveled by bus and was stopped on arrival in Albuquerque by immigration agents interested in his citizenship, his draft document, and his reason for being there. Sax explained that he was considering transfer to a local university, where he eventually spent several days attending lectures to burnish his alibi.

Hall had smuggled a number of manuscripts out of his installation, which he rewrote with milk on a newspaper (evidently an available variant of "invisible ink"), burning the originals.[129] Yatskov spent much time developing and processing the material once Sax had returned with it on May 11: "With our workload, this method of conveying material is extremely undesirable," the station complained to Moscow. "We couldn't discern several words in the report, but there were not many such words; the material generally is highly valuable."[130] Hall had passed on data concerning the design of the atomic bomb.*[131]

---

* "[Theodore Hall's] material contains: (a) A list of [eight] places where work on ENORMOZ is being carried out . . . (b) A brief description of the four methods of production of 25—the diffusion, thermal diffusion, electromagnetic, and spectrographic methods. The material has not been fully worked over. We shall let you know the contents of the rest later." Kvasnikov to Fitin, May 26, 1945, No. 799, VENONA files. Nor were the materials Harry Gold obtained from Klaus Fuchs in February unappreciated by those working on the Soviet atomic bomb project, as an April 10, 1945, cable from Moscow to the New York station indicated: "[Fuchs's] information . . . on the atomic bomb . . . is of great value. Apart from the data on the atomic mass of the nuclear explosive and on the details of the explosive

It was Hall himself who suggested to Sax, after hearing of his interrogation at the bus terminal, that Soviet intelligence send a female courier to him in future. This would appear more natural, and the opening was soon filled by Lona Cohen.[132]

Sax also reported (to Kvasnikov) Hall's indiscretion in a talk with a Los Alamos colleague in early 1945. The other scientist had expressed irritation that the American and British governments were not sharing atomic secrets with the Soviet Union. If he had an opportunity, Hall's associate insisted, he would inform the Russians about the project. Hall responded that he had already taken steps in this direction and began encouraging his colleague to do the same. At that time, his fellow-"progressive" backed down, denied any intent to spy, and thereafter avoided Hall. Yet Hall believed that he would not be reported to security personnel because of his colleague's apparent political views.

After reviewing Sax's report, Kvasnikov decided to continue young Hall's education in tradecraft through future contact directly with a Soviet agent. He dispatched Lona Cohen to Denver in mid-July and told her to await further instructions, without discussing the purpose of the trip.[133] Moscow approved Lona's new role as Hall's courier. However, it forbade any meeting between Hall, an indiscreet source, and an actual Soviet NKGB operative.[134]

As early as March 1945, the New York station began preparing for Harry Gold's visit with Klaus Fuchs in June. Yatskov informed Moscow that Gold, who had "troubles with his throat constantly," would identify a resort or sanitarium in New Mexico's dry climate where he could spend time, nominally on vacation, while arranging his meetings. Gold proposed taking his mother, "who also needed treatment and rest." With Moscow's approval, the pair left for Colorado, after which Gold would travel to Albuquerque for scheduled meetings with Fuchs and the Greenglasses.[135]

While awaiting additional materials from American and British scientists working on "Enormoz," the First and Second Directorates of the NKGB prepared to celebrate the 220th anniversary of the Academy of Sciences of the USSR (known, prior to 1917, as the Russian Academy of Sciences). Semyon Semyonov was assigned the task of developing

---

method of actuating [the bomb], it contains information received for the first time from you about the electromagnetic method of separation of ENORMOZ." No. 349, VENONA files.

personal links to key American scientists who would be invited to the festivities in Moscow and Leningrad.[136] However, at this delicate stage in work on the atomic bomb, none of the American invitees—Ernst Lawrence, Arthur Compton, Enrico Fermi, and others—were given permission by the U.S. government to attend.*

From London, on June 12, Guy Burgess informed Moscow that Prime Minister Winston Churchill had forbidden a delegation of eight British scientists to travel to Moscow for the event. Apparently, Soviet intelligence in both America and England had nurtured the naive hope that the anniversary celebration could reap a scientific bonanza through Western participation. Instead, the Anglo-American rebuff reinforced the views of those in the USSR who believed that, after Hitler's defeat, Western hostility would quickly replace wartime cooperation with the Soviet Union.[137]

But Harry Gold's visit to Klaus Fuchs and the Greenglasses in early June 1945 produced a rich harvest of fresh information and material from the heart of the "Enormoz" project. Returning to New York on June 11, Gold handed Anatoly Yatskov materials received from Fuchs and Greenglass on the design of the atomic bomb.[138]

Gold first visited David and Ruth Greenglass at their Albuquerque home on June 3. "I proved my credentials," he wrote in his report for Yatskov, "and they received me very well. D. asked me to return that afternoon as he had very important material for me. He said they had expected me two weeks later, but that he could prepare the stuff within a few hours since it had been organized. I left them a considerable sum of money which both were very glad to receive." Greenglass turned over his material to Gold later that day.[139]

Yatskov and his colleagues were not entirely impressed with the data: "[Greenglass's] material, though it gives some data, is low in quality and far from processed," the station informed Moscow on June 26. "We suppose this is due to the insufficient qualifications of [Greenglass], on the one hand, and to [Gold's] sudden arrival, on the other, when he had no prepared materials."[140]

Klaus Fuchs conveyed a more extensive and valuable batch of material at his meeting with Harry Gold. The project was obviously entering its final stage, Fuchs noted, with people at his camp working eighteen- to twenty-hour-a-day shifts. Fuchs also informed the courier

---

* NKGB headquarters cabled its New York station a list of dozens of such scientists "expected to come to MOSCOW" for the celebration, few of whom, if any, actually attended. April 3, 1945, Nos. 311, 314, VENONA files.

(inaccurately, as it turned out) that the atomic bomb's first test would take place soon at a spot he knew only as "I," with the bomb (he had been told) somehow placed inside a B-29 on the ground. Fuchs was certain that it would be impossible to hide the explosion from anyone within a radius of several hundred miles. Somewhat more accurately, Fuchs added that, if this test went well, the second test would be carried out in battle conditions in the South Pacific very soon.[141] (In the end, the Japanese city of Hiroshima, and not some Japanese-occupied Pacific atoll, was chosen as the atomic bomb's first overseas target.) Additional information provided by Greenglass and Hall during this period expanded Soviet knowledge of the weapon being tested in the desert.[142]

The test finally occurred on July 16, one day before the opening of the Potsdam Peace Conference, where Truman told Stalin of the new weapon. Stalin's calm and lack of surprise, when informed of this super-bomb with massive destructive force to be used shortly against Japan, was understandable given the constant flow of information Soviet scientists were receiving from their intelligence service throughout the war years. Nonetheless, even before leaving Potsdam, Stalin instructed Igor Kurchatov, the physicist in charge of the USSR's atomic project, to accelerate work on the Soviet bomb.[143]

"ENORMOZ" IN THE POSTWAR WORLD

Nor did the bombs dropped on Hiroshima and Nagasaki, followed rapidly by Japan's surrender and the end of the war, dull Moscow's hunger for more information on "Enormoz." Kvasnikov received an impatient communique from NKGB headquarters on August 18 reminding him that it awaited data on the two recent atomic blasts. Moscow was puzzled by his silence.[144] Kvasnikov had expected a report from Lona Cohen, who had gone to New Mexico to meet with Hall. Unfortunately, Hall had postponed the meeting.[145] Finally, on August 25, Kvasnikov responded that the station had not yet received agent reports on the explosions in Japan. As for Fuchs and Greenglass, their next meetings with Gold were scheduled for mid-September.[146]

Moscow found Kvasnikov's excuses unacceptable and reminded him on August 28 of the even greater future importance of information on atomic research, now that the Americans had produced the most destructive weapon known to humankind:

In the light of statements by representatives of the American government about the successful creation of the atomic bomb and its use in battle conditions, we are faced with an absolutely urgent task of intensifying and expanding our work on "Enormoz" . . . which must be regarded as of paramount importance in the work of your station. The station chief is personally responsible for this area. . . .

We consider the agent situation in the Country [the United States] exceptionally favorable in this direction. A number of facts known to us prove that: for instance, an unknown person bringing to the consulate an important document on "Enormoz," motivated by the wish to inform our country; [Hall's] coming to us; the successful recruitment of [David Greenglass] and "Persian," as well as agents' reports that among workers taking an active part in "Enormoz's" work, there are people who openly manifest sympathy for us and express the opinion that our country should be informed about the results achieved. . . .

Statements by Truman and Churchill, relating to the atomic bomb, state clearly that all work on "Enormoz" is being carried out in strict secrecy from the rest of the world, including our country, and that this policy will remain in the future. This circumstance should be skillfully used as an argument while recruiting agents among scientists, willing to help us but having the illusion that there are no secrets from our country.[147]

Moscow demanded that its Soviet operatives in America develop new recruits and more information on "Enormoz" immediately after the war's end. NKGB cables even suggested that couriers establish their own base camps in mid-American cities such as Chicago, Cincinnati, and Denver rather than traveling from New York to New Mexico for every meeting with a source.[148] Thus, Pavel Fitin wrote Vsevolod Merkulov, setting out the task that lay ahead:

Practical use of the atomic bomb by the Americans means the completion of the first stage of enormous scientific-research work on the problem of releasing intra-atomic energy. This fact opens a new epoch in science and technology and will undoubtedly result in rapid development of the entire problem of "Enormoz" — using intra-atomic energy not only for military purposes but in the entire modern economy. All this gives the problem of "Enormoz" a leading place in our intelligence work and demands immediate measures to strengthen our technical intelligence.[149]

In this report, Fitin singled out the Soviets' main "atomic sources" in the United States: Klaus Fuchs, Theodore Hall, David Greenglass, and Alfred Slack. The first three agents were all at "Camp Y" in Los Alamos, New Mexico ("Camp 2"). Slack, at the station's instruction, had acquired a job in "Camp 1" beginning in December 1944, but, as Fitin noted, "because of especially difficult conditions and despite constant attempts, contact with [Slack] failed to be established."[150]

Ruth and David Greenglass traveled to New York in mid-September 1945, where David met with Anatoly Yatskov, whose cable to Moscow reported:

> The meeting was quite short, since [Greenglass] had to remain at home that afternoon (it was on the eve of his departure) and broke out [to meet only] for a short while. In our conversation, it was established that [Greenglass] worked in secondary workshops of the "Nature Reserve" [the New Mexico atomic camps], producing tools, instruments for the "Nature Reserve," and sometimes details for the balloon [the atomic bomb]. Thus, for example, detonators for the fuse of the balloon's explosive were made in their workshop, and [Greenglass] passed to us a cartridge for such a detonator. [He] doesn't have access to the balloon itself or the main shops. Information about the balloon he is giving us comes from stories of friends who work in the "Nature Reserve" and refers to personnel having access to scientific materials (the so-called red button personnel. [Greenglass] refers [also] to "blue button personnel," i.e., auxiliary personnel).
>
> [Greenglass] was assigned to gather detailed characteristics on people he considered suitable for drawing into our work.
>
> In addition, [he was given] the task of gathering samples of materials used in the balloon, such as tube alloy, explosives, etc. Materials sometimes come to [Greenglass's] workshop.[151]

It would have been preferable, in Yatskov's opinion, to send Lona Cohen to Albuquerque to collect this material on December 21, the assigned date for the next meeting with David Greenglass.[152] Instead, Ruth Greenglass was told to receive all of it from David. NKGB headquarters in Moscow gave its New York station permission to pay the Greenglasses $300 for services rendered.[153]

David Greenglass's technical limitations and restricted access to major sectors of the Los Alamos project made him an important but not pivotal figure in NKGB intelligence collection. The same could not be said of the Soviets' invaluable insider, Klaus Fuchs, who continued his meetings with Harry Gold in Santa Fe on September 19.[154] Again, Gold took his mother on the mission, nominally to relax at an Arizona resort before moving on to Albuquerque, changing buses there for Santa Fe and the rendezvous with Fuchs.[155] Gold's detailed report, written after his return to New York, was not conveyed to Moscow until October 26:

> For the first time since I have known him, [Fuchs] was late—by fifteen minutes. He came with a car and picked me up. We drove out into the mountains beyond S.F., and he explained the reason for his tardiness by saying that he had great difficulty in breaking away from his friends at the "Zapovednik" ["Reserve"]. He said further that we had made an error by choosing to meet in the evening. It would have been better to come together in the afternoon when everyone was busy shopping. In fact, [Fuchs] said, it was very bad for me to come to S.F. in any case but that we could not have foreseen this since the last meeting. He was very nervous (the first time I have seen him so), and I was not too calm myself inwardly.
>
> His first remark was "Well, were you impressed?" I answered that I was even more than impressed and was even somehow horrified. [Fuchs] said that the test shot had far exceeded expectations but that these had been purposely toned down because the results of the calculations showed them to be so incredible. [Fuchs] had been present at the test shot, some 20 miles away.
>
> Regarding the future, [Fuchs] says that a research institute will be established in [Great Britain], but that he will most likely be here until at least the beginning of the year. He agreed, however, that it was a good idea to make an arrangement to meeting in [Great Britain]. The city is London; the place Mornington Crescent, along the Crescent; the date is the first Saturday of the month after he returns. So, on the first Saturday of each month thereafter, the time 8 o'clock in the evening. [Fuchs] is to carry a copy of Life magazine. Our man is to carry three books tied together with a stout twine and held by a finger. [Fuchs's] remark will be: "Can you tell me the way to Harvard Square?" ([Fuchs] is to speak first). Our man's remark is: "Yes, but excuse me a minute—I have an awful cold" (and our man is to blow his nose into a handkerchief).
>
> [Fuchs] gave me material that is excellent and fully covers everything. He dropped me off in the outskirts of S.F. The next

meeting will be in [Cambridge, Massachusetts], probably in November or December. I am to keep in touch with his sister so as to be advised when.

After a few bad moments of waiting for the bus, I left S.F. with no mishaps. S.F., incidentally, is very well watched, and when I came in, I purposely got off the bus about one-half mile from the station.[156]

Upon Gold's return from New Mexico, he informed Yatskov that security surrounding the atomic camps was "much tougher than it was during his visit there in June. Local residents . . . treat outsiders very suspiciously."[157]

In addition to the technical data, Fuchs gave Gold a copy of a memorandum sent by a number of scientists at Los Alamos to the American government, signed by the majority of prominent scientists at the camp and, according to Fuchs, expressing the virtually universal views of scientific and technical personnel at the facility. An October 29, 1945, Moscow memorandum summarized its contents, at least from a Soviet perspective:

This memorandum assesses the balloon [the atomic bomb] as a super-destructive means of war and expresses certainty in the possibility of exercising international control over the [bomb's] production. It urges creation of an international organization to control the use of atomic energy and proposes to let other countries know about secrets connected with the [bomb's] production. It also emphasizes the role of the USSR in solving political and economic problems and talks about the need for agreement among the USSR, France, the U.S., England, and China.

The memorandum underlines that within a few years other countries, one way or another, will be producing the [bombs] and points out that competition in their production will yield most disastrous results.

[Fuchs] points out that the memorandum is being examined currently by the President, and the association has not received an official answer yet. However, unofficially, the secretary of the government committee on "Enormoz" stated the government's complete agreement with the memorandum's ideas. But there was opposition from some people in Washington, who argued that in the contemporary "delicate domestic and international situation," accepting those proposals could cause damage to the country. Many in the association take the afore-cited unofficial declaration by the government with great skepticism, and [Fuchs] points out that feelings of distrust toward the government are very strong in it.

[Harry Gold] points out that in [Los Alamos] and [Santa Fe], watchfulness over inhabitants is noticeable and that the number of agents, checking out all the newcomers, has increased considerably. One concludes from this an intensification of the U.S. War Department's effort to keep secret the work on "Enormoz."[158]

Both increased postwar American counterintelligence activity and Elizabeth Bentley's defection in November 1945 quickly undermined the entire fabric of Soviet intelligence work on "Enormoz" and numerous other projects in the United States. Even before Bentley had begun to cooperate with the FBI, tensions that affected NKGB operations had increased between the United States and the USSR in the first months of the Truman presidency. When FBI agents in October 1945 briefly detained one of Anatoly Yatskov's agents, "Guron," Moscow ordered Yatskov to halt indefinitely all meetings with agents.[159]

That same month, on October 26, 1945, New York's "political" station received word from one of its key sources, Justice Department employee Judith Coplon ("Sima"), that the FBI had been listening to Robert Oppenheimer's telephone conversations. Beginning as early as 1941, Oppenheimer had been a constant, if unsuccessful, target for recruitment. Coplon handed over an excerpt from a May 10, 1943, FBI memo on the practice: "Eavesdropping on the telephones of Professor Haakon Chevalier . . . and Professor J. Robert Oppenheimer . . . through a secret informer SF-25 shows that they called to Thomas Addis. . . . Chevalier called the subject on August 13, 21 and 29, 1941. . . . Chevalier and Oppenheimer have a reputation as extremely liberal and are suspected of belonging to the Communist Party."[160]

Although interesting to review, Coplon's material was not of immediate concern to the NKGB since Oppenheimer was not a Soviet agent. Julius Rosenberg was, however, and at this time Leonid Kvasnikov and his colleagues at the NKGB's New York technical station were deeply concerned with Rosenberg's situation. After he was fired on security grounds, the station had instructed him to halt all active intelligence work. Although Rosenberg found other employment, he wished to resume his work as an agent. Thus, the station wrote Moscow on June 26, 1945: "[Rosenberg] is slightly pained [and] suffers from the fact that he is left without people but fully understands the correctness of our plan to compartmentalize his group. The main thing he can't reconcile himself to is his relative inactivity. At every meeting, he asks us to allow him to bring materials out of the plant and thus benefit us."[161]

The NKGB station and Moscow controllers admired Rosenberg's zealousness but, at the same time, feared his potential for damaging the entire network. For example, during one of their 1945 meetings, Feklissov noted that Rosenberg was under surveillance, presumably by the FBI.[162] Nevertheless, he was one of the few American sources whom Soviet operatives told about Elizabeth Bentley's November 1945 defection. Feklissov arranged an urgent meeting with Rosenberg through another source, Joel Barr ("Meter"), on December 15. The meeting procedure specified that Ethel Rosenberg visit the drugstore on their street to indicate that it was safe to proceed. Without approaching Feklissov, she was to buy something and then return home. Five minutes later, Feklissov would come to their apartment.

That afternoon, Feklissov left his home and checked for surveillance. He went first to the Brooklyn maternity hospital where his wife was awaiting the birth of their child; he then spent time at a Turkish bath. For a professional operative, all of this amounted to standard procedure to detect possible surveillance. Finally, Feklissov entered the drugstore at 11 P.M. and noticed Ethel making a purchase. After spotting the Russian, Ethel left. He, in turn, made a purchase and went directly to the Rosenberg home,[163] describing their conversation in a later report for the station:

We went to the kitchen and immediately began talking. I asked [Rosenberg] did he know some of [Jacob Golos's] friends. He replied he knew only [Golos] and [Bernard Schuster]. To my question as to whether he knew any woman [friends], at first he answered negatively but then added that he had an agreement with [Golos]. Every time he urgently needed to see [Golos], [Rosenberg] had to call him from a telephone booth and tell his secretary that he wanted to see him. To that secretary, he always gave only his first name, Julius. He never met her personally. But he said he had passed to [Golos] personal data on himself, "Yakov," "Meter," and "Nil." Those data were typed and therefore, perhaps, didn't fall into [Elizabeth Bentley's] hands. You must find those data in 1941–42 correspondence and compare the print of the typewriter they were typed on with one of the typewriters [Bentley] worked on. . . .

At the end of the conversation, I let [Rosenberg] know that [Golos's] secretary (I didn't name her) had betrayed us and that in this connection we worried very much about him. I instructed him on how to behave if summoned to the Hut [the FBI]. We decided he must deny belonging to the compatriots [CPUSA] because he already did so both in 1941 and 1945. If he doesn't deny it again now, as you suggest in your cable, it will be illogical. He will also deny his connections with [Golos] and [Schuster]. In case he is asked to name his friends, he will name [Joel Barr] and "Nil," who are his old friends. He will also deny all the photos and other documents of this sort, where he is shown with me, [Golos], or [Schuster]. I ordered him very strictly to burn all notes with addresses of probationers [agents] and materials that could serve as evidence of his belonging to the compatriots.

I agreed with [Rosenberg] that our connection with him would cease for three and a half months. The next meeting is fixed for the third Sunday in March 1946 at 8 P.M. at the Colony Theater, 79th Street and Second Avenue. I warned him that, possibly, another man would come to that meeting instead of me. Therefore I asked him to come to the meeting with the *Post* newspaper. Our man must have a *Reader's Digest* in his left hand. Having come up to [Rosenberg], our man must ask him: "Aren't you waiting for Al?" [Rosenberg] will answer, "No, I'm waiting for Helen." Our man must then say: "I am Helen's brother. She asked me to tell you something."[164]

In late 1945, Anatoly Yatskov and his Soviet colleagues were particularly worried not only about the exposure of Julius Rosenberg but, also, about their most important "atomic" courier, Harry Gold. By this time, Elizabeth Bentley's defection in the United States and Igor Gouzenko's in Canada had led Moscow to order the freeze of virtually all intelligence activities by the NKGB in North America, a pause that lasted until late 1947. Nevertheless, Yatskov received authorization to meet with Gold on December 19, 1945. According to Yatskov's information, Bentley had told the FBI about another major source initially coordinated by Bentley and Golos—Abraham Brothman ("Kron"). Yatskov's report of the conversation with Gold was reassuring:

I asked [Gold] under which name [Brothman] knew him, whether he knew his place of work, address, etc. He told me the following:

1. [Brothman] knows [Gold] under the name "Frank Kessler."
2. [Brothman] is aware that [Gold] lives in the Philadelphia area but doesn't know his address.

3. [Brothman] thinks [Gold] is married and has two children (in reality, however, he is still a bachelor).

Gold took the news that [Brothman] was exposed to the [FBI] with visible interest but without much anxiety. I said that . . . in case [Brothman] confessed about [Gold's] existence and described . . . [what] he knew about him, the [FBI] would try to find him. [Gold] should know that these links to him come only from [Brothman] and must not worry, since the [FBI] knows nothing about him and his work. Other connections to him are not affected, and nothing can prove his association with us. However, [Gold] must be on the alert and demonstrate tenfold prudence and attentiveness in everything.[165]

Those connected with atomic espionage at this time, in fact, were relatively safe compared with other Soviet networks in the United States because most lacked any connection to the Golos-Bentley network. Neither Earl Browder's domestic Communists nor Bentley's contacts (except for Brothman) had any links to Yatskov's "XY line" station.

After his meeting with Gold, Yatskov focused again on Klaus Fuchs, his chief source within Los Alamos. Fuchs was scheduled to deliver fresh material for Gold by leaving a package at his sister's Cambridge home.[166] Reluctant to contact Gold again so soon after their previous meeting, considering Moscow's instructions to avoid all encounters, Yatskov delayed scheduling another one until the end of 1946. He traveled to Philadelphia for the talk on December 26. Yatskov had not seen Gold for an entire year. By the time they concluded their conversation, the Soviet operative undoubtedly regretted his neglect.

Gold had been fired from his job as a chemist at a sugar plant in March 1946 when the company laid off a number of employees because of business losses. He remained unemployed until May, when Abe Brothman hired him as a chief chemist in his company. In short, the NKGB's chief courier in America now worked daily for one of his own leading sources!

Worse, still, Gold and Brothman apparently had become good friends. Gold not only confessed to his employer that he had lied about having a wife and children but told him his real name (and, presumably, his real address). Moreover, both men crossed the line between espionage and risky public activity, a perennial difficulty for Soviet networks in the United States during the 1930s and 1940s. In June and again in August, Brothman's firm fulfilled orders from the Soviet Purchasing Commission in New York, assisting in developing a plant in the USSR to produce vitamins B$_1$ and B$_2$. On several occasions, Brothman and Gold visited the Commission's headquarters to negotiate with Soviet officials.

Yatskov was outraged and rebuked Gold angrily for having violated the rules of tradecraft with his new and open relationship with Brothman. If Gold wished to go into business, the Russian observed, he should leave Brothman and start his own enterprise. "He realizes he committed a grave mistake," Yatskov reported, "and is ready to correct it at any cost."[167] As for Klaus Fuchs, Gold informed Yatskov that he had visited his sister the previous April. Fuchs had not left any materials and now lived in England. In fact, Gold recalled having read a story with an English dateline in a July 1946 *Herald Tribune* describing Fuchs's arrest for espionage.[168] That no such story had been printed was Yatskov's only consolation after this troubling discussion with a courier who came in from the cold.

When the NKGB leadership finally decided to resume intelligence activities in the United States in late 1947, their priority remained "Enormoz" and the "XY line," gathering data on nuclear research. Nowhere was this more precisely expressed than in a directive Moscow sent to its American operatives in October 1948:

> The policy being carried out by the Alpinists [the Americans] on this question proves plainly their firm intention to maintain a complete monopoly on "Enormoz" and to use the [atomic bomb] for aggressive purposes against us. According to the data we have, the [Americans] are carrying out a wide program of scientific and theoretical research on "Enormoz" and conducting feverish work on perfecting already existing types of [bombs] and creating new samples. However, this important area of work has not been fully developed by us during the period of conservation [1946–47, when Soviet agents in the U.S. were inactive and thus being "conserved"]. Neither has it been developed up to now.[169]

As part of this expanded effort, Moscow ordered the New York station to determine the address, telephone, and business situation of Abraham Brothman's firm and to restore its connection with Harry Gold.[170] Unaware of the FBI's parallel interest in him by then, NKGB operatives asked Gold to check with Brothman, especially whether he had been questioned in connection with Elizabeth Bentley's allegations. If Brothman was not aware that Bentley had exposed his secret activities, then Gold was ordered to warn him to deny everything if interrogated. The FBI had no evidence against Brothman—or so the station believed.[171] Also, the operatives were to inform Gold that Klaus Fuchs had not been compromised or arrested.[172] He was continuing secret work from Harwell, his research laboratory in the United Kingdom.

David and Ruth Greenglass also attracted renewed NKGB interest at this time. After leaving the United States in February 1947, Alexander Feklissov, in a Moscow memorandum summarizing his work, had suggested using the Greenglasses actively as couriers and "group handlers,"[173] roles similar to those previously performed by Julius Rosenberg. Moscow signified agreement with this idea the following year, especially considering David's modest scientific abilities: "[Greenglass], although he has the possibility of returning to work at an extremely important institution on 'Enormoz,' Camp 2, because of his limited education will not be able to obtain a position in which he could become an independent source of information in which we are interested."[174]

The New York station had followed Greenglass's movements since his 1945 meeting with Harry Gold. It knew that he had been demobilized from the army in March 1946 and had returned to New York with his family. He then worked at a small firm launched by Julius Rosenberg. For some reason, Greenglass awaited advice from his Soviet associates on where he should continue his education (at least according to their report).[175] The NKGB learned, also, in July 1948 that Greenglass had kept a small piece of plutonium in a lead box as a souvenir after leaving Los Alamos but eventually threw it into the East River.[176] He also kept a sample of Uranium-238, which the station sent on to Moscow on December 18, 1948.[177]

In its role as David's educational counselor, the station recommended that Greenglass enroll for studies at the University of Chicago, where at least four of his Camp 2 scientific colleagues now either studied or taught. Greenglass had suggested all four as possible recruits for the station, and they were duly assigned code names awaiting David's further cultivation.[178]

Moscow also ordered the New York station in April 1948 to reestablish connections with Morris and Lona Cohen in order to reach Theodore Hall through them.[179] It turned out, however, that the Cohens had not maintained contact with either Hall or Saville Sax during the 1946–47 "conservation" period. The station received a report that Hall had recently resumed his studies in Chicago and joined the American Communist Party, making it even more likely that he was already under FBI surveillance.[180]

One New York station NKGB operative, "August," resumed contact with Julius Rosenberg in May 1948. It turned out that Rosenberg (according to "August's" report of their meeting and despite Yatskov's and Feklissov's instructions to the contrary) had in 1946–47 "continued fulfilling the duties of a group handler, maintaining contact with comrades, rendering them moral and material help while gathering valuable scientific and technical information."[181]

As in the past, "August" and other New York station operatives remained gravely concerned with Rosenberg's security. Moscow warned the station in December 1948:

> We have special concern provoked by the fact that possibly [Julius Rosenberg] is still engaged in conversations with the athletes [Rosenberg's sources] on the issues of our work at his apartment. We have exact information that the competitors [the FBI] use technical means to listen into apartments of people whom they [then] take into cultivation. Therefore, it is necessary once more to warn [Rosenberg] categorically about the inadmissibility of [continuing] such conversations at his apartment or at some of the athletes' [apartments].[182]

Julius Rosenberg's disregard of cautious tradecraft procedure was only one of the factors that would soon lead to exposure of the Soviets' network of American agents and sources on "Enormoz," with disastrous results for virtually all concerned.

CHAPTER 10

❖❖❖

Harvest Time, II: The Perlo Group

O NE MAJOR GROUP of American sources for Soviet intelligence had become a "lost tribe" for a time during the late 1930s and early 1940s. Some of its members, including John Abt and Victor Perlo, had taken part during the thirties either in Harold Ware's (GPU) or Whittaker Chambers's (GRU military intelligence) Washington networks or both. Chambers's defection in 1938 and the consequent fear of exposure doubtless caused several in the group to curtail cooperation for a time.

A shortage of Soviet operatives in the United States during this period coincided with the purges underway in the USSR. The result was an unusual situation: a significant number of American sources pursuing a tiny cadre of professional Soviet intelligence operatives. In 1939–40 alone, Moscow recalled seven experienced case officers from the United States, leaving a number of highly placed intelligence sources within the government without couriers or contacts.[1] Until the German invasion of the USSR in June 1941, moreover, the few Soviet operatives still on U.S. soil were more likely to be pursuing Trotskyists and Nazi-fascist agents in their own midst than Roosevelt Administration secrets.

With the emergence of an anti-Nazi wartime alliance of the United States, England, and the Soviet Union beginning in the summer of 1941, NKVD and GRU interest in classified materials related to the war effort increased dramatically.

Initially, many of these sources developed links to Jacob Golos's network, often steered in that direction by Golos's friend and collaborator, CPUSA head Earl Browder. Golos shared the information conveyed by his sources with his Soviet colleagues but not their identities.

This element of secrecy was quite frustrating for professional Soviet operatives such as Itzhak Akhmerov. After Golos's death in 1943, however, Akhmerov, with Browder's support and Elizabeth Bentley's reluctant cooperation, gradually became the group's primary contact in Soviet intelligence. The process took months, but by the following spring, Akhmerov was able to report to Moscow (on May 13, 1944) that all members of the group "are reliable compatriots, highly developed politically, [and] have a desire to help us with information. According to them, they were abandoned, and nobody was interested in their possibilities. In all, there are eight Communists in their group, with [Browder's] organization [the CPUSA] connected through [John] Abt."[*2]

The group's members included attorney John Abt, economist Victor Perlo, Edward Fitzgerald, Charles Kramer, Nathan Witt, Henry Collins, and several other figures. For the moment, Elizabeth Bentley remained as coordinator, reporting to Akhmerov. "They come to New York in turn once a fortnight," Akhmerov informed Moscow on May

* The May 13, 1944, cable from Akhmerov to Moscow received this partial deciphering in the VENONA release: "On [Browder's] instructions [Bentley] contacted through [Abt] a new group [in Washington]: [undeciphered sentences] . . . MAGD-OFF—'KANT.' [Bentley's] impressions: They are reliable [Communist Party members], politically highly mature; they want to help with information. They said that they had been neglected and no one had taken any interest in their potentialities . . . [undeciphered] . . . [Perlo], [Kramer], [Fitzgerald], and [Magdoff] will go to [New York] once every two weeks in turn. [Kramer] and [Fitzgerald] know [Silvermaster]. We shall let you have identifying particulars later. [Akhmerov]." May 13, 1944, No. 687, VENONA files. An earlier cable sent from Akhmerov to Moscow the previous month also described the situation: ". . . group:—KRAMER, PERLO, FLATO, GLASSER, EDWARD FITZGERALD, and others in a group of 7 or 8 [Communist Party members]. [Bentley] talked with [John Abt] and PERLO. They told her that this group was neglected and that nobody was interested in them. KRAMER is the leader of the group. All occupy responsible posts in [Washington]. . . . For more than a year [Zarubin] and I tried to get in touch with PERLO and FLATO. For some reason or other [Browder] did not come to the meeting and has just decided to put [Bentley] in touch with the whole group. If we work with this group it will be necessary to remove her and [undeciphered]. . . . Recently I met PERLO by chance in [Mary Price's] apartment. For your information: I have never met [Browder]. . . ." April 29, 1944, No. 588, VENONA files.

30, "passing the materials to [Bentley]. [Perlo] asks her every time to make certain his materials are sent to Comrade Stalin."*³

The following month, Moscow sent new instructions on handling the group. Bentley was removed as coordinator, and her future role was restricted to that of courier. The number of meetings with Soviet agents was reduced, and material delivered was limited to essential information (apparently the group had been passing along a great deal of low-quality data). Finally, fearing surveillance by the FBI, Joszef Peter, who ran a separate CPUSA intelligence network linked to Browder, was cautioned *not* to resume contacts either with Soviet operatives or members of this group.⁴

Akhmerov's own description of the participants' working procedures, in a September 17, 1944, memorandum to Moscow, suggested its intrinsic amateur character regarding basic tradecraft, which would remain a problem in the months ahead. Bentley met with Perlo, Fitzgerald, and Kramer once every two to three weeks in the New York apartment of another agent: "Each time someone among the three brings notes, information, and other material compiled by the entire group," Akhmerov wrote. "They type their notes themselves or, they say, their wives do it. They do not have a camera." Ironically, Akhmerov noted, their most valuable information source, Donald Wheeler ("Izra"), worked for the OSS and normally did not come to such meetings.⁵

Nor did what became known as "the Perlo Group" lack its own domestic problem, one far more dangerous than the personal rivalries

---

* A late-May 1944 cable from Akhmerov to Moscow described the variety of talents and complicated relationships among the "Perlo group's" members: "The probationers of the new group have given the following personal histories of themselves: 1. [Edward Fitzgerald], AN OLD [Communist Party member], capable, reliable, works in the Civilian Allocation Division of the [War Production Board]. 2. [Harry Magdoff] became a [Communist Party member] a long time ago . . . works in the Machine Tool Division of the [WPB]. 3. [Victor Perlo], an old [Communist Party member], reliable, capable; works in the Aeroplane Allocation Division of the [WPB]. 4. [Charles Kramer], an old [Communist Party member], reliable, works on the KILGO[RE] Committee. . . . [Donald Wheeler] has been a [Communist Party member] for several years . . . capable, works in the Labor Division, Research and Analysis Branch of [the OSS]. . . . [Unidentified person] maintains a close friendship with [Helen Tenney] and has repeatedly tried to marry her. . . . Harold GLASER [sic], an old [Communist Party member]. Temporarily abroad. . . . Concerning the remaining members of this group we will advise shortly." May 30, 1944, Nos. 769, 771, VENONA files.

that beset Nathan Gregory Silvermaster and his colleagues. Akhmerov described the dilemma to Moscow in his September 17, 1944, dispatch:

> Some months ago you wrote to me to stop the connection with [Perlo] for a while, because his ex-wife threatened in a letter to compromise him. I cannot afford to cease the connection with him because . . . it will be next to impossible to organize the group's work and to establish the connection with its valuable members without his active help . . . he settles everything. . . . He is undoubtedly the most active one in the group.[6]

The crisis in question involved Perlo, then chief of the Aviation Section of the War Production Board, and his former spouse, Katherine Wills Perlo, who in previous years had worked for Soviet intelligence along with her husband. Following a bitter divorce and custody dispute, Perlo had remarried, and his former wife had moved to Texas with their daughter. Perlo was able to gain custody of their child, and following a painful encounter with her ex-husband, the emotionally distraught Katherine Perlo wrote him. She warned Victor that she had sent President Roosevelt a letter exposing his unit's underground activities, mentioning Perlo and his colleagues by name.[7] Fortunately for Perlo, his former wife's letter would be ignored both by those in the White House assigned to security matters and by American counterintelligence agents until Elizabeth Bentley's defection provided vivid corroboration of Mrs. Perlo's allegations.[*]

Since Soviet operatives both in the USSR and in the United States could not be certain that Mrs. Perlo's letter had been disregarded, however, they took special measures to protect themselves from possible fallout.[8] Akhmerov instructed Bentley in mid-September 1944 to prevent Perlo from traveling to New York with government data for the next several months: "He must not realize that we are removing him from work for some time. He will be very upset by it. He is a hypochondriac and a very nervous man. . . . We should not mention that we are doing this because of his ex-wife."[9] When, in late 1944, Bentley and the entire Perlo Group came under the direct control of Washington's

---

[*] The flow of information from Perlo and his colleagues to the Soviets ended in late 1945. The question of whether the former Mrs. Perlo had actually sent the 1944 letter denouncing Victor and others as "members of an illegal Communist Party group" was settled to Moscow's satisfaction only years later. Its New York NKGB station reported on December 27, 1948, that a Soviet source within the Justice Department, Judith Coplon ("Sima"), had confirmed the letter's receipt.

"legal" NKGB station headed by Anatoly Gorsky, he issued even more stringent instructions. Bentley was not to meet at all with Perlo for several months. Moreover, Perlo was forbidden to accept documents and other written material from group members, an assignment now given to Edward Fitzgerald ("Ted"), who would serve as courier between Perlo and Bentley.[10] Victor Perlo's insulation was complete.

He remained important to the group, however, as a source of information and (Moscow believed) its "ideological leader." Perlo's NKGB file in Moscow observed of his work at the War Production Board (WPB) that he "has access to the minutes of the WPB and its different committees, to interdepartmental economic summaries . . . and to different documents on war industry."[11] Also, despite his ex-wife's letter threatening the entire group's safety, Perlo remained its acknowledged leader, hence the importance Gorsky placed on his continuing involvement in Soviet espionage.

Not that Perlo and his colleagues ever absorbed any of the lessons regarding compartmentalization and basic tradecraft that first Akhmerov and then Gorsky tried to teach them. A number of the sources in Perlo's network were close personal friends, as were their wives. The working environment that resulted resembled a type of informal espionage commune. "The group seems to have worked absolutely as a compatriot cell," Joseph Katz ("X") reported to Gorsky in January 1945. "They gathered at meetings in each other's homes, and their wives typed the reports. Then [Perlo] received the material from them and passed [it along] further. Taking into account the state of *konspiratsia*, one cannot do much. I am persuading [Perlo] to stop holding the meetings so regularly and to work individually as much as possible."[12]

Gorsky's anguish reflected both his chagrin at the amateur style of the Perlo Group and his awareness that Moscow had assigned an incredibly ambitious espionage agenda for which these American sources appeared singularly unsuited. The NKGB's August 1944 memorandum of instruction to Gorsky stated the challenge plainly:

> First of all, the station must ensure receipt of interesting information about activities of the following institutions and organizations:
>
> a. the State Department;
> b. the Senate and the Congress, in particular, the Committee on Foreign Affairs;
> c. the Interior, Treasury, and Justice Departments;

   d. the UNRRA [United Nations Relief and Rehabilitation Administration];

   e. the national committees of the Republican and Democratic parties;

   f. the Department of War Production;

   g. the department for economic activities in foreign states;

   h. the OSS;

   i. the FBI and immigration intelligence . . . ;

   j. trade unions;

   k. foreign embassies and missions.[13]

In addition, Gorsky was ordered "to enter one of the respectable clubs visited by state officials and diplomats to widen [your] outward connections."[14] As a result, this Soviet intelligence operative, as his financial records for Moscow demonstrated, discovered the pleasures of dining out in Washington: "January 1, 1945—lunch with Ch. [Charles] Bohlen, Assistant Secretary of State (8 dollars); January 7—dinner with D. Fry, president of the TWA air-company (10 dollars). . . ."[15]

The lack of reality in Moscow's expectations, however, was plain even in its August 6 instructions to Gorsky. These identified Michael Straight and Martha Dodd as people who would serve as main sources.[16] Straight had long since broken with the Communist Party and, by then, Dodd had little if any access to either Franklin or Eleanor Roosevelt. As early as September 1943, Gorsky's colleague, New York station chief Vassily Zarubin, had noted the problem, which his superiors apparently chose to ignore:

> Despite increase of our probationer [agent] network in government institutions and penetration into the intelligence organizations during the war, nevertheless our [agent] prospects do not satisfy the demands nor assure acquiring full, up-to-date information necessary for our country in wartime. We don't have any probationers in Congress* and very weak probationer possibilities in the "Temple" [the White House], executive organs of President Roosevelt, the State Department, various ministries, intelligence centers and new wartime institutions, etc. . . . The major gap at our [station] is the lack of probationers with distinguished status capable not only of explaining matters in which we are interested but influencing affairs in a direction desirable for us.[17]

---

* Samuel Dickstein ("Crook") ended his cooperation in 1940.

Among existing Soviet sources within the government, concern for security was almost nonexistent. Thus, Gorsky and his Soviet colleagues were appalled not only by the Perlo Group's casual disregard of basic precautions but by a general indifference to normal intelligence methods among virtually all the Washington sources whom Soviet operatives cultivated during World War II. Gorsky reported to Moscow in March 1945 that "all of them know each other as compatriot-informers [Communists and sources of information] as well as being aware of what work every one of them carries out."[18]

To illustrate the point, Gorsky noted that while an agent named Joseph Katz was passing along to "Tan," another Perlo Group agent, an assignment on oil information, "Tan" responded that still another Soviet source, Silvermaster Group member Frank Coe, could fulfill this task better since he had materials on the issue:

> One could extend the list of examples. As we reported earlier, in a conversation with me, [Harold Glasser] named more than a dozen names [of those] who are known to him as informers [sources of information]. [Victor Perlo] gave us a list including fourteen men definitely connected with the groups. . . . Once in a conversation with me, [Katz] claimed that from discussions with [Perlo, "Tan,"] and others, he got the impression that there are about a hundred such illegal informers in Washington, knowing each other and about each other.[19]

Gorsky pointed out that, when Perlo's group had reported to Golos through Browder's CPUSA links, all of its members would meet each week in their apartments. They discussed which materials should be passed along to Bentley or her predecessors and designated a different courier at each meeting. Unaccustomed to American informality, such collective espionage unnerved Soviet professionals.

Nor did the security lapses stop there. Gorsky provided Moscow with this 1945 Washington example: "Recently ["Tan"] told us that a certain Irving Kaplan from 'Bill's' group had invited him to come to a meeting of some 'group collecting information for the Russians.' Of course, we forbade him from going to such meetings." Gorsky concluded that the situation, though not hopeless, required "much time, patience, [and] prudence" in training sources in basic tradecraft, and he outlined a series of steps to achieve such "reeducation."[20]

Moscow responded to these concerns on March 28, 1945, with general advice to *reduce* the number of its many active wartime sources of information in the American government! Rather, it proposed identifying and nurturing one or two key informants "in the main institutions of the country (State Department, Foreign Economic Administration, War Production Board, FBI, OSS, War Department [and] Justice Department) having chosen the most valuable of them" and to concentrate "on educating these remaining sources completely in our spirit."[21]

One model for the type of Western agent Soviet intelligence hoped to cultivate in postwar Washington was already being handled by Gorsky, though with fewer problems than those Victor Perlo and his colleagues presented. Donald Maclean ("Homer") had worked for Soviet intelligence along with others—Blunt, Burgess, Cairncross, and Philby—recruited at Cambridge in the late 1930s. In his current wartime post at the British Embassy in Washington, Maclean delivered to Gorsky a number of official documents sent by Lord Halifax, the British Ambassador, to Prime Minister Churchill in London containing detailed and up-to-date information on American domestic and foreign policy.

Receiving materials directly from Maclean troubled the cautious Gorsky, however, especially considering the evident strengthening of U.S. counterintelligence in the latter years of the war. He urged Moscow to identify an American to serve as the British diplomat's courier, perhaps even Maclean's wife, Melinda.[22] Station chief Vladimir Pravdin ("Sergei"), who had met Maclean in New York in 1944, expressed the general view of the man held by NKGB officials with whom he dealt during this period:

> [Maclean] impressed one as a man of great initiative who does not need to be prompted in his work. He also orients himself very well to the international situation and understands what questions represent our major interests. I do not feel a desire on his part to evade working with us. Instead, he thinks that meeting too infrequently does not give him an opportunity to pass along operational information in a timely way.[23]

Nevertheless, Moscow plainly did not share its operatives' enthusiasm for Maclean's efforts at this point. They complained in 1945 about the substance of Halifax's cables, noting that the British Ambassador might not be an objective observer: "He looks at these problems through the eyes of an Englishman and, besides, of a reactionary . . . a highly typical representative of the bourgeois world."[24] Thus, although Maclean's (and Philby's) material was sent regularly to Stalin and his closest associates, some in Soviet intelligence at the time believed that the two highly placed British officials were actually double agents.

NKGB officials in Moscow were more concerned at this time with the Perlo Group's work, or so a May 29, 1945, cable to Gorsky would indicate. It expressed "interest" in the materials Perlo had conveyed but concluded that "he obviously cannot cope with the role of group handler." Fitzgerald, Kramer, and Magdoff were among those who had complained about the quality of Perlo's leadership. Moscow recommended compartmentalizing future contact with group members, the same solution it had provided for comparable problems that confronted Nathan Gregory Silvermaster and *his* associates.[25]

Like Silvermaster, Perlo now also faced troubling personal circumstances: a new baby, an ill wife, and a need for extra cash. Gorsky arranged a $500 "bonus" after consulting with Moscow.[26] Later that year, Elizabeth Bentley's defection led to renewed interest by American counterintelligence agencies in Katherine Wills Perlo's earlier letter. As a result, the Perlo Group was closed down, along with other Soviet wartime networks in Washington by the final weeks of 1945. Reinforced security regulations put in place by the Truman Administration and the war's end also contributed to its demise. A cursory review of some major documents passed by group members to Soviet operatives in 1945 indicates, however, that Victor Perlo and the others remained a prime source of information for Soviet intelligence up to the very end.*

---

* The Soviet archives credit the Perlo Group's members with having sent, among others, the following 1945 U.S. government documents to Moscow:
February
- Contents of a WPB memo dealing with apportionment of aircraft to the USSR in the event it declared war on Japan;
- WPB discussion of the production policy regarding war materials at an Executive Committee meeting;
- Documents on future territorial planning for commodities in short supply;
- Documents on a priority system for foreign orders for producing goods in the United States after the end of the war in Europe;
- Documents on trade policy and trade controls after the war;
- Data on arms production in the United States in January 1945;

March
- A WPB report on "Aluminum for the USSR and current political issues in the U.S. over aluminum supplies" (2/26/45);

April
- Documents concerning the committee developing plans for the U.S. economy after the defeat of Germany, and also regarding war orders for the war against Japan;
- Documents on the production of the B-29 bomber and the B-32;

A CONGRESSIONAL SOURCE

All but one member of Victor Perlo's group, like Perlo himself, were middle-level officials in the Roosevelt Administration. The sole exception worked in the U.S. Congress. Charles Kramer's Russian-Jewish immigrant family background resembled that of others in the group, and he had labored for Communist causes since 1931 before actually joining the CPUSA two years later. Kramer had married another committed Communist in 1934, a native-born southerner from a poor farm family, who served during the thirties as a courier for the NKVD's New York station. An autobiography, prepared for Soviet intelligence in 1945, described Kramer's work during the 1930s at different minor government posts but, also, as an investigator of antiunion violence for a U.S. Senate committee before becoming a union organizer.[28]

In 1942, Kramer joined the staff of the Senate's Kilgore Committee, which was focused on wartime economic mobilization. Following this appointment, Kramer resisted Perlo's continuing pressure to intensify his collection of information and documents for Soviet intelligence, pointing out that much of his free time was spent preparing a book on postwar issues for West Virginia senator Harley Kilgore, a project that took precedence over other obligations.[29]

  · Tactical characteristics of various bombers and fighters;
  · Materials on the United States using Saudi Arabian oil resources;
June
  · Data concerning U.S. war industry production in May from the WPB's secret report;
  · Data concerning plans for 1945–46 aircraft production from the WPB;
  · More data on specific aircrafts' technical aspects;
August
  · Data concerning the new Export-Import Bank;
  · Data concerning supplies of American aircraft to the Allies in June 1945;
  · Data from the top secret WPB report on U.S. war industry production in June;
October
  · Detailed data concerning the industrial capacities of the Western occupation zones of Germany that could be brought out as reparations;
  · Information on views within U.S. Army circles concerning the inevitability of war against the USSR as well as statements by an air force general supporting U.S. acquisition of advanced bases in Europe for building missiles.[27]

Kramer also disliked Perlo's role as the group's leader and, by 1945, was delivering mainly innocuous public record documents. One clue to Kramer's disaffection was an argument he had with Perlo in mid-1945 after Truman became president. Perlo asserted that "people in our situation [Communists] cannot influence politics." Kramer disagreed, pointing out that continuing to place Communist supporters in key government agencies could lead to effective postwar economic policies related to full employment.[30]

But the NKGB was not interested in Kramer's views on curing unemployment in the postwar period unless they affected American foreign policy toward the Soviet Union. Nevertheless, as Moscow reminded Anatoly Gorsky on April 14, 1945, Charles Kramer ("Mole") was still the only source in his station who could systematically pass data concerning the policy and views of U.S. Senators and Congressmen: "Therefore, one must take necessary measures to educate [Kramer] properly and place him firmly in [Perlo's] group. [Kramer] must be made to understand that he is working for us. Therefore, his information must satisfy all our demands." But Kramer continued to avoid giving confidential information to Perlo, prompting Moscow's complaint in the April 14 cable: "[Kramer's] survey . . . is just a shallow compilation of official material on this issue. Nor are we satisfied with his data about different Senators, since they [are] commonly known [and do not] concern the background work of these individuals."

Of particular interest to the NKGB at the time, understandably, were the views of different key House and Senate members on major issues of the postwar settlement: "U.S. policy [toward] . . . the treatment of Germany, in particular, the dismembering of Germany, economic actions, reparations . . . [U.S. policy] toward the Balkan nations and Poland . . . [toward] relations between the United States and Great Britain . . . [and, finally, toward] relations between the U.S. and the USSR, both in the period right after the end of the war and thereafter."[31]

In response, Kramer promised a Soviet operative that he would design his work "according to what is best in our opinion."[32] He would even satisfy the NKGB's curiosity concerning "the concrete connections of different influential Congressmen with industrial and financial interests."[33]

Gorsky met with Kramer for dinner at a Washington restaurant on June 13, where Kramer informed him that he had left Kilgore to become the staff director of a committee headed by another liberal Democrat, Senator Claude Pepper of Florida. Gorsky had brought another Soviet operative to the meeting—"Bogdan," who became Kramer's sole contact.[34] Thus, the NKGB's "man in Congress" effectively terminated his relationship with Gorsky and Victor Perlo's group.

Kramer briefed "Bogdan" on June 19 regarding Truman's instruction to his Treasury Secretary. Morgenthau, an advocate, like the Soviet government, of a strongly punitive economic and political peace settlement with defeated Germany, was told not to raise these issues before Truman, Stalin, and Churchill had discussed them privately at the forthcoming Potsdam Conference. Kramer also briefed "Bogdan" on the likely appointment of Senator James Byrnes of South Carolina, a conservative anti-Soviet Democrat, as Stettinius's replacement as Secretary of State, information he had obtained from other Senators.[35]

At this and subsequent meetings, despite conveying a range of inside gossip, Kramer still deflected Moscow's requests for written summaries on U.S. policy matters or profiles of key Senators. Thus "Bogdan's" June 27 report: "Concerning Truman's stand on Far and Middle East issues at the forthcoming [Potsdam] conference of the three leaders, [Kramer] could not find out anything."[36] The American did report at a July 6 meeting the unhappy news that "lately the FBI has begun an intensified scrutiny on a wide scale of 'Reds' (Communists) working in the U.S. government. In particular, they [are watching Lee] Pressman intensively. . . ."

Otherwise, Kramer simply recounted familiar Washington news of the day: Fred Vinson, who was accompanying Truman to Potsdam, was the likely new Treasury Secretary; Secretary of State Byrnes "is hostile toward the Soviet Union and . . . is also a champion of a soft peace with Germany"; and similar items well known to informed Washingtonians if not to Soviet operatives. Nevertheless, the station's view of Charles Kramer's potential remained optimistic and, as his next assignment, never fulfilled, Kramer was to "compose by our next meeting a report about Truman's connections, activities, and feelings."[37]

These chatty, covert colloquies continued until Elizabeth Bentley's November 1945 defection. Then, when the 1946 congressional elections produced Republican majorities in both the House of Representatives and Senate, Kramer lost his position as staff director among other displaced Democratic appointees. He briefly remained an adviser to Senator Pepper before seeking employment outside of Congress.[38]

The Soviet NKGB station chief in Washington at the time, Ambassador Alexander Panyushkin, reported to Moscow in early March 1948 that Kramer had begun working as a speechwriter for former Vice President Henry Wallace, then gearing up his third-party, pro-Soviet

"Progressive Party" campaign.[39] By that time, Kramer's name and background had reached Administration and congressional investigators through the testimony of Elizabeth Bentley and Whittaker Chambers.

A TRIO OF SOURCES

Often, even minor sources provided extremely important information to their Soviet handlers. The case of a Communist economist code-named "Buck" illustrates the point. In 1943, "Buck" became deputy director of a division of the new United Nations Relief and Rehabilitation Administration. Jacob Golos had cultivated him as an agent and then turned him over to Silvermaster's group, where David Silverman managed contact with him.[40] As with other relationships in the group, the line between overt involvement in CPUSA activities and covert efforts on behalf of Soviet intelligence was often perilously thin. Thus, "Buck" paid his party dues directly to Silverman.

In the fall of 1943, "Buck" began passing on confidential materials, including a sixty-five-page report on the U.S. machinery industry.[41] But the high point of his career as a Soviet source came in late June 1945, when he conveyed to a Soviet operative code-named "Konstantine" information on issues that would be discussed at the forthcoming Potsdam Conference.[42] After the war—and with espionage halted temporarily because of Elizabeth Bentley's defection—"Buck" settled into a comfortable sinecure as director of an economic development department in the United Nations secretariat.[43]

Another relatively obscure agent code-named "Arena" began working with Soviet operatives, including Itzhak Akhmerov, in the late 1930s. Again, in a common circumstance among agents of the period, "Arena" retained close links with and membership in the CPUSA.[44] In several 1937–38 memoranda, Moscow chided Akhmerov for allowing this interconnection of "open" Communist involvement and secret work, but to no avail.[45] "Arena" had provided his Soviet contacts from 1937–39 with material from the Civil Service Commission, where he worked, including crucial "lists with schemes and detailed description of the kind of work by officials of the American secret police, military and naval intelligence, Secret Service . . . the State Department and other significant state institutions," noted a November 14, 1940, NKVD dispatch to Moscow.[46]

Contact with "Arena" was lost for a time when Akhmerov left for the Soviet Union in December 1939 and restored only when Akhmerov returned to America in April 1942.[47] "Arena" joined the Navy Department in July 1943[48] and was passed from Akhmerov to Anatoly Gorsky's supervision. Victor Perlo also figured in managing "Arena," who assisted in photographing materials taken by Perlo and other members of his group. Later, "Arena" became a source for information on radar, sonars, and other naval equipment.[49] Quite unexpectedly, "Arena's" wife, "Rina," also a party member, found occasion to acquire strategically important materials concerning Japan. Thus, Joseph Katz ("X") wrote Gorsky on November 16, 1944:

> It seems to me that "Arena's" job at present is not of any interest for us, whereas his wife's job is of enormous interest. She works in the Military Intelligence section of the War Department. This institution belongs to the General Staff and is located in the Pentagon. Her group is composed of only 10 people and apparently is considered very important since the head of Military Intelligence (G-2) Bissell personally visits this group and follows its work. The group is busy mainly with defining types, quantity, etc. of Japanese radio and radar equipment, different kinds of electrical mechanisms and all the ground equipment on the basis of captured documents and other sources. Supposedly the results of this research must be passed also to the English, but in her opinion, it will not be done. . . . I explained to her that, in my opinion, her place of work was of enormous interest and assured her that we would take all possible precautions to guarantee her personal security and the security of the work itself. She claimed that she did not have a typewriter, and I promised to get her one.[50]

Whatever the relative importance of "Arena's" thefts for Soviet intelligence compared to materials provided by his wife, he remained an active agent until war's end. On June 1, 1945, "Arena" met with Perlo to express an interest in appointment as an officer in the U.S. Army. But Perlo told him that "all of us, because of our special work, are incomparably more useful here than we could possibly be at the front."[51] Certainly "Arena" was vital to his Soviet handlers, conveying to them later that year issues of the secret military journal, "Combat Information Center," for July and August 1945. Colonel Vassilevsky, chief of a section of the NKGB's First Directorate, called the journal quite helpful: "Contains data on operational and tactical use of radio-location means in the Second World War, which are of great value."[52]

"Arena" passed on several other secret publications from the Navy Department in September, with Colonel Vassilevsky, now an avid secret "subscriber" to these journals, requesting the latest issues. Unfortunately, like other Soviet sources in the United States, "Arena" and his wife were abandoned by their Soviet handlers after Elizabeth Bentley's defection in late 1945.[53] Joseph Katz was instructed to restore contact with "Arena" in 1948 but could not locate him.[54]

Katz himself was another little-known but interesting American agent who left for Europe after the war and (among other assignments) tried at various times to organize for the NKGB the retributive murder of arch-defector Elizabeth Bentley. It was Katz, in discussing the always delicate question of whether stolen materials were being given "merely" to Earl Browder's CPUSA or directly to Soviet intelligence operatives, who wrote Gorsky in January 1945 this piquant notation on a conversation he had had with another American member of the Perlo Group:

> By the way, he told me that [Perlo] had told him some time ago that he was not passing materials to [Browder] anymore but was passing them to us. I answered nothing to this, but ["Tan"] apparently was very proud of this fact, which contradicts [Bentley's] opinion that everyone will immediately stop working if they find out about the connection with us. Seemingly, one way or another, they already know about it.[55]

By then, a majority of those involved in Soviet intelligence's Washington networks clearly knew that their information and documents were being sent directly to Moscow. That knowledge, which had been a source of pride during the war years, now became, after Bentley's defection, a matter of anxiety and concern.

CHAPTER 11

❖❖❖

OSS and NKGB: Penetration Agents

DONOVAN AND THE NKGB

O N SEVERAL OCCASIONS, during the Second World War, some high-level officials in the Roosevelt Administration sought to create an informal relationship between Soviet and American foreign intelligence services. The effort succeeded finally in 1944, when the NKGB and the new U.S. wartime intelligence service, the Office of Strategic Services (OSS) led by General William J. ("Wild Bill") Donovan, concluded an agreement to exchange information and establish close liaison. The attempt to implement this agreement exposed the deep and mutual suspicions between the services in spite of the Soviet-American wartime alliance. Both sides were prepared for disappointment, and neither side was surprised, at war's end, by the agreement's collapse.

The effort began in July 1941 at a time when the United States had already become deeply engaged in supplying first England and then the Soviet Union (after the German invasion) through Lend-Lease and other assistance programs. That month, the USSR's Ambassador to the United States, Konstantin Umansky, informed the NKVD of a recent private conversation with Treasury Secretary Henry Morgenthau. He quoted Morgenthau, an FDR confidant, as asking "not on behalf of the American government but on my personal behalf to give me and Roosevelt the heads of German agents in the U.S., since the FBI works poorly today . . . leaving the core of Nazi leaders in the U.S. free and still carrying on their undermining work." (The NKVD official who read Umansky's dispatch was so struck by this remarkable request that he scrawled several exclamation and question marks over it.)[1]

Several months later, in February 1942, Assistant Secretary of State Adolf Berle, the official responsible for security issues at State, made the same request of the newly designated Soviet Ambassador, Maxim Litvinov. The USSR's Deputy Commissar for Foreign Affairs, Vladimir Dekanozov, described the meeting in a February 23 memorandum to then-NKGB head Vsevolod Merkulov:

> According to Comrade Litvinov's information, one of U.S. Secretary of State Hull's assistants, Berle, declared to Comrade Litvinov that the Americans would like to organize a meeting between representatives of the American and Soviet intelligence services to exchange information about the "fifth column."* To Comrade Litvinov's remarks about the difficulty in arranging such a meeting in view of the fact that Soviet intelligence is in the USSR, Berle stated significantly that he was aware of the presence of Soviet intelligence in the U.S.[2]

Since Berle was (in Litvinov's words) "known for his hostility toward the USSR," the Soviets viewed the request with suspicion, as having "a clearly provocative character." Fueling this caution was a recent related inquiry to the embassy by yet another anti-Soviet official at the State Department. Loy Henderson (a senior diplomat known for his knowledge of, and hostility toward, the Soviet Union) contacted Andrei Gromyko, who then held the rank of Counselor, "asking several times about the whereabouts of Comrade Zubilin," the pseudonym of Vassily Zarubin, nominally the embassy's Third Secretary and attached to the Soviet Consulate in New York, who served at the time as NKGB station chief.

American officials evidently wished to develop some pattern of official cooperation between the NKGB and, at least, the State Department's

---

* The phrase "fifth column" was popularized in the late 1930s in Ernest Hemingway's play of the same name about the Spanish Civil War. The title referred to the fact that four fascist armies were encircling Republican Madrid from every direction while within the city a "fifth column" of fascist agents and sympathizers undermined morale and spied for the enemy. The phrase was widely applied at the time in antifascist countries to possible Nazi or fascist sympathizers.

intelligence bureau while, at the same time, recognizing covert Soviet activities and personnel in the United States. Gromyko sought Moscow's advice: "I ask you to consult Comrade Beria and communicate the response you consider desirable for our embassy to give regarding the questions they touch on, particularly, your decision concerning the [future] residence of Comrade Zubilin."[3] The embassy (and the station) received Moscow's dismissive response in early March:

> The proposal made by Berle [for] a meeting between representatives of American and Soviet intelligence services . . . is unacceptable, and the NKVD of the USSR is not interested in establishing this liaison. As far as . . . Comrade Zubilin's residence is concerned, . . . we are interested in his remaining in New York. This circumstance can be explained to the Americans by the need to help the New York Consul General due to the large amount of work.[4]

The Soviet memorandum did not attempt to explain further the decision to reject cooperation with American intelligence.

One factor influencing the USSR's attitudes toward an exchange of secret information may have been the Soviet effort, already underway, to infiltrate the OSS, America's newest and most important foreign intelligence unit. The NKGB's 1942 activities plan for the United States stated this goal explicitly: "Donovan's committee . . . created under the President's direct leadership, is now . . . creating a powerful centralized intelligence apparatus, drawing to its work different U.S. government and private institutions. Using this organizational period, our task is to insert there our people and carry out cultivation with their help." Although the NKGB had no agents in the OSS at the start of 1942, within months that situation changed.[5]

After Moscow's firm rebuff, Berle and his State Department colleagues dropped all interest in a formal liaison with Soviet intelligence. The idea reemerged only in December 1943, when General Donovan, after obtaining support from President Roosevelt and the Joint Chiefs of Staff, flew to Moscow to raise it directly with Soviet leaders. Donovan proposed far more than joint cooperation in exposing German agents in the United States. He discussed with Soviet Foreign Minister Molotov a comprehensive plan for sharing military and political intelligence on Germany. Molotov quickly agreed to the proposal. By then, the NKGB had undoubtedly briefed the Foreign Minister on its agents within the OSS who could inform Soviet intelligence if the Americans attempted to use the arrangement unfairly.

To discuss implementing this exchange, Donovan and General John Dean, head of the U.S. military mission in Moscow, met on December 27 with NKGB head Pavel Fitin and a second official introduced as "General Alexander Ossipov."[6] Any experienced FBI counterintelligence operative could have told the unsuspecting Donovan and Dean that "Ossipov" was actually former station chief Gaik Ovakimyan, a veteran of NKGB penetration in the United States.

At Fitin's request, Donovan briefed his Soviet counterparts on the work of the OSS: how it operated on enemy territory, how liaison was maintained between the various OSS-infiltrated groups and their home bases, and how agents were trained. Fitin was especially interested in whether the Americans could assist Soviet agents operating in countries like France and western Germany. Donovan offered to help.

The OSS director proposed cooperating with the NKGB in a wide range of activities: exchanging information, consulting on needed sabotage activities against the Germans, and coordinating work on infiltrating agents in the occupied countries. Donovan also suggested exchanging formal representatives—an NKGB liaison in Washington and an OSS agent in Moscow—to coordinate cooperation while maintaining links between the two services in neutral countries such as Turkey and Switzerland (where Allen Dulles already directed OSS activities).

Donovan then offered an immediate test of the new relationship, reviewing with NKGB officials the reliability of OSS sources in pro-German Bulgaria. Pavel Fitin listened politely to this extraordinary recitation of possible joint ventures but responded simply that an exchange of information seemed possible.[7] He awaited a final decision on the issue by Soviet leaders.

Bad winter weather kept Donovan's plane in Moscow for another ten days.[8] Shortly before leaving, he received a 2 A.M. phone call from Gaik Ovakimyan ("General Ossipov"), who informed him that the Kremlin had officially consented to contacts with the OSS. Donovan persuaded Ovakimyan to come to the American Embassy immediately for a middle-of-the-night meeting with him and Colonel John H. F. Haskell, whom Donovan presented to the Russian as the OSS's designated man in Moscow.

Despite the hour, Donovan was full of ideas for launching the new cooperative arrangement, especially in the Balkans. He and Ovakimyan agreed that tangible pressure should be applied to the Bulgarian government to force that country's withdrawal from the war as a German ally. Donovan proposed coordinating bombings and sabotage activities in Bulgaria and asked for Moscow's data on its key government officials. He described an OSS group already working on Bulgaria from Turkish territory.[9]

Nor did the discussion stop there. Donovan also informed Ovakimyan about the OSS's relationship with the partisan leader Tito in Yugoslavia, whom his operatives helped to supply with weapons. He proposed that the OSS and NKGB work together in that country and in Greece with the various guerrilla groups, painting an attractive picture of Soviet-American cooperation against both the Germans and the British! "General Donovan underlines especially the fact of the gradual retreat from Yugoslavia and Greece by the English and simultaneous reinforcement of American positions in those countries," Ovakimyan wrote in his report of the meeting. "By this, in particular, he explained the American interest in cooperating with us."[10]

An exuberant Donovan asked for the accelerated dispatch of NKGB operatives to the United States to act as the intelligence service's official representatives. He guaranteed that they would visit OSS bases to learn about the organization's training and activities. Donovan invited "General Ossipov" personally to Washington, still unaware of his true identity and background, and the visitor managed to leave the U.S. Embassy meeting only at 4 A.M. He returned later that day with Pavel Fitin and Andrei Graur, chief of the NKGB's Anglo-American section, who had been assigned to work as chief NKGB "official" representative in the United States. They continued to discuss possible joint efforts until Donovan's departure from Moscow that evening.

The OSS director was sincere in his hopes for close wartime and postwar collaboration with the USSR. Moscow would soon receive confirmation of this from an important aide to Donovan, Duncan Lee, who moonlighted as an NKGB agent ("Kokh"). "During his trip to Moscow," Lee reported in a January 17, 1944, memorandum to Soviet operatives, "Donovan . . . asserts that he made no effort to deceive the Russians—he spoke with total frankness to them."[11] Another detailed NKGB report prepared at this time and based on Lee's conversations with his boss confirmed that judgment:

> Donovan was very pleased that he and Moscow agreed to exchange missions and information. . . . [But] there are strong objections to allowing the NKVD an official mission in the U.S. Donovan's adversary is E. Hoover (the FBI head) who particularly objected to this exchange. He sent a memorandum to Roosevelt in which he pointed out that it would be too dangerous to

have an NKVD mission in the country [and] that American public opinion would perceive this move very negatively.

When this memorandum was shown to Donovan, he called
Hoover a fool and said if [Hoover] thought the NKVD didn't [al-
ready] have its representatives in the U.S., he was deeply wrong.
When Amtorg arrived in the U.S. [during the 1920s], the NKVD
started to function, too. His opinion is as follows: "If the NKVD is
to have its representatives in the U.S., whether we like it or not, it
would be better if there was an official mission to have the possibility of controlling their activities." . . .

The Soviet government made an enormous impression on
Donovan, and he is fascinated by it. He considers Stalin the most
intelligent person among all [those] heading today's governments. . . .[12]

Turf battles between the FBI and OSS directors, the memo continued, also helped to explain the bitter, mutual hostility between Hoover
and Donovan: "Sometimes Donovan's and Hoover's interests clash,
since Hoover wants to control some directions of Donovan's work
while the latter, in turn, intends to penetrate Hoover's field of activity."

Within months of the OSS director's return from Moscow, however,
J. Edgar Hoover had clearly won his bureaucratic battle on the issue of
exchanging OSS and NKGB official representatives. On March 3,
1944, Itzhak Akhmerov reported to Moscow that Hoover had sent
FDR's closest aide, Harry Hopkins, a strong letter objecting to the
Donovan-Fitin agreement. Hoover argued—correctly—that Soviet intelligence's main goal was to penetrate American state secrets, and he
urged the White House to stop the deal.

Hopkins gave Hoover's letter to Roosevelt (it probably reached
Akhmerov through Lauchlin Currie, the only presidential aide then
also working for Soviet intelligence). Roosevelt, in turn, told the Chairman of the Joint Chiefs of Staff, Admiral William D. Leahy, of
Hoover's concerns and instructed Leahy to discuss the proposal with
the Joint Chiefs. In another memo, which also reached the Joint
Chiefs (and Soviet intelligence), Hoover accused the NKGB of seeking highly confidential War Department secrets (presumably a reference to the atomic bomb project). He again cautioned, on internal
security grounds, against allowing an official NKGB presence in Washington.[13]

Despite these objections, a majority of the Joint Chiefs supported
Donovan's proposal but urged that they all discuss the idea further with

FDR before it was implemented. The White House decided finally in mid-March to reject a formal OSS-NKGB link, fearing conservative Republican attacks abetted by J. Edgar Hoover in the midst of the 1944 presidential election campaign more than Soviet spying. If ideological factors conditioned Roosevelt's decision, historian Bradley Smith observed, "the ideology was less a fear of communists than of anticommunists."

For his part, Donovan viewed the White House's retreat as tactical and temporary. He cabled General Dean in Moscow the following month that both the President and the Joint Chiefs approved the agreement but asked for time to implement it. After a conversation on this cable by Dean and the NKGB's Pavel Fitin on April 7, Gaik Ovakimyan reported that the delay was "caused by political considerations and connected with the election campaign. . . . Donovan thinks that [as soon as] the election campaign is over, it will be possible to exchange representatives."[14]

Of greater interest to Moscow's intelligence chiefs was Donovan's readiness—reported by Dean to the Soviets—"to give any information on our request or respond to any question we are interested in." Thus began the period of informal cooperation between the OSS and the NKGB. Each side delivered to the other, in the months that followed, a broad range of highly classified material.

General Dean, evidently following instructions from Donovan, expressed "hopes for the activation of . . . cooperation before the exchange of representatives, and . . . declared that he was ready to give intelligence information not only from the OSS files but also from Army, Navy and other intelligence organizations as well as to start an exchange of samples of sabotage equipment." Based on these assurances and backed by confirmation from their covert operatives at OSS headquarters in Washington, Fitin and Ovakimyan agreed to begin immediate cooperation while postponing the exchange of representatives.

Other U.S. intelligence agencies, however, shared the U.S. State Department's view, as reported to the NKGB in spring 1944 by a source in the OSS's Russian section (code-named "Yasha"), that such cooperation was both dangerous and ludicrous. State especially opposed providing entry visas for NKGB operatives and feared that the OSS, in the USSR, would interfere with the activities of accredited American diplomats in Moscow.[15]

Nor did NKGB sources within the OSS think much of the organization's operatives, most of whom lacked professional training and experience. "The main principle of the entire OSS is the principle of amateurism," one NKGB source code-named "Z" reported in late July 1944.

> In reality, the OSS is an organization which doesn't know what it will be searching for, doesn't know where to begin, and what is wanted from it. The OSS cadre is poorly trained. . . . The OSS is the Cinderella of the American secret services: the FBI seriously hates them, suspecting that the OSS wants to take away the FBI monopoly on Western Hemisphere security. Nor is it liked at the War and Navy Departments. The OSS owes its existence only to General Donovan's personal popularity and not to its work.[16]

Although Fitin and his colleagues agreed with this critical assessment of their American intelligence associates, the cooperation pact had less to do with acquiring information—which, after all, their sources inside OSS could do for the NKGB—than with furthering U.S.-USSR political and military cooperation against the Nazis. The Soviet goal was to encourage the earliest possible opening of a "second front" in Western Europe to relieve German military pressure on the Soviet Union.

During the spring of 1944, despite Soviet reservations and Roosevelt's personal reticence, the NKGB and General Dean's military mission in Moscow began passing intelligence information from one country to the other. The process got underway in March when the Soviets forwarded a memorandum dealing with Bulgaria, a prime subject during Donovan's visit.[17] Both sides transferred data concerning Germany and its allies as well as on German-occupied countries.[18]

Pavel Fitin, in June 1944, drafted a summary report assessing the materials received from the OSS, dividing them into two categories. One category contained information about Germany and occupied countries of primary interest to the Red Army's GRU intelligence (which received it, in turn). A second category, much more valuable to the NKGB, included reference manuals written by the OSS's analytic section based on information provided by field agents. Understandably, Fitin supported continuing the exchange of information.[19]

The previous month, General Donovan had asked for data on the sabotage methods used by the NKGB against their German enemies.[20] The material was provided by a department head, Pavel Sudoplatov,[21] who in August 1944 received in exchange an illustrated catalog of American special weapons and mechanisms for such purposes.[22] Earlier that year, Dean had informed Ovakimyan that OSS operatives had captured German intelligence (Abwehr) agents in Turkey, transferring them to Cairo for questioning. The NKGB submitted a list of questions concerning German intelligence efforts against the USSR to be posed to the captured agents, the answers to which Dean conveyed to his Soviet colleagues in late March.[23]

Such cooperation sometimes involved complex policy issues. Thus on April 23, three days before U.S. Ambassador Averill Harriman was scheduled to leave Moscow for London to brief Secretary of State Edward Stettinius on Soviet views of Poland's status, General Dean met with Gaik Ovakimyan. Dean wished to know whether Soviet units on the Ukrainian front had really agreed to joint military activities with paramilitary Polish nationalist groups as some Western papers had reported. The United States maintained contact with some of these groups through the OSS. "The Americans don't quite trust these clandestine military organizations," Ovakimyan reported Dean's remarks, "and therefore didn't supply much help . . . despite the Polish government's persistent pressure for such help."[24]

Ovakimyan went on to report that, despite the Polish government-in-exile's request from London for weapons delivery via transport planes to these bands of resistance fighters inside Poland, "the Americans don't quite trust the Polish government." Nor do they know "the real intentions and goals of these combatant groups and reckon that [they] exist mainly on paper," thereby denying them major weapons assistance.[25] Ovakimyan's report on his conversation with Dean went directly to Stalin, Molotov, and Beria.[26] It undoubtedly influenced Soviet attitudes toward the Polish resistance, helping to explain the passivity displayed by Soviet forces surrounding Warsaw later that same year when the aborted anti-Nazi uprising occurred in that city.

Donovan also attempted to interest the NKGB in developing a quasi-official exchange of information and contacts in Stockholm and London, but representatives of both services met only in London.[27] OSS agent John Haskell regularly sent a range of material to the Soviet military attaché in London, but the NKGB continued to pass its information only through General Dean in Moscow.[28] Several times in the fall of 1944, as Soviet forces advanced through Czechoslovakia and other German-occupied territories and Nazi armies continued their retreat, OSS units lost contact with their controllers. Donovan then requested Fitin's assistance in determining his agents' fate. The NKGB chief normally proved obliging, providing when possible names and locations of OSS agents whom Soviet troops encountered or whose deaths could be confirmed.[29]

Despite this informal pattern of cooperation, Donovan recognized the potential for postwar conflict between the two countries. Thus, in late 1944, when anti-Soviet Finnish intelligence sources offered the OSS mission in neighboring Sweden over 1,500 pages of Soviet codes, including the cipher keys to NKGB and GRU intelligence agency transmissions, Donovan jumped at the opportunity to acquire the material. By that time, however, the Soviets had discontinued use of these codes, aware that they had been compromised.

Donovan briefed Roosevelt concerning the acquisition, which he recommended keeping and using. Instead, the President instructed the OSS director to return the codes to the Russians without making any copies. Secretary of State Stettinius had urged this approach on FDR, and Roosevelt ordered both Donovan and Stettinius to inform Moscow of the situation immediately. General Dean had received a cable about the codes from Donovan on January 5, 1945. Sometime before February 15, when the 1,500 pages involved were handed over to Andrei Gromyko, the Soviet Ambassador to the United States, NKGB officials learned of Donovan's action.[30] What they did not learn at the time was that Donovan had disobeyed FDR's explicit instruction and ordered the entire cache reproduced secretly before being given to Gromyko.*

Despite his actions in connection with the Soviet codes, Donovan continued to honor his commitment to share crucial intelligence information with the NKGB. He passed on to Fitin in late December 1944, for example, several long memoranda from Allen Dulles, the OSS director in Switzerland, distilling Dulles's private discussions with German officials, as well as other information on the political situation and plans within the Nazi leadership.[31] Soviet officials remained suspicious of these informal contacts between Americans such as Dulles and German military officials or civilians, fearing that they foreshadowed efforts (about which Stalin and his associates fretted constantly) to generate a separate Anglo-American peace agreement with Nazi Germany aimed against the Soviet Union. Several of Fitin's memos to Soviet leaders concern such German-American exchanges, usually initiated by the Germans, reports Donovan dutifully forwarded to the NKGB.[32]

Nor did the German surrender in Europe end Moscow's contacts with the OSS. On July 23, 1945, General Fitin received from John Dean's successor, Colonel M. W. Pettigrew, acting head of the U.S.

---

* These intelligence codes would prove extremely valuable in later years in assisting the FBI, Army Signal Corps, and others involved in the "VENONA" project to decipher intercepted Soviet transmissions.

Military Mission in Moscow, a remarkable letter from the faithful Donovan offering to turn over to the NKGB an entire captured German intelligence unit commanded by the Gestapo's deputy foreign intelligence chief, Dr. William Hoettl. Donovan's concern over Soviet suspicions of America's postwar intentions emerges in Pettigrew's letter:

> I have just been advised by General Donovan that Dr. William Hoettl, former Chief of the organized German intelligence network in the Balkans, is now in American custody. . . . Hoettl claims he operated his intelligence network against the Soviets. . . .
>
> Motivated, in General Donovan's opinion, by a desire to create dissension between the Soviets and Americans, Hoettl has expressed a willingness to turn the entire network over to United States forces with the assumption that it might be useful against Soviet interests. General Donovan states that Hoettl's claims concerning the network's existence have been substantiated by the receipt of various messages and recognition signals.
>
> General Donovan not only feels that you should have this information but that it would be most desirable for American and Soviet representatives on the spot to discuss ways and means of eliminating Hoettl's entire organization. . . . [33]

After verifying the situation (Generals Eisenhower and Marshall were both irritated at Donovan's decision to hand over the Hoettl network without first consulting American military authorities in Europe), Fitin, along with Lavrenty Beria and Vsevolod Merkulov, wrote Stalin in September 1945 about their plan to dismantle (or acquire) Hoettl's agent organization.[34] By that time, William Donovan had already decided to retire, although he could not have anticipated President Truman's decision to disband the OSS on October 1, 1945.

The death of Franklin Roosevelt that April presaged the political demise of his longtime friend and associate. Donovan doubtless valued, more than many of the Truman Administration's more fervently anti-Communist leadership, Pavel Fitin's condolence letter regarding FDR's death.[35] That fall, all official contact between the OSS and Soviet intelligence ceased, only weeks before Elizabeth Bentley began to brief the FBI about Soviet agents within the OSS. Her information could only have delighted J. Edgar Hoover, providing further confirmation of his view that Donovan had been too trusting in his dealings with Soviet intelligence.

SOVIET AGENTS IN THE OSS

After the United States entered the war, it became more difficult for Soviet operatives in America to maintain links with countries in Europe. Therefore, the NKGB found the OSS an especially vital location for its agents both in Washington and in the field. Using channels provided by the CPUSA, the NKGB managed to plant in various OSS special missions—according to Moscow's records of the effort—at least a dozen agents in countries such as England, Spain, and Yugoslavia where the OSS was active. However, it was possible to maintain regular contact only with those in England.[36]

Yet penetrating the OSS was less focused on stations abroad than on that supposedly secret agency's more accessible Washington headquarters. The NKGB's 1942 plan of action for the United States stressed using the time during the OSS's initial organizational period "to insert our people there and carry on cultivation with their help."[37] Among the matters of critical importance to Soviet leadership, those for which OSS sources might provide useful information, none ranked higher than efforts by anti-Nazi Germans to negotiate a separate peace with the United States and England.

Franz Neumann

One refugee economist working in the OSS's German section, Franz Neumann ("Ruff"), had been recruited initially for Soviet intelligence by Hedda Gumperz and her husband, Paul Massing. The couple, like Neumann, former socialists in pre-Hitlerian Germany, had begun working for Moscow in the mid-1930s both in Europe and in the United States, broke during the purges, but apparently continued to render modest assistance during the war years.

Neumann had fled Nazi Germany for England, where he graduated from the London School of Economics before moving to the United States in 1936. He worked for a time teaching, was a government consultant, and published a book on the German economy. In February 1942, Neumann joined the OSS.[38] Gumperz and Massing reported to Moscow in August on a valuable study of the Soviet economy by the OSS's Russian department, which Neumann had brought to their attention.[39] His more active assistance to the NKGB began the following spring. Elizabeth Zarubina, wife of the Soviet station chief in New

York and herself an experienced operative (using the code name "Vardo" but known to her sources as "Helen"), then established contact with him.[40] On April 3, 1943, the New York station informed Moscow: "[Zarubina] met for the first time with [Neumann] who promised to pass us all the data coming through his hands. According to [Neumann], he is getting many copies of reports from American ambassadors . . . [and] has access to materials referring to Germany."

That same day, Neumann conveyed to Zarubina detailed information from OSS files regarding various subjects: conversations between U.S. Cardinal Francis Spellman and the Pope, with Spellman trying to bring the Pontiff toward a more supportive public role on behalf of the Allies; official Spanish talks with German and Italian generals and industrialists on prospects for overthrowing Hitler; secret official OSS exchanges in Mexico while recruiting German immigrants (including Communists); and others.[41]

Although Neumann had promised to cooperate fully during his initial meeting with Zarubina, after becoming a naturalized American citizen later that year he appeared to avoid contact. One memorandum sent to Moscow in early January 1944 described a conversation between Neumann and his friends Gumperz and Massing, in which they "directly asked him about the reasons for his inability to work" and tried to determine whether he had changed his mind about cooperating. Neumann responded: "I did not change my mind. If there is something really important, I will inform you without hesitation," though he claimed he had nothing valuable to talk about at present.[42]

Soon, however, he did. Shortly before the unsuccessful attempt on Hitler's life by dissident German officers on July 20, 1944, Neumann described in detail for the NKGB the negotiations between German opposition groups and OSS representatives in Switzerland led by Allen Dulles. Based on Neumann's information, Vassily Zarubin sent several memoranda to Moscow that month.[43] Neumann's reports fit squarely into a continuing pattern of inquiry begun in fall 1941.

At that time, Moscow had cabled its New York station "to get documentary material that elucidated proposals for peace by fascist Germany and English attempts on this matter." This cable mentioned a former League of Nations official, then working for the International Red Cross, who had visited Berlin and London to explore such proposals.[44] Still, almost three years later, no rumor regarding talks that might lead to a separate Anglo-American peace agreement with Nazi Germany was too vague or unsubstantiated to be ignored by Stalin and other Soviet leaders.

Franz Neumann lost his NKGB courier in July 1944 when Elizabeth Zarubina left the United States. Apparently, the link to Neumann was not picked up by another station operative, and the German refugee scholar turned U.S. citizen had no further contact with Soviet intelligence. The following year, Neumann left for London to work on war crimes issues at the headquarters of chief U.S. prosecutor General Robert Jackson.[45]

Julius Joseph

Since Hedda Gumperz and Paul Massing did not work directly for Jacob Golos during the war years, their recruitment of Neumann evolved from prewar association as anti-Nazi exiles. Others among Golos's contacts and sources, however, did find their way into OSS ranks, and both he and Elizabeth Bentley supervised these agents. One of them, Julius Joseph ("Careful"), even had a friend and confidant who worked at the FBI when Golos recruited him and his wife ("Colleague") in 1941.[46] First Mrs. Joseph (as a typist)[47] and then Julius (as an analyst) joined the OSS in 1943.[48] Mr. Joseph became a prime source on a range of subjects of interest to the Soviets—among them U.S. policy toward China, Japan, and Korea and the personal characteristics of certain OSS officials.[49] Mrs. Joseph, on the other hand, launched a love affair with another man that same year and, despite Jacob Golos's best efforts as an informal marriage counselor, divorced Julius.[50] Fortunately, and unlike Katherine Perlo, the former Mrs. Joseph chose not to expose her husband to American authorities. He continued working for the OSS (and the NKGB) for the remainder of the war.

Donald Wheeler

So effective was Julius Joseph that, in May 1945, Moscow proposed assigning him to supervise two other Soviet sources within the OSS: Donald Wheeler ("Izra") and Helen Tenney ("Muse").[51] Wheeler, the more important of the two, had worked with the GRU earlier in his career. After Golos's death, his Soviet link shifted to the NKGB through the combined efforts (according to its files) of Vassily Zarubin, Earl Browder, and Elizabeth Bentley. Throughout this process, Wheeler remained closely linked to Victor Perlo's covert circle of Washington bureaucrats moonlighting for Moscow.[52]

The Soviets considered Wheeler easily the most valuable of all the agents associated with Victor Perlo's group, as Itzhak Akhmerov confirmed for Moscow in this September 17, 1944, memorandum:

> As you know, [Wheeler] passed to us more interesting materials than anybody else from this group. Three weeks ago [Bentley] met with him for the first time. He made a very good impression on her. I asked [Bentley] to be very prudent and to do everything possible to fortify his position in the [OSS]. He seems to be very brave and does not care about his situation. He says it makes no sense to be afraid: a man dies only once. He treats his [OSS] colleagues very critically and considers them all empty-headed.[53]

Unlike many of the sources linked to Soviet intelligence elsewhere in the government, Wheeler was neither Jewish nor a first- or second-generation American. "My father's people were originally Puritan," began the autobiography he prepared in January 1945 for the NKGB's Moscow personnel file; "they came to this country in the Great Migration of the 1630s and settled in Massachusetts. At the time of the Revolution, they were farmers in upstate New York and, in the 1830s, they moved to Wisconsin when the state was first being settled. . . ." Wheeler's father, a skilled bricklayer, held radical views derived from American Populist and Christian Socialist traditions and became an early and constant supporter of the Bolshevik Revolution: "He has never been disturbed by purges, by pacts, or by any of the aspects of Soviet policy which have upset so many middle-class liberals," his son Donald wrote.

Born on his parents' farm in the state of Washington, Donald Wheeler was a bona fide member of the "agrarian proletariat" from birth, living "in a tent house . . . [with] neither electricity, nor running water, nor telephone . . . [and little] heat in winter." He escaped from family poverty through a Rhodes Scholarship to Oxford in 1935, where he excelled before returning in 1938 to work at a series of federal government posts before going to work in October 1941 "for the Coordinator of Information, now the OSS."

Politically, Wheeler's life followed a familiar arc among the romantic, radical Americans who volunteered their service to Soviet intelligence, from milder reform traditions into communism, though in his case, family background dictated a wider range of involvement. Thus, Wheeler explained in his NKGB memoir that his "childhood political development"—presumably preadolescent—"was a curious mixture of agrarian radicalism, utopian socialism (from books mainly), and faith in militant trade unionism." His pantheon of heroes included "Eugene Debs along with John Brown, Lincoln, and Lenin. But on the issues of the day, I was naturally rather confused."[54]

After supporting the Progressive Party candidate in 1924—at age eleven!—Wheeler turned Socialist by 1932. While at Oxford, he completed his political odyssey in 1935 by joining the Communist Party of Great Britain (as another American, Michael Straight, did at Cambridge, also in the mid-1930s). After several years in England and France assisting in "political work" for the International Brigades that fought in Spain, Wheeler returned to the United States where, as a Communist, he became a union organizer in government agencies.

Although Donald Wheeler worked in the OSS from its earliest days on German manpower problems, only upon joining Victor Perlo's group in 1943 did he begin to deliver a steady flow of material to Soviet intelligence. "He has access to excellent material," Perlo wrote his Soviet supervisors in January 1945, "and once given an explanation of what was wanted, worked hard and bravely to get it. . . . He has not been reckless but has gotten materials regularly under security conditions more difficult than those faced by most others [in the group]."[55]

Wheeler's 1945 NKGB autobiography described more precisely the areas in which his information could prove useful to the Soviet Union:

> Up to the present, the work of my section has been mainly strategic analysis and estimating population and manpower factors of strategic importance to the enemy's position. In particular, we have worked on the German civilian manpower situation, military manpower, the strength and disposition of enemy forces, and enemy losses. A sideline has been the analysis of European population movements, contributing to the appraisal of the Axis' food situation and, later, to planning for military government.[56]

Beginning in 1944, virtually the entire range of OSS analytic and planning documents on Nazi Germany and its postwar prospects flowed continuously from General Donovan's Washington headquarters through Donald Wheeler to Pavel Fitin's offices in Moscow. After receiving ten documentary reports on Germany in July 1944, for example, the chief of the NKGB's Eighth Department of the First Directorate, one Colonel Allakhverdov, called them all valuable and organized their distribution elsewhere in the Soviet government: "The materials are being used by us in our work as rich reference material on the economic situation in Germany." Wheeler's deliveries also included reports on the losses of the German armed forces and on "comparative capabilities of the sides on the Eastern front," which went directly to the GRU, the Foreign Ministry, and other departments.[57] The NKGB leadership acknowledged directly in September 1944 that "we have received very valuable materials, especially on the Soviet Union and Germany" from Wheeler.[58]

Penetration of the OSS by Soviet intelligence was extensive and reached across various departments in the organization. Thus, even before approaching Donald Wheeler through Victor Perlo, information on his potential value had been received from other OSS officials working for the Russians, including Franz Neumann (who described Wheeler as "a calm and progressive man") and, most important, from Donovan's aide Duncan Lee ("Kokh"), who had befriended Wheeler and his wife.[59]

Through Duncan Lee, Moscow learned in mid-September 1944 that the OSS's internal security branch had composed a list of "Reds" within its ranks, dividing them into three categories:

1. known members of the Communist Party (Wheeler was listed among them);
2. non-members of the CPUSA who hold Communist views;
3. "progressive liberals" on the Left.

Lee's associates among OSS security personnel, evidently not suspecting his own Communist ties, told him that measures would be taken against the agency's "Reds" if they were found to have passed information to the Russians or in the event of a future American conflict with the USSR.[*60]

---

* "According to [Duncan Lee's] advice, a list of 'reds' has been compiled by the Security Division of [the OSS]. The list contains 4 surnames of persons who are supplying information to the Russians. One of them sounds like JIMENEZ. The list is divided into two categories: 1. Open [Communist Party members] (among them [Donald Wheeler]) and 2. Sympathizers, left-wing liberals, etc. (among them [Maurice Halperin]). [Lee] is trying to get the list." New York station to Moscow, September 15, 1944, Nos. 1325–26, VENONA files. A week later, New York station sent Moscow the following cable: "Further to [the above cable]. On the Security Division of [the OSS's] list of [Communist Party members] are [the following]: . . . Donald WHEELER. [A number of other names are blacked out.] . . . included in a list of persons 'concerning whom it is known that they give information. . . .'" September 22, 1944, No. 1354, VENONA files. A third cable that week indicated Moscow's deep concern over the situation: ". . . tell [Bentley] temporarily to cease liaison with [Wheeler]. . . . In future liaison may be re-established only with our permission. Give [Lee] the task of compiling a report on the Security Division of [OSS]." September 20, 1944, No. 954, VENONA files.

Despite this evident threat of personal exposure, Donald Wheeler continued to cooperate with Soviet intelligence. One of his 1945 assignments was to identify individual OSS agents in Europe operating under cover. Wheeler responded with alacrity, fingering among others a *Life* magazine correspondent.[61] One of his most useful reports, recounting a conversation with an OSS paratrooper lieutenant named Buchbinder who had just returned from a secret mission behind Soviet lines in Germany, was sent by Anatoly Gorsky to Moscow in May 1945. Buchbinder described his OSS effort to monitor the Soviet transfer of plants and equipment out of Germany into its direct control, an assignment that indicated Donovan's concern over the USSR's postwar intentions.[62]

After the war's end, Wheeler continued to pass a significant number of documents and information to the NKGB, including among his October/November 1945 collection alone the following:

- an August 1945 OSS report on Polish immigration in France;
- a report on the Italian domestic political situation on the eve of elections in that country;
- the monthly confidential report of the military governor in the U.S. occupation zone of Germany;
- OSS reports [Numbers NN1785.49 and 1785.52] about current political events in the USSR;
- correspondence between OSS representatives in Germany and OSS leaders in Washington on a range of issues;
- OSS weekly reports on political events in Europe;
- a State Department intelligence report on the Middle East.[63]

Presumably Wheeler conveyed to Soviet intelligence anything of interest that came to his attention at the OSS.

Nor did Wheeler's assistance end there. Sometime in late 1945, he managed to expand his acquisitions to include documents related to military projects, summarized in a belated October 1946 Moscow memorandum from Lieutenant Colonel Leonid Kvasnikov (who earlier had overseen the theft of atomic secrets from his post at the NKGB's New York station during the war) to a colleague. This data had arrived earlier in the year from the files of American military intelligence's joint technical subcommittee, also credited in Kvasnikov's memo: "The source 'Izra' [Wheeler's code name], mail . . . for 1945. The material is of interest." The reports formed an impressive collection, covering:

1. German guided missiles . . .
2. Description of the German missile X-4 . . .
3. Sound-absorbing covers for submarines . . .
4. Trends in German tank projectiles.[64]

These deliveries may have been Wheeler's last. By then, President Truman had disbanded the OSS and transferred many of its units and staff to other government intelligence agencies. Wheeler and his OSS colleagues now found themselves, temporarily, an unwelcome addition in a hostile State Department. Elizabeth Bentley's defection had placed him in immediate jeopardy, as it did all those with connections to Victor Perlo's group. Other Americans who had served Soviet intelligence within the OSS found themselves similarly imperiled.

Duncan Lee

Several Soviet sources at the OSS who had reported to Jacob Golos—including Helen Tenney ("Muse"), an employee of the agency's Soviet section—believed at first that their materials were being delivered to Earl Browder for use by the CPUSA.*[65] Only after Golos's death, when the OSS sources began dealing directly with Soviet operatives, did the actual destination of documents and information become clear to some of them.

One source, "Yasha," who worked on Soviet economic problems for the OSS, and a few others would brief their NKGB contacts but refused to pass written material.[66] Another, who worked in the Latin American section, Maurice Halperin ("Hare"), sometimes conveyed documents, but Moscow criticized the paucity of information he delivered.[67] Nor did Soviet intelligence always know the actual source of data, a recurrent problem for the NKGB and its major complaint about Golos's OSS contacts. One exasperated dispatch from Moscow headquarters expressed irritation that "every cable [from OSS sources] begins approximately the same way: 'A man of the OSS in Berne. . . .' Obviously, the names of OSS representatives in these countries are of considerable interest to us and are indicated in the originals of these cables"—but were not being identified by NKGB sources such as "Yasha" and "Hare."[68]

---

* One barely deciphered 1944 cable from the New York station to Moscow detailed some of "Muse's" data: "According to [Tenney's] information the [OSS]. . . ." May 27, 1944, No. 756, VENONA files. On Tenney's reporting to the NKGB, see also July 4, 1944, No. 940, VENONA files.

The basic reason for this reticence may have stemmed from the fact that Jacob Golos encouraged among his American sources at OSS the naive belief that their information went to CPUSA leaders, not to Soviet intelligence. In that case, presumably Earl Browder did not need to know the name and post of an OSS officer in Switzerland! Even the OSS's most senior official who spied for the NKGB, Duncan Lee, while working for Golos, conveyed the contents of OSS reports from Moscow without indicating their authors or other information of the highest value to Soviet intelligence.[69] Later, supervising Lee's covert life became the responsibility of more experienced Russian operatives, and throughout the war he proved to be a valuable but difficult source.

While Donald Wheeler traced his American roots to Puritan New England forebears, Duncan Lee was a product of the Old South and a descendant of Confederate General Robert E. Lee. He was born in China, where his father was a missionary, and first traveled to the United States as a teenager. After graduating from the University of Virginia and studying at Cambridge in England, he returned to the United States to earn a law degree at Yale in 1939. He immediately went to work at the New York firm of Donovan & Leisure, where he became a protégé of General Donovan's. Three months into this job, Lee transferred to Donovan's staff first at the Coordinator of Information's office (COI) and, after its founding, at the OSS.[70]

Jacob Golos wrote Moscow about Lee on September 8, 1942, extolling the potential of Donovan's talented assistant, who had just received a captain's commission in the U.S. Army while continuing to work at OSS:

[Lee] works on issues of guerrilla movement, sabotage, and "commandos" (knows about training camps in the United States). Cables coming to the State Department go through his hands. He collects them and shows them to Donovan at his discretion. All the agent information from Europe and the rest of the world also comes through his hands. He joined the party at Yale University in 1939; his wife joined the party at the same time. . . . Thanks to his appointment [assisting Donovan at COI and OSS], he was withdrawn from the [party] group and made an illegal member. [Lee] wants to work with us and pass to us information he is able to acquire. He can bring no documents out of his department but will remember them as much as possible, then make notes and pass them to "Dir" [another radical activist, Mary Price].[71]

Despite Lee's reluctance to hand over documents, limiting himself to briefings for couriers such as Mary Price or Elizabeth Bentley, his Soviet overseers were not displeased: "For the period of contact with us," observed one mid-May 1943 NKGB memorandum, "[Lee] has given [us] much interesting information which speaks to his great possibilities in the field of valuable information."* According to this document, Lee had described OSS cables discussing such vital matters as Chinese Nationalist leader Chiang Kai-shek's intention to hold a conference at Xian with Communist Party leaders to discuss relations between their forces; a report from the American Ambassador to the USSR about rumors in Moscow that Churchill had told Stalin no second front would be opened until the Soviet Union initiated war against Japan; and a range of reports concerning European political and diplomatic events.[72]

Although it received these useful tidbits, Moscow did not initially consider Duncan Lee a full-fledged source: "[He] needs everyday guidance and education," the May memorandum concluded. ". . . So far there is no data from the station that his recruitment is completed." Jacob Golos had informed Moscow earlier in 1943 that Lee was traveling to London, Cairo, and the Chinese city of Chintsin, making constant supervision by Soviet operatives impossible.[73] The New York station informed Moscow on September 1 that, on the flight to China, Lee's plane had crashed into the Burmese jungle; he was injured but rescued. After Lee returned to the United States at the end of October, the station wrote Moscow that his "wanderings in Burma's jungles frayed him very much, and one will need some time to draw him back into active work with us."[74]

By the following month, however, Lee had resumed the practice of relating interesting items to his Soviet intelligence contacts—though never in writing or through stolen documents. He would not accept assignments from the NKGB but maintained the Russians' interest with news of OSS stations abroad, German peace feelers, and descriptions of the political situation in various European countries.[75] Of paramount importance, Lee reported on March 3, 1944, that movements among high-level U.S. generals suggested that "the second front will be opened between mid-May and the beginning of June,"[76] a clever and, it turned out, accurate conclusion regarding the Allied armies' invasion of occupied France.

* "[Duncan Lee] reports that at the [Roosevelt]-[Churchill] conference . . . [remainder of sentence undeciphered]. . . . In the middle of June [Lee] is going . . . to CHUNGKING to acquaint himself there with the work of the [OSS] group. . . . We discussed with [Lee] the question of his removing documents for photographing. [Lee] said that in some cases he [agrees] to do this, but as a rule he considers it inexpedient." New York station to Moscow, May 26, 1943, No. 782, VENONA files.

Lee was also extremely useful in warning the NKGB about security investigations of possible Communist informers within the OSS, including the persistent probe of Donald Wheeler. "About ten days ago," Itzhak Akhmerov reported in September 1944, "[Lee] told us very unpleasant news concerning [Wheeler's] situation . . . he is included on the list of officials who allegedly provide us with information . . . from their department. [Bentley] says [Lee] is one of the senior people in the department in charge of checking the officials, etc." Lee also said that, if the OSS decided to fire the suspected Communists (including his "old friend," Donald Wheeler), he might have to perform the task personally.[77] Wheeler and Lee had become friends while both attended Yale University. But Wheeler did not know, according to a memorandum he gave the NKGB, that Lee had also become a Soviet source within OSS.[78] Nor did Lee know of Wheeler's involvement, or so Elizabeth Bentley informed Moscow at this time.[79]

Meanwhile, Lee continued his conversational involvement with the NKGB, mentioning in September 1944 that he had been appointed to an even more important operational post as chief of the OSS's Japanese section.[80] The New York station informed Moscow the following month on various matters related to Asian agents—Chinese, Japanese, and Korean. It also noted, turning to Europe, that the OSS was becoming increasingly concerned about the future of its operatives in territories occupied by the Red Army—especially in Bulgaria, which had also been of focal interest in General Donovan's discussions in Moscow.[81]

In late 1944, Duncan Lee's family troubles began to plague his efforts on behalf of Soviet intelligence, as was the case with other agents (such as Perlo and Silvermaster) at this time. Anatoly Gorsky reported to Moscow on November 2 that, based on information provided by Elizabeth Bentley, Lee and his sometime-courier Mary Price had become lovers, which posed an obvious problem for Lee's marriage. "[Price] established an intimate relationship with [Lee], and she did not tell us about it until recently." Interweaving espionage and lovers' liaisons posed problems for both activities, which Gorsky went on to describe: "[Lee] and [Price] met in two places, at her flat and at his. The meetings were held in the presence of [Lee's] wife, who was aware of her husband's secret work."

When Lee's wife discovered her husband's love affair and complained in a series of jealous scenes, Price stopped serving as his courier. But she continued the love affair, hoping that Lee would divorce his wife and marry her.[82]

Distraught over his deteriorating marriage, the pressures of the love affair, and intensified security probes at the OSS, Duncan Lee, by late 1944, had become an extremely reluctant Soviet source. Moreover, he distrusted Elizabeth Bentley, who now acted as his primary courier and contact with Soviet intelligence.

Throughout his final series of bi-monthly meetings with Bentley, Lee claimed to have little interesting information. The pair would meet at carefully designated locations, Bentley wrote Moscow at the time,

> . . . and he never brings material since he fears writing down information. . . . He tells me the information he has, and I remember it. A long time ago, I had to promise him that I would not write down data communicated by him. Therefore, I have to remember his data, until I am elsewhere and can write it down. . . . At present, [Lee] has access only to reports on Japan which, according to him, are of no interest. . . . At present [Lee] has nothing very valuable for us. However, one must maintain the connection with him, since he has very solid status at the OSS, has friendly relations with Donovan, and can be useful to us in future. [Lee] needs special guidance—he is one of "the weakest of the weak sisters," nervous and fearing his own shadow. This, as well as his personal troubles . . . considerably hamper working with him at present.[83]

Early in 1945, troubled by Bentley's reports, Anatoly Gorsky assigned another agent, Joseph Katz ("X") to meet with Duncan Lee. But after a February 3 meeting, Katz's report reinforced Bentley's earlier analysis:

> Saw [Lee] last night. After beating his chest about what a coward he is, how sorry he feels about it, etc., he told me he must stick to his decision to quit. Though I agreed to meet again in case of necessity, in my opinion, there is no sense in using him. He is totally frightened and depressed. He suffers from nightmares where he sees his name on the lists [presumably of accused Communists within OSS], his life is destroyed, etc.[84]

Lee had begun to believe that Donovan and others at OSS suspected him. He recalled for Bentley a March 1944 episode in which OSS representatives had discussed a group of its agents in Bulgaria with Soviet Foreign Minister Molotov in Moscow. Molotov apparently knew about the group and could even name one of its key agents, signaling an obvious Soviet intelligence source within OSS's highest ranks.[85]

Lee met twice more with Joseph Katz in March 1945, and Gorsky reported to Moscow that he "came so scared to both meetings that he could not hold a cup of coffee since his hands trembled." Basically, Lee met with Katz to plead for his complete release from Soviet intelligence involvement. The station chief's account of the discussions with Katz left no room for argument:

> [Lee] said the work of gathering information for the compatriots, and possibly for us, filled him with horror. He has terrible dreams every night. He cannot believe for a minute that the FBI does not know . . . all the American informer-compatriots, but due to the fact that the general situation does not [warrant] taking strong measures, [the FBI] undertakes no action for the time being. . . . In the end, [Lee] asked us to leave him in peace . . . and explained his decision to stop working for us with the fact that he cannot have "a double life," that his conscience is "not clean" because he "deceived the U.S.," that there is a constant struggle in his soul. . . .[86]

Moscow responded to Gorsky in April 1945, recognizing the obvious, that "it seems impossible to use [Lee] for getting materials." But NKGB leaders encouraged his continued use as a "talent-spotter" and informant on security investigations within the OSS.[87] Concurrently, however, its New York station received news from Judith Coplon in the Justice Department that the FBI would soon begin investigating every Soviet organization in the United States and pursuing all previous leads on Communist sources within the government. As a result, Moscow instructed Gorsky on April 7 to cease all contact with Duncan Lee and to place him, along with other American recruits, "on conservation."[88] This left Lee still burdened by a jeopardized career, an eroded marriage, and an anguished conscience.

Fitzgerald and "Dan"

For every troubled and ambivalent source within OSS, for every Franz Neumann or Duncan Lee, Soviet intelligence operatives during the war could point out those who were untroubled and cheerfully compliant: sources such as Donald Wheeler, Helen Tenney, and at least two others—Edward Fitzgerald and "Dan."

Fitzgerald ("Ted") came from a New York working-class, once-Republican family that, during the 1930s, had shifted political allegiance to the Communist Party! As the autobiography he provided to

Moscow indicated, not only Fitzgerald but his mother, sister, wife, and two cousins were all members of the CPUSA during this period.[89] About his work for the party, Fitzgerald wrote, in his sketch for the New York station in February 1945, "Member last 10 years. Always in closed groups under Peters in NY, Philadelphia and Washington.* No mass organization work, no bad record. . . ."[90]

After holding a series of posts in various wartime agencies, Fitzgerald went to work for the OSS in 1943. He passed material to Nathan Gregory Silvermaster at least twice, until Elizabeth Bentley informed Silvermaster that she considered Fitzgerald incautious and advised that he not be used as a source. Silvermaster stopped meeting Fitzgerald. He never learned that Fitzgerald had apparently belonged at the same time both to his own group of sources *and* to Victor Perlo's, which Bentley discovered once she established contact with the Perlo Group in the spring of 1944.[91] Most of the information conveyed by Fitzgerald concerned European economics: food supplies, Swiss government reluctance to cooperate with the Allies in locating and confiscating German investments, and other data on Nazi properties.[92] Edward Fitzgerald remained a minor and occasionally used NKGB source at OSS.

More important to Soviet intelligence was a government economist code-named "Dan," who was an active source for the Perlo Group of economic information from the War Production Board, where "Dan" worked throughout much of the war. In one memorandum, which reached Moscow through Itzhak Akhmerov, "Dan" complained about the methods allegedly being used by senior officials at the Board "to sabotage the fulfillment of USSR orders."[93] This news undoubtedly fueled Stalin's already keen suspicion of America's postwar intentions toward the Soviet Union.

"Dan" was born in New York in 1918, the son of a successful Russian immigrant businessman. He joined the Communist Party in 1935.[94] Known to the New York station as an intelligent and loyal source of data during his tenure at the War Production Board, "Dan" attracted even greater interest when he was recruited by OSS in the summer of 1945 to work in its Russian section (as Anatoly Gorsky promptly informed Moscow). "Dan" was ordered to leave for London where his responsibilities for the soon-to-be-disbanded OSS involved gathering information on the Soviet Union.

* A reference to his involvement in secret CPUSA cells run by Joszef Peter, a.k.a. "J. Peters."

His instructions from OSS higher-ups were extensive and of considerable interest to Soviet intelligence: to collect data on the USSR's transportation network; the military potential of the Trans-Siberian and Baikal-Amur railroads; Soviet machine-building industries and that country's metallurgy, mining, rubber, and chemical industries; human losses in the war and the Soviet health system; the location of Red Army units in the Far East; and Soviet policy toward liberated countries. These were all among "Dan's" broadly based fields of research interest. Again, Soviet anxieties over American and British postwar policies seemed more realistic when viewed against the backdrop of the OSS's intelligence-gathering agenda.

Even before leaving the United States, "Dan" began to collect data from OSS files for his Soviet contacts. In August, Gorsky reported that "Dan" had found a detailed fall 1943 summary report on the Baikal-Amur railway, information Gorsky passed along to Soviet navy counterintelligence. "Dan" also provided a memorandum on the activities and operatives of the OSS's Russian department.[95]

Once in London, "Dan" almost immediately reestablished contact with the NKGB through an operative code-named "Allen." "Dan" pointed out to his contact that his main purpose in accepting the OSS posting to England was to help Soviet intelligence: "If I hadn't met with you, there wouldn't have been any sense in coming here." By that time, President Truman had issued his September decree ordering the termination of the OSS on October 1 and the shift of several agency units to the State and War Departments. "Dan" had already learned that his stay in London would soon end.[96]

To a second meeting with "Allen," "Dan" brought various documents, informing his contact: "Basically everything is clear here. I had to reproduce by memory part of the information since it passed through my hands a long time ago." Moscow officials were especially irritated at "Dan's" report that American and British intelligence officers had interrogated Soviet prisoners of war who had been liberated by Western troops.

"Dan" indicated that, on his return to America, "the comrade who connected us . . . his personal friend"—Victor Perlo—"would reestablish there without any problems."[97] "Dan" described in detail the contents of OSS files to which he had access, including a number from British intelligence, but (according to "Allen") "claims this material is too old and not of interest . . . however, if it is needed, he will try to do something to acquire it. . . . I concluded that the risk connected with obtaining it is not worth the material itself."[98]

"Dan" and "Allen" had five meetings, according to the reports filed by the Soviet operative,[99] before the OSS agent returned to the United States that fall.[100] Because of Elizabeth Bentley's defection, however, and Soviet fears of intensified U.S. counterintelligence inquiries, "Dan" was not approached again for several years and then unsuccessfully.

In the decades that followed, Soviet intelligence operatives made a variety of efforts to restore their link to "Dan." But he had long since left government employ, only to find himself under periodic but persistent investigation—as did other Soviet sources within OSS during World War II—by the FBI and other American government agencies.

As late as September 1958, the chief of a major KGB department wrote a memo to his superior proposing a meeting with "Dan"—"a prominent economist with rich experience working in U.S. federal organizations"—to determine his ability to publish writings "advantageous to us as well as [other] possibilities for cooperation. . . ." Although the KGB memorandum apparently was never acted upon, it reflected the long institutional memory of a Soviet operative who may not have met "Dan" personally in the United States during the Second World War but who read carefully the files of that period. The memorandum's author was Colonel Alexander Feklissov.[101]

Throughout its brief history, the OSS provided Soviet intelligence with a harvest of vital information on virtually every topic related to the European war effort. Some of this material reached Moscow through the legitimate, if naive, efforts of Donovan and his colleagues to cooperate with the NKGB on matters of mutual concern related to defeating the Axis powers. More extensive still were the contributions of such figures as Donald Wheeler, Duncan Lee, and others within the OSS who betrayed their country's trust through misguided devotion and loyalty to the Soviet Union.

CHAPTER 12

❖❖❖

Harvest Time, III: Hiss, Glasser, and Warning Signs

GLASSER AND HISS

Soviet agents within the U.S. government during the New Deal era and the Second World War were sufficiently numerous and active that often, as in meetings between Alger Hiss and other sources (among them Noel Field, Laurence Duggan, and Michael Straight), it was not unusual for entirely unrelated operatives and agents to run into one another. Thus, NKGB's Washington station chief Anatoly Gorsky reported to Moscow in December 1944 about an accidental encounter while on official business with an extremely important Treasury Department agent, Harold Glasser, code-named "Ruble":

> On December 9 . . . [Soviet Ambassador to the U.S. Andrei] Gromyko charged me with meeting "Richard" [Harry Dexter White] for the purpose of receiving additional explanations from Morgenthau's department about German postage-stamps prepared by him. On the same day, [White] phoned me and asked me to come and get the information Gromyko was interested in. On December 11, I went to Morgenthau's department. [White] was not in the office, but one of his secretaries showed me to his assistant, on whose office door was written: Assistant to the Director of the Division of Monetary Research. [White's] assistant

turned out to be [Harold Glasser]. We have tried to organize [Glasser's] work through [Elizabeth Bentley, Victor Perlo,] and others . . . [but] these circumstances may be used to develop this official acquaintance in order to switch then to direct connection [with a Soviet operative].[1]

Moscow agreed with Gorsky's suggestion and recommended that he try to establish personal operational contact with Glasser, using his previous password at an arranged meeting. The intimate bond between top CPUSA leaders and Soviet intelligence was again apparent here: The password was "Greetings from Gene Dennis," a key official of the American Communist Party.*[2] Gorsky informed Moscow on December 24 that contact with Glasser had been made and that a second meeting would be held shortly.[3]

In August 1944, prior to establishing a direct link to Gorsky, Glasser had handed over government materials to Silvermaster.[4] That fall, he also used Perlo and Bentley to convey information to the NKGB.[5] After talking to Glasser, Gorsky concluded that the Treasury official understood that he worked for Soviet intelligence; in Glasser's words, "[I am] not a child [and] realize exactly where and to whom [my] materials have been going for several years."[6]

Glasser's personal background resembled that of a number of others involved in Soviet espionage in America during these years. He described it in a December 1944 handwritten autobiography for Moscow. The son of Lithuanian-Jewish immigrants, Glasser was born in Chicago in 1905 and studied economics at the University of Chicago. He joined the Communist Party in 1933. Glasser joined the Treasury Department in 1936 and developed a pattern of clandestine meetings with various Soviet and American operatives that, largely because of Harry Dexter White's strong support, survived a 1940 FBI background inquiry.[7] Although his friendship with White became strained, according to Glasser because of a quarrel between their wives, nevertheless White remained a strong backer. He assisted Glasser in obtaining posts and promotions at Treasury while aware of his Communist ties.[8]

Several networks competed for Glasser's services in the war's closing year. Still "officially" attached to Victor Perlo's group, Glasser, though now privy to numerous State and War Department secret cables on

* "Further to our [cable] No. 665[a], [Harold Glasser] advises that . . . [unde-ciphered section] first name and surname—Dennis, on whose behalf one should get in touch." New York station to Moscow, July 22, 1943, No. 1206, VENONA files.

postwar planning as well as Treasury's own documents, apparently declined to give these to Perlo or his colleagues. This caution extended to Silvermaster, who schemed with evident success to prevent Glasser from obtaining a sought-after promotion at Treasury.[9] Considering Silvermaster's difficulties with his existing network of sources, Moscow turned down his request (via Akhmerov) for Glasser's transfer to him from Perlo's oversight.*[10]

Rejected for promotion at Treasury, Glasser considered for a time accepting an invitation from a friend at State to take over an important post there. For a variety of reasons, however, including a fear of renewed security inquiries by a less-friendly State Department, Glasser accepted Gorsky's strong recommendation (backed by Pavel Fitin at NKGB headquarters in Moscow) that he remain at Treasury.[11]

Glasser brought urgent but discomfiting news to his Soviet handlers in April 1945. He summoned Anatoly Gorsky, in his Soviet consul's "cover" role, to his office on April 2 nominally to continue their earlier "official" discussions on Treasury's plans to use new postage stamps in occupied territories. At this apparently normal meeting and with another Treasury official present, Glasser, while shaking hands, slipped a note to Gorsky that contained this warning:

> An FBI agent communicated to [Secretary of State Edward] Stettinius that one of their agents had seen a bundle of documents which had been brought in a briefcase to New York for photographing. After that, they were returned within 24 hours to Washington. A political report and important cables were among these documents. Judging by the character of the documents, only three people had access to them. One of these people is "Ales" [Alger Hiss]. . . . According to Stettinius, the FBI agent told him such operations with documents had already gone on for 18 months, that in this manner, "hundreds and hundreds" of documents were withdrawn. Stettinius asked the FBI agent whether these documents were going to *PM* [a radical New York daily newspaper], to which the latter answered: "No, much lefter

---

* "According to [Silvermaster's] report, he may be presented with an opportunity of obtaining from [Harry Dexter White] [Harold Glasser's] appointment to [White's] post as the latter will soon be appointed assistant secretary. . . . [Silvermaster] has repeatedly suggested that [Glasser] be turned over to him. . . . [Silvermaster] does not want to promote [Glasser] to [White's] post unless he takes him into his group. . . ." New York station to Moscow, January 18, 1945, No. 79, VENONA files.

than this." Concluding his conversation with [Hiss] about it, Stettinius told him: "I hope it is not you."[12]

Since Glasser's source for this information could hardly have been either Stettinius or the FBI agent, it was evidently his friend and fellow-agent Alger Hiss who had informed him of the episode.

Gorsky had tried the previous month, through Glasser but without success, to make contact with the Soviet agent "Ales" at the State Department in order to receive information on U.S. foreign policy. The process was frustrating, since both Glasser and Hiss were often abroad during this period on government business (Gorsky would learn only weeks later that Hiss reported to the GRU, which normally precluded cooperating with competing NKGB operatives). "Concerning [Hiss], we spoke to [Glasser] several times," Gorsky informed Moscow on March 5, 1945:

> As we have already written, [Glasser] gives to [Hiss] an exceptionally good political reference as a member of the Communist Party. [Glasser] tells us that [Hiss] is a strong, determined man with a firm and resolute character, who is aware that he is a Communist with all the consequences of illegal status. Unfortunately, he evidently understands the rules of security as his own [business] as [do] all local Communists.[13]

In short, Alger Hiss declined Glasser's request to meet with Gorsky, leading the station chief to suspect—correctly—that he was already associated with another Soviet operative.

Whatever excellent credentials Hiss might have had as a Soviet agent, so impressive were Glasser's own document deliveries that, on April 25, 1945, Pavel Fitin, then head of the NKGB's First Directorate, recommended to Vsevolod Merkulov that their American source be decorated with the Order of the Red Star. This memorandum sheds light on the underground careers of both Harold Glasser and Alger Hiss:

> Our agent [Glasser], drawn to working for the Soviet Union in May 1937, has been passing (with short breaks caused by business trips) initially through the military "neighbors" and then through our station, valuable information on political and economic issues. Since the beginning of 1945 alone, from reports based on his information and cabled to the station, 34 special reports were sent [by the NKGB information department] to the "Instance" [Stalin and other top leaders]. [Glasser] also gave us talent-spottings on

valuable people . . . who are now being cultivated by us; communicated data about the trip to the USSR by regular officers of the Office of Strategic Services under cover of the U.S. Embassy in Moscow, etc. He gives much attention and energy to our work [and] is a devoted and disciplined agent.

According to data from [Gorsky], the group of agents of the military "neighbors" whose member [Glasser] had been earlier, was recently decorated with USSR orders. About this fact, [Glasser] learned it from his friend [Hiss] who is the leader of the mentioned group.* Taking into account [Glasser's] devoted work for the USSR for 8 years and the fact that as a result of transfer to our station, [he] was not decorated together with other members of [Hiss's] group, [we] consider it expedient to recommend him for the decoration with the Order of the Red Star. Ask your consent.[14]

Merkulov agreed and informed Washington that Glasser had been recommended for the award, pointing out: "At present, [Glasser] is one of the principal sources of information in your station." Moscow recommended maintaining the cultivation of Glasser, encouraging him to continue passing along documents on U.S. foreign financial and economic policy but, even more important, to penetrate Secretary Morgenthau's "financial intelligence service, which is of great operational interest for us."

---

* "As a result of [unidentified] chat with [Alger Hiss], the following has been ascertained:

1. [Hiss] has been working with the [GRU] continuously since 1935.

2. For some years past he has been the leader of a small group of the [GRU's] probationers, for the most part consisting of his relatives.

3. The group and [Hiss] himself work on obtaining military information only. Materials on the [State Department] allegedly interest the [GRU] very little and he does not produce them regularly.

4. All the last few years [Hiss] has been working with "Pol" [Paul] who also meets other members of the group occasionally.

5. *Recently [Hiss] and his whole group were awarded Soviet decorations.* [italics added.]

6. After the YALTA Conference, when he had gone to MOSCOW, a Soviet personage in a very responsible position ([Hiss] gave to understand that it was Comrade Vyshinskij) allegedly got in touch with [Hiss] and at the behest of the Military [GRU] passed on to him their gratitude and so on.

Anatolij Borisovich Gromov [*aka* Anatoly Gorsky]" Washington station to Moscow, March 30, 1945, No. 1822, VENONA files.

One measure of Harold Glasser's importance as an agent at this time can be seen in a 1945 NKGB file. It reported that, during the first five months of that year, based on materials provided by Glasser, its Moscow headquarters had sent seventy-four memoranda on to Stalin and other Soviet leaders.[15]

The material Harold Glasser conveyed to Soviet intelligence in 1945 alone covered an extraordinary range of important subjects, including wartime and postwar economic and international financial issues and political, military, and intelligence information—all of critical interest to the leadership of the USSR.*

---

* A partial list of the 1945 material forwarded by Glasser includes the following:
January
  · Treasury draft on Allied policy toward neutral countries;
  · Cable by General Eisenhower on treatment of persons deported forcibly to Germany during the war;
  · London discussions by U.S. Treasury and Polish advisers on postwar Polish-German and Polish-Soviet relations;
  · Talks on London draft directive removing German personnel from the German financial system;
  · Draft directives by the American commander-in-chief concerning control over German finances (11/22/44);
  · Memorandum on Allied military administration's attitude toward German participation in international cartels (11/21/44);
  · Draft directives on disbanding the Nazi party and purging Nazi personnel (10/13/44).
February
  · Memorandum by Secretary Morgenthau to President Roosevelt concerning a possible $10 billion loan to the USSR and possibilities of repayment;
  · Memorandum by Treasury to State concerning postwar policies toward Germany to prevent another world war;
  · Memoranda on U.S.-USSR negotiations concerning lend-lease protocol;
  · Cables by U.S. Ambassador to London Winant concerning postwar policies toward Germany;
  · Conversations between Morgenthau and State Department official Will Clayton concerning postwar loan to the Soviet Union;
  · Contents of the OSS memorandum about the economic consequences of stripping Germany of its heavy industry.
March
  · Memo on forthcoming trip by presidential envoy Samuel Rosenman to probe financial situation of European countries;
  · Cable from the U.S. Ambassador to London to State concerning England-USSR negotiations regarding postwar credits;
  · Memorandum from Morgenthau to Roosevelt (3/20/45);

Glasser remained incredibly valuable to Soviet intelligence at his Treasury post in 1945. But Gorsky reported to Moscow on October 18 that the State Department had proposed sending him to Japan to serve as General MacArthur's chief adviser on all financial and economic matters, representing both State and Treasury with the rank of ambassador. Gorsky noted that Glasser was prepared to follow Soviet instructions on whether to accept the post if offered, but "his refusal of such a big promotion both by the State Department and [the new Treasury Secretary Fred] Vinson will look absolutely inexplicable." Both Gorsky and Pavel Fitin agreed that Glasser must accept the new assignment, which, in the end, was never offered.[17]

After Elizabeth Bentley's defection later that year, Harold Glasser's services to Soviet intelligence were "conserved" (as Soviet officials re-

----

· Extracts from the FBI's confidential report, its "General Intelligence Survey" of the United States (12/44);
· Extracts from secret U.S. government interdepartmental economic bulletins on "Oil," "Copper," and "Goods" (2/3/45).

April
· Internal memorandum from Treasury concerning conferences at State on postwar reparations (4/7 and 4/16/45);
· Draft instruction from Treasury for the U.S. delegation to the Moscow reparation commission;
· Extracts from the memorandum concerning the Anglo-American financial agreement signed in London (3/7/45);
· Contents of Morgenthau memorandum on the situation in the U.S. occupation zone of Germany (4/20/45);
· Contents of top-secret directives from the commander-in-chief of Allied forces to the commander of the 12th Army Group (4/19/45).

May
· Internal memorandum by Treasury concerning lend-lease policy toward the Soviet Union (5/9/45).

June
· Morgenthau's memorandum to President Truman on postwar lend-lease policy in Europe (5/9/45);
· Draft directives by the U.S. Joint Chiefs of Staff on locating and detaining suspected war criminals;
· Contents of the cable by the U.S. Ambassador in Moscow to State about Soviet losses in the war (5/20/45). ["[Harold Glasser's] material. We transmit a telegram of the Ambassador of the [United States] in [Moscow] number 1818 of 30 May 1945 addressed to the [State Department]. . . . The fact that the Russians' estimate of their war losses will of course be astronomical (see Embassy telegram number 1230 of 18 April 1945) is merely confirmed by the figure of 100 milliard [sic] dollars quoted above." Washington station to Moscow, June 21, 1945, No. 3598, VENONA files.]

ferred to such an operational halt) on November 23, thus ending his remarkable deliveries of policy documents from State and Treasury at a pivotal moment in postwar relations between the U.S. and the USSR.[18]

THE TROTSKYIST OBSESSION

Even after his death, the "Old Man," as Leon Trotsky was known to friends and adversaries alike in the years prior to his assassination in 1940, remained a fearsome—if spectral—presence to Soviet operatives abroad. Throughout the World War II years, therefore, one of Soviet intelligence's major interests in the United States and Western Europe remained the struggle to infiltrate or eliminate the dwindling organizational remains of Trotskyism. Thus, his Moscow superiors wrote Gaik Ovakimyan, New York station chief, on January 27, 1941 (Trotsky died from wounds inflicted by an NKVD-trained assassin in Mexico on August 21, 1940), about the need "to activate the struggle against

---

July
- Memorandum on issues the American delegation would raise at the Potsdam Conference concerning a major credit to the Soviet Union;
- Contents of War Department directives concerning locating and detaining suspected war criminals and their trials;
- Contents of the message from Prime Minister Churchill to President Truman concerning reduction of American deliveries to England (5/28/45);
- Contents of the draft cable by Truman to Churchill, drafted by State, concerning changes in postwar lend-lease policy.

September
- Memoranda on sales of surplus American war supplies;
- Treasury Department views concerning the loan to the Soviet Union.

October
- Contents of the memorandum by Treasury Secretary Vinson to President Truman concerning the policy of loans to Belgium, France, and the USSR (a memorandum approved by Truman);
- Contents of the draft economic directives to General MacArthur for Japan's occupation (9/4/45);
- Contents of the draft economic directives to General MacArthur for Korean postwar occupation (9/9/45);
- Contents of the protocol at State's interdepartmental conference on issues related to Germany's reparations obligation (9/25/45);
- Memorandum on the conditions of the American loan to England.[16]

Trotskyites using the disorder among [them] after the 'Old Man's' death. . . . Communicate your concrete proposals for possible recruitments and penetration."[19]

Even dead, Trotsky remained in the minds of Stalin and his associates a figure of incalculable potential disruption within the Soviet Union, despite the horrendous purge years that decimated virtually any possible source of opposition to the regime. Years later, the obsession with Trotskyist views persisted, as in this October 1, 1948, NKGB memorandum concerning a world-famous writer (code-named "Argot") to whom the Soviets had unsuccessfully sought access for years: "He is said to adhere to Trotskyites and has leveled attacks on the Soviet Union," the dispatch from the NKGB's Washington station observed of Ernest Hemingway.[20]

The NKVD made efforts to acquire Trotsky's remaining archives, where they hoped to find leads to the "Trotskyite underground" that Stalin firmly believed still existed in the USSR awaiting its moment to strike. Thus an agent code-named "Satyr" conveyed to the New York station a list of Trotsky's documents held at a bank in that city: "If there is an opportunity," Moscow responded to a report from Ovakimyan on this information, "it is useful to obtain these archives. As far as the archives at Harvard University are concerned, we need to recruit a man there who could photograph them."[21]

Such a person reached the United States specifically to infiltrate the ranks of leading Trotskyists, Mark Zborovsky, a trained NKVD agent code-named "Tulip" and a resident, until then, of Paris. Born in 1908, Mark Zborovsky, a Russian Jew whose parents had left the USSR in 1921 for Poland, joined the Young Communist League in 1926 and the Polish Communist Party in 1934. Jailed for strike activity in 1931, Zborovsky escaped to Germany and later to France, where he was recruited by the NKVD in 1934 to infiltrate the ranks of Trotsky's followers, who were extremely active in French radical circles. Zborovsky eventually became a trusted assistant to Trotsky's son, Lev Sedov, and an active figure in the movement. "With [Zborovsky's] active participation," reads the NKVD's biographical description prepared when Zborovsky was transferred to the United States, "we obtained the entire secret archive of the [Trotskyists'] International Secretariat, Sedov's entire archive, and a considerable portion of the 'Old Man's' archives."[22] After reaching the United States, Zborovsky spent the war years cultivating American Trotskyists and their international associates (to all of whom the NKVD gave the generic code name "polecats").[23] Other agents also reached America during the war, assigned specifically to the apparently unending task of guarding against Leon Trotsky's machinations even from his grave.

THE FBI'S ANONYMOUS LETTER

Similar neurotic preoccupation reached into the heart of Soviet intelligence's American operations in 1943. An anonymous, unsigned August 7 letter from an apparent Soviet operative in the United States to FBI Director J. Edgar Hoover named NKGB station chief Vassily Zarubin (Gaik Ovakimyan's replacement) and ten other NKGB officers in North America plus two American assets, including a "high-level agent in the White House" (unnamed but presumably a reference to Lauchlin Currie). The Soviet whistle-blower portrayed internecine bickering within the spy network and, most extraordinary of all, alleged that his evident superior, station chief Zarubin, actually "works for Japan . . . while his wife [Elizabeth Zarubina, another Soviet operative] works for Germany." Such an accusation in the middle of World War II was indeed startling.

The writer went on to describe a large network of Soviet agents, "among whom are many U.S. citizens," mentioning by name CPUSA head Earl Browder.* Tart commentary on his Soviet NKVD colleagues suggested the author's inside status. He described one colleague, for example, as "a great coward [who] on arrest will quickly give away all the agents to save himself and remain in this country." Although the FBI increased its surveillance on Zarubin and other Soviet operatives mentioned in the letter, the Bureau never learned the writer's identity. Soviet intelligence was apparently more efficient, at least according to former KGB official Pavel Sudoplatov's 1994 memoir. Sudaplatov credits a disgruntled embassy aide to Zarubin (whose official rank was Second Secretary of the Soviet Embassy in Washington), one Lieutenant Colonel Mironov, as the author of the anonymous letter. Mironov, according to Sudoplatov, also wrote Stalin to denounce the Zarubins as Axis agents, an act of bravado that led to his recall to the Soviet Union and eventual confinement in a mental hospital.

Apparently, Mironov was joined in his charges by another Soviet op-

---

* The August 7, 1943, letter was released along with other Soviet intelligence dispatches as part of the VENONA program's recent distribution of previously classified cables. See Robert Lewis Benson and Michael Warner, eds., *VENONA: Soviet Espionage and the American Response, 1939–1957*, pp. 51–55, for its text.

erative at the New York station who, in 1944, raised the same allegations stated in the previous year's anonymous letter to Hoover. In March 1944, Pavel Fitin, chief of the NKGB's First Directorate, investigated the charges and reported to Commissar of State Security Vsevolod Merkulov that the entire affair was "a far-fetched false provocation" whose initiators "used their official position . . . and rudely violated basic rules of security and Service secrecy." Fitin proposed firing both accusers, sending one to work in a remote area of the Soviet Union for five years while his colleague—more ominous still—would be dispatched as a soldier to the front.[24] Available records do not indicate whether the severe punishments—or others, such as confinement to a mental hospital, as Sudoplatov recalled—were actually carried out.

SIGNS OF DISCOVERY

Alexander Feklissov, one of the NKGB's most experienced operatives in the United States during World War II (and during the Kennedy Administration, in meetings with American journalist John Scali, he played a role in the Cuban missile crisis), enjoyed regaling his colleagues in Soviet intelligence with the story of his meeting with then–People's Commissar for Foreign Affairs Vyacheslav Molotov in the fall of 1940. Feklissov was about to leave for the United States. During their talk, Molotov discovered that the agent was unmarried and asked: "How can you be a bachelor, my dear friend? We don't send single people abroad, especially to the U.S. They will immediately find a beautiful blonde or brunette for you—and then a provocation will happen." An official accompanying Feklissov reassured Molotov that the Soviet organizations in New York had many eligible women, and a wife for the operative would be found among them.[25]

Whatever the FBI's experience with beautiful blondes or brunettes may have been during this period, Feklissov did not mention such "provocation" in his 1994 memoir. He did comment disparagingly on the Bureau's ineptitude in dealing with Soviet intelligence activity in the United States during the war years:

> In 1943, there were a number of young, inexperienced officers working in [the FBI's] surveillance brigades whom our intelligence officers spotted easily using simple methods. Evidently, these sleuths were found among young men from small towns who, after two or three months of preparation, started working

against us. We could see at once that they were provincials: their clothing style, guilty-thievish glances, and clumsy manners. When they realized that we noticed them, they would lose self-control and did not know what to do, turning away and looking aside or quickly entering the first available building.[26]

Similar reports were given to Moscow superiors by Feklissov, Gorsky, Zarubin, and other Soviet operatives, despite the FBI's success in gathering evidence that led to the expulsion first of Gaik Ovakimyan and then, in 1944, of Vassily Zarubin, who left for the USSR after being declared persona non grata.[27]

In Zarubin's case, as Mironov's letter indicated, there were complaints from inside the NKGB concerning his practices as a station chief. Not all of them were as improbable as Mironov's allegation that he had been a Japanese agent while his wife worked for the Germans. Even before Zarubin arrived in Moscow, his superiors had begun investigating security violations at the New York station under his leadership. Information emerged that "illegals" coming to the United States were being housed in apartments belonging to "legal" case officers (attached to the Soviet Embassy in Washington or the consulate in New York), that operatives knew the real names and code names of American sources being handled by other operatives (as noted earlier) and, in fact, that at least once Zarubin had organized a meeting where such names (actual and code) were announced.

The luckless station chief, moreover, was called on the carpet in Moscow for other practices, among them addressing all of his subordinates by their code names and not their real ones in the presence of unwitting diplomats. In one reported instance, Zarubin shouted from the third floor to the fifth floor of the Soviet Consulate, "Leonid, come here!," after which the ordinary consular staff called a diplomat whose real name was Alexsey by his code name, "Leonid."[28] Such deviations from proper tradecraft suggested to at least some highly ranked NKGB officials in Moscow that Zarubin and perhaps other operatives in America had adapted the casual style of their American sources.

There was worse to come in the summer of 1944 when the NKGB received reliable information that the FBI had planted microphones in key Soviet locations, including the embassy and consulates, and had learned the names and code names of many operatives and sources. It was that warning which led to the change of virtually every existing agent's code name between August and October 1944.* Thus, the

* "In accordance with our telegram no. 403 we are advising you of the new cover-names . . . [list of cover-name changes follows]. All these cover-names are

USSR's head of state security, Merkulov, wrote Anastas Mikoyan, the Commissar for Foreign Trade, on September 9, 1944:[29]

> According to reliable data received by us, American counterintelligence has planted microphones in all Soviet institutions in America as well as in cars belonging to Soviet citizens and garages where these cars are parked. A reminder, then, from the NKGB about the need to observe maximum caution when speaking on the telephone indoors and in the cars. . . .[30]

Merkulov asked Mikoyan to convey the same instruction to representatives of the foreign trade ministry in the United States.

The source of this "reliable data" was probably Judith Coplon (codenamed "Sima"), who worked at the Justice Department and was first drawn to Soviet intelligence by a CPUSA member whom we know only by the code name "Zora." Initially, according to a memorandum in Coplon's NKGB operational correspondence file, "Zora" did not explain to "Sima" that her information was going directly to Soviet operatives.[31] In January 1944, however, the NKGB acted swiftly through "Zora" to sidetrack Coplon's expressed interest in joining the Communist Party.[32]

Coplon had told her friend repeatedly that she was interested in establishing closer links to American Communist leaders, and operatives at the New York station had requested Moscow's permission to recruit her formally.[33] On January 4, 1945, New York station chief Vladimir Pravdin finally met with Coplon, who impressed him as a "very serious, shy, profound girl, ideologically close to us." Based on that meeting, the station reported to Moscow:

> We have no doubts about the sincerity of her desire to work with us. In the course of conversation [Coplon] underlined how much she appreciated the credit we gave to her and that, now knowing for whom she was working, she would redouble her efforts. At the very first stage of her work with "Zora," [Coplon] thought she was helping the local compatriots [the CPUSA]. Later, from conversations with "Zora" and by the character of the stuff she was asked for,* she

---

economical from the point of view of encoding. . . . Continuation will follow later." New York station to Moscow, September 2, 1944, No. 1251, VENONA files. See also New York station to Moscow, October 5, 1944: "Further to our no. 700. Herewith are changes in cover-names. . . . Continuation later." No. 1403, VENONA files.

* This statement suggests Coplon's involvement with Soviet intelligence during 1944. Further confirmation comes from the VENONA cables, for example:

guessed that this work bore a relationship to our country. To [Pravdin's] question as to how she came to such a conclusion, [Coplon] responded that she knew about "Zora's" previous connections with the consulate; besides, she thought the stuff acquired by her couldn't represent an interest to the compatriots but could for an organization like the Comintern or another institution bearing a relationship to us. She added that she hoped she was working specifically for us, since she considered it the highest honor to have an opportunity to provide us with her modest help.*[34]

Shortly before this meeting with Pravdin, Coplon was transferred to Washington by the Justice Department, though she continued coming to New York for subsequent meetings with Pravdin.[†] He urged her to temper her enthusiasm with caution, though to little avail (according to subsequent reports sent to Moscow):

In particular, [Coplon] was forbidden at initial stages from bringing out documents before she was completely certain that she was trusted [at Justice]. Unfortunately, [Coplon] didn't follow this instruction and at the first opportunity brought out secret material

---

"[Coplon] works for the Economic Section of the Military Department of the Ministry of Justice. . . . If we are interested in the materials of [Coplon's] office then it is necessary to put through her recruitment. We have checked [Coplon] on the [preliminary] matters and again request your sanction for her recruitment. Telegraph a decision." New York station to Moscow, July 20, 1944, No. 1014, VENONA files. By November 1944, Coplon was complaining in discussions with a Soviet operative about her lack of supervision in the relationship. New York station to Moscow, November 12, 1944, No. 1587, VENONA files.

* "[Pravdin's] conversation with [Judith Coplon] took place on [January 4]. [Coplon] gives the impression of being a serious person and is politically well developed and there is no doubt about her sincere desire to help us. She had no doubts about whom she is working for and said that the nature of the materials in which we are interested pointed to the fact that it was our country which was in question. She was very satisfied that she was dealing with us and said that she deeply appreciated the confidence shown in her and understood the importance of our work." New York station to Moscow, January 8, 1945, No. 27, VENONA files.

† "[Judith Coplon] has got work in the Registration of Foreign Agents Branch of the War Office Division of the Department of Justice." New York station to Moscow, December 31, 1944, No. 1845, VENONA files.

from her office.* According to her, there is no surveillance on employees in her institution and many materials are scattered without any registration on shelves and in boxes at the archive.[35]

By this time, Coplon discovered, countersubversive activity at the FBI and Justice Department had shifted its focus from Nazis and fascists to Communists: "In a conversation with her, one of the senior officials said that the 'Club' [the military intelligence liaison at the Justice Department] also is charged with exposure of 'Right' movements but hinted that she shouldn't reveal an excessive zeal in that direction, pointing out that recently one employee had been fired because she was pursuing only those on the 'Right.' "[36]

Coplon had become one of the NKGB station's most valued sources by then, displaying a measure of devotion bordering on obsession: "She treats very seriously and honestly our tasks and considers our work the main thing in her life. Her serious attitude is demonstrated by her decision not to marry her former fiancé because, otherwise, she couldn't continue working with us."[37]

Judith Coplon's attention was focused on the main Justice Department counterintelligence archive that collected information from the various government agencies—the FBI, OSS, and naval and army intelligence—involved in this effort. She passed to her Soviet handlers in October 1945 a number of documents from this archive, including FBI materials on Soviet organizations in the United States, on Trotskyist groups, and on individual Communist leaders (including information on the late Jacob Golos).[38] A review of this data shocked Soviet operatives at the New York station who had previously dismissed the various U.S. counterintelligence efforts as amateurish: "The materials show how thoroughly the smallest facts from conversations, correspondence, and telephone talks held by our organizations, individual representatives, and workers in this country are recorded. We observed [also] how numerous is the 'Hut's' [FBI's] cadre involved in the [activities] described."[39]

Responding to this depressing news from New York and to the several known or rumored defections from their ranks in North America,

* "After [Coplon's] transfer to [Washington, D.C.], she was instructed to refrain from [removing] documents until she was quite sure that she was trusted." New York station to Moscow, June 26, 1945, No. 992, VENONA files. On Coplon's later arrest and trial, see Robert J. Lamphere and Tom Schachtman, *The FBI-KGB War...*, pp. 98–123.

NKGB officials in Moscow on September 10, 1945, instructed their stations in the United States and Canada to maximize their vigilance:

> Every meeting with agents must be thoroughly prepared. Operatives shouldn't meet with agents more often than 2–3 times per week. Work with agents should be organized in a way that operatives' work doesn't differ from the work of other members of the Soviet community.
>
> Identify authoritative and trustworthy group handlers from among local citizens and serve agents through them. Leading operatives should meet group handlers as rarely as possible and only to instruct and discuss tasks. . . .
>
> Pay attention to the personal lives of the workers. Take preventive measures to remove all difficulties (dissatisfaction with work, family problems, etc.). In case of need, address the Center for help.[40]

In short, even before NKGB operatives in the United States confronted the defection of Elizabeth Bentley that November, they had begun preparing for the worst in a postwar era of anticipated Soviet-American confrontation. Ironically, the clearest warnings of increased counterintelligence activity in America had come from Judith Coplon, an enthusiastic, recently recruited brunette Soviet agent at Justice, while within weeks of the NKGB's mid-September instructions to operatives, the defection of Elizabeth Bentley—a veteran American blond agent—would shut down the networks completely. Vyacheslav Molotov, at least, would not have been surprised (as he had once cautioned Alexander Feklissov in Moscow) that "then a provocation will happen."

PART THREE

Discovery:
Cold War
Confrontation

CHAPTER 13

❖❖❖

Flight from Exposure, I: The Washington Sources

THE MONTHS IMMEDIATELY following the end of World War II brought disappointment and danger to Soviet intelligence operatives in the United States. The new Administration under President Harry S Truman, who was inexperienced in the nuances of U.S.-USSR relations during the war years and instinctively anti-Communist, threatened to expose Soviet sources within the U.S. government. Expanded FBI and military counterintelligence efforts were aided by the defections of Igor Gouzenko in Canada and Elizabeth Bentley in the United States. Each provided detailed information that precluded continuing the operations of NKGB networks in both countries. Moreover, the Western powers had produced an atomic bomb while—even with help from the vital covert contributions of Fuchs, Hall, "Eric," Greenglass, and others—Soviet scientists were still years away from creating a similar weapon.

BREAKFAST WITH THE STATION CHIEF

Against this uncertain backdrop of postwar Soviet-American relations, there occurred one of the more remarkable and unexpected meetings of the period: an October 24, 1945, breakfast session between former U.S. Vice President (now Truman's Secretary of Commerce) Henry A.

Wallace and Anatoly Gorsky, the NKGB's Washington station chief. More remarkable still, it was Wallace, undoubtedly familiar with Gorsky's profession, who had arranged the meeting. The results (duly reported in Gorsky's memo to Moscow) reached Foreign Minister Vyacheslav Molotov, who in turn wrote Gorsky's superior a terse instruction: "Comrade Merkulov! It must be sent to Comrade Stalin!"[1]

That Wallace had chosen the Soviet intelligence chief in Washington as his conduit to the USSR leadership testified to the daring (and recklessness) of the man whom FDR had removed from the Democratic ticket in 1944 in favor of the more conservative Truman. Wallace's proposal, considering the Truman Administration's cooler relations with the USSR in past months, was also startling. He asked Gorsky how Moscow would respond if the U.S. government invited a group of Soviet scientists to visit the United States to witness the achievements of their American colleagues, especially in the field of atomic energy. President Truman personally, Wallace continued, would like Professor Peter Kapitza to join the delegation, given his well-known efforts on "the atomic project" in the Soviet Union. (No confirmation exists of Wallace's dubious claim to have been speaking on behalf of Truman.)

The conversation then turned to a discussion of U.S. secrecy concerning the atomic bomb and how this was viewed by the USSR. Gorsky reported: "Keeping technical data about this matter in the U.S., according to Wallace, not only leads to further worsening of already extremely tense Soviet-American relations but creates in the rest of the world an impression of the United States as the most obvious possible aggressor on earth." If nothing else, the Commerce Secretary's remarks were extraordinarily indiscreet:

> Wallace claimed that he was trying in the [U.S.] government to have control of the use of atomic energy for military purposes transferred to the U.N. Security Council, but so far all his efforts had failed. Wallace characterized [Senator Edwin] Johnson's bill on this matter, proposed for discussion in Congress, as a reactionary attempt by the War Department inspired by representatives of big industrial capital: DuPont, General Electric, Union Carbide. . . .

The apparently bemused Gorsky, no stranger to Washington's (or Moscow's) factional infighting, asked how Wallace explained the difference between his point of view and Truman's statements on the subject: "Wallace faltered a bit and then claimed that Truman was a petty *politico* who got his current post by accident. He often has 'good' intentions but too easily falls under the influence of people around him."

The former Vice President identified two such groups "fighting for Truman's 'soul' (his literal expression)," a small group of which he was a member and another more influential cluster that included Attorney General Tom Clark and Secretary of State James F. Byrnes. Those who joined with Wallace "reckon that there are only two super-powers in the world, the USSR and the U.S., [and that] the well-being . . . of all mankind depends on good relations between them." The second group, however, was extremely anti-Soviet, according to Wallace, "and advances an idea of a dominating Anglo-Saxon bloc consisting mainly of the U.S. and England" confronting an "extremely hostile Slavic world" led by the Soviet Union. Wallace's table talk then reached beyond the fragile boundaries of discretion by urging direct Soviet support for the efforts of those who shared his views in Washington: " 'You (meaning the USSR) could help this smaller group considerably, and we don't doubt . . . your willingness to do this.' Wallace did not elaborate on this statement, and it was not appropriate for me [Gorsky] to insist."[2]

Wallace continued with a description for his NKGB guest of Anglo-American economic negotiations and, at the conclusion of their talk, volunteered his view that "U.S. Congressmen spread lots of anti-Soviet lies here." Even Soviet intelligence recognized that Wallace's views were those held by only a small and isolated minority within the Truman Administration. Thus, there appears to have been no follow-up to Wallace's apparently self-generated proposal for a visit by Soviet atomic scientists or to his plea for the support of politicians such as himself friendly toward the Soviet Union.

THE BELEAGUERED STATION CHIEFS

At that moment, Anatoly Gorsky and his colleagues had a sufficiently full plate protecting their personal security without plunging into U.S. national politics. Only three days before the Wallace breakfast, Gorsky had received a cable from Moscow describing the chaotic situation of NKGB agents in Canada after Igor Gouzenko's defection. The NKGB leadership's preliminary order—soon to be superseded, following Elizabeth Bentley's defection, by a blanket instruction to Soviet operatives to halt all contact with sources—was to meet only once or twice a month with the most important sources. And, at all costs, they were to protect from disclosure such valuable agents as Donald Maclean ("Homer"), Harold Glasser ("Ruble"), Donald Wheeler ("Izra"), and one previously unmentioned in these pages, William Weisband ("Zhora").[3]

Weisband, a cipher clerk for the U.S. Army Signal Security Agency, had worked for Soviet intelligence throughout the war. Born of Russian parents in Egypt, he had immigrated to the United States in the 1920s and become a U.S. citizen in 1938. After military service in North Africa and Italy, Weisband was transferred to the Washington area where he joined other Russian specialists in 1945 in efforts to decipher and analyze intercepted Soviet cipher messages in the so-called VENONA program.[*]

By the time Moscow learned from Weisband about VENONA, the NKGB had replaced Gorsky in Washington (fearing repercussions from Bentley's defection). Its New York station chief, Vladimir Pravdin ("Sergei"), also departed on March 11, 1946, aboard the Soviet vessel *Kirov* without first having read the vital message his superiors had sent both to him and to Gorsky on March 5. The letter contained instructions based on Moscow's awareness that Soviet codes, although replaced by then, had been broken by American government analysts:

> During the war, there was an extensive quantity of ciphered cable correspondence between your office and [Moscow] Center. No doubt, the [American] intelligence organizations systematically determined the quantity of data, outgoing and incoming ciphered cables from Soviet representatives in your country. Using this data, [U.S.] intelligence could determine without difficulty which organizations are writing the ciphered cables and in what amount. A sharp reduction of ciphered correspondence in connection with events in the U.S. and Canada cannot escape notice by intelligence organizations.[4]

The NKGB's solution to this dilemma was both practical and pathetic. The station's remaining "skillful operatives" were instructed "every week, [to] compose summary reports or information on the basis of press and personal connections, to be transferred to the Center by telegraph."[5] Soviet intelligence's once-flourishing American networks, in short, had been transformed almost overnight into a virtual clipping service, now that the NKGB had to rely on publicly available information in order to provide useful data to Moscow. Considering the near-

---

[*] VENONA is described elsewhere in this chapter.

impossibility of recruiting new agents after the Gouzenko and Bentley defections, compounded by the VENONA revelation, the NKGB turned in near-desperation to the most readily accessible, comprehensive, and continuous source of reliable information on major developments in the United States—the media.

Not that Gorsky's replacement as Washington station chief, Grigory Dolbin, lacked covert interests. Without a network of American agents and sources to supervise, Dolbin instead probed other Soviet officials in Washington and the embassy environment from his "cover" identity as a "diplomatic aide." Thus, he reported to Moscow on conflicts between Soviet Ambassador Andrei Gromyko and Dolbin's nominal boss at the embassy, Kiril Novikov.[6] He noted that District of Columbia workers were digging trenches in front of the 16th Street embassy and concluded that the purpose must be to install a powerful U.S. counterintelligence listening system.[7] Dolbin even found time in 1947 to complain to Moscow about the anti-Soviet comedy *Ninotchka* being shown in local movie theaters. He noted especially "a scene in which the Soviet consul is beaten by a visitor who was refused a visa." This suggested to an agitated Dolbin the need for a diplomatic protest "to make American authorities responsible for an undisguised instigation to the beating of Soviet officials."[8]

Despite his inexperience, the station chief had cause for concern. Moscow had instructed Dolbin to examine closely the changing nature of U.S. domestic and foreign policy: "Unfortunately, in the current conditions of counterintelligence measures against us and a bitter anti-Soviet campaign in the country, we cannot thus far give you our agents and let you use them to fulfill present tasks. Reestablishing connection with important [American] agents can lead to fatal consequences."[9] His superiors provided him little support but nonetheless expected significant results.

Moscow urged Dolbin to cultivate, through his legal cover, politicians and organizations still willing to meet with Soviet officials. The NKGB provided him with the usual "wish list" of desired contacts, among them the White House, Congress, State, the political parties, the National Association of Manufacturers, and the Council of Foreign Relations. Within Congress, Dolbin was urged to seek relationships with those who remained strong "Roosevelt Democrats." At the cabinet level, he was asked to pursue discussions with Henry Wallace, whose views obviously fascinated Moscow, and with former Secretary of the Interior Harold Ickes, from whom the NKGB hoped to gain insight into the influence of energy companies on U.S. foreign policy.[10]

Moscow instructed Dolbin to redouble his efforts to collect "inside" information of all types from Washington policymakers "despite the temporary lack of ready-to-work agents." Persistent demands fell upon the new station chief to fulfill the NKGB's hunger for highest-level news about the new American Administration by "using properly your legal connections," developing them "in order to be ready to convert these connections into agents any time that the situation allows it." The hapless Dolbin was further instructed to focus on U.S. citizens and not immigrants in his work.[11]

While Moscow insisted that Dolbin create a new network of informants through openly cultivating powerful Washingtonians, his station was being stripped of other Soviet operatives. Virtually all were recalled home in 1945 and 1946. "I ask for only one thing," a despairing Dolbin wrote his superiors in August 1946. "Send me people. Without people, the work won't improve, the amount of information won't increase, and its quality won't be raised. Only the number of remarks that 'such a situation can't be tolerated' will increase."[12]

By the fall of 1946, Dolbin had been left completely alone: "The departure of technical workers has led me to a situation in which I am everything from the typist to the cipher officer," he cabled Moscow.[13] But NKGB Center remained unsympathetic and furious in its complaints over the quality of Dolbin's effort:

> For the six months of your stay in the country (from March to August 1946), only fifteen information [cables] have been received from you, among which eleven were reviews of newspapers or short summaries of articles, and only four contained information received from official channels. . . . But [even] the contents of this information was not satisfactory.[14]

By March 1947, Moscow added linguistic insult to injury, humiliating Dolbin in a merciless cable: "In conclusion, it is worth noting that all of your work is full of grammatical mistakes and inaccurate formulations, which are the result of insufficient knowledge of the facts and incorrect understanding of current events."[15]

In the end, the NKGB's disappointment with Dolbin's performance remains more of an implicit commentary on the obtuseness of its Moscow leadership than on its beleaguered Washington station chief. Beyond the hostile environment and isolation in which Dolbin dwelled—lacking Soviet operatives and American sources, who were being pursued relentlessly by the FBI and other U.S. counterintelligence agencies at a time of growing tension with the Soviet Union—he confronted one additional problem in seeking to cultivate fresh recruits in the nation's capital: Dolbin did not speak English.

He had been chosen for the U.S. assignment only two days before a scheduled departure for Japan. Dolbin's entire NKGB briefing prior to his being rerouted to America had consisted of two brief conversations with Center operatives, one of them the experienced Gaik Ovakimyan, in which they described the general situation in the United States.[16] Nor was Dolbin told about Elizabeth Bentley's defection, which he only learned accidentally through correspondence with Moscow in the summer of 1947, more then a year after he arrived in Washington. Dolbin's frustration emerged clearly in his summary report of "progress" in the U.S. assignment:

> Now, after a year, I feel that my knowledge of English has sharply improved. I read American newspapers almost without a dictionary, translate serious articles from English into Russian, and can talk with an American about any subject. Still, I consider [my knowledge of English] insufficient, especially in fluent conversation on everyday topics.[17]

Moscow finally replaced Dolbin in December 1947, first assigning him a role as deputy to his successor, Alexander Panyushkin ("Vladimir"), who doubled as Soviet Ambassador to the United States.[18] Recalled to the Soviet Union early in 1948, Grigory Dolbin had become mentally unstable by then, possibly as a direct consequence of his American experiences.

An ambassador functioning also as NKGB station chief was an unusual experiment in mixing public and covert roles that Soviet authorities were conducting in several countries during the postwar decade. Generally, the experiments were short-lived and unsuccessful. However, much was expected in Moscow of Panyushkin in his new assignment, given his background and experience, having served as the USSR's Ambassador to China from 1939 to 1944. At the time, this was perhaps the most delicate post in the Soviet diplomatic world due to Moscow's need to maintain decent relations *both* with Chiang Kai-shek's Nationalist government and its main foes, Mao Tse-tung's Communist insurgents, who controlled a significant portion of the country. Panyushkin was also, from 1944 to 1947, a high-ranking official in the Central Committee of the Communist Party of the Soviet Union.[19]

In addition to the seriously troubled Dolbin, Panyushkin inherited two other Soviet operatives—Boris Krotov ("Bob") and Yuri Bruslov

("Pavel")—on the NKGB station's roster. Both were kept busy accumulating public information on U.S. political developments for transmission to Moscow.[20] In March 1948, Moscow cabled Panyushkin, in his dual capacity, demanding that he assess the reliability of information being received from other stations describing reports of allegedly urgent American military preparations against the Soviet Union.[21] Considering the complete absence of such preparations, Panyushkin's task in this instance proved manageable, without turning to American agents or sources.

Yet so concerned was Panyushkin with the absurdity of relying on only a pair of overworked Soviet operatives that he petitioned Moscow to review the post-1945 shutdown of its existing networks: "Since we have connections now only with a very small number of masters,* I ask you to reexamine our network of old masters in order to determine the possibility of resuming contact with some of them."[22]

Moscow then tried to determine, without a coherent plan, which previous sources had *not* been exposed to American counterintelligence by Elizabeth Bentley, Whittaker Chambers, or other defectors.

Among the few still functioning in Washington and in contact with the NKGB was British diplomat Donald Maclean. He began reporting in December 1947 to Boris Krotov, who had handled the so-called Golden Five (Maclean, Philby, Burgess, Blunt, and Cairncross) in London from 1944 to 1947.[23] Maclean was assigned to explain Anglo-American relations from his insider's vantage point. In the process, he provided data on all intelligence and counterintelligence officers working at the British Embassy in Washington and, at the NKGB's request, recommended one of the British diplomats for recruitment by the Soviets.[†24]

Krotov found himself under FBI surveillance while approaching a scheduled June 26, 1948, meeting with Maclean and broke off contact. The station then instructed Maclean to pass all his material—a constant and invaluable collection of information—through dead-letter drops, a method Maclean found unsatisfactory, preferring direct con-

---

* The new code name for agents.
† For several years, beginning in the last months of World War II, Maclean served as an invaluable source of information for Soviet intelligence in Washington, passing on a voluminous amount of material dealing with top-secret Anglo-American discussions. See, for example, Washington station to Moscow, August 2–3, 1944; March 29, 1945 (3 cables); March 30, 1945 (3 cables); March 31, 1945, Nos. 1105–10, 1791, 1793, 1808–1809, 1826; VENONA files.

tact despite the risk involved.[25] Finally, Maclean and Krotov agreed to a schedule of personal meetings every third week, but twice between meetings, Maclean's data would be delivered at dead-letter drops.[26]

THE "VENONA" WHISTLE-BLOWER

One of the few American agents who provided information to Soviet intelligence during this period was William Weisband ("Zhora"), who worked on cipher analysis at the U.S. Army Signal Security Agency. As with other American sources, contact with Weisband, initially recruited by the NKVD in 1934, had been broken off between 1945 and 1947. Moscow apparently approved Panyushkin's request to restore communication with this "old master," carried out by Yuri Bruslov in February 1948. A memorandum concerning Weisband's work, drafted later that year, indicates the importance of his contribution:

> For one year, a large amount of very valuable documentary material concerning the work of Americans on deciphering Soviet ciphers, intercepting and analyzing open radio-correspondence of Soviet institutions [the "VENONA" project], was received from [Weisband].* From these materials, we came to know that, as a re-

* In February 1943, the U.S. Army Signal Intelligence Service (later the Army Security Agency) began a secret program to intercept and analyze encrypted Soviet diplomatic telegrams exchanged between Moscow and Soviet missions in the United States and various other countries in the Western Hemisphere and Europe. By 1945, over 200,000 messages had been transcribed, and progress had been made in "decrypting" the cables, many of which turned out to be reports from Soviet intelligence station chiefs and instructions from their superiors in the Soviet Union. The program was assigned the code name "VENONA," and the process of analyzing and deciphering the cables continued for decades at a Virginia headquarters known as "Arlington Hall." One of VENONA's chief analysts, Meredith Gardner, had broken the code sufficiently by late 1946 to expose the Soviet penetration of the atomic energy program at Los Alamos. By 1948, Soviet intelligence had learned of VENONA through Army Security Agency cipher clerk William Weisband. "What seems increasingly clear," the recent Commission on Protecting and Reducing Government Secrecy concluded, "is that the entire VENONA project was kept secret from [President] Harry S Truman and his Attorney General, Tom Clark." In 1995–96, over 2,990 fully or partially decrypted Soviet intelligence cables from the VENONA archives were declassified and released by the Central Intelligence Agency and the National Security Agency. See SECRECY: *Report of the Commission on Protecting and Reducing Government Secrecy* (Washington, D.C.: U.S. Government Printing Office, 1997), Appendix, pp. A33–A34.

sult of this work, American intelligence managed to acquire important data concerning the stationing of the USSR's armed forces, the productive capacity of various branches of industry, and work in the field of atomic energy in the USSR. . . . On the basis of [Weisband's] materials, our state security organs carried out a number of defensive measures, resulting in the reduced efficiency of the American deciphering service. This has led to the considerable current reduction in the amount of deciphering and analysis by the Americans.[27]

Weisband passed documents to Yuri Bruslov at personal meetings regularly between February and August 1948, then switched primarily to dead-letter drops. (The August opening of hearings by the House Committee on Un-American Activities, where Elizabeth Bentley and Whittaker Chambers were major witnesses, may have led to Bruslov's sudden measure of caution.) Beginning that month, Bruslov met with Weisband only every six to eight weeks after extremely careful preparations to avoid FBI surveillance, mainly to provide Weisband with instructions regarding information wanted by the NKGB.[28]

Weisband was increasingly concerned over his own possible exposure by then and asked Bruslov to request asylum for him in the USSR.[*29] Weisband received occasional monetary payments of $600 for his efforts in 1948, plus a onetime $400 for repairs on his automobile.[31]

By mid-1949, Weisband was meeting his handler once a month at a restaurant near Washington.[32] Replacing Bruslov as NKGB contact was one of the half-dozen new operatives assigned to the Washington station in response to Panyushkin's desperate 1948 cable, one Nikolai Statskevich ("Larry"), who, in addition to Weisband, specialized in handling diplomats from Eastern Europe.[33]

Despite the difficult environment, Weisband continued his work. On meeting days, he smuggled documents out of his army facility under his shirt, once during the lunch break and again at the end of the day, placing the material in the trunk of his car prior to delivering them to Statskevich. Weisband asked the NKGB operative to provide him with a camera in order to avoid transporting documents. The station declined, however, fearing that he would be detected more easily while taking photos.[34] At a mid-July meeting, Weisband reported that

---

* Moscow finally consented to his request in April 1950, though Weisband never actually fled the United States.[30]

the U.S. military had suddenly lost the ability to read Soviet cables, and the head of the deciphering service was concerned that a Communist might have penetrated its ranks. Weisband asked that his Soviet friends refrain from changing ciphers too quickly lest he be exposed.[35] That exposure actually came from other quarters in mid-December 1949, when the FBI established permanent surveillance of Statskevich and, apparently, observed his meeting with Weisband.[36]

The NKGB's Washington station proposed in March 1950 that Weisband be assigned to an "illegal" operative, unlike Statskevich who worked "legally" under diplomatic cover, but no appropriate person was available for the task.[37] At the same time, Moscow warned the station that Weisband was known to a number of other Soviet sources, including at least one defector, Alexander Koral, then testifying before congressional committees. Therefore, Moscow cautioned: "Working with [Weisband], it is necessary to assume the worst possibility, not excluding variants, for instance, recruitment of [Weisband] by [American] counterintelligence after showing him compromising materials that prove his connection with us."[38]

From that moment, Statskevich and his colleagues prepared, at least temporarily, to sever their links to Weisband. At an April 10, 1950, meeting, Weisband was given $1,694 in cash and a permanent password should he be contacted at some future date by an unknown operative:[39] "[Operative]: Do you know that Jerusalem is occupied by the Chinese? [Weisband]: Do you know that the Chinese bombed New York?"[40] Shortly thereafter, Soviet contact with William Weisband came to an end, and the password was never used.[41]

BLEAK TIMES

Nikolai Statskevich was not the only Soviet diplomat targeted by American counterintelligence in the late forties. In an October 1948 cable to Moscow, written as Ambassador, Panyushkin noted that the FBI and other agencies were "hunting" Soviet citizens (including diplomats), and establishing permanent surveillance on them, including eavesdropping devices in their apartments.[42]

The American scene rendered NKGB leaders in Moscow pessimistic and suspicious. They recalled "Stepan," their acting station chief in New York, that same year on the grounds that he was "preparing to betray the Motherland." In addition, seven other NKGB operatives were ordered home because of a decision to close the USSR's

Consulate in New York. "The stations in the U.S. in 1948 didn't recruit any valuable agent," Moscow concluded. "Moreover, no station acquired prospective talent-spottings for later work with them."[43]

In the absence of concrete plans either to revive the work of "old masters" other than William Weisband or to identify new American sources, Panyushkin spent some time in late 1948 concocting a scheme to discredit Whittaker Chambers. At this time Chambers faced a possible grand jury indictment for initially lying about his relations with Alger Hiss and for his work as a Communist courier. Panyushkin, a station chief then managing a largely defunct agent network, cabled his Moscow superiors in December with a bizarre proposal to launch a disinformation campaign "exposing" Chambers as a former Nazi, not a Communist, agent:

> As "Karl" [Chambers's primary underground pseudonym while a Soviet agent] is of German origin [and] lived and studied for some time in Berlin, [we could] "find" in German archives "Karl's" file from which it would become clear that he is a German agent who by Gestapo instructions was carrying out espionage work in the U.S. and penetrated into the American Communist Party. If we claim it in our press and publish some "documents" which could be produced at home, the effect of this will be very great. This information will be snatched not only by foreign Communist parties but by the progressive press in all countries, and, as a result, positions of the Committee on Un-American Activities, the grand jury [then considering testimony from Hiss, Chambers, and others on the matter] and other organs will be strongly undermined.
>
> It can be also claimed that "Karl" is well known to the Committee and grand jury and other American organs as a Gestapo agent, but heads of these institutions being vehement haters of the USSR, the Communist Party, and the progressive movement in general, presented the case as if "Karl" and others supposedly spied for the USSR and not for Germany.[44]

Panyushkin's proposal did not receive Moscow's support and for the perfectly sensible reasons outlined in its immediate response:

> The station's proposal to produce and publish in our press "documents" stating that the traitor Chambers was a German agent, by Gestapo instructions carried out espionage work in the U.S., and by German instructions penetrated into the CPUSA cannot be

approved. Certainly publication of such "documents" will affect extremely negatively our former agents exposed by Chambers for knowing that they worked for us after "converting" [them] into German agents. [As a result] these people may . . . cooperate with authorities, giving frank testimonies and so forth. Besides, transformation of these individuals from supposed agents of Soviet intelligence into determined agents of a country that fought against the U.S. by no means can help them from the juridical point of view.[45]

Nonetheless, Moscow was intrigued by another element in Panyushkin's plan: "The station's proposal about production and publication of documents exposing some leaders of the Committee on Un-American Activities and the federal jury as Gestapo agents must be carefully examined and weighed." Neither was there follow-up to this clumsy disinformation proposal.

The station made one further foolish attempt to restore contact with an "old master," the reluctant Laurence Duggan, who, after cooperating with Soviet intelligence during the 1930s, had resisted a series of NKVD attempts to keep him involved during the war years. Duggan, now head of the International Institute for Education, was even given the new code name "Prince." Panyushkin received instructions to try once more but to avoid pursuing Duggan too aggressively "in order not to expose our operative . . . by our sharply manifested interest in him."[46] A renewed Soviet courtship, however, combined with the FBI's simultaneous interest in his previous covert efforts, apparently proved too much for Laurence Duggan to endure.

Panyushkin's analysis of what followed, contained in a December 25, 1948, cable to Moscow, reflected not only his assessment of the Duggan affair but a reversal of his earlier view that contacting former sources would benefit the station:

> To continue the work with old agents and talent-spottings in such conditions gives American counterintelligence an opportunity to cultivate even more deeply our connections and ourselves. Besides, by contacting old agents . . . the station may collide with new cases similar to [that of Duggan] who, being under surveillance by [American] counterintelligence, was interrogated on December 11. The station, unaware that he had been summoned for interrogation . . . attempted to reestablish a connection with him [and] charged "Saushkin" with calling on [Duggan] on December 15, i.e., four days after his interrogation. Evidently,

"Saushkin" ran into [American] counterintelligence and, in that way, gave supplementary material against [Duggan] to the Americans. I do not exclude [the possibility] that, to some extent, this promoted his decision to commit suicide. We can cause great damage to our country by striving to get information from old agents who, as experience shows, are exposed, and information acquired from them . . . has no value.[47]

Panyushkin now urged that the NKGB concentrate on recruiting new agents in the United States, increasing activities by Soviet "illegals" in America, and approaching Americans in other countries, all of which made sense under conditions prevalent at the time.[48]

A debate among NKGB leaders in Moscow ensued after receiving these recommendations. In the end, Panyushkin, whose main career was in diplomacy and, as such, was hardly an NKGB insider, found his views rejected by Moscow: "In our opinion," a memorandum on the Ambassador's proposal observed, "this is equivalent to halting all intelligence work in the U.S., since the station did not acquire new talent-spottings and, even more, new valuable agents in the main U.S. institutions. . . . We cannot agree with [Panyushkin's] sweeping denial of all our old agents and our talent-spottings. We consider it necessary to continue working with them, attentively weighing all the details of every agent's work in the past and his current usefulness for resolving our tasks."[49]

Such ridiculous instructions to resume contact with former agents at a time when most were under FBI investigation and surveillance did nothing to change the bleak prospects described by Panyushkin. This was confirmed the following year by yet another analysis of Soviet intelligence's prospects in the United States filed in Moscow by the knowledgeable Anatoly Gorsky: "[The Washington station] practically stopped work on finding recruiters and new agents since the middle of 1949. . . . In its practical work, the station followed the line of least resistance, either drawing to our work people largely known by their connections with the U.S. Communist Party . . . or trying to use as agents officials from 'People's Democracy' [Eastern European] countries sympathizing with us but not having access to information interesting to us."[50]

Even Gorsky, who should have known better, now joined in criticizing the Washington station for not reestablishing links with older agents who might have been exposed by Bentley or other defectors. In fact, no NKGB operatives, whether in Moscow or the United States, could state with confidence which of their sources had been identified.

Gorsky criticized the appointment of nonprofessionals such as Panyushkin to the post of station chief—as someone kept "busy on his main job [and, therefore, who] cannot go deeply into all operational matters"—but reserved his major complaints for the deputy station chief, Gyorgi Sokolov ("Fyodor"), whom he blamed for the recruiting failure.[51]

Sokolov, a skilled professional, admitted that his poor knowledge of English hindered his work in America as did FBI harassment. But he rejected Gorsky's primary complaints about his "cowardice, laziness, [and] inability to organize the station's work." His response was blunt: "I left for Washington in October 1948 with good references; in February 1950 . . . I was given a [poor] reference* [and unfairly] was transformed by the people who composed it into a good-for-nothing shit."[52] As for Alexander Panyushkin, his failures in Washington apparently were overridden by his status in the Communist Party hierarchy. Three years after this admittedly unsuccessful station chief left Washington, he was appointed the head of Soviet intelligence!

The most candid commentary on the problems confronted by the NKGB in postwar America, specifically how the achievements by American agents and sources during the New Deal and war years had been so quickly overtaken by the collapse of networks and defection of key agents, was provided in a mid-March 1950 memorandum from Sergei Savchenko, then head of the NKGB intelligence service. The document approved a new plan to resume activities in the United States.

Savchenko began with a standard early–Cold War Soviet political assessment, which blamed "American imperialism" and its post–World War II expansionist policies as primarily responsible for the U.S.'s growing obsession with internal security issues: "Preparing for a new world war, America's expansionist circles are . . . [attempting] to strangle inside the country any possible resistance to its external ventures . . . set[ting] middle-class Americans against the USSR and people's democracies with the help of . . . anti-Soviet, anti-Communist propaganda through the press, radio, cinema, and church."

Savchenko credited Igor Gouzenko's defection in Canada with "American counterintelligence intensifying their work against us, managing to inflict serious blows to our agent network in the U.S." The worst wounds, however, came from an American defector: "The most tangible blow to our work was inflicted by the defection of our former

* Gorsky's critiques.

group-leading agent [Elizabeth Bentley] in November 1945, who gave
away more than 40 most valuable agents to American authorities. . . .
The majority of agents betrayed by [Bentley] worked at key posts in leading state institutions: the State Department, organs of American intelligence, the Treasury Department, etc." Other defectors, Savchenko
continued, added to the debacle:

> Besides [Bentley's] treachery, at the same period of time—i.e.,
> since the end of 1945—there were failures of four agent groups
> (working independently from the agent network headed by
> [Bentley]) that followed [according to] testimony given to the
> Federal Bureau of Investigation by former agents of the MGB,*
> and the GRU—traitors "Berg" [Alexander Koral], "Buben"
> [Louis Budenz], "Karl" [Whittaker Chambers], and "Redhead"
> [Hedda Gumperz]. There were more than 30 valuable agents in
> these four groups, including former officials of the State Depart-
> ment, Treasury Department, Interior Department, etc.
>
> The last link in this chain of failures was the arrest of [Valentin]
> Gubitchev and [Judith] Coplon, which took place on March 4,
> 1949, and their trial, which ended in March 1950. Thus, as a result
> of all these failures, we lost an agent network that had been in op-
> eration for many years and was a source of valuable political and
> economic information for us.[53]

Despite his bleak assessment of the disarray among Soviet intelligence networks that these defections had provoked and the bitter anti-
Soviet public mood in the United States, Savchenko remained
confident that a rebuilding process could begin under his direction. He
proposed penetrating the State Department and American intelligence
community with newer agents to probe mainly for information on U.S.
foreign policy toward the Soviet Union and the pro-Soviet "people's
democracies" of Eastern Europe, China, and Germany. A first step
would be to recruit so-called agent-spotters: "These recruiters must be
people indebted and devoted to us, politically literate, and brave." Nor
would the previous generation's collection of largely immigrant-
background agents suffice. The new breed, Savchenko believed, "must
be chosen first of all from American citizens having connections necessary for us (among officials of state institutions, American representatives abroad, and students of privileged American universities). . . ."[54]

---

* The name in 1950 for what had been the NKVD and then the NKGB.

Savchenko's strategy was based on an impossibly naive assessment of current American reality. Nonetheless, Moscow instructed all of its stations in Western countries on March 27, 1950, to focus on recruiting either Americans or foreigners capable of recruiting American citizens. It also asked the intelligence services of Eastern Europe's "people's democracies" to help.[55] So demanding were the cables pushing for immediate action to re-create the earlier networks that, in October 1950, Alexander Panyushkin, still in Washington, lost his patience and fired back this memorandum:

> Instead of blowing up at us in every letter, the authors of this severe and biting correspondence should come here themselves and show by personal example how to acquire people working in the State Department and other governmental institutions in the current fascist atmosphere in the U.S. To yell, reproach, and shift the blame onto others is easy, but to resolve a concrete matter is much more difficult. Thus, for example, the Center has not helped the station for the past two years by sending any "illegals" here or transferring agents here from European or other countries.
>
> It should not be forgotten that we work here in the period of unfinished investigations of cases involving almost 50 agents exposed long before us. . . .
>
> As far as I am personally concerned, I persistently ask you to send me a replacement as soon as possible, probably from among those nimble authors of loud letters who can demonstrate their complete understanding of tasks while fulfilling them with ability and courage.[56]

This dismal state of affairs could not be resolved in the pre–Cold War manner of recruiting dedicated Communists or other radical supporters of the Soviet Union, whose numbers had been reduced dramatically and whose future remained perilous in a time of anti-Communist purges. By February 1951, the Washington station had only one agent, code-named "Jack," a member of the "open" U.S. Communist Party who spent his time writing books on the threat to world peace posed by "American imperialism."[57] Even by the following year, a March 1, 1951, memorandum from the KGB's "Information Committee" could point with pride only to the recruitment of local citizens in Australia and France working for American agencies—but none within the United States. Nevertheless, the memo argued that even this modest foreign effort "against the main adversary . . . is evidence that with efficient organization of business and proper purposefulness, it is possible to carry out this work successfully and achieve positive results."

Any coldly rational Soviet intelligence operative would have marveled at the bombast and self-deception inherent in this claim, considering that the cable continued with this admission:

> The most serious drawback in organizing [Soviet] intelligence in the U.S. is first of all the lack of agents in the State Department, intelligence service, counterintelligence service, and the other most important U.S. governmental institutions as well as in the so-called business circles virtually defining U.S. foreign and domestic policy.
>
> Our U.S. stations did practically nothing to acquire agent-recruiters. Nor did stations in other capitalist countries accomplish the Information Committee's instructions on this matter. [They] acquired no agent-recruiters for work in the U.S.[58]

In addition to admitting its record of recent failures in the United States, this March 1, 1951, memorandum is the earliest document released from Soviet intelligence archives in which the United States is described as the USSR's "main adversary."

BROWDER—FROM
SPYMASTER TO PUBLISHER

One element of the collapse of Moscow's American networks after the Second World War occurred as the result of Stalin's decision in 1945 to remove Earl Browder as leader of the Communist Party of the United States. His downfall as a trusted associate of Soviet leadership can be traced both to his personal actions and to the policy shift in relations between the United States and USSR from wartime allies to postwar adversaries.

Browder had been an eager and productive participant in a range of Soviet espionage efforts during the 1930s and throughout the war years as the "Helmsman" (his code name), recruiting from his "open" Communist cadres a significant number of those who later became prominent NKVD agents and sources within the American government. After a 1940 conviction for using a false passport during a trip he made to Spain during the Civil War, he served only fourteen months of a four-year prison sentence, freed after being granted amnesty by President Roosevelt.

At a party congress in May 1944, Browder had mobilized a majority of delegates in favor of disbanding the U.S. Communist Party, creating in its place a Communist Political Association. He was convinced that the period of "class cooperation" within the United States that characterized the war years would continue after the war. But following a campaign against his leadership—designed and encouraged by Moscow but publicly spearheaded by French Communist Jacques Duclos—a majority of American Communist leaders reversed their long record of support and drove Earl Browder from the CPUSA during the summer of 1945. One reason for Elizabeth Bentley's alienation from Soviet intelligence was Browder's expulsion after years of their close collaboration on underground matters.

Despite Browder's removal, he continued to enjoy significant personal allegiance among rank-and-file party activists. Thus, Soviet operative Alexander Feklissov, after returning home from the United States, noted in February 1947 that the American source code-named "Condenser" "respects and is very devoted to [Browder]. . . . Therefore, it was a powerful blow to him when, in 1945, [Browder] was expelled from the party for his politics of reconciliation with capitalism, which resulted in the slackening of class struggle in the U.S. . . ." Feklissov found "traces of dissatisfaction" in "Condenser" because of the action taken against Browder, and he underscored the fact that his source would continue to cooperate with the NKGB only if Browder remained on good terms with Soviet leaders.[59]

Earl Russell Browder was born in 1891 in Wichita, Kansas. He was an active member of the Socialist Party; convicted of taking part in antiwar demonstrations related to U.S. involvement in the First World War, Browder served a prison term until 1920. He became a member of the CPUSA's Central Committee in 1921 and the party's head in 1930 after protracted factional struggles within its leadership. Browder ran unsuccessfully for the American presidency as the Communist candidate in both 1936 and 1940.[60]

His second wife, who was also a party member and agent, was Russian-born Raissa Berkman; they married in 1926.[61] Browder's sister, too, apparently, was involved with Soviet intelligence, at least financially. Shortly after Germany's invasion of the Soviet Union in June 1941, Jacob Golos delivered $2,000 to her, responding to an extraordinary request made earlier that month. Golos, then the most active figure in the NKVD's New York station, informed the station (which cabled Moscow) after a meeting with the lady: "Browder's sister, to whom we pay a certain amount of money every month, asks for two thousand

American dollars to start her own business—trading in antiques. She is sure that the business will be a success and that she will return the money fully."[62] The files are silent on the matter of later repayment.

Even while orchestrating Browder's expulsion as leader of the American Communist Party, Moscow conceded his value in assisting with the expansion of its intelligence operations in the United States. Much less would have been accomplished, a detailed and candid 1945 NKGB memorandum acknowledged, without Browder's constant and comprehensive involvement in "secret work":

> The use of [Browder's] . . . leadership of the compatriot organization [the CPUSA] by our stations in the U.S. began approximately in 1933. It was organized through particularly trusted persons specially appointed personally by [Browder] with whom the heads of our stations at different times maintained an illegal connection. . . . Joszef Peter [who led "illegal" CPUSA intelligence gathering in the 1930s], [Browder's] brother "Bill," and [Jacob Golos] were these entrusted representatives.
>
> a. [Peter] was used by our stations occasionally until 1936. Afterwards, he was released by [Browder] from this work. To a greater degree, he was used very actively by operatives of the GRU. [Peter] had his own group of agents [composed of] illegal compatriots working in various state institutions through whom he obtained information both for [Browder] and the GRU.
> b. "Bill" was used sporadically as a connection with [Browder] in 1936–1937 and in 1942–1944, only by our station chief [Zarubin].
> c. [Golos], being our important group handler for a large number of agents made up of local citizens, was the main person entrusted for a connection with [Browder] from 1937 to 1940. But he had no relation to the GRU operatives and met none of them.
>
> The heads of our stations were receiving, through [Browder's] trusted representatives, the following:
>
> 1. Verified persons from the local compatriots for use as agents, illegal couriers, and illegal group handlers;
> 2. Personal data on people interesting to us (being cultivated) with a view to their recruitment;

3. Talent-spottings with a view to recruitment of so-called illegal compatriots working in various state institutions, private firms, defense plants, and laboratories.

The trusted persons recommended by the compatriots' leadership were being used by the stations for various intelligence purposes: to penetrate local Trotskyite organizations, as illegal couriers, owners of secret addresses, group handlers, to acquire passports and other documents showing citizenship, directly as agents, and, finally, to fulfill various special tasks.

Through these trusted representatives, the stations also sporadically received information, various documents, and other intelligence materials.

Note: Sometimes, the heads of our station—with Moscow's special permission—met personally with [Browder] in especially secret conditions for important conversations.[63]

Considering Earl Browder's deep and personal engagement in Soviet intelligence activities in the United States from 1933 to 1945, described in this and other memoranda, the loss of his services was a major blow.

Because of Browder's personal stature and special role linking "open" and secret party activities in the United States, he traversed the normal demarcation lines within the Soviet intelligence world. He saw little difference between assisting the NKGB and helping the Communist International (Comintern) agent network run by Bulgarian Communist Georgy Dimitrov. For example, Browder informed Elizabeth Zarubina at a December 1943 meeting where extreme security precautions were observed that Dimitrov had asked him to send to Moscow monthly reports containing information on U.S. political events—but through NKGB channels. Any *secret* data for Dimitrov, however, would be sent only via Elizabeth Bentley or Bernard Schuster ("Echo"), a CPUSA official and another approved NKGB courier.[64]

As a result of this unusual arrangement, Browder himself acted as a direct channel for conveying intelligence materials from the CPUSA's American sources to Moscow, bypassing the normal agent networks. Often, this resulted in delays for material sent to the Soviet Union, thereby reducing its value. Thus, in early February 1944, Browder passed to the New York NKGB station obviously obsolete "secret" material from OSS sources on the September 1943 losses by the German armed forces.[65] Similarly, other documents from his OSS contacts obtained in November 1943 reached Soviet hands too late to be helpful.[66] Despite these delays and occasional confusion, Browder's involvement proved crucial in 1943 and 1944 in helping to persuade a reluctant Elizabeth Bentley to transfer key government sources from Jacob Golos's American agent network to direct oversight by Soviet operatives such as Itzhak Akhmerov. Browder's role in Soviet intelligence and his knowledge of its covert efforts was uncommon among leaders and most ordinary members of the CPUSA. Only a handful of party officials served as Soviet sources, couriers, and group handlers, virtually all—except for those involved in atomic espionage—handpicked by Browder himself and not by NKGB operatives.

Under these circumstances, intelligence officials in Moscow responded cautiously to Browder's expulsion, awaiting word on how to deal with those of his devoted American partisans who also served as NKGB sources. Station chiefs in the United States were told to halt temporarily all contact with agents whom Browder had recommended.[67] At the same time, Soviet operatives sought out CPUSA members close to its former head but willing to inform on him, as Anatoly Gorsky reported to Moscow in July 1945 of a conversation with one member: " 'Reina' says that currently Browder . . . lives in the countryside. . . . He refuses to receive anyone but reckons that, within less than a year, the Communist Party will call him back to its leadership. . . ."[68]

Browder and his family used his special relationships with Soviet operatives during this period to try and maintain back-channel contact with the USSR's leadership. In August of that year, Itzhak Akhmerov ran into Browder's brother, who asked whether Earl could send a letter to Moscow through the New York station. On September 1, station chief Vladimir Pravdin asked special permission from his superiors for an unusual procedure: The expelled former leader of the CPUSA wished to reach Stalin and his associates through Soviet intelligence to express complaints about his treatment and his successors![69] On September 11, Moscow responded to the request with a curt memo from Alexander Panyushkin (who, two years later, would be Ambassador and station chief in Washington): "You should not take a letter from Browder."[70]

Browder persisted in his plan to regain leadership of the CPUSA by gaining the support of Soviet leaders. Thus, a November 2, 1945, memorandum from the New York station to Moscow reported that in another conversation with "Reina," Browder said he planned to travel to Moscow: "He still believes that his position was incorrectly understood and interpreted [and] that he will be understood in Moscow, where he is considered the only well-prepared Marxist outside the Soviet Union."[71]

A subsequent February 7, 1946, dispatch from the NKGB's Pavel Fitin to Alexander Panyushkin, then working in the Soviet Communist Party's Central Committee, reported yet another conversation with Browder. A Communist "illegal" named "B. Josephson," who managed the Café Society cabaret in New York (whose revenues, according to this report, went toward financing the CPUSA), had heard Browder reiterate his intention to "unmask" the new party leadership and its chief, William Z. Foster, by traveling to the USSR. He demanded that Josephson support his family using Communist Party funds during his absence. More ominously, according to Fitin's cable, Browder claimed that he knew where $540,000 in secret party funds were being kept and would "do everything necessary in order to assure that the party couldn't use them."[72]

Soviet intelligence operatives found themselves, in short, caught in the middle of an internecine struggle between Browder and his CPUSA successors, which could only increase exposure of Moscow's most secret efforts in America. When one of William Z. Foster's supporters expressed concern about Browder's impending trip to the USSR and asked that an NKGB operative code-named "Nazar" transmit a brief concerning Browder to Moscow from the new CPUSA leaders, Pavel Fitin sternly warned the New York station in May 1946: "We have nothing to do with compatriots' affairs and can't take the brief."[73]

The Browder dilemma, quite appropriately, was kicked upstairs for Stalin's personal review, given the Soviet dictator's personal involvement in the process that had led to Earl Browder's removal as American Communist Party leader. Vsevolod Merkulov summarized the problem posed by Browder for Soviet intelligence in an extremely candid April 1946 memorandum for Stalin, which contained the background and significance of this previously revered figure who now bore the stigma of a "capitalist collaborator":

On February 12, 1946, the National Committee of the American Communist Party . . . expelled Earl Browder . . . for "a gross violation of party discipline and decisions . . . and defection to the side of class enemy—American monopoly capital. . . ."

In this connection, the NKGB of the USSR considers it necessary to communicate to you the following:

Starting in 1933 and into 1945, Browder rendered the NKGB . . . and the GRU . . . help, recommending to our representatives in the U.S. a number of illegal members of the U.S. Communist Party for agent work.

At Browder's recommendation, eighteen people were drawn to agent work for the NKGB and . . . [number missing] people [for the GRU]. In addition, through the Central Committee's functionaries controlling illegal party groups, Browder knew about illegal members of the U.S. Communist Party working for the Soviet Union [through] the NKGB of the USSR—more than twenty-five people [and for] the GRU of the General Staff of the Red Army . . . [number missing] people.

In connection with the Canadian case [Igor Gouzenko's defection] and betrayal by an agent of the NKGB . . . in the U.S. that was reported to you on November 14, 1945, by [message] #7698 [Elizabeth Bentley's defection], we temporarily halted agent work in America and conserved the main group of agents who became known to American authorities due to this agent's betrayal. Among the agents conserved, the majority were recommended to us either personally by Browder or were known to him as working for us through top-level functionaries of the Central Committee [of the CPUSA].

The link to Browder in our work from 1933 to 1945 was maintained occasionally by senior operatives of the NKGB of the USSR. Three Soviet citizens from the NKGB in the United States were known to him. . . .

The NKGB of the USSR believes that Browder's expulsion from the party may lead him into a transition toward extreme means of struggle against the Communist Party and may inflict damage to our interests. Therefore, the NKGB of the USSR considers it expedient to allow Browder's arrival in the Soviet Union. [We should see] if it is possible to recommend . . . to the Executive Committee of the American Communist Party that Browder be reestablished in the party under a convenient pretext and [that the CPUSA adopt] a more tactful line of behavior with regard to him.[74]

By the time Earl Browder arrived in Moscow on May 6, 1946, the NKGB's arguments for "a more tactful line of behavior with regard to him" had the approval of Soviet leaders. Hours after he arrived at the Moskva hotel, Browder was visited by two key figures in Soviet intelligence, Vassily Zarubin and Gaik Ovakimyan—both old friends and associates. They questioned Browder about his family, the situation in the CPUSA, how he had managed to obtain a passport for travel to the USSR, and older matters still puzzling to them. How, for example, had

Browder managed to obtain President Roosevelt's amnesty and release from prison? Understandably, Zarubin and Ovakimyan were particularly interested in information Browder might have about American sources and agents with whom he had maintained contact in earlier years. He reassured the anxious NKGB officials that he did not meet with those people any longer.[75]

The following day, Browder met with another old friend, a venerable Comintern official named Solomon Lozovsky, who was then chairman of Sovinformbureau, the Soviet news agency. Lozovsky had been sent by Stalin personally to meet with Browder and then to brief Stalin on the discussion. Shortly thereafter, Lozovsky talked to NKGB officials, who filed a report on the conversation:

> Comrade Lozovsky stated that he reported to Comrade Stalin on the "Helmsman" affair and mainly one question was discussed: whether [Browder] would defect to the enemy's side. Comrade Lozovsky, having known [Browder] for more than 20 years, believes that [he] became entangled but did not become a renegade. In this connection, Comrade Lozovsky received instructions* to maintain [Browder] financially for the first year until [his] commercial enterprise was able to provide for him. It was decided to give [Browder] $300 a month for one year.[76]

Browder's new business involved five-year exclusive contracts with a number of Soviet publishing houses to publish their books in the United States. The NKGB memo noted that Browder "is bringing two photocopies of these agreements to present to the State Department."

Responding to the NKGB officials' obvious question, Lozovsky stated that he had not discussed internal U.S. Communist Party politics with Browder, despite the former leader's attempts to open up the subject. Rather, Lozovsky had simply criticized Browder's "non-Marxist point of view concerning the progressiveness of American capitalism." Browder acknowledged only that "some of his formula may have been wrong."

Asked by the NKGB whether their officials should meet with Browder before his departure to discuss "the issue of his behavior, Comrade Lozovsky thought such a conversation would be necessary":

> In [Lozovsky's] opinion, it is necessary in a friendly way to let [Browder] understand a desirable line for his behavior in his

* Presumably from Stalin.

country, but to do it in a way that does not thrust our opinion on him.*

... In conclusion, Comrade Lozovsky claimed that the main task was maintaining [Browder] for the forthcoming year, giving him a possibility in connection with publishing activities to consolidate his positions in [the] wider democratic circles of his country and, if he behaved properly, ensuring him in future an opportunity to correct his mistakes.†[77]

Joseph Stalin's direct instructions to Lozovsky governed the official Soviet reaction to Earl Browder's apostasy: combining a potentially lucrative publishing carrot with the threatened stick of continued expulsion from CPUSA ranks.

Ovakimyan and Zarubin held a final meeting with Browder on June 18, 1946, prior to his departure. Pavel Fitin immediately reported on the meeting to Victor Abakumov, the USSR's then-Minister for State Security:

Meeting with Comrades Ovakimyan and Zarubin, [Browder] proposed using both himself and his connections in our work. We consider it inexpedient to use him in agent work, [however,] taking into account the special situation of [Browder] in his country due to his political position [expelled from CPUSA ranks] and the notorious [Bentley] case in which he must appear as the main figure. Consequently, competitors in the country [the FBI and other U.S. counterintelligence agencies] will inevitably hold him under their meticulous observation. However, we consider it expedient to consult him on issues of the general political, external, and internal situation of his country while passing him money. . . .[78]

When he left Moscow the following day to return to the United States, Browder had good reason to feel pleased with the overall bargain he had struck in the Soviet Union, thanks to Stalin's direct involvement.[79] He had come to Moscow a despised "renegade" from CPUSA ranks. He returned (in exchange for his political silence) as the designated representative of major Soviet publishing houses and—as in the past, though in a more limited format—with his special relationship to key Soviet intelligence operatives substantially intact.

---

* That Browder should stop criticizing Foster and other CPUSA leaders.
† For example, to return to the party organization.

During the late 1940s, contact with Browder was maintained by both Soviet Information Bureau officials and NKGB operatives. Occasionally, he turned over long written assessments of American political conditions and, also on occasion, he received special funds from Soviet agencies—for example, $1,500 from Sovinformbureau to help pay for his wife's medical treatment in 1948. "Helmsman," no longer at the CPUSA helm, also received a new code name, "Shaman," but the old Communist sorcerer could no longer sustain his hold on Soviet intelligence.[80]

Moscow came to the conclusion in January 1949 that Browder's writings, despite his pledge to abjure such commentary, reflected the same political perspectives that had alienated Stalin years earlier and were aimed at discrediting the current American Communist leadership.[81] By then, the new leaders of the CPUSA had confronted trial and conviction, charged under the Smith Act with advocating the violent overthrow of the U.S. government. Compounding the irony of this senseless prosecution, had Stalin chosen in 1946 to reinstate Earl Browder as a CPUSA member (even if not again as its leader), he would have joined the imprisoned ranks of his former colleagues and comrades. Instead, he continued to lead an unfettered, if not especially profitable, private life.

Curious about Browder in June 1949, Soviet First Deputy Foreign Minister Andrei Gromyko instructed Ambassador and NKGB station chief Alexander Panyushkin to determine his current attitudes without making direct contact. Panyushkin responded on July 5:

> In the opinion of the Embassy's friends, Browder's official connection with Soviet publishing houses restrains him from anti-Soviet statements and the disclosure of secrets known to him. Our friends do not rule out, [however,] that if we break officially with Browder, it might push him to the side of reaction and complete betrayal.[82]

Panyushkin recommended continuing the publishers' arrangement with Browder until (as he vainly hoped) the campaign against Soviet agents had receded.

Soviet intelligence, however, would soon lose any remaining confidence in Browder. Eighteen months after Panyushkin sent his memorandum to Gromyko, the KGB received a report, which it appeared to credit, that Browder had offered his services to the anti-Soviet "renegade" Communist government of Yugoslavia and had expressed a willingness to work with its nationalist leader, Marshal Tito.[83] Earl Browder, who had been a pivotal figure—indeed a linchpin—of Soviet espionage in the United States from 1933 to 1945, now served as yet another reminder to Moscow of the extent to which its once-successful structure of intelligence networks in America now lay in total ruin.

CHAPTER 14

❖❖❖

Flight
from Exposure, II:
The Atom Spies

A FTER THE WAR'S END, the key agents involved in providing information to Soviet intelligence on the atomic bomb project—
Klaus Fuchs, David Greenglass, Ted Hall, and others—left their
well-guarded enclaves to pursue new careers and opportunities. Harry
Gold went into a business partnership with another Soviet source,
Abraham Brothman. Greenglass prepared to continue his education
while working for his brother-in-law, Julius Rosenberg, who in turn
impatiently awaited a signal to resume fully his activities as a Soviet
agent handler. Theodore Hall launched a teaching career. None appeared to be as concerned as their NKGB supervisors with the danger
posed by the Anglo-American-Canadian counterintelligence effort
mounted against Soviet espionage following the 1945 defections of Igor
Gouzenko and Elizabeth Bentley.

FUCHS AND FEKLISSOV

The most important Soviet source of atomic information in the West,
Klaus Fuchs ("Charles"), had been out of touch with his courier, Harry
Gold, for more than two years before contact with another Soviet op-
erative was restored in England. The NKGB was able to confirm
Fuchs's whereabouts only in autumn 1946. It learned then that Fuchs,

after leaving the United States in late 1945, had been trying unsuccessfully to resume his link to Moscow, working through old associates in the German Communist Party.

One of these, Hans Sibert, a leading German Communist exile in London at the time, had been introduced to Soviet agents by another party member, Urgen Kuchinsky ("Karo"). Kuchinsky's wife (Sibert told the NKGB operatives) had been approached by another German exile named Fuchs, a scientist recently returned from the United States, who asked for help in establishing contact with Soviet intelligence.[1] Considering the haphazard contacts between Harry Gold and Fuchs in the United States, such difficulty in restoring a link to NKGB couriers seems less surprising.

When told of Fuchs's request and the German Communist intermediaries involved, however, Moscow responded cautiously, concerned that British counterintelligence might be monitoring Fuchs. Nor was the NKGB enthusiastic about using "open" party members to rendezvous with the atomic physicist, especially not Kuchinsky's wife, since her husband was no longer trusted in the USSR.[2]

A 1945 Moscow memorandum on Urgen Kuchinsky noted that he had worked for American military intelligence in 1944–45, holding the rank of lieutenant colonel in the U.S. Army. Assigned to Berlin with U.S. occupation troops in a military intelligence unit in July 1945, Kuchinsky requested demobilization but remained with American forces there as an adviser. When the NKGB's Berlin station restored its connection with this former agent in December 1945, at first Kuchinsky declined to cooperate. Only after significant pressure did he agree to renew his old ties, but after doing so, he failed to provide significant information. Thus, Moscow remained suspicious of utilizing Kuchinsky or his wife to contact the valuable Fuchs. The NKGB's Berlin station severed relations with Kuchinsky in August 1946.[3]

Devising a method to contact Klaus Fuchs without resorting to German Communist intermediaries was complicated by the trust Fuchs had in his former comrades. He had joined the German Communist Party as a student in 1931. After going underground, Fuchs maintained these connections as a student and teacher in Paris and later in Edinburgh.[4] In the end, it was through this German Communist network that contact was eventually restored with Fuchs on July 19, 1947.

Briefed beforehand by NKGB personnel, a German party member named Hanna Klopshtock met Fuchs in London's Richmond Park. He was informed that a subsequent meeting with NKGB operatives would take place in two months on September 27 in a bar opposite the Wood

Green tube station. The following dialogue was to confirm the designated contact's identity:

CONTACT: Stout is not so good. I generally take lager.
FUCHS: I think Guinness is the best.

The two would then leave the bar, and the dialogue would continue:

CONTACT: Your face looks very familiar to me.
FUCHS: I think we met in Edinburgh a year ago.
CONTACT: Do you know big Hannah?[5]

The meeting could then begin, with Fuchs carrying a copy of the *International Herald Tribune* and his contact holding a book with a red cover.

Alexander Feklissov ("Kalistrat"), who had left the United States for Moscow in October 1946 and had remained under "legal" cover as a diplomat, was the experienced operative assigned to handle Klaus Fuchs. In Feklissov's new role, he served as London's deputy station chief for scientific and technical intelligence. He prepared for his meeting with Fuchs with briefings from a Soviet specialist in atomic problems, who introduced the operative to the bomb's basic structure and terminology while developing detailed questions to be discussed at their first meeting.[6]

The NKGB station deployed several operatives to watch the meeting venue in order to assure itself that the pub was not under surveillance by British counterintelligence. Once satisfied, Feklissov entered the building where Fuchs was already waiting. After the exchange of passwords, Feklissov began a discussion of the health of the scientist's family and, finally, of his work. According to Fuchs, the atomic research taking place in England was insignificant, but a major conference in the United States on problems in the field was scheduled for mid-November. Fuchs had been appointed to the British delegation for the five-day conference, a point stressed in Feklissov's report: "We think the fact that [Fuchs] was included in the delegation proves that [he] enjoys the skiers'* trust."

After the arrest in Canada of another NKGB agent among the scientists, Allan Nunn May, however, Fuchs hesitated when asked to communicate while in the United States with Soviet intelligence couriers, as he had done in the past:

* The new NKGB code name for the British.

To the question of whether he will be able to meet with our man in Tyre [New York], while staying in the [United States], [Fuchs] said that he would like to . . . during this short trip. He expressed apprehension that, after May's case, the [Americans] would watch intensively all the scientist-specialists in "Enormoz" coming to them from the island [Great Britain]. Nor is he certain that he will be able to contact his sister during this trip. Therefore, we didn't arrange for him to pass us any materials through [her].[7]

Fuchs explained to Feklissov the principle of the hydrogen bomb on which, according to Fuchs, Professors Fermi and Teller were then working at the University of Chicago.

When the conversation concluded, the reason behind Feklissov's earlier discussion of the Fuchs family became apparent. The Soviet operative wrote in his report:

> [I] thanked him once again for helping us and, having noted that we know about his refusal to accept material help from us in the past, said that now conditions had changed: his father was his dependent, his ill brother [who had tuberculosis] needed his help . . . therefore we considered it imperative to propose our help as an expression of gratitude.

Feklissov then handed over two packets containing one hundred British pounds each, which Fuchs accepted. After a brief pause, the scientist responded (according to the report): "We were given the [Allan Nunn] May file to read, where it said that Soviet spies always tried to give money to foreigners who passed them information, in order to commit them morally to work for them later. But I am not afraid of this. On the contrary, I will take the money you propose to prove my devotion to you." Fuchs then asked how much Feklissov had given him. When told the sum, Fuchs returned one packet on the grounds that he could not explain the sudden appearance of the entire two hundred pounds.[8]

Fuchs attended the Anglo-American scientific conference in November 1947 that he had described to Feklissov. He apparently skipped their scheduled December meeting, however, since only in mid-March 1948 did he pass along important conference information dealing with the design of various bombs (including the H-bomb then being developed).[9]

Twice that year, Moscow feared that Fuchs had been exposed as a Soviet agent. Both proved to be false alarms. On April 5, an NKGB official in Moscow added a handwritten warning to Feklissov on an oper-

ational memo: "Comrade Kalistrat! Just now, I learned some unpleasant news. The athlete [source] who in her time drew [Fuchs] to our
work [apparently a reference to Ursula Kuchinsky] was interrogated by
the competitors [FBI]. They allege that she told them nothing. When
she was interrogated, under what circumstances, and other details are
not yet known to me."[10]

The second episode was more serious. In May 1948, Klaus Fuchs
disappeared or, at least, failed to appear for his scheduled and backup
tri-monthly meetings in London, a fact of sufficient concern for NKGB
intelligence chief Peter Fedotov to report directly to Molotov and
Beria. On March 23, London's *Daily Express* had reported that British
counterintelligence was investigating three (unnamed) scientists who
worked at the same research center as did Fuchs—all suspected of
Communist Party membership. Fedotov promptly informed his superiors but was unable to shed much light on the situation:

> We don't yet know the real reasons that [Fuchs] failed to come to
> the meetings, but we suppose that he—knowing about the purge
> of his co-workers—decided not to meet with us out of caution.
>
> It cannot be ruled out that [Fuchs] also could be subjected to
> verification [investigated] and, in this case, he undoubtedly will
> be barred from participating in secret scientific research work on
> the atomic problem, thus losing the possibility of passing further
> information to us on this issue.
>
> [However,] being a prominent specialist, participating directly
> in research work on the atomic problem, [Fuchs] is well informed
> about the latest achievements in this field and, staying in the
> USSR, could be a great benefit [to us] due to his knowledge.
>
> [Therefore,] we take into account the possibility of losing
> [Fuchs] as an agent and . . . ask you to settle the question of bring-
> ing [him] to the USSR to [work] on the atomic problem in one of
> our scientific-research institutions.[11]

This question was never answered, since Klaus Fuchs appeared on
July 10, 1948, for his next scheduled meeting with Alexander Feklissov.
He had failed to come to the earlier one because his institute was
preparing for some top-secret experiments, and all personnel had been
instructed not to leave the premises on those days. He confirmed that
three Communist scientists had been fired but believed that personally
he remained beyond suspicion.[12]

Each encounter between operative and source followed an identical
procedure. Soon after the meeting began, Fuchs would hand over any

materials he had brought. Feklissov would leave the meeting briefly to give the material to a waiting colleague for delivery to the station and then return immediately to continue his discussion with Fuchs.

At this meeting, for some reason, Feklissov raised the same question that Anatoly Yatskov had raised three years earlier regarding Fuchs's relationship with women, producing this response: "No changes have happened in [Fuchs's] private life. He is still a bachelor. When [Feklissov] asked whether changes in his 'bachelor status' might be expected, [Fuchs] responded that in his situation he didn't consider it necessary to change this status, adding jokingly that 'therefore, I avoid falling in love deeply.' "[13]

At their next meeting in late October, Fuchs alerted Feklissov to some surprising information about Soviet atomic development, described to Moscow in this report:

> In early October, [Fuchs] saw a British intelligence service report on a Soviet atomic center near Sukhumi. . . . It described the construction of the center and a list of incoming equipment. [Fuchs] concludes that the report had not been written by a scientist since it says nothing about the progress of scientific work.*[14]

At the February 12, 1949, meeting, the physicist provided the startling news that British intelligence had contacted a Soviet scientist and tried to persuade him to spy on the atomic research effort in the USSR. Fuchs identified his informant simply as "Herbert Skinner," but in response to Feklissov's question stated that he had not personally seen any Soviet scientific material. A hurried memorandum from the London station reported:

> To [Feklissov's] request to find out where and with whom among the Soviet scientists the English had made contact, as well as what materials they receive from the Soviet Union, [Fuchs] replied that, in his opinion, revealing an interest in this matter while conversing with his colleagues would be unwise. However, he assured [Feklissov] he would let us know everything he saw or heard on this matter.[15]

The possible existence of a Western "mole" among Soviet scientists provoked Fuchs's anxiety about his own safety:

---

* A more detailed account of Fuchs's postwar relations with Soviet intelligence, also based on the KGB files, is in Nigel West and Oleg Tsarev, *The Crown Jewels*, pp. 239–55.

[Fuchs] asked [Feklissov] to pass on his request that his materials be shown only to trustworthy people to avoid his [exposure], which would follow if the English got his materials. [Feklissov] answered that [his] materials were being used . . . only by trustworthy people.

When questioned whether the person whom the English intended to use to receive data on Soviet atomic work was the source who passed information to the English about Sukhumi, [Fuchs] responded that, from Skinner's information . . . , it wasn't the same person and that the new source was a scientist.[16]

Western counterintelligence, meanwhile, seemed more energetic than ever, and in one instance this directly affected Feklissov's meetings with Fuchs. The FBI had arrested Justice Department employee Judith Coplon and her Soviet handler, U.N. official Valentin Gubitchev, on a New York street on March 4, 1949. Coplon had top-secret U.S. government documents in her purse at the time. Eight days later, Moscow sent its London station the following cautionary letter:

In connection with the latest events in [New York] and in order to avoid repetition of such cases in other places, it is necessary to revise urgently and most carefully the practice of holding meetings with the athletes [Soviet agent-sources] and of receiving materials from them.

The practice by some [stations] of meeting in the street is blamed [by the Central Committee of the Communist Party of the Soviet Union] as an ignorant method of work, not guaranteeing security for our people and the athletes. We ask you to revise, together with [Feklissov], all methods for carrying out meetings, especially with [Fuchs]. It is necessary to stop having meetings with him in the street, since this is very risky. Now, the risk grows because the police have begun practicing spot-checks of people's documents, especially on lonely streets, for the purpose of fighting crime. Even an accidental check of [Fuchs's] and [Feklissov's] documents will lead immediately to disclosure of our liaison with [Fuchs].[17]

Moscow proposed several procedural options for meeting with Fuchs. It recommended that Fuchs purchase a secondhand car with the station's funds and meet with Feklissov either in the car or at a girlfriend's apartment once or twice a year. The last option was questionable since it involved a third person in the encounter. In any case,

Feklissov learned from Fuchs at their next meeting on April 1, 1949, that no such person existed. Fuchs admitted that he spent time with "various girls," but Feklissov "concluded that those were prostitutes" and, therefore, there was no possibility for using any of their apartments for meetings. After passing on some information verbally, Fuchs promised to bring his notes to the next scheduled meeting with Feklissov.[18]

The two never met again; Fuchs failed to appear on June 25 and at the scheduled backup meeting on July 2.[19] Fuchs's absences deeply troubled Feklissov and his NKGB colleagues. Earlier in June, the American press had prominently featured stories mentioning six Soviet agents named by Elizabeth Bentley, including Abraham Brothman. Brothman's exposure, beginning with Bentley's earliest 1945 testimony to the FBI, had not overly disturbed Moscow since he was no longer an active agent. Moreover, his handler had been Harry Gold, whom Brothman initially knew under the name "Frank Kessler." Then, Gold joined Brothman's firm in 1946 and told him his real name. Since Brothman could identify Gold as a Soviet courier and Gold, in turn, could incriminate Klaus Fuchs (whose name and working history he knew), the NKGB took immediate steps to contact Gold, whose last meeting with a Soviet operative had taken place three years earlier.

GOLD AND FUCHS

The NKGB's New York station decided to arrange a meeting with Gold for several reasons at this point: to confirm his loyalty but, also, to inform him that Fuchs was safe; to discuss his response to possible FBI interrogation; and to suggest that he consider going underground or, at least, moving to a remote state where he could live undetected.[20] Gold received a coded letter on July 18, 1949: "Dear Harry, Just got back to New York and am going to stay here for about three weeks. Will be very glad to see you if you suggest when you can come. Yours sincerely, John."[21] Based on three-year-old instructions, that note alerted Gold to a meeting scheduled for July 25. But he never appeared for the rendezvous with a Soviet operative named Kamenev ("Photon"), nor did he make a backup meeting.[22] Finally, on September 10, Kamenev traveled to Philadelphia and found Gold at his home.

Harry Gold had received the letter but claimed to have forgotten the conditions for a meeting (more likely, he was trying to avoid the encounter). Gold informed the Soviet visitor that he now worked with radioactive isotopes on heart research at Philadelphia's General Hospital. In July 1948, he had left Brothman's firm after an argument and had not seen him since. Most troublesome to Kamenev, as he later reported, was evidence that Gold (as well as Brothman) had attracted the attention of American counterintelligence.[23]

In April or May 1947, Gold told the Soviet operative, Brothman was summoned before a federal grand jury and shown a photo of Gold and Jacob Golos. (Evidently, Brothman had recounted this episode to Gold before their rupture.) Although the prosecutor overseeing the grand jury told Brothman they knew "everything about their [covert] activities" and urged him to confess, the engineer denied any involvement with Golos's work and claimed to have met him only once or twice. When asked who had introduced him to Golos, Brothman named Gold.

Gold told Kamenev that following Brothman's grand jury appearance, two FBI agents visited him, asking what secret materials Brothman had given to him. He showed them around his house and insisted that, although he worked for Brothman's firm, he did not have access to secret materials. The agents left, but on July 30, 1949, Gold informed the operative, he was summoned before the New York grand jury investigating subversive activities.

Gold testified that he and Brothman had met Golos as professional chemists seeking jobs in a new firm Golos claimed he was launching. (Gold insisted to Kamenev that he did not share Abraham Brothman's nervousness about future interrogation.) After Kamenev learned additional details of Gold's grand jury appearance at a subsequent meeting, the New York station informed Moscow that Gold remained a loyal agent, "devoted to us . . . but, taking into account everything that has happened to him lately, it is difficult to foresee how he will behave at an interrogation if the [FBI] undertakes further inquiry of the case."[24]

Moscow then ordered the station to prepare Harry Gold for possible departure for Europe.[25] But Gold insisted that the FBI no longer had any interest in him and "expressed his desire to [resume] active work with us."[26] At an October 24 meeting, although Kamenev urged him to be ready to flee, Gold was reluctant, concerned that, as a result, his brother would be fired from a navy post as a security risk and his aging father left without support. Kamenev assured him that his father would be provided for, and the two began exploring escape routes, including the possibility of Gold's joining a Quaker medical commission leaving soon for China.[27]

The discussions proved timely. Only months later, on February 3,

1950, British newspapers reported the arrest of Klaus Fuchs, charged with passing atomic secrets to the Soviet Union both in the United States and England.[28] The New York station had a meeting with Harry Gold scheduled for February 5 but was instructed by Moscow, considering Fuchs's arrest, to determine first whether Gold remained free. An operative unknown to Gold was sent to the meeting place, armed with a photograph, to check simply whether the chemist showed up.[29] Fuchs's arrest clearly had provoked panic within the NKGB leadership, since another cable soon followed forbidding *any* operative to appear at the meeting place. But the order arrived too late. A Soviet operative who drove to the site of the scheduled rendezvous with Gold found him waiting patiently for Kamenev. Nothing appeared suspicious.[30]

News of Klaus Fuchs's arrest reached Joseph Stalin that same day, February 5, in a report on Fuchs's recruitment and work for Soviet intelligence. The report stressed that, in the United States, Fuchs had supplied information on the atomic bomb's design and assembly. While in London, in 1948–49, he had passed to Feklissov valuable material on several subjects: planning for the hydrogen bomb, English atomic stockpiles, the process of isolating plutonium, data on American atomic stockpiles and types of bombs, the tests at Eniwetok atoll, theoretical calculations of explosions, and other data. The report also concluded, erroneously, that although Harry Gold had denied testifying against anyone to the FBI, examining the circumstances surrounding Fuchs's arrest and Gold's behavior at his meetings with Kamenev suggested strongly that he had probably betrayed Fuchs.[31]

Throughout the months that followed, the NKGB presumed that Gold's treachery had caused Fuchs's arrest. On February 23, Moscow provided instructions to the New York station based on this belief:

> Analysis of the data we have on [Fuchs's] case . . . leads us to highly serious suspicions toward [Gold].
>
> To analyze his real role in this case, we have to continue maintaining relations with [Gold] and not reveal our suspicions to him. . . .
>
> [Moreover,] the matter of [Gold's] departure from the country can be used as a touchstone in determining his real attitude toward us and [American] counterintelligence.
>
> To protect against a possible trap, restoring connection with [Gold] must be carried out by contacting him on his daily trip to the office or from the office back home, not by calling him to a meeting at a site known to him beforehand.[32]

Moscow hoped that its operatives could determine Gold's "real feelings . . . [and] attitude toward the matter of leaving for abroad." Under the circumstances and reflecting its barely contained fury, Moscow also assigned Gold a new code name: "Mad" (as in "Angry," not "Crazy").

The NKGB's New York station chief Boris Krotov ("Bob") disagreed vehemently with Moscow's instructions. In his view, "in case [Gold] is involved in [Fuchs's] collapse, no conversations with [Gold] can possibly determine where he really stood on the matter of treason." He would be coached by U.S. counterintelligence and might even agree to leave the country, if that corresponded with the plans of those now supervising him. On the other hand, "in case [Gold] is innocent, one may assume that [Fuchs] has given him away, and that now he is under active cultivation [by the FBI], including surveillance." Either way, in Krotov's opinion, Moscow's proposal would "disclose one of its operatives to counterintelligence with all the consequences that may proceed from that."[33] Krotov's arguments persuaded Moscow, and he was instructed to investigate whether Gold would come to scheduled meetings.[34] One operative drove by the site for an April 2 rendezvous; Gold never appeared.[35]

The arrest of Klaus Fuchs and his subsequent confession to British and American interrogators greatly troubled Soviet intelligence. The NKGB investigated not only Harry Gold as a possible informant but a number of others related to Fuchs's recent relationships in London, especially those German Communists who had known of Fuchs's link to the NKGB, almost all of whom now lived in the Soviet occupation zone in Germany.[36]

Fuchs's British interrogators gained admissions of his espionage activities on behalf of Soviet intelligence, and at a two-day trial that ended on March 1, 1950, Klaus Fuchs was convicted and sentenced to fourteen years' imprisonment. The USSR's TASS News Agency published on March 8 an official "refutation" of Fuchs's confession that he had passed atomic secrets "to agents of the Soviet government," declaring "this statement . . . a rude falsehood, since Fuchs is unknown to the Soviet government and no 'agents' of the Soviet government had any relation to Fuchs."[37]

Of greater concern to the NKGB at the time, however, was the potential effect of Klaus Fuchs's swift exposure, interrogation, trial, and sentencing upon still-undiscovered agents in England and the United States. Soviet intelligence flagged especially a portion of Fuchs's confession stating that lately he had begun to doubt the correctness of the USSR's policies. Moscow concluded in an April 6 memorandum to its London station that this "undoubtedly . . . was done by direct instruction of Anglo-American intelligence organizations . . . to sow confusion in the minds of our active agents and to shake their devotion to our cause."

The NKGB leadership believed that some of their agents and sources might "change their political views" because of the growing public anti-Soviet campaign in the West. They suggested that Soviet operatives inform English sources "that the Americans deliberately created the 'Fuchs case' so that they could refuse to provide the British with information on atomic matters." The tone and content of these memoranda revealed Moscow's anxieties about persuading its English and American agents—in the midst of Eastern European repression, new purge trials, and the Berlin blockade—that the USSR remained "a real fighter for peace and defense of working peoples' interests all over the world."[38]

Obsessed with determining how Fuchs had been discovered and which agents, in turn, he had named, NKGB operatives in Moscow developed elaborate if unworkable plans to use Fuchs's father (who lived in the Soviet occupation zone of Germany) to spearhead an aggressive and uncooperative defense. But Fuchs's rapid confession, arraignment, and trial ended such schemes and brought Soviet intelligence back to its major preoccupation—damage control.[39]

The task was eased substantially when, in March 1950, the NKGB acquired a ten-page memorandum prepared by MI-5 for French counterintelligence that summarized the Fuchs case.[40] Based largely on analysis of this memo, Moscow informed its London station on April 6 that Fuchs had testified candidly, giving away much operational data that he could easily have withheld. This "leads us to a firm conviction that [Fuchs] confessed passing us material and gave away to [British] counterintelligence all the data he knew about our work and our people connected to him by this work."[41]

The MI-5 memorandum, remarkable even today for its meticulous description of Fuchs's career and involvement in Soviet espionage, also explained to Moscow why the British had launched its investigation of Klaus Fuchs:

> In late August 1949, the Security Service received information from the Federal Bureau of Investigation which indicated in some detail that, during the war, there had been a leak to the Russians relating to the work of a British Atomic Energy Mission in the United States. Research into British files of that period, combined with the Federal Bureau of Investigation's research and investigation in the United States, showed that Dr. Emil Julius

Klaus FUCHS fit such facts as were known; intensive investigation into FUCHS' career and current activities began at once, while research into war-time records was continued in order to establish that no other person also fit the known facts.[42]

Although by December 1949, MI-5 had concluded after three months of investigation that Fuchs and only Fuchs "fit the information received from the FBI," ironically, British counterintelligence agents were (incorrectly) "satisfied that they had found no evidence to suggest that FUCHS was currently engaged in espionage."

The problem confronted by MI-5, "therefore, became one primarily of preventive security." Although Fuchs would have to be removed from top-secret research at his institute, Harwell, "equally clearly, his dismissal would greatly decrease the prospects of obtaining evidence of current espionage; moreover, there was the further danger that to dismiss him summarily might lead to his defection to the Russians."

Klaus Fuchs resolved the dilemma himself by volunteering information to security officers at Harwell that his father had been offered a chair at Leipzig University in the Soviet zone of Germany, "which, he explained, might become embarrassing to him [Klaus] in view of the secrecy of his work." He proposed resigning if British authorities felt the situation too awkward and submitted himself for interrogation on the matter. Whatever the outcome of his questioning, the British had already decided at its conclusion to dismiss Fuchs from his post.

Thus began several intensive rounds of interrogation in December 1949 and January 1950. Initially, Fuchs acknowledged youthful Communist associations but flatly denied having committed espionage. His questioners described Fuchs's behavior at his initial interview on December 21 as "both friendly and composed," giving "every appearance of innocence" through four hours of close questioning. On December 30, they informed Fuchs that he would have to resign but would be helped in finding another position elsewhere in England.

Fuchs asked to meet with his chief interrogator on January 23, 1950. An MI-5 report described the encounter: "Under considerable mental strain and moved by a series of complex psychological factors, he was this time persuaded to make a full confession that for seven years he had been passing top secret information to the Russians. The prosecution of Klaus FUCHS was sustained solely on his own admissions."

The memorandum outlined in detail the procedures used by Fuchs in England after his active espionage career began in 1942. Once he left for the United States in 1944, "he was met by a man who remained his contact for the next two years, first in New York, then in Boston, and finally in Santa Fe. On his return to the U.K. in 1946, contact was resumed with another man, probably a Russian, the last meeting being in February or March 1949 (six months before investigation by the Security Service began)." Fuchs admitted the £100 payment he accepted in 1946, which he described as "a symbolic payment signifying his subservience to the cause."

He had become a Communist initially, Fuchs said, because of his disgust at the failure of socialist resistance to Hitler and his belief that only the Communists could effectively oppose the Nazi regime. In the statement read out at his trial, Fuchs described a type of psychological strategy—which he called controlled schizophrenia—that allowed him to lead an effective double life as devoted British scientist and loyal Soviet agent.

The formula was applicable in some measure to a number of the other English and American antifascist romantics who served Soviet intelligence from the 1930s through World War II:

> I used my Marxist philosophy to establish in my mind two separate compartments. One compartment in which I allowed myself to make friendships, to have personal relations, to help people, and to be in all personal ways the kind of man I wanted to be and the kind of man which, in a personal way, I had been before with my friends in or near the communist party. I could be free and easy and happy with other people without fear of disclosing myself because I knew that the other compartment would step in if I approached the danger point. I could forget the other compartment and still rely on it. It appeared to me at the time that I had become a "free man" because I had succeeded in the other compartment to establish myself completely independent of the surrounding forces of society. Looking back at it now, the best way of expressing it seems to be to call it a controlled schizophrenia.

Fuchs informed his interrogators that after returning to England in 1946 and despite his renewed involvement with the NKGB through his London contact, Alexander Feklissov, he had begun having doubts about Soviet foreign policy similar to those he had felt during the period of the Nazi-Soviet Pact. Should he continue to supply information while feeling uncertain about the legitimacy of his Communist cause? New friendships with colleagues at Harwell only increased the pressures bearing down on him. He avoided one scheduled 1949 meeting with Feklissov prior to contacting the Harwell security officer concerning his father's new Soviet zone posting. "In his groping toward escape from the doctrine which his mind now rejected," the MI-5 report con-cluded, "FUCHS had set in train the last stage in the uncovering of his tragic career. 2nd March 1950."[43]

Thus did the NKGB learn the basic facts surrounding the arrest and confession of Klaus Fuchs. Once caught, he cooperated completely with British counterintelligence, displaying the same candor and self-lessness that he had shown previously to Soviet intelligence, in both cases because of his personal reckoning of moral responsibility.

Although the MI-5 document told a great deal about the scientist's activities as a Soviet agent, it failed to make clear what FBI data, passed to the British in August 1949, initiated the probe of Klaus Fuchs. The answer to this puzzle came in a May 29, 1950, report, which followed shortly a memo from New York station chief Boris Krotov to Moscow, describing Harry Gold's arrest in Philadelphia.[44] The May 29 report, delivered directly to Stalin, set to rest any remaining suspicions in Moscow that Gold may have been the informant who identified Fuchs:

> As a result of verification and examination of the circumstances surrounding the collapse of our agent "Charles" (former head of the theoretical physics department of the English atomic center in Harwell, Klaus Fuchs), the following was established:
>
> The American deciphering service [the "VENONA" project] worked for a long time on one of the telegrams from the New York station, referring to 1944–1945 when [Fuchs] was in the U.S. Having failed to decipher this telegram completely in late 1949, the Americans passed it to British counterintelligence, which managed to decipher it to the end and to find out that [Fuchs] was an agent of Soviet intelligence, passing us important data about the work of the American and English atomic centers where he worked. . . .
>
> The verification showed that, in the war years, there had been an extensive telegraph-ciphered correspondence on matters of in-telligence work by [Fuchs] between our station in New York and [Moscow]. Short excerpts of materials on the atomic bomb, re-ceived from him, had been passed, and in one of the telegrams his family name and detailed data about him were even men-tioned.
>
> Our specialists admit the possibility of the English deciphering our telegram, processed by a used table of reciphering gamuts.
>
> From documents acquired by us through agents . . . it is

known that [Fuchs], having been arrested by the English, confessed to cooperating with Soviet intelligence, told the main
things about the work with us in the U.S. and England, and testified about his intelligence connections. . . .

On May 24 of the current year in the city of Philadelphia, USA,
through [Fuchs's] testimony, Harry Gold, our old agent "Arno,"
who received from [Fuchs] materials on the atomic bomb in
1944–45 and whose [work] . . . was stopped by us in December
1945, was arrested.

To prevent compromising [NKGB] operatives . . . , an operative of the London station, Feklissov, who controlled [Fuchs], as
well as an operative of the New York station, Kamenev, who controlled the agent [Gold], were recalled by us to the USSR in early
1950.

Currently there are no Soviet operatives in England or the
U.S. whom these agents could know.

Measures to bring out of the U.S. four agents previously connected with [Gold], facing a threat of exposure in case of the latter's confession, were also taken.*[45]

According to the American media, Gold had been exposed through
information provided by Fuchs. But a full account of how the FBI
came to identify Gold reached Soviet intelligence only upon Fuchs's
release from prison in 1959, after serving nine years of his fourteen-year
sentence.

Klaus Fuchs promptly left England for citizenship and a prestigious
research post in Communist East Germany. There, the forty-eight-
year-old physicist soon married.[46] Because of Moscow's continuing
interest in "the circumstances and possible reasons for his arrest,"
Alexander Shelepin, then Chairman of the KGB, arranged Fuchs's invitation to join a scientific delegation from the German Democratic
Republic to the USSR's Joint Institute for Nuclear Research.[47]

During the visit to the Soviet Union in June 1960, Fuchs's translator
was actually a KGB operative named Starikov. Although the physicist
used most of his time to familiarize himself with new developments
in Soviet atomic research and design, facing the past was also on
the Moscow agenda. At a private meeting there, two KGB scientist-
operatives familiar with Fuchs's past assistance, Leonid Kvasnikov and

---

* The agents referred to were undoubtedly the Greenglasses and the Rosenbergs.

D. Pronsky, introduced themselves to Fuchs "as representatives of the organization he had cooperated with." They expressed appreciation for his earlier efforts and regret over his arrest and imprisonment.[48]

Fuchs, in turn, apologized for admitting to British interrogators "serious . . . doubts concerning the rightness of the Soviet Union's policy." He blamed this lapse on "the influence of bourgeois propaganda and his isolation from sources of accurate information. . . . His opinion that his cooperation was a mistake resulted from these erroneous views." Fuchs acknowledged that the British had not coerced his confession; it was made voluntarily. Questioned by the two Russians about others involved in espionage with him whom Fuchs may have exposed:

> [Fuchs] claimed the only man was Gold. In the course of investigation, [Fuchs] was shown two American motion picture films of Gold. In the first, Gold was shown on an American city street and impressed [Fuchs] as a man in a state of nervous excitement being chased. After seeing the film, [Fuchs] didn't confess that he knew Gold. In the second film, Gold was already in prison. . . . After seeing that, [Fuchs] identified Gold and gave testimony about him.[49]

Fuchs's memory played tricks on him here since Gold was not yet in prison when Fuchs identified him in the film, an action that played a crucial role in making the FBI's case against Harry Gold.

Questioned on the information he had revealed to his interrogators, Fuchs confirmed for the Russians that he had given "detailed testimony about . . . material passed to us, except materials on the H-bomb." After Fuchs's imprisonment, American intelligence officers had visited him seeking data "mainly on the Soviets' working methods [and the] scientific and technical issues on which Soviet intelligence officers sought to acquire information. . . ."[50]

GREENGLASSES AND ROSENBERGS

Klaus Fuchs's confession and the subsequent identification and arrest of his American courier, Harry Gold, led both the NKGB and the FBI to New York City. There, others involved in atomic espionage—including David and Ruth Greenglass—nervously awaited events.

Throughout the first half of 1949, NKGB operatives in New York tried to persuade David Greenglass to return to his studies and to focus on atomic research. They urged him to apply to the University of

Chicago, where he could renew friendships with scientists he had known at Los Alamos while seeking useful data and potential new agents for Soviet intelligence. The NKGB offered to pay his tuition and living expenses at Chicago, but the university turned down Greenglass's application.[51] At the same time, his wife, Ruth, then expecting their second child, insisted that she would not leave her family doctor in New York.[52]

Greenglass continued to work as a mechanic at a Brooklyn company that assembled radar stabilizers for tank guns — "The idea of this device is that it must keep the gun constantly directed at the target regardless of the tank's vibrations while moving during battle" (the station wrote on January 13, 1950).[53] David's Soviet handlers rejected as too dangerous his offer to take a camera into the top-security plant to photograph drawings. Instead, they asked him (as in the case of the atomic bomb's triggering mechanism) simply to make sketches of the process from memory.[54]

The New York station reported to Moscow in February 1950 that "in late January, agents of American counterintelligence" had visited Greenglass first at his plant and then at his apartment "under the pretext of investigating uranium thefts from [Los Alamos] in the past." Greenglass had previously stolen such samples (according to his file in the KGB archives), but he denied it to the agents.[55] Reassured by his evident refusal to cooperate with the American agents, but fearful that Harry Gold might expose David, Moscow ordered the New York station in April 1950 to discuss with the Greenglasses their departure from the United States. By then, new code names had been assigned to both David ("Zinger") and Ruth ("Ida"). Moscow's concern was evident in its memorandum to New York:

> In the case of [David] and [Ruth], the competitors have not only a clear and (for them) unquestionable association with our work but the fact of [their] having passed to us secret materials on the atomic bomb. On these grounds, the competitors will exert strong pressure on [David] and [Ruth], threatening and using other measures right up to their arrest, and in the end will force them to testify with all the consequences proceeding from this for "King" [Julius Rosenberg's new code name], his group, and all of our work in the country.[56]

Once more, however, as so often in the history of Soviet intelligence operations in the United States during this era, Moscow's plans were sidetracked by the inconvenient and unexpected realities of its agents' daily lives. In the Greenglass case, brother-in-law Julius Rosenberg served as the major source of news, reporting to NKGB operative "August" (who in turn wrote to his Moscow superiors) on April 25:

[Julius] informed [me] that currently [David's] departure is . . . difficult for family reasons. First, his wife is due to bear a child in a month. Second, about two and a half months ago, [Ruth] was passing by a gas cooker and her dress accidentally caught fire. [Ruth] was heavily burned and spent about ten weeks in a hospital, returning home only a week ago. In the hospital, she was given nearly forty blood transfusions, so serious was her condition. Since her blood type turned out to be very rare, [David] made a speech on the radio with an appeal to donate blood to save her. The campaign to help [Ruth] was also backed by the Red Cross . . . [and] some time ago, I saw a story in the *Post* about this accident; however, not then knowing [David's] exact name, I didn't pay attention to it. [Julius] also told me that this story had been described in the *Post*. Thus [Julius] thinks that [David] will be unable to leave the country in the near future. Undoubtedly, this case drew public attention to [David], and we don't rule out that sometime an idle reporter might come to their apartment for an interview.[57]

"August" asked Rosenberg to inform Greenglass that Soviet intelligence would assume all expenses connected with his departure if he agreed to leave the country. Also, it would resettle him in a new country and assume the care of those relatives remaining in America:

After [I said] this, [Julius] remarked: "If he goes there, make a good Communist out of him." I asked [Julius] immediately whether he considered [David] a bad Communist. He answered that recently [David] had hardly read any party publications, and, naturally, his education must be supplemented.[58]

To the NKGB, an itinerary for the Greenglasses meant traveling to Czechoslovakia via France as "tourists."[59] But both David and Julius believed that any departure, because of Ruth's physical condition, could occur only in the fall. The station informed Moscow on May 23: "About ten days ago, [Ruth] gave birth to a girl, and . . . is still not sufficiently recovered from the illness she had . . . and, naturally, she can't undertake a trip now."[60]

David objected to the Paris-Prague proposal. He argued that, in addition to accumulated debts of over $3,000 that had to be paid, applying for a passport to travel to Europe (given his "Manhattan Project" background) would surely attract the FBI's attention. If they had to flee, David urged that their destination be Mexico.[61] Moscow agreed, and Harry Gold's arrest on May 23 accelerated the timetable for departure.

The following day, New York NKGB station chief Boris Krotov proposed to his superiors that the Greenglasses leave for Mexico within two to three weeks and received Moscow's immediate approval.[62] Soviet officials acknowledged that if the Greenglasses remained in the United States, this would "inevitably lead to their arrest." They also suggested that if David could not take his entire family with him on short notice, then he should leave only with his wife and newborn child or, worst-case scenario, even without them. The same strictures applied to Julius Rosenberg: "[Julius, David,] and their wives must be told that counterintelligence may use blackmail, invent various stories about the fate of those who left and [those who] remained, referring to their alleged confessions. Therefore, they shouldn't believe in these stories but stand firmly on their positions."[63]

It is evident from the cables sent by the NKGB's leadership that, after Klaus Fuchs's confession and Harry Gold's arrest, Moscow had begun to prepare for—and to expect—the worst regarding its remaining American atomic spies. The NKGB instructed its New York station immediately to provide Rosenberg and the Greenglasses with $10,000 to be used for their departure, while taking photos of all family members for the production of false passports in Mexico. The May 25 cable stressed the extraordinary nature of the situation and cautioned Krotov that the entire future of Soviet intelligence work in the United States depended on the successful evasion of arrest by the Greenglasses and the Rosenbergs.[64]

That same day, Moscow asked its Mexico City station to determine what documents Americans would need to live in Mexico and to leave the country for Europe. It also asked the station to identify a secure location for hiding two families with children. The Stockholm station was told to determine urgently if there were any passenger ships traveling directly between Mexico and Sweden, how often the ships left, and their names.[65] The following day, May 26, Moscow asked the New York station to discuss with Julius Rosenberg the possibility that he and David Greenglass might go underground if they were unable to leave the United States almost immediately.[66] On June 1, David told Julius that his family would be prepared to leave on June 15.[67]

But on June 9, a Soviet operative code-named "Kirillov" met with Julius Rosenberg and filed the following report:

I saw no surveillance during the meeting and afterwards, despite checking [this] out for three hours following the meeting. [Julius] came to the meeting very agitated and immediately proposed that we leave the meeting place quickly. We walked about two blocks from the meeting place, and then [Julius] told me about the circumstances that had disturbed him. . . .[68]

While approaching David Greenglass's apartment building on Wednesday afternoon, June 7, Rosenberg noticed a car parked directly across the street with three men inside who stared at the entrance. Rosenberg assumed Greenglass was under FBI surveillance but nevertheless entered the building. As the two men conversed, David passed Julius a note which confirmed that the apartment had been watched constantly by these strangers all day long.

Julius left the apartment and, rounding the corner, noted a van with "Acme Construction Company" labeled on its sides. To confirm that David was being monitored, Julius returned to the building that evening. He found the same car and van where they had been parked earlier and saw two men leave the car and enter the back of the van. Julius also noticed four men, one standing on each of the four corners near the Greenglass apartment. He assumed that these, too, were American counterintelligence agents.

In discussions that day about the dangers of arrest, Rosenberg had cautioned Greenglass against revealing any of his operational activities if taken in for questioning. Greenglass insisted that under no circumstances would he become an informant. They both concluded, after observing the strict surveillance around the building, that, for the moment, escape was out of the question. Rosenberg suggested that Greenglass remain at home and await further word on preparations for his departure for Mexico, which "would depend now on the [continued] presence of surveillance."

"Kirillov," the operative who received Julius Rosenberg's report of the FBI's watch on David Greenglass, agreed with Julius that he must not visit David again. Instead, Ethel Rosenberg should visit her brother and take back all but $1,000 of the money previously given to him for his trip. (Should he be arrested, it would be difficult to explain the larger sum.)[69] The following week, on June 15, 1950, the FBI arrested David Greenglass and charged him with espionage. In Boris Krotov's June 17 cable reporting this event, he added the even more disturbing news that Greenglass apparently intended to plead guilty and cooperate with the government.[70]

Almost from the start of interrogation, David Greenglass acknowledged his complicity in atomic espionage and named Julius Rosenberg as the person who had recruited him for Soviet intelligence work in 1944. Greenglass's main goal, from the moment of arrest, was to persuade the U.S. government not to indict his wife as an accomplice and co-conspirator. His subsequent testimony against Julius and Ethel Rosenberg apparently reflected David's wish to protect Ruth far more than an effort on his part to avoid a long prison sentence, which he seemed to expect. When Greenglass was sentenced to fifteen years' imprisonment on April 6, 1951, Leonid Kvasnikov observed in a handwritten notation on a cable to Moscow from the NKGB's New York station that the sentence demonstrates "a clear tendency to show that those who contribute to the court's work are being spared by it."[71]

The FBI questioned Julius Rosenberg on the day following David's arrest and continued to gather evidence from the Greenglasses' statements and other sources. Rosenberg was arrested finally in July and charged with conspiracy to commit espionage with Greenglass and Harry Gold in 1944 and 1945. Other alleged co-conspirators were then taken into custody, including Ethel Rosenberg (on August 11) and Morton Sobell (on August 18), Julius's friend and former college classmate.

Morton Sobell, like the Rosenbergs, avowed his innocence. He had fled to Mexico with his family but was delivered to the FBI by Mexican police at the Texas border, an indication of the Greenglasses' probable fate had they attempted the plan to seek temporary Mexican asylum. Ethel Rosenberg and Morton Sobell were also charged with conspiracy to commit espionage as members of what the American media by the fall of 1950 had labeled the "Rosenberg spy ring."[72]

The trial of Julius and Ethel Rosenberg before Judge Irving R. Kaufman began in New York in March 1951. The chief witnesses for the prosecution were David Greenglass, who had pleaded guilty the previous October, and his wife, Ruth. Greenglass testified that he had given Harry Gold (once) and the Rosenbergs (several times) diagrams and other information concerning the lens mold, firing mechanism, and internal structure of the atomic bomb. Gold, who had pleaded guilty at a separate trial in December 1950 and had been sentenced to a thirty-year prison term, corroborated Greenglass's statements about their meeting but testified that he had never met the Rosenbergs.

The government's case against Ethel and Julius Rosenberg, therefore, relied largely upon the testimony of Ethel's brother and their sister-in-law. Similarly, the case against Morton Sobell depended almost entirely upon the testimony of another alleged co-conspirator, a former friend and fellow Communist named Max Elitcher who charged that Sobell had tried to recruit him into the espionage ring.

Defense lawyers ridiculed the evidence provided by confessed co-conspirators, but in cross-examination they dealt ineffectually with the testimony of Greenglass and Elitcher. (Gold was not cross-examined.) The Rosenbergs' decision to testify on their own behalf also proved unhelpful. Ethel Rosenberg, under cross-examination, chose to plead self-incrimination when questioned about her Communist affiliations.* On March 29, 1951, all four defendants (the Rosenbergs, Sobell, and Greenglass) were found guilty. While Judge Kaufman sentenced David Greenglass to a fifteen-year and Morton Sobell to a thirty-year prison term, Julius and Ethel Rosenberg were both sentenced to death.†

Judge Kaufman set their execution for the week of May 21, 1951, but a series of legal appeals prevented the sentence from being carried out for more than two years. Meanwhile, a campaign to obtain clemency for the pair was mounted both in the United States and abroad. The movement, which included many non-Communist dignitaries, was spearheaded by Communist-dominated "defense committees."

Even the NKGB became involved. Within weeks of the trial verdict, on April 14, the New York station sent Moscow a plan on behalf of the Rosenbergs to "organize a powerful campaign in our and especially the foreign press. It is desirable to place articles about the trial, first of all in the non-Communist press." For Soviet writers, the station suggested eighteen separate themes for articles related to the case, including the fact that "the mother of two children is sentenced to execution in the electric chair . . . by the slanderous denunciation of her scoundrel-brother." Interestingly, although the first theme was that "espionage mania has reached its highest degree" in America with the Rosenberg trial, the station did not focus on arguing Julius's innocence. The eighteenth and last theme essentially accepted David Greenglass's guilt:

---

* "Information on [Julius Rosenberg's] wife. Surname that of her husband, first name Ethel, 29 years old. Married five years. Finished secondary school. A [member of the Communist Party] since 1938. Sufficiently well developed politically. Knows about her husband's work and the role of METRE and NIL. In view of delicate health does not work. Is characterized positively and as a devoted person." Kvasnikov to Fitin, November 27, 1944, No. 1657, VENONA files.

† Julius and Ethel Rosenberg were executed on June 19, 1953, after the U.S. Supreme Court vacated in a 6–3 decision the stay of execution granted two days earlier by Justice William O. Douglas.

"The fact that [Greenglass], who allegedly passed 'secret' materials on the atomic bomb and is on substance the main accused person, got a relatively light sentence, tells us that this trial was a frame-up for certain goals."

The station's other proposal, beyond a media campaign to compel reduced sentences for the Rosenbergs, was to pressure Greenglass to recant his trial testimony against Julius and Ethel. A letter, supposedly written by David's friends, was to be passed personally to Ruth Greenglass or one of their relatives. The station cautioned that the document "by its form should give no hints that it could have been written by operatives of the station or members of the U.S. Communist Party." Essentially a threatening letter, it would claim to have been written "by American friends of [David Greenglass] who can turn into his deadly enemies. . . ."[73]

This sophomoric strategy to belatedly transform Greenglass's essentially accurate testimony against his sister and brother-in-law concluded with an absurd plea to those who might implement the plan, an impossible scheme at a time when the NKGB station had no American agents and sources: "[We] underline [the fact] that nobody should know about the letter, that it must be recited to [Greenglass], that his lawyer shouldn't know about it." The New York station, which, in earlier and more productive times, had been home to the most creative practitioners of Soviet intelligence tradecraft—among them Gutzeit, Ovakimyan, Yatskov, Kvasnikov, and Feklissov—had been reduced by the early 1950s to concocting doltish media campaigns and poison pen letters.

MOSCOW MEMORIES—1953-88

Even these proposed projects paled, however, when compared with the falsehood developed by Joseph Stalin's closest colleagues and heirs in 1953 following the dictator's death that March. Fearing a coup d'état in which virtually the entire Soviet leadership would be arrested and shot at the direction of Lavrenty Beria and his associates in the state security services, the Politburo's major figures—Bulganin, Malenkov, Khrushchev, Zhukov, and others—quickly arrested Beria and his major supporters. After a secret trial, all were executed by year's end on fictitious charges of plotting to overthrow the regime and to restore capitalism. (One of those who died with Beria was former NKVD head Vsevolod Merkulov.)

One of the charges against Beria on which even his main accusers disagreed was the extraordinary assertion that he had cooperated with British intelligence since the Revolution and may have been linked to the exposure of Klaus Fuchs and others who had engaged in atomic espionage. "Traitors Beria, Merkulov, [and others] during their work at leading posts in the state security organizations had been systematically informed about all the valuable materials on atomic energy . . . as well as data about the sources of this information," noted one December 1953 KGB document prepared for the "trial." "In particular, they were aware of agents' names and biographic data."[74]

A decade later, by which time the Soviet Union had moved from the terror of Stalin's last years to Nikita Khrushchev's "thaw," Colonel Alexander Feklissov suggested to the agency's head, A. Sakharovsky, in 1965 (the twentieth anniversary of Hitler's defeat) that the KGB urge the government to award Klaus Fuchs a medal honoring "his help to the USSR . . . in the struggle against fascism and imperialism . . . taking into account Fuchs's essential contribution to strengthening the USSR's military power." Feklissov proposed to decorate Fuchs with a high government medal and make him an honorary member of the Soviet Union's Academy of Sciences. The Academy's head, however, opposed the award, apparently believing that such an action would minimize the role played by Soviet physicists in creating their own country's atomic weapons.[75]

Klaus Fuchs did not remain insensitive to such slights. For example, in 1971 he protested directly to the chief of East Germany's Ministry for State Security, Erich Mielke, who in turn complained to Moscow, when Harold "Kim" Philby's memoir My Secret War referred in disparaging terms to Fuchs's behavior under interrogation.[76] Fuchs died in 1988 and, posthumously, Soviet intelligence officials decided to urge their government to award his long-deferred official decoration.[77] Appropriately, it was Fuchs's postwar courier, Alexander Feklissov, who flew to East Berlin for the presentation ceremony.

After visiting Fuchs's gravesite, Feklissov went to Dresden to present the Order of People's Friendship directly to the physicist's widow, Margaret Fuchs, who, despite the honor, was not pleased. "Why did you come so late?" she demanded of Fuchs's Soviet admirer. "Klaus waited for you for twenty-five years. In the last years, he thought there were no Soviet comrades left alive who knew him."[78] The complaint, although delivered unfairly to Feklissov, who for decades had urged such recognition, was justified. It was also bittersweet, coming as it did in the waning months of the Communist world to which—like so many Soviet operatives, agents, and sources of an earlier generation—Klaus Fuchs had devoted his life.

Few of those in the West known to have delivered atomic secrets to Soviet intelligence escaped postwar pursuit and punishment. Klaus Fuchs, after serving his prison sentence, found a new life in Communist East Germany. Donald Maclean escaped certain arrest and imprisonment by fleeing, in 1951, to the Soviet Union, where he lived out his days. Harry Gold and David Greenglass, after completing their jail sentences, disappeared from public view. Greenglass had successfully negotiated his trial testimony against the Rosenbergs in exchange for the U.S. government's agreement not to prosecute his wife, Ruth. His sister and brother-in-law proved less fortunate in the prevailing anti-Communist mood of the times. Despite numerous appeals for clemency from around the world, the Rosenbergs went to their deaths in 1953.

Others avoided detection. The British scientist known by the code name "Eric," who proved so helpful to the NKVD during the war years, successfully protected his anonymity, as did the American engineer "Persian." Theodore Hall faced an FBI interrogation at the time of the atom spy trials, but it failed to turn up adequate evidence against him—including several incriminating cables decrypted in the VENONA program—until years later. Nonetheless, Hall left his U.S. teaching career and settled in England, where he abandoned atomic physics to pursue a distinguished career as a microbiologist at Cambridge University. Only after the VENONA materials were released in 1995–96 did Hall acknowledge his covert assistance to the NKVD during the war years.

Unabashed even today, however, Ted Hall concluded in a recently published *apologia* that as a young scientist delivering Western atomic secrets to Soviet intelligence, he had "the right end of the stick. I am no longer that person; but I am by no means ashamed of him."[79] A half-century earlier, the Soviet operative-journalist Sergei Kurnakov had asked Hall at their first encounter: "Do you understand what you are doing? Why do you think it is necessary to disclose U.S. secrets for the sake of the Soviet Union?" Hall responded: "There is no country except for the Soviet Union which could be entrusted with such a terrible thing."[80]

This blind faith in the superiority of a Communist society, whose norms differed so greatly from those of his own country, led Hall and other Americans who delivered secrets to Soviet intelligence in the 1930s and 1940s to an interlude of profound betrayal. Markus Wolf, the talented East German Communist spymaster, described figures like Hall—and other Western spies for the USSR—as believing that leading covert lives secured their admission to "an elite . . . secretive club fighting for a noble ideal."[81]

Moscow could rely for an entire generation upon this varied collection of American and British espionage agents and sources, only a handful of whom ever defected or renounced their earlier treachery. Even during the murderous purge era, Soviet communism retained for some in the West a power to illuminate action and induce devotion that would persist until Cold War confrontation and the venomous final years of Joseph Stalin's rule combined to extinguish the flame.

Epilogue: Aftermath and Legacy

A S HE LAY seriously ill in Moscow during the late 1960s, following years of incarceration in the Gulag, Alexander Ulanovski, Soviet military intelligence's U.S. station chief from 1931 to 1934, read his wife's Russian translation of Robert Conquest's extraordinary book on the 1936–39 Soviet purge years, *The Great Terror*. (A samizdat translation was then being distributed secretly among other dissidents.) "Now I can die in peace," Ulanovski announced. "The story is known and it will survive."*[1]

But when does a chronicle survive, fully and persuasively, as a work of history? Surely the operatives, agents, and sources described in *The Haunted Wood* (and others still unrevealed) deserve a more complete narrative than the one provided by the authors' partial access to KGB archives.

For now, we have to accept the illuminating but incomplete scrutiny of Soviet records available for this book, supplementing its mosaic of evidence with the VENONA cables, the published literature, and private sources. If the present guardians of intelligence files in Russia, the United States, and Great Britain are among our readers, however, perhaps this effort to dispassionately describe Soviet espionage in the

---

* Nadya Ulanovskaya described her husband's deathbed statement in a 1977 interview with Allen Weinstein.

United States during the Stalin era will encourage expedited review and release of even more materials under their control.

As for the entire effort to penetrate key American institutions by Moscow's intelligence operatives in the 1930s and war years, "by the onset of the Cold War [as Daniel Patrick Moynihan wrote recently] the Soviet attack in the area of espionage and subversion had been blunted and turned back":

> There would be episodic successes in the years to come, but none equal to earlier feats. New York of the 1930s. Los Alamos. Some unions. The State Department. The Treasury Department. By the close of the 1940s, Communism was a defeated ideology in the United States, with its influence in steep and steady decline, and the KGB reduced to recruiting thieves as spies.[2]

Moynihan might have added the OSS and several other wartime government agencies to his roster of Soviet "successes." But he is correct in believing that the end of World War II's Soviet-American alliance and the defections of Gouzenko and Bentley combined to end most of the spying that had provided the USSR's leaders with a cornucopia of policy and technical secrets from the United States during the war.

Soviet intelligence largely contented itself in the half-century of Cold War confrontation that followed with the gleanings of traitors-for-hire, paid informants such as the later-convicted members of the Walker family and Aldrich Ames. Such mercenaries existed also among agents and sources in America during the Stalin era, especially in the 1930s. But they were dwarfed in number and importance by antifascist believers in Communist ideology, who risked their careers to hand over material. By the time a far-reaching "culture of secrecy" (in Moynihan's phrase) had swept through U.S. society in the Truman-Eisenhower years, the dangers of an "American Communist underground" had become the stuff of both history and myth—but no longer a reality.

In the aftermath of Soviet espionage's "golden age," 1933–45, Moscow operatives in the United States who survived execution during the purge years (such as Itzhak Akhmerov, Alexander Feklissov, Anatoly Gorsky, and others) were not compelled to suffer the indignity experienced by many of their key American agents and sources who followed Soviet instructions* and lied about their past involvement at congressional hearings, government security inquiries, and criminal trials. By breaking completely with the Communist underground, a

---

* For example, those given to Nathan Gregory Silvermaster.

few defecting agents—notably Elizabeth Bentley and Whittaker Chambers—escaped this moral dilemma only to assume another, that of bearing witness against their former friends and colleagues. The testimony of defectors provoked criticism not only from those who had remained Communists but also from a significant portion of the non-Communist American intelligentsia.

A number of Soviet agents, despite the evidence, persisted in denying their covert deeds—Alger Hiss, Duncan Lee, Julius Rosenberg, Nathan Gregory Silvermaster, and Harry Dexter White, to name a few—even though, for some, the Stalinist "god" had long since failed.

Based on the available evidence, nor were the Russian operatives assigned to the United States during this generation as emotionally troubled and, in some cases, as unhinged as some of their American agents and sources. No hint of personal scandal, despite one or two divorces, ever attached itself either to married operatives, such as Itzhak Akhmerov and Helen Lowry or Vassily Zarubin and Elizabeth Zarubina, or to most of the other major station chiefs and operatives of that era—Alexander Feklissov, Anatoly Gorsky, Peter Gutzeit, Leonid Kvasnikov, Gaik Ovakimyan, Alexander Panyushkin, Vladimir Pravdin, Anatoly Yatskov, among others. With a few exceptions, although the word would trouble them, they and their colleagues appeared thoroughly bourgeois in personal habits and lifestyle.

For many of their American associates, however, covert activity referred not only to underground work but also to personal habits that often threatened their exposure. Moscow complained on several occasions about Martha Dodd's numerous liaisons, and Nathan Gregory Silvermaster solved his household tensions by devising a ménage à trois for himself, his wife, and another agent in the group. The domestic quarrels of Victor and Katherine Perlo led to her incriminating letter to American authorities, just as Elizabeth Bentley's troubled years following the death of her lover, Jacob Golos, finally led to her break with Communist espionage. A married Whittaker Chambers collected documents from Washington sources in the evenings during the mid-1930s while (by his own later confession) he roamed the streets of Baltimore and New York seeking male companionship. In addition, confidence men like Samuel Dickstein ("Crook") and Boris Morros professed ideological devotion even as they continually raised the monetary stakes for their services. Under the circumstances, it is not surprising that Soviet operatives valued so greatly those Americans whose devotion even in adversity—Earl Browder (until his expulsion from the CPUSA), Alger Hiss, and Julius Rosenberg among them—was rock-solid.

From a half-century's perspective, one remarkable achievement by Soviet intelligence in the mid-1940s was to keep American counterintelligence ignorant of the dramatic manner in which its networks were swiftly dismantled after the Gouzenko and Bentley defections. During the years that followed, testimony by Elizabeth Bentley and Whittaker Chambers was crucial in the FBI's pursuit of individuals who had served earlier as Soviet agents and sources. Moreover, without Klaus Fuchs's confession, which led to the arrests of Harry Gold and David Greenglass and to their subsequent cooperation with the government, all of those involved in atomic espionage might have escaped arrest (as some, including Theodore Hall, "Eric," and "Persian," actually did).

In at least one case, punishment far exceeded the crimes. Even most of those who were persuaded that Julius Rosenberg had recruited his brother-in-law, David Greenglass, to commit atomic espionage, and that Rosenberg had been a longtime Soviet agent and agent handler, believe that his death sentence should never have been issued or carried out. As for Ethel Rosenberg, the material drawn from KGB archives for this book, along with previously available information, suggests that although she knew of her husband's long and productive work for Soviet intelligence, at most she played only a minor supporting role in that work. In a less-pressured legal and political environment, her actions might have led only to a brief jail term, perhaps not even to her arrest. The couple became the focus of a worldwide clemency campaign, especially after publication of their *Death House Letters*.[3] Ethel and Julius Rosenberg were executed in 1953, recognizing that they had become, for their supporters, mythic figures in an iconography that dramatized the larger symbolism of their situation through these "open letters" from prison.[4]

The other major case related to Soviet espionage that became a public drama during this period involved Whittaker Chambers's allegations, and evidence, against Alger Hiss. The complex facts of the Hiss-Chambers relationship, like those in the Rosenberg case, were reduced by partisans to competing images. In both cases, almost from the moment they began, the facts became the subject matter for simple morality tales. The protagonists assumed the status of icons in the demonologies and hagiographies of their opposing camps.

Republicans invoked Hiss's presumed treachery to indict the Democratic Party for allegedly tolerating large numbers of Soviet agents in the federal government during the Roosevelt presidency. For many liberals and radicals, on the other hand, the nature of Hiss's main accusers—a Communist defector (Chambers), an ambitious Congressman (Richard Nixon), and a Red-hunting FBI director (J. Edgar Hoover)—was enough to persuade them, erroneously, that Hiss had been an innocent victim of perjured testimony and concocted evidence. The assault on Alger Hiss, his defenders argued, foreshadowed a larger effort by Republicans to discredit New Deal liberalism and bipartisan internationalism. On both sides, issues of evidence blended into a defining argument over political beliefs.

Thus the question of whether Alger Hiss had committed perjury by denying that he had spied for the Soviets became entangled in a larger set of public issues: the meaning and merit of the Cold War, the treatment of domestic Communists, the response by intellectuals to their own radical pasts, the true extent of Communist infiltration into the U.S. government during the New Deal and war years, and the proper role of congressional committees in probing subversion. The facts that might have established Alger Hiss's *legal* guilt or innocence became absorbed in this debate over the broader meaning of the case.[5]

Hiss's conviction, in turn (as historian Earl Latham observed), "revolutionized public opinion" on the question of Soviet espionage in the American government. "Without the Alger Hiss case," Latham noted of the postwar spy probes, "the six-year controversy that followed might have been a much tamer affair, and the Communist issue somewhat more tractable."[6] Instead, within a month of the jury verdict against Hiss, Klaus Fuchs was arrested, opening the investigation that led to the Rosenbergs, and Senator Joseph McCarthy journeyed to Wheeling, West Virginia, to make his maiden speech on Communist subversion in America. The new era of anti-Communist politics quickly acquired its leading figure—and its name.

Despite later denials, the truth is that a number of American agents and sources, some from doctrinal devotion and others for cold cash, carried on espionage for Soviet operatives throughout the New Deal and war years. Because of their work, Russian intelligence agencies received substantial and sometimes critical information (including many classified documents) concerning U.S. government policies on highly sensitive subjects, its confidential negotiating strategies, and secret weapons developments, including essential processes involved in building the atomic bomb. Moscow's American surrogates, in short, turned over, especially during the war, a voluminous collection of classified materials to Soviet operatives. In addition to the material from KGB archives quoted in the preceding pages, the authors collected—but have not cited—150 single-spaced pages of confidential letters, cables, and other documents taken by Moscow's American agents and sources, a fraction of the total amount actually transmitted.*

This data was the tangible and hurtful legacy left by those who volunteered for membership in that "secretive club" described by Markus Wolf, however tarnished Soviet communism might have become for some of them in the wake of the Moscow purge trials and the Nazi-Soviet Pact. Few joined Bentley and Chambers in defecting or, like Duggan and Straight, in distancing themselves. Most continued their involvement in espionage until Moscow itself terminated its American networks in 1945.

At the same time, the personal legacy left by many of Soviet intelligence's American confederates was mainly one of anguish and bitterness. The Rosenbergs' execution, jail sentences for Alger Hiss and others, Laurence Duggan's suicide, and the exiled wanderings of Martha Dodd and Alfred Stern highlighted the underlying sense of frustration and grief that also affected others who, earlier, had enjoyed the secret life's psychic rewards. After Alger Hiss's conviction, for example, Whittaker Chambers wrote a friend concerning his testimony against Hiss that he felt "it was all for nothing, that nothing had been gained except the misery of others."[7]

Even those Americans who, unlike Chambers, had not turned against communism may have shared in the "misery." Certainly, none wrote and published in the following years a proud memoir of his (or her) achievements as a Soviet intelligence agent comparable to Kim Philby's *My Secret Life* or John Cairncross's recent posthumous autobiography. Nor did an aspiring Herodotus, a participant-historian, emerge from among them to record their motives and actions, as that first historian wrote of his age, "in the hope of preserving from decay the remembrance of what men have done . . . of preventing [their] great and wonderful actions . . . from losing their due meed of glory; and withal to put on record what were their grounds of feud."[8] In the end, the enduring legacy of those Americans who sacrificed country for cause in "the haunted wood" remains one of inglorious constancy to a cruel and discredited faith.

---

* Some of the American material was actually stolen by British agents—Burgess, Maclean, and Philby—while in Washington or in London.

NOTES

Chapter 1. Communist Romantics, I:
The Reluctant Laurence Duggan

1. File 36857, Vol. 1, pp. 11–13, KGB Archives, Moscow. Hereafter, all materials from these archives will be denoted by the introductory file, volume, and page numbers as above.
2. Ibid., p. 19.
3. Ibid., p. 14.
4. Ibid., pp. 17, 20.
5. Ibid., p. 23.
6. Ibid., p. 22.
7. Ibid., p. 24.
8. Ibid.
9. Ibid., p. 25.
10. Ibid., p. 27.
11. Ibid., p. 30.
12. Ibid., pp. 30–31.
13. Ibid., pp. 258–60.
14. Ibid., p. 36.
15. Ibid., p. 40.
16. Ibid., pp. 42–44.
17. Ibid., p. 46.
18. Ibid., p. 49.
19. Ibid., p. 51.

20. Ibid., pp. 84–85.

21. Pavel Sudoplatov and Anatoli Sudoplatov, *Special Tasks: The Memoirs of an Unwanted Witness—A Soviet Spymaster* (New York: Little, Brown, 1995), p. 47.

22. File 36857, Vol. 1, p. 87.

23. File 3587, Vol. 1, p. 227.

24. File 36857, Vol. 1, p. 67.

25. Ibid., pp. 68–69.

26. Ibid., pp. 70–71.

27. File 3587, Vol. 1, pp. 231–32.

28. File 36857, Vol. 1, pp. 71–72.

29. Ibid., pp. 74–75.

30. Ibid.

31. Ibid., p. 80.

32. Ibid., p. 86.

33. Ibid., pp. 87–88.

34. Ibid.

35. Ibid., pp. 90–93.

36. Ibid., pp. 94–95.

37. Ibid., p. 100.

38. Ibid., p. 102.

39. Ibid., p. 101.

40. Ibid., pp. 103, 106.

41. Ibid., pp. 108–109.

42. Ibid., pp. 114, 116–22.

43. Ibid., pp. 123–24.

44. File 3587, Vol. 7, pp. 36, 154.

45. File 36857, Vol. 1, p. 137.

46. Ibid., pp. 140, 143.

47. Ibid., pp. 156–58.

48. Ibid., p. 167.

49. Ibid., pp. 170–78.

50. Ibid., p. 185.

51. Ibid., pp. 192–93.

52. Ibid., pp. 196a–98.

53. Ibid., p. 200 (in the envelope).

54. Ibid., pp. 201–205.

55. Ibid., p. 229. "[Duggan] has been appointed . . . Assistant Diplomatic Advisor of the [UNRRA]. . . . According to [Akhmerov], [Duggan] even before this, was announcing that his position in the [State Department] was precarious. . . ." New York station to Moscow, August 4, 1994, No. 1114, VENONA files.

56. File 36857, Vol. 1, p. 246.

57. Ibid., p. 262.

58. Ibid., pp. 263–64.
59. Ibid., pp. 271–72.
60. Ibid., p. 284.

Chapter 2. Creating the Soviet Networks: Hiss, Chambers, and Early Recruits

1. File 17517, Vol. 3, pp. 70–72.
2. William E. Leuchtenburg, *Franklin D. Roosevelt and the New Deal* (New York: Harper & Row, 1963), pp. 205–207.
3. File 17407, Vol. 1, p. 116.
4. Ibid., p. 22.
5. Ibid., pp. 9–12.
6. Ibid., pp. 75–76.
7. Ibid., pp. 67–68.
8. File 3465, Vol. 1, p. 28.
9. File 3460, Vol. 1, pp. 42, 59.
10. File 3464, Vol. 1, pp. 176–78.
11. Ibid., p. 29.
12. Ibid., p. 31.
13. File 3461, Vol. 2, pp. 176–77.
14. File 3463, Vol. 1, p. 90.
15. Ibid., p. 236.
16. File 3464, Vol. 1, p. 217.
17. File 40594, Vol. 2, pp. 230–31.
18. File 3461, Vol. 1, pp. 56–57.
19. Ibid., pp. 57–58.
20. File 3465, Vol. 1, pp. 45–47.
21. Ibid., pp. 290–92; File 40594, Vol. 4, pp. 167–68.
22. File 40594, Vol. 4, pp. 144–45.
23. File 3463, Vol. 2, p. 183.
24. File 3463, Vol. 1, p. 57.
25. File 3465, Vol. 1, p. 39.
26. File 40594, Vol. 1, pp. 110–11.
27. File 3461, Vol. 1, pp. 32–33.
28. File 3463, Vol. 2, pp. 71–72.
29. File 3461, Vol. 1, p. 156.
30. File 3465, Vol. 2, pp. 78–79.
31. File 17407, Vol. 1, p. 76.
32. File 35112, Vol. 1, p. 5.
33. File 3464, Vol. 1, pp. 113–14.
34. Ibid.
35. File 17690, Vol. 1, pp. 5–7, 90–93.

36. File 3460, Vol. 2, pp. 32–33.

37. File 3463, Vol. 1, p. 285.

38. File 3460, Vol. 2, p. 39.

39. File 17407, Vol. 1, pp. 70, 73.

40. Ibid., pp. 76–77.

41. File 3464, Vol. 1, p. 133.

42. File 17643, Vol. 1, p. 24.

43. Ibid., p. 17.

44. Ibid., p. 20.

45. Ibid., p. 42.

46. Ibid., pp. 20–21.

47. Ibid., pp. 39–41.

48. Ibid., p. 42.

49. Ibid., pp. 21–22.

50. A. Vassiliev and A. Koreshkov, *Station Chief Gold* (Moscow: Andropov Red-Banner Institute, 1984), pp. 31–32.

51. Ibid., pp. 50–51.

52. File 17643, Vol. 1, p. 29.

53. Ibid., p. 30.

54. Ibid., pp. 33, 38.

55. Ibid., pp. 53–54.

56. Ibid., p. 51.

57. Ibid., p. 64.

58. Ibid., p. 69.

59. Ibid., p. 70.

60. File 3464, Vol. 1, p. 76.

61. File 43173, Vol. 5, p. 266.

62. Allen Weinstein, *Perjury: The Hiss-Chambers Case* (New York: Knopf, 1968), p. 114. See also Sam Tanenhaus, *Whittaker Chambers: A Biography* (New York: Random House, 1997).

63. Weinstein, *Perjury*, passim.

64. Ibid., p. 121; see also pp. 120–24.

65. Ibid., p. 122.

66. Ibid., p. 123.

67. Ibid., pp. 120–24.

68. Ibid., especially pp. 116–20.

69. Ibid., pp. 98–99.

70. Ibid., especially pp. 192–203.

71. Ibid., pp. 114–15, 124–25.

72. Ibid., pp. 124–27.

73. Ibid., pp. 189–235.

74. Ibid., pp. 204–35.

75. Ibid., pp. 272–80.

76. Ibid., pp. 280–87.

77. Ibid., pp. 233–35, 287–90.
78. Ibid., p. 234.
79. Ibid., p. 291.
80. Ibid., pp. 291–92.
81. Ibid., pp. 292–93.
82. Ibid., pp. 55–59, 293–94.

Chapter 3. Love and Loyalties, I:
The Case of Martha Dodd

1. File 14449, Vol. 1, p. 13.
2. Ibid., p. 25.
3. Ibid., p. 15.
4. Ibid., p. 16.
5. Ibid., p. 25.
6. Ibid., p. 27.
7. Ibid., pp. 17–18.
8. Ibid., pp. 20–21.
9. Ibid., pp. 24, 31.
10. Ibid., p. 27.
11. Ibid., p. 28.
12. Ibid., p. 30.
13. Ibid., p. 35.
14. Ibid., p. 36.
15. Ibid., p. 37.
16. Ibid., pp. 38–44.
17. Ibid.
18. Ibid., p. 48.
19. Ibid., pp. 33–34.
20. Ibid.
21. Ibid., pp. 45–46.
22. Ibid., p. 50.
23. Ibid., p. 51.
24. Ibid., pp. 33–34.
25. Ibid., p. 52.
26. Ibid., p. 14.
27. File 35112, Vol. 5, p. 45.
28. Ibid., p. 102.
29. File 14449, Vol. 1, p. 56.
30. File 35112, Vol. 5, pp. 117–18.
31. File 35112, Vol. 6, pp. 98–99.
32. File 14449, Vol. 1, p. 57.
33. Ibid., p. 61.

34. Ibid., pp. 70–72.
35. Ibid., pp. 75–77.
36. Ibid.
37. Ibid., pp. 106–107.
38. Ibid., pp. 118–21.
39. Ibid., pp. 124–25.
40. Ibid., pp. 122–23, 126–28.
41. File 14449, Vol. 2, p. 231.
42. File 3463, Vol. 2, pp. 40–41.
43. File 35112, Vol. 5, p. 37.
44. File 43173, Vol. 5, pp. 101, 103.
45. File 35112, Vol. 5, pp. 166–67.
46. Ibid., pp. 186–87.
47. Ibid., pp. 169, 267.
48. File 35112, Vol. 5a, pp. 452–55.
49. File 35112, Vol. 6, pp. 96–97.
50. File 35112, Vol. 7, pp. 438–39.
51. File 43173, Vol. 5, p. 103.
52. File 35112, Vol. 7, pp. 73, 94; File 43173, Vol. 1, p. 126. See also New York station to Moscow, May 26, 1944, No. 748, VENONA files.
53. File 14449, Vol. 2, pp. 21–24.
54. Ibid., p. 17.
55. Ibid., pp. 18, 25.
56. File 43173, Vol. 5, p. 102.
57. File 14449, Vol. 2, pp. 29, 31, 22–34, 62–63, 71–72, 79.
58. Ibid., p. 76.
59. Ibid., p. 77.
60. Ibid., p. 78.
61. Ibid., pp. 100, 105.
62. Ibid., p. 129.
63. Ibid., pp. 130–33, 137.
64. Ibid., pp. 144, 150.
65. Ibid., pp. 153, 158–59.
66. Ibid., pp. 160, 164.
67. Ibid., pp. 170–71.
68. Ibid., pp. 173–74, 186, 188.
69. Ibid., p. 190.
70. Ibid., pp. 210–11.
71. Ibid., pp. 227, 241–43.
72. Ibid., pp. 265–66.
73. Ibid., pp. 244, 263.
74. Ibid., pp. 276–77.
75. Ibid., p. 325.
76. Ibid., pp. 362–63.
77. Ibid., p. 365.

Chapter 4. Communist Romantics, II:
The Exuberant Michael Straight

1. File 58380, Vol. 1, p. 13.
2. Ibid., p. 12.
3. Ibid., pp. 14–17.
4. Ibid.
5. Ibid., pp. 19, 21, 25.
6. Ibid., pp. 28–32.
7. Ibid., p. 157.
8. Ibid., p. 26.
9. Ibid., pp. 33–34.
10. Ibid., pp. 39, 158.
11. Ibid., p. 39.
12. Ibid., p. 40.
13. Ibid., p. 46.
14. Ibid., p. 43.
15. Ibid., p. 46.
16. Ibid., p. 49.
17. Ibid., p. 48.
18. Ibid., pp. 44–45.
19. Ibid., p. 53.
20. Ibid., p. 51.
21. Ibid., p. 52.
22. Ibid., pp. 56–57.
23. Ibid., p. 59.
24. Ibid., pp. 60–62.
25. Ibid., p. 67.
26. Ibid., pp. 71, 81.
27. Ibid., p. 62.
28. Ibid., pp. 73–74.
29. Ibid., p. 83.
30. Ibid., pp. 92, 96.
31. Ibid., p. 113.
32. Ibid., pp. 118, 120–22.
33. Ibid., p. 147.
34. Ibid., p. 142.
35. Ibid., pp. 143–44, 146–47.
36. Ibid., pp. 148, 158, 162.
37. Ibid., pp. 165–67.
38. Michael Straight, *After Long Silence* (New York: William Morrow, 1983), pp. 130, 135.
39. Ibid., p. 207.

40. Yuri Modin, *My Five Cambridge Friends: Burgess, Maclean, Philby, Blunt and Cairncross* (New York: Farrar, Straus & Giroux, 1994), p. 76.

41. Ibid., p. 214.

Chapter 5. Love and Loyalties, II:
Elizabeth Bentley and Jacob Golos

1. File 70994, Vol. 1, p. 127.
2. Ibid., pp. 7, 127.
3. Ibid., pp. 105, 127–28.
4. Ibid., p. 10.
5. Ibid., pp. 8, 12–14, 21.
6. Ibid., p. 30.
7. File 70545, Vol. 1, p. 233.
8. File 70994, Vol. 1, pp. 71, 83, 98.
9. Ibid., pp. 86, 98.
10. Ibid., pp. 36, 97, 392.
11. Ibid., pp. 141, 241.
12. Ibid., p. 155.
13. Ibid., p. 161.
14. File 70545, Vol. 1, p. 279.
15. Ibid., pp. 277–78.
16. Ibid., pp. 212–13.
17. File 35112, Vol. 5a, p. 420.
18. File 70545, Vol. 1, p. 229.
19. Ibid., pp. 224–27.
20. Ibid., pp. 230–32.
21. Ibid., pp. 235–36.
22. Ibid., pp. 239–41.
23. Ibid., p. 208.
24. File 70994, Vol. 1, p. 130.
25. Ibid., pp. 146, 173, 272.
26. Ibid., pp. 48, 98–99.
27. Ibid., pp. 101–102, 120–25, 181–82, 188.
28. File 35112, Vol. 1, p. 8.
29. File 70994, Vol. 1, pp. 235–36.
30. File 32428, Vol. 1, p. 266.
31. File 70994, Vol. 1, p. 339.
32. Ibid., p. 171.
33. Ibid., pp. 338, 367–68, 371.
34. File 70545, Vol. 1, pp. 280–82.
35. Ibid.

36. Ibid. Browder used Golos, among others, to convey his information to Soviet intelligence. See, for example, New York station to Moscow, July 18, 1943, Nos. 1163 and 1164; and May 26, 1943, No. 784, all VENONA files.

37. File 70994, Vol. 1, pp. 296–98.

38. Ibid., pp. 307, 312.

39. Ibid., p. 324; File 70545, Vol. 1, p. 65.

40. File 70994, Vol. 1, p. 310.

41. File 70545, Vol. 1, p. 283.

42. File 70994, Vol. 1, pp. 352–53.

43. File 70545, Vol. 1, p. 9.

44. Ibid., pp. 19–22.

45. Ibid., pp. 48–49; File 70994, Vol. 1, p. 325.

46. File 70545, Vol. 1, pp. 32, 35–36.

47. Ibid., pp. 79–80.

48. Ibid., p. 97. "The [Silvermaster/Ullman] material goes through [Bentley]. . . . Most of the material received . . . has been processed by [Akhmerov]. . . ." New York station to Moscow, February 23, 1944, No. 278, VENONA files.

49. File 70545, Vol. 1, pp. 83–84, 88–89. Browder also worked directly, when he chose to, with Soviet operatives. New York station to Moscow, February 9, 1944, No. 196, VENONA files.

50. File 70545, Vol. 1, pp. 95–99.

51. Ibid., p. 100.

52. Ibid., p. 103.

53. Ibid., pp. 105–12.

54. Ibid., pp. 128–29.

55. Ibid., p. 114; File 70994, Vol. 1, p. 339.

56. File 70545, Vol. 1, pp. 253–54.

57. Ibid., pp. 168–69.

58. Ibid., p. 249.

59. Ibid., p. 184.

60. Ibid., pp. 288–94.

61. Ibid., pp. 338–340.

62. Ibid., pp. 340–48.

63. Ibid., p. 359.

64. Ibid., pp. 360–62.

65. Ibid., pp. 363–67.

66. Ibid.

67. Ibid., pp. 368–71. Merkulov's caution probably reflected recognition of the fact that, despite her erratic behavior, Elizabeth Bentley continued to provide valuable information to Soviet intelligence at this time. For example, one October 1944 cable described Bentley's identification of a new OSS employee whom she believed would be willing to work with the NKGB. New York station to Moscow, October 14, 1944, No. 1464, VENONA files.

68. File 70545, Vol. 1, pp. 387–90.
69. Ibid., pp. 410–14.
70. Ibid., p. 402.
71. Ibid., p. 403.
72. Ibid., pp. 393–96.
73. Ibid., pp. 397–401.
74. Ibid., p. 212.
75. Ibid., pp. 405–406.
76. Ibid., pp. 407–408.
77. Ibid., p. 415.
78. Ibid., p. 416.
79. Ibid., pp. 439–40.
80. Ibid., pp. 420–22.
81. Ibid., pp. 423–24.
82. Ibid., pp. 446–48.
83. Ibid., pp. 472–74.
84. Ibid., pp. 551–52.

Chapter 6. Double Agent/Hollywood Hustler: The Case of Boris Morros

1. File 30595, Vol. 1, pp. 13, 17.
2. Ibid., p. 13.
3. Ibid., pp. 14–15.
4. Ibid., p. 18.
5. Ibid., p. 16.
6. Ibid.
7. Ibid., p. 21.
8. Ibid., p. 26.
9. Ibid., p. 27.
10. Ibid., pp. 36–38.
11. Ibid.
12. Ibid., p. 35.
13. Ibid., p. 39.
14. Ibid., pp. 44–47.
15. Ibid.
16. Ibid., p. 48.
17. Ibid., pp. 40, 42–43.
18. Ibid., pp. 57, 114.
19. Ibid., p. 58.
20. Ibid., p. 52.
21. Ibid., pp. 62, 64, 76–77.
22. Ibid., pp. 65–67.

23. Ibid., pp. 66, 71, 74, 77, 89.
24. Ibid., pp. 79, 113, 114, 126.
25. Ibid., p. 82.
26. Ibid.
27. Ibid.
28. Ibid.
29. Ibid., pp. 93–98.
30. Ibid., p. 101.
31. Ibid., pp. 101–106.
32. Ibid.
33. Ibid., pp. 101–108.
34. Ibid., pp. 109–10.
35. Ibid., p. 111.
36. Ibid., p. 112.
37. Ibid., pp. 119–23.
38. Ibid., p. 129.
39. Ibid., pp. 133–38.
40. Ibid., p. 131.
41. Ibid., pp. 146–48.
42. Ibid., p. 152.
43. Ibid., pp. 156–57.
44. Ibid., pp. 158–59.
45. Ibid., p. 163.
46. Ibid., pp. 166–74.
47. Ibid., p. 176.
48. Ibid., pp. 180–86.
49. Ibid., pp. 195–99.
50. Ibid., pp. 199–200.
51. Ibid., pp. 206–11.
52. Ibid.
53. Ibid., p. 213.
54. File 30595, Vol. 3, p. 42.
55. Ibid., p. 43.
56. Ibid., pp. 20–29.
57. File 30595, Vol. 1, pp. 238–40.
58. File 30595, Vol. 3, p. 37.
59. Ibid., p. 60.
60. Ibid., pp. 63–65.
61. Ibid., pp. 86–92.
62. Ibid., pp. 95–96.
63. Ibid., pp. 101–106.
64. Ibid., pp. 98–99.
65. Ibid., p. 155.
66. Ibid., pp. 196–98.
67. Ibid., p. 194.

68. Ibid., p. 199.
69. Ibid., pp. 178, 180, 185, 211.
70. Ibid., p. 219.
71. Ibid., pp. 230, 260.
72. Ibid., pp. 248–49.
73. Ibid., p. 252.
74. Ibid., p. 249.
75. Ibid., pp. 263–64, 266.
76. Ibid., p. 342.
77. File 30595, Vol. 4, pp. 8, 11.
78. Ibid., p. 17.
79. Ibid., pp. 29–31.
80. Ibid., pp. 34–37.
81. Ibid., pp. 39–40.
82. Ibid., p. 48.
83. Ibid., pp. 44–45.
84. Ibid., p. 84.
85. Ibid., pp. 88–89, 90–93.
86. Ibid., pp. 110–11, 119.
87. Ibid., pp. 124–29.
88. Ibid., pp. 130–31.
89. Ibid., pp. 142–49.
90. Ibid., pp. 151, 153–54, 157.
91. Ibid., p. 210.
92. Ibid., p. 230.
93. Ibid., p. 232.
94. Ibid., p. 235.
95. Ibid., p. 254.
96. Ibid., pp. 269–71.
97. Ibid., pp. 266–67.
98. Ibid., pp. 289–91.
99. Ibid., p. 293.
100. Ibid., pp. 320–25.
101. Ibid., pp. 298–99.
102. File 30595, Vol. 5, pp. 43–45.
103. Ibid., pp. 78–81.

Chapter 7. "Crook": A Soviet Agent in Congress

1. *New York Times*, April 23, 1954.
2. Walter Goodman, *The Committee* (New York: Farrar, Straus & Giroux, 1968), pp. 10–12.
3. Ibid., p. 3.

4. File 15428, Vol. 1, pp. 54, 56.
5. Ibid., pp. 58–60.
6. Ibid., pp. 61–63.
7. File 35112, Vol. 5, pp. 269–70.
8. File 15428, Vol. 1, pp. 1–2.
9. Ibid.
10. Ibid., p. 9.
11. Ibid., p. 5.
12. Ibid., pp. 6, 10–11.
13. Ibid., p. 11.
14. Ibid., pp. 12–14.
15. Ibid., pp. 17–18.
16. File 35112, Vol. 5, pp. 136–37, 108, 238.
17. File 15428, Vol. 1, pp. 18–22.
18. Ibid.
19. File 32428, Vol. 1, pp. 183–85.
20. File 15428, Vol. 1, p. 23.
21. Ibid., pp. 27–29, 31–33, 37–38.
22. Ibid., p. 83.
23. Ibid., pp. 90–91.
24. Ibid., p. 93.
25. File 35112, Vol. 5a, pp. 434–35; File 35112, Vol. 1, p. 84.
26. File 15428, Vol. 1, p. 147.
27. Ibid., pp. 104–105.
28. Ibid., pp. 123–24.
29. File 35112, Vol. 5, pp. 329–30.
30. Ibid., p. 369.
31. File 15428, Vol. 1, p. 143.
32. Ibid., pp. 143–44.
33. Ibid., p. 145.
34. File 35112, Vol. 5, pp. 269–70.
35. Ibid., pp. 33–36.
36. *New York Times,* April 23, 1954.
37. Oksana Kasenkina, *Leap to Freedom* (Philadelphia: J. B. Lippincott Company, 1949), p. 293.

Chapter 8. Harvest Time, I: The
Silvermaster Network in Wartime Washington

1. File 9995, Vol. 1, pp. 43, 48; File 43173, Vol. 10, p. 112.
2. File 35112, Vol. 1, p. 69.
3. File 43173, Vol. 1, pp. 32–33.
4. Ibid., pp. 41–42.

5. File 35112, Vol. 5, p. 105.

6. File 35112, Vol. 1, p. 8.

7. File 32428, Vol. 1, pp. 3–6, 234–35, 266, 354.

8. File 35112, Vol. 1, p. 38.

9. Ibid., pp. 415–17.

10. File 35112, Vol. 7, pp. 107–108.

11. File 35112, Vol. 1, pp. 413, 419.

12. File 35112, Vol. 7, pp. 109–10.

13. File 35112, Vol. 8, p. 68.

14. File 35112, Vol. 6, pp. 100–102.

15. File 55298, Vol. 1, pp. 253–54.

16. File 35112, Vol. 6, p. 314.

17. File 35112, Vol. 7, pp. 95–96.

18. Ibid., pp. 180, 207.

19. File 35112, Vol. 4a, pp. 408–409, 419.

20. Ibid., pp. 411–12.

21. Ibid., p. 416.

22. Ibid., p. 421.

23. Ibid., p. 625.

24. File 35112, Vol. 6, p. 176.

25. Ibid., p. 177.

26. File 43173, Vol. 1, p. 8.

27. Ibid. Lauchlin Currie's ("Page's") role in conveying information from the White House to Soviet intelligence was also vital during these years. See, for example, New York station to Moscow, August 10, 1943, No. 1317, VENONA files.

28. File 55298, Vol. 1, pp. 29–33.

29. Ibid., pp. 66–67.

30. Ibid., p. 50.

31. Ibid., pp. 72, 74–78, 369 (in the envelope).

32. Ibid., pp. 106–107.

33. File 35112, Vol. 7, p. 471a.

34. File 55298, Vol. 1, pp. 116–17.

35. File 43173, Vol. 3, p. 23.

36. File 55298, Vol. 1, pp. 133–35.

37. File 35112, Vol. 7, p. 259.

38. File 35112, Vol. 1, pp. 400–401.

39. Ibid., p. 421.

40. File 35112, Vol. 2, p. 18a.

41. Ibid., pp. 31–32. Harry Dexter White's ability to tap discussions among Roosevelt cabinet members had a special interest for Soviet intelligence: "According to [White's] data, [Secretary of State Cordell Hull] in a conversation with [Vice President Henry Wallace] touched upon the question of giving us a 5 billion dollar loan. The idea appealed to [Wallace]. . . ." New York station to Moscow, April 29, 1944, No. 500, VENONA files.

42. File 35112, Vol. 9, pp. 108, 110.

43. File 55298, Vol. 1, p. 139.

44. Ibid., pp. 168–73, 181, 201. "In [Akhmerov's] opinion, [Silvermaster] should be assisted in acquiring the firm since the presence of such a [words unrecovered] can continue our work with certain changes in the group's structure. [Akhmerov] requests us to advise as quickly as possible whether we approve [Silvermaster's] proposal and whether we are ready to give him financial support." New York station to Moscow, October 18, 1944, Nos. 1481–82, VENONA files.

45. File 35112, Vol. 2, pp. 38, 54. The new code names are also outlined in two summary cables: New York station to Moscow, September 2, 1944, No. 1251, and October 5, 1944, No. 1403, VENONA files.

46. File 35112, Vol. 9, pp. 164–65.

47. Ibid., p. 182.

48. File 55298, Vol. 1, p. 158.

49. File 35112, Vol. 9, pp. 28–31.

50. Ibid.

51. Ibid., p. 81.

52. Ibid., p. 31. Despite the group's internal strife, Silvermaster continued in 1944 and 1945 to provide extensive and extraordinary classified documents and information to Soviet intelligence. Among other deliveries, see the following: May 9, 1944, No. 655; June 7, 1944, No. 827; June 28, 1944, No. 918; July 1, 1944, No. 927; July 18, 1944, No. 1003; October 17, 1944, No. 1469; October 18, 1944, No. 1483; November 21, 1944, No. 1635; December 1, 1944, No. 1691; December 13, 1944, Nos. 1751–53; December 19, 1944, Nos. 1787, 1789; December 20, 1944, No. 1798; December 26, 1944, No. 1821; January 15, 1945, No. 55; January 18, 1945, No. 83; and February 10, 1945, No. 205. Silvermaster's housemate, Ludwig Ullman, was productive in his own right with secret military data: December 8, 1944, Nos. 1721–28; December 27, 1944, No. 1822; December 29, 1944, No. 1836; February 10, 1945, Nos. 210–12; and March 28, 1945, No. 289; VENONA files.

53. File 35112, Vol. 2, p. 135. A shift in Soviet focus by 1944 to concerns over postwar settlement issues can be seen in various materials delivered by Silvermaster and other American agents of Soviet intelligence at this time. One November 1944 dispatch regarding Silvermaster's information, for example, contains this nugget: "[The OSS] has passed to the army a list of 20,000 'reliable Germans' with whom [OSS] considers it safe to have dealings. It is impossible to obtain the list here at the moment. Perhaps it could be procured in [London]. An analogous list of Austrians has been compiled by the [British]." New York station to Moscow, November 21, 1944, No. 1635, VENONA files.

54. File 35112, Vol. 9, p. 33.

55. Ibid., p. 32.

56. Ibid., pp. 142–43.

57. Ibid., p. 109.

58. Ibid., pp. 112–14.

59. File 55298, Vol. 1, pp. 280–88.

60. Ibid., pp. 295–301.

61. File 35112, Vol. 9, p. 145.

62. File 55298, Vol. 1, pp. 312–15.

63. Ibid., pp. 318–20.

64. Ibid., pp. 366–67.

65. A. Vassiliev and A. Koreshkov, *Station Chief Gold*, pp. 68, 86–87.

Chapter 9. Atomic Espionage: From Fuchs to the Rosenbergs

1. File 82702, Vol. 1, p. 25. Two magnificent works of history provide both general readers and specialists with a comprehensive portrayal—among other subjects—of the role played by Soviet espionage in aiding development of that country's atomic bomb: Richard Rhodes, *Dark Son: The Making of the Hydrogen Bomb* (New York: Simon & Schuster, 1995), passim., and David Holloway, *Stalin and the Bomb* (New Haven, Conn.: Yale University Press, 1994), especially pp. 82–95, 102–108, 222–23, 296–97, and 310–12.

2. Ibid., p. 26.

3. Ibid., p. 27.

4. File 40159, Vol. 3, p. 43.

5. File 40129, Vol. 3a, p. 202.

6. Alexander Feklissov, *Behind the Ocean and on the Island* (Moscow: DEM, 1994), p. 56.

7. File 32428, Vol. 1, p. 53.

8. File 40594, Vol. 2, p. 122.

9. Ibid., pp. 134, 201. The VENONA project identified "Talent" as one William Maries Malisoff. By that time, the NKGB's scientific operatives in the United States were focused on the priority of obtaining atomic research information, and "Talent" complained about a lack of support for the data he offered to provide. May 4, 1944, Nos. 620, 622, VENONA files.

10. File 40159, Vol. 3, pp. 169–70.

11. File 40594, Vol. 6, p. 166.

12. File 40129, Vol. 3a, p. 210.

13. File 40129, Vol. 4, pp. 256–58.

14. File 40594, Vol. 4, p. 251.

15. File 40594, Vol. 6, pp. 43–44. Semyonov had another source in New York, code-named "Kvant" ("Quantum") who delivered information on "Enormoz" but expected from Soviet intelligence "recompense for his labor—in form of a financial reward," for which Semyonov "was given 300 dollars" for "Quantum." New York station to Moscow, June 21, 1943, No. 961, VENONA files. See also New York station to Moscow, June 22–23, 1943, Nos. 972, 979, 983, VENONA files.

16. File 40129, Vol. 3a, p. 208.
17. File 40594, Vol. 6, p. 118.
18. File 40594, Vol. 7, p. 14.
19. File 86194, Vol. 1, p. 272.
20. Ibid., pp. 16–17.
21. Ibid., p. 25.
22. Ibid., p. 135.
23. Ibid., p. 140.
24. Ibid., p. 132.
25. Ibid., pp. 263, 350.
26. Ibid., p. 290.
27. Ibid., p. 344.
28. Ibid., p. 348.
29. File 40159, Vol. 3, p. 285.
30. Ibid., p. 283.
31. File 40594, Vol. 6, pp. 134, 310.
32. File 40159, Vol. 3, p. 195; File 40594, Vol. 6, p. 143; File 35112, Vol. 1, p. 407.

33. File 35112, Vol. 7, p. 98. On Rosenberg's recruitment of Alfred Sarant, see New York station to Moscow, May 5, 1944, No. 628, VENONA files. On Rosenberg's recruitment of another radical friend, Max Elitcher, see New York station to Moscow, July 26, 1944, No. 1053, VENONA files. On bonuses paid to Rosenberg's agent-group for handing over valuable material, see New York station to Moscow, September 14, 1944, No. 1314, and March 6, 1945, No. 200, VENONA files. By late 1944, Rosenberg's group was in full swing: "[He] has on hand eight people plus the filming of materials," New York station reported to Moscow, December 5, 1944, No. 1715, VENONA files. See also New York station to Moscow, December 13, 1944, Nos. 1749, 1750, VENONA files.

34. File 35112, Vol. 1, p. 407.
35. File 40129, Vol. 3a, pp. 205–206.
36. File 35112, Vol. 1, pp. 407–408.
37. File 40159, Vol. 3, p. 160.
38. File 82702, Vol. 1, pp. 32, 69.
39. Ibid., p. 70.
40. Ibid.
41. Ibid., p. 32.
42. Ibid., p. 34.
43. Ibid., p. 72.
44. Ibid., pp. 77–79.
45. File 40159, Vol. 3, pp. 222–23; File 82702, Vol. 1, p. 37.
46. File 40159, Vol. 3, pp. 275–79.
47. Ibid., pp. 313–14; File 82702, Vol. 1, p. 93.
48. File 40159, Vol. 3, p. 223.

49. File 82702, Vol. 1, p. 96.
50. Ibid., pp. 192–93.
51. Ibid., p. 146.
52. Ibid., p. 158.
53. Ibid., p. 54.
54. Ibid., p. 143.
55. File 25748, Vol. 2, pp. 116, 148.
56. File 82702, Vol. 1, pp. 422–23, 496–98.
57. File 84490, Vol. 1, p. 17.
58. Ibid., p. 22.
59. Ibid., p. 26.
60. Ibid., pp. 26–27.
61. File 82702, Vol. 1, p. 121.
62. File 40159, Vol. 3, pp. 355–56.
63. File 40129, Vol. 3a, p. 212.
64. File 84490, Vol. 1, pp. 31–32.
65. File 82702, Vol. 1, p. 150.
66. Ibid., p. 154.
67. File 84490, Vol. 1, p. 48.
68. Ibid., p. 49; File 82702, Vol. 1, p. 171.
69. File 40594, Vol. 6, p. 285. "For the time being [Kvasnikov] and [Semyonov] are not being shadowed anymore but shadowing of [Fomin] has started. One is forced to the conclusion that the [FBI] is carrying out 'trial' surveillance." New York station to Moscow, April 29, 1944, No. 586, VENONA files.
70. File 40129, Vol. 3a, pp. 219–20.
71. Feklissov, *Behind the Ocean and on the Island*, pp. 57–58.
72. File 40159, Vol. 3, p. 416. See also the account of a mid-June meeting between Fuchs and Gold. New York station to Moscow, June 15, 1944, No. 850, VENONA files.
73. File 40129, Vol. 3a, p. 154. On Gold's September visit to Fuchs's sister, see New York station to Moscow, September 22, 1944, No. 1345, VENONA files.
74. File 40159, Vol. 3, p. 404. On "Fogel," see also New York station to Moscow, February 11, 1944, No. 212, and June 16, 1944, No. 854, VENONA files.
75. File 40594, Vol. 7, pp. 24–25.
76. File 40594, Vol. 6, p. 240.
77. File 40129, Vol. 3a, p. 208.
78. Ibid., pp. 218–19.
79. File 40129, Vol. 4, p. 354.
80. Ibid., p. 353.
81. Feklissov, *Behind the Ocean and on the Island*, pp. 21–22.
82. File 40129, Vol. 4, pp. 353–54, 377–78.
83. File 82702, Vol. 1, p. 210.

84. Ibid., p. 284.

85. Ibid., p. 310.

86. Ibid., p. 190.

87. Ibid., pp. 215–17.

88. Ibid., p. 380.

89. Ibid., p. 358.

90. Ibid., pp. 224–25.

91. File 40129, Vol. 3a, p. 174.

92. Ibid., p. 177.

93. Ibid., p. 190.

94. Ibid., p. 237.

95. Ibid., pp. 287–89.

96. Ibid.

97. Ibid., pp. 290–91. See also New York station to Moscow, December 2, 1944, No. 1699, and January 23, 1945, No. 94, VENONA files.

98. File 40129, Vol. 3a, p. 237.

99. Ibid., p. 291.

100. Ibid., p. 168.

101. Ibid., p. 169.

102. File 40129, Vol. 4, p. 377.

103. File 86192, Vol. 1, p. 21.

104. File 86191, Vol. 1, p. 16.

105. Ibid., p. 15.

106. File 86192, Vol. 1, p. 20.

107. Ibid., p. 26.

108. Ibid., p. 23.

109. File 40594, Vol. 7, p. 48.

110. Ibid., p. 49.

111. File 84490, Vol. 1, p. 69. Gold had traveled to Cambridge, Massachusetts, to visit Fuchs's sister earlier that fall, but apparently no contact had been made. New York station to Moscow, October 4, 1944, No. 1397, VENONA files.

112. File 84490, Vol. 1, p. 71.

113. Ibid., p. 74.

114. File 40594, Vol. 7, pp. 81–82.

115. File 84490, Vol. 1, pp. 79–82.

116. File 40594, Vol. 7, p. 75.

117. File 84490, Vol. 1, p. 73; File 40594, Vol. 7, p. 79. The sudden availability of information on "Enormoz" not only from Fuchs but also from Hall and Greenglass was a source of keen interest in Moscow. See, for example, the evaluation by Soviet atomic scientists of Fuchs's and Hall's data, discussed in a single cable: March 31, 1945, No. 298, VENONA files.

118. File 40594, Vol. 7, p. 13.

119. Ibid., pp. 8–10.

120. File 40159, Vol. 3, pp. 472–74.

121. Ibid., p. 473.

122. File 40129, Vol. 3a, pp. 212–13.

123. File 40159, Vol. 5, pp. 107, 208; File 40129, Vol. 3a, p. 213.

124. File 40159, Vol. 3, p. 474.

125. File 40594, Vol. 7, p. 83.

126. File 84490, Vol. 1, p. 73.

127. Ibid., p. 74. Soviet intelligence considered information received from both Fuchs and Hall during this period, once evaluated, of "substantial interest." Moscow to New York station, March 31, 1945, No. 298, VENONA files.

128. File 82702, Vol. 1, p. 298. See also New York station to Moscow, January 23, 1945, No. 94, VENONA files.

129. File 82702, Vol. 1, p. 309.

130. File 40594, Vol. 7, p. 130.

131. File 84490, Vol. 1, p. 91. See also New York station to Moscow, May 26, 1945, No. 799, VENONA files.

132. File 40594, Vol. 7, p. 214.

133. Ibid., p. 342.

134. Ibid., p. 343.

135. File 84490, Vol. 1, pp. 76, 84, 90; File 40129, Vol. 3a, p. 380. Soviet atomic scientists were still digesting the important information Fuchs had given Gold at their February 1945 meeting when Moscow sent this cable to its New York station in mid-April: "[Fuchs's] information . . . on the atomic bomb . . . is of great value. Apart from the data on the atomic mass of the nuclear explosive and on the details of the explosive method of actuating [the bomb] . . . it contains information received for the first time from you about the electro-magnetic method of separation of ENORMOZ." April 10, 1945, No. 349, VENONA files.

136. File 82702, Vol. 1, pp. 325–29.

137. Ibid., pp. 333, 339.

138. File 84490, Vol. 1, p. 91.

139. Ibid., p. 92.

140. File 40594, Vol. 7, p. 131.

141. File 82702, Vol. 1, p. 363.

142. File 84490, Vol. 1, p. 91.

143. Andrei Gromyko, *Memorable*, Vol. 1 (Moscow: Politizdat, 1988), p. 221.

144. File 82702, Vol. 1, p. 362.

145. Ibid., p. 350.

146. Ibid., p. 367.

147. File 40159, Vol. 3, pp. 548–50.

148. Ibid., p. 551.

149. File 82702, Vol. 1, pp. 375–76.

150. Ibid., pp. 377–80.

151. File 40594, Vol. 7, pp. 250–51.

152. Ibid., p. 251.

153. File 40129, Vol. 3a, p. 468.

154. File 84490, Vol. 1, pp. 97, 99.

155. Ibid., p. 106.

156. Ibid., pp. 104–105.

157. File 40594, Vol. 7, pp. 251–52.

158. File 84490, Vol. 1, p. 98.

159. File 82702, Vol. 1, pp. 427–28.

160. Ibid., p. 320.

161. File 40594, Vol. 7, p. 134.

162. Ibid., pp. 297–99.

163. Ibid., pp. 352–53.

164. Ibid., p. 355.

165. File 86194, Vol. 2, pp. 79–80.

166. Ibid., pp. 89–90.

167. Ibid., pp. 113–14. Gold's dream of setting up a private laboratory had emerged even during the war years, when he discussed it with Soviet operatives. New York station to Moscow, December 20, 1944, No. 1797, VENONA files.

168. File 86194, Vol. 2, pp. 113–14.

169. File 40159, Vol. 5, p. 238.

170. Ibid., p. 37.

171. Ibid., p. 229.

172. Ibid., p. 232.

173. File 40129, Vol. 4, p. 377.

174. File 40159, Vol. 5, p. 282.

175. File 86192, Vol. 1, p. 46.

176. Ibid., p. 55.

177. Ibid., p. 58.

178. Ibid., pp. 59–61.

179. File 40159, Vol. 5, pp. 107, 118.

180. Ibid., pp. 208–209.

181. Ibid., pp. 148, 173.

182. Ibid., p. 300.

Chapter 10. Harvest Time, II:
The Perlo Group

1. File 35112, Vol. 1, p. 69.

2. File 45100, Vol. 1, p. 14.

3. Ibid., p. 17.

4. Ibid., pp. 18–19.

5. Ibid., p. 28.

6. Ibid.

7. Ibid., p. 21.

8. Ibid., p. 160.

9. Ibid., pp. 28–29.

10. Ibid., p. 32.

11. Ibid., pp. 44–45.

12. Ibid., p. 80.

13. File 43173, Vol. 1, pp. 55–56.

14. Ibid., p. 58.

15. Ibid., p. 73.

16. Ibid., pp. 8–8a.

17. File 35112, Vol. 1, p. 226.

18. File 45100, Vol. 1, pp. 100–102.

19. Ibid. The problem of casual security and open knowledge of one another's agent-links affected the Silvermaster group and other American sources as well. Moscow to New York station, February 25, 1945, Nos. 179–80, and March 29, 1945, No. 292, VENONA files.

20. File 45100, Vol. 1, pp. 100–102. Despite the security lapses, Perlo remained a continuing and important source of information for Soviet intelligence throughout this period. Washington station to Moscow on the following dates, for example: March 30, 1945, Nos. 1823–25; June 24, 1945, No. 3707; and June 29, 1945, Nos. 3708 and 3713–15; VENONA files.

21. File 45100, Vol. 1, p. 107.

22. File 43173, Vol. 1, p. 95.

23. File 35112, Vol. 8, p. 154.

24. File 43173, Vol. 1, p. 128.

25. File 45100, Vol. 1, p. 119. Despite Moscow's grousing, any objective reader of Maclean's cables from Washington, whether Soviet or Western, would acknowledge their policy importance and broad-ranging scope. See, for example, the following transmissions: New York station to Moscow, September 5, 1944, No. 1263; September 9, 1944, Nos. 1271–74; Washington station to Moscow, March 29, 1945, Nos. 1788, 1791, 1793; March 30, 1945, Nos. 1808–1809, 1815; and March 31, 1945, No. 1826; VENONA files.

26. File 45100, Vol. 1, pp. 113–14.

27. Ibid., pp. 207–209.

28. File 55302, Vol. 1, pp. 35–43.

29. Ibid., pp. 29–30.

30. Ibid., pp. 50–51.

31. Ibid., p. 52.

32. Ibid., pp. 55–60.

33. Ibid., p. 52.

34. Ibid., p. 68.

35. Ibid., pp. 70–71.

36. Ibid., pp. 72–73.

37. Ibid., pp. 74–77. See, for example, Kramer's innocuous report to Soviet intelligence on a visit by Senator Kilgore to London. Washington station to Moscow, June 22, 1945, No. 3612, VENONA files. Also see June 23, 1945, No. 3640, and June 29, 1945, Nos. 3709–10, VENONA files.

38. File 55302, Vol. 1, p. 103.

39. Ibid., p. 116.

40. File 55205, Vol. 1, p. 11.

41. Ibid., p. 12.

42. Ibid., p. 20.

43. Ibid., pp. 28–29.

44. File 59264, Vol. 1, p. 9.

45. Ibid., pp. 15a–16.

46. Ibid., p. 30.

47. Ibid., pp. 31, 45.

48. Ibid., p. 44.

49. Ibid., p. 53.

50. Ibid., pp. 57–58.

51. Ibid., p. 49.

52. File 59264, Vol. 2, p. 22.

53. File 59264, Vol. 1, p. 53.

54. Ibid., p. 81.

55. File 40623, Vol. 1, p. 22.

Chapter 11. OSS and NKGB:
Penetration Agents

1. File 35112, Vol. 4, p. 567.

2. File 35112, Vol. 5, p. 192.

3. Ibid.

4. Ibid., p. 193.

5. File 43173, Vol. 1, p. 9.

6. File 28612, Vol. 1, p. 36.

7. Ibid., pp. 1–9.

8. Ibid., p. 10.

9. Ibid., pp. 20–21.

10. Ibid., p. 22.

11. Ibid., p. 209.

12. Ibid., p. 210.

13. Ibid., p. 43.

14. Ibid., pp. 117–19.

15. Ibid., p. 122.

16. Ibid., p. 232.

17. Ibid., pp. 44–45.

18. Ibid., pp. 125, 160–65, 183.

19. Ibid., p. 184.

20. Ibid., p. 136.

21. Ibid., pp. 186–87.

22. Ibid., pp. 273–74.

23. Ibid., pp. 36, 99, 109.

24. Ibid., pp. 123–24.

25. Ibid.

26. Ibid., p. 127.

27. Ibid., pp. 214–15.

28. Ibid., p. 235.

29. Ibid., pp. 321–22, 358–59, 386; File 28612, Vol. 2, pp. 28, 49–50.

30. File 28612, Vol. 2, pp. 3, 15, 17.

31. File 28612, Vol. 1, pp. 401, 429–31.

32. Ibid., pp. 299–300.

33. File 28612, Vol. 2, p. 89.

34. Ibid., p. 113.

35. Ibid., p. 63.

36. File 35112, Vol. 1, pp. 235–36, 383–84. New York station to Moscow, April 29, 1943, No. 592, VENONA files.

37. File 43173, Vol. 1, p. 98.

38. File 28734, Vol. 1, pp. 7, 28.

39. Ibid., p. 8.

40. Ibid., p. 14.

41. Ibid., p. 15.

42. Ibid., p. 20.

43. Ibid., p. 23.

44. File 35112, Vol. 1, p. 133.

45. File 28734, Vol. 1, p. 28.

46. File 35112, Vol. 4a, pp. 549–50.

47. File 35112, Vol. 7, p. 308.

48. File 35112, Vol. 1, p. 404. On Helen Tenney, see also New York station to Moscow, May 27, 1944, No. 756, and July 4, 1944, No. 940, VENONA files. On Wheeler and Tenney, see New York station to Moscow, May 30, 1944, Nos. 769, 771, VENONA files. The latter memo also discusses the agent involvement of, among others, Edward Fitzgerald, Charles Kramer, and Harold Glasser.

49. File 43173, Vol. 3, p. 65.

50. File 35112, Vol. 7, p. 419.

51. File 43173, Vol. 3, p. 65.

52. File 35112, Vol. 1, pp. 413–14.

53. File 45049, Vol. 1, p. 22.

54. File 45049, Vol. 2, pp. 33–37.

55. Ibid., p. 32.

56. Ibid., p. 40.

57. Ibid., p. 8.

58. File 45049, Vol. 1, p. 16.

59. Ibid., pp. 9, 12.

60. Ibid., p. 18.

61. File 45049, Vol. 2, p. 11.

62. Ibid., p. 10.

63. Ibid., pp. 17–19, 21, 25–28.

64. Ibid., p. 20.

65. File 43173, Vol. 3, p. 65; File 35112, Vol. 1, p. 406. See also New York station to Moscow, September 23, 1944, No. 1352, VENONA files.

66. File 43173, Vol. 3, p. 53.

67. File 35112, Vol. 1, p. 405; File 35112, Vol. 6, p. 313.

68. File 35112, Vol. 8, p. 97. See also New York station to Moscow, June 8, 1943, No. 880, and June 9, 1943, No. 887, VENONA files.

69. File 35112, Vol. 8, p. 98. New York station to Moscow, June 9, 1944, No. 830, VENONA files.

70. File 40457, Vol. 1, pp. 7–8, 41v.

71. Ibid., pp. 7–8.

72. Ibid., p. 20.

73. Ibid., p. 23.

74. Ibid., pp. 24–25. A belated September 23, 1944, cable from New York advised Moscow about Lee's impending trip "to INDIA or CHINA for 5–6 months," though the trip had actually started weeks earlier. New York station to Moscow, September 23, 1944, No. 2353, VENONA files.

75. File 40457, Vol. 1, pp. 8, 26.

76. Ibid., p. 9.

77. Ibid., pp. 43–44.

78. Ibid. (in the envelope at the end of the file).

79. Ibid., p. 41e.

80. Ibid., p. 35.

81. Ibid., p. 37.

82. Ibid., p. 38. Earlier that year, Bentley told Akhmerov of Earl Browder's concern that Mary Price's "nerves had been badly shaken" and recommended that her work as a courier be halted. New York station to Moscow, July 28, 1944, No. 1065, VENONA files.

83. File 40457, Vol. 1, pp. 41a–41g. "[Donovan] has appointed [Lee] chief of the Japanese section. . . ." New York station to Moscow, October 10, 1944, No. 1437, VENONA files.

84. File 40457, Vol. 1, p. 45.

85. File 40457, Vol. 2, pp. 9, 49–50.

86. Ibid., pp. 54–55.

87. Ibid., p. 56.

88. Ibid., p. 57.

89. File 40624, Vol. 1, pp. 31, 36.
90. Ibid., p. 37.
91. Ibid., p. 28.
92. Ibid., p. 50.
93. File 61512, Vol. 1, pp. 13, 157 (in the envelope).
94. Ibid., pp. 16–18, 82.
95. Ibid., p. 19.
96. Ibid., pp. 27–29.
97. Ibid., pp. 32–33.
98. Ibid., pp. 34–35.
99. Ibid., pp. 38, 40, 156.
100. Ibid., p. 45.
101. File 61512, Vol. 2, pp. 88–89.

Chapter 12. Harvest Time, III:
Hiss, Glasser, and Warning Signs

1. File 43072, Vol. 1, p. 38.
2. Ibid., pp. 11, 36, 39.
3. Ibid., p. 54.
4. Ibid., p. 37.
5. Ibid., p. 35.
6. Ibid., pp. 55–60.
7. Ibid., pp. 49–50.
8. Ibid., pp. 55–60. New York station to Moscow, July 21, 1943, No. 1195, VENONA files.
9. File 43072, Vol. 1, p. 66.
10. Ibid., p. 69.
11. Ibid., pp. 70–72.
12. Ibid., pp. 81–82.
13. File 43173, Vol. 1, pp. 88–89.
14. File 43072, Vol. 1, pp. 96–97. See also Washington station to Moscow, March 28, 1945, No. 1759; June 21, 1945, Nos. 3598, 3600; June 23, 1945, No. 3645; and June 28, 1945, No. 3688; VENONA files.
15. File 43072, Vol. 1, p. 86.
16. Ibid., pp. 134–54.
17. Ibid., p. 101.
18. Ibid., p. 128.
19. File 35112, Vol. 4, pp. 66–67.
20. File 43173, Vol. 12, p. 193.
21. File 35112, Vol. 4, p. 117.
22. File 35112, Vol. 6, pp. 280–81.
23. Ibid., p. 507.

24. File 35112, Vol. 1, pp. 310–11.

25. Alexander Feklissov, *Beyond the Ocean and on the Island* (Moscow: DEM, 1994), p. 15.

26. Ibid., p. 61.

27. Ibid., p. 53.

28. File 35112, Vol. 1, pp. 357–66.

29. File 35112, Vol. 2, pp. 38, 54.

30. Ibid., p. 56.

31. File 35112, Vol. 7, p. 469.

32. File 35112, Vol. 8, p. 112.

33. Ibid., p. 179.

34. File 35112, Vol. 9, p. 5. See also New York station to Moscow, October 1, 1944, No. 1385, VENONA files.

35. File 35112, Vol. 9, p. 12.

36. Ibid., p. 13.

37. Ibid., p. 62.

38. Ibid., p. 138.

39. Ibid., p. 131.

40. File 43173, Vol. 1, p. 144.

Chapter 13. Flight from Exposure, I:
The Washington Sources

1. File 43173, Vol. 1, p. 155.

2. Ibid., pp. 156–60.

3. Ibid., p. 162.

4. File 43173, Vol. 2, pp. 9–10.

5. Ibid.

6. Ibid., p. 11.

7. Ibid., pp. 41a, 67, 69.

8. Ibid., p. 299.

9. Ibid., p. 25.

10. Ibid., pp. 27–30.

11. Ibid., pp. 30–31.

12. Ibid., p. 78.

13. Ibid., p. 91.

14. Ibid., p. 84.

15. Ibid., pp. 128–30.

16. Ibid., p. 135.

17. Ibid.

18. Ibid., p. 330.

19. Diplomatic Dictionary. Moscow, "Science," 1986, Vol. 2, p. 338.

20. File 43173, Vol. 4, pp. 22–23; File 43173, Vol. 2v, p. 18.

21. File 43173, Vol. 10a, pp. 647–49.

22. File 43173, Vol. 4, p. 24.

23. Ibid., p. 27.

24. Ibid., p. 271.

25. Ibid., pp. 198, 270.

26. Ibid., p. 350.

27. File 43173, Vol. 2v, pp. 25–27.

28. Ibid.

29. File 43173, Vol. 4, p. 230.

30. File 43173, Vol. 11, p. 87.

31. File 43173, Vol. 7, p. 18.

32. File 43173, Vol. 2v, p. 27.

33. Ibid., pp. 18, 29.

34. File 43173, Vol. 7, p. 114.

35. Ibid., p. 85.

36. File 43173, Vol. 11, p. 11.

37. Ibid., p. 51.

38. Ibid., p. 52.

39. File 43173, Vol. 12, p. 101.

40. Ibid., p. 51.

41. File 43173, Vol. 2v, p. 272.

42. File 43173, Vol. 4, pp. 421–22.

43. File 43173, Vol. 2v, pp. 41–42.

44. File 43173, Vol. 4, p. 479.

45. Ibid., p. 203.

46. File 43173, Vol. 5, p. 276.

47. File 43173, Vol. 4, pp. 477–78.

48. Ibid., pp. 479–80.

49. File 43173, Vol. 2v, pp. 33, 43.

50. Ibid., pp. 46–47.

51. Ibid., p. 47.

52. Ibid., pp. 309–10.

53. Ibid., pp. 71–87.

54. Ibid.

55. File 43173, Vol. 14, pp. 24–25.

56. File 43173, Vol. 12, pp. 201–203, 216.

57. File 43173, Vol. 2v, p. 239.

58. File 55951, Vol. 1, pp. 301–306.

59. File 40129, Vol. 4, pp. 378–79.

60. File 70548, Vol. 1, p. 86.

61. Ibid., pp. 3–6.

62. File 35112, Vol. 4, pp. 350, 357.

63. File 70548, Vol. 1, pp. 149–50. Earl Browder's role in—and value to—Soviet intelligence activities in the United States is also documented in Harvey Klehr, John Earl Haynes, and Fridrikh Igorevich Firsov, *The Secret World*

of American Communism (New Haven, Conn.: Yale University Press, 1995), especially pp. 231–48.

64. Ibid., pp. 31–33. For example: "We are transmitting information written down by [Browder] after a conversation with [Schuster]. . . ." New York station to Moscow, May 2, 1944, Nos. 598–99, VENONA files.

65. File 70548, Vol. 1, p. 41a. On disconnecting Soviet intelligence's links to agents closely associated with Earl Browder, see, for example, New York station to Moscow, January 4, 1945, No. 14, VENONA files.

66. Ibid., p. 42.

67. Ibid., p. 69.

68. Ibid., p. 65a.

69. Ibid., pp. 73–74.

70. Ibid., p. 75.

71. Ibid., p. 77.

72. Ibid., p. 81.

73. Ibid., p. 119.

74. Ibid., pp. 152–54.

75. Ibid., pp. 156, 163.

76. Ibid., pp. 170–72.

77. Ibid.

78. Ibid., pp. 175–76.

79. Ibid., p. 203.

80. Ibid., pp. 272, 300, 375.

81. Ibid., p. 323.

82. Ibid., p. 344.

83. Ibid., p. 379.

Chapter 14. Flight from Exposure, II: The Atom Spies

1. File 84490, Vol. 1, p. 126. The most thorough account of Klaus Fuchs's relationship with Soviet intelligence operatives in England after his return from the United States is provided by another book whose authors had access to the SVR archives in Moscow comparable to that of this book's authors. Nigel West and Oleg Tsarev, *The Crown Jewels: The British Secrets at the Heart of the KGB Archives* (London: HarperCollins, 1998), see especially Chapter X, "Atomic Secrets," pp. 227–55.

2. File 84490, Vol. 1, p. 128.

3. Ibid., pp. 140–42.

4. Ibid., pp. 131–32.

5. Ibid., p. 235.

6. Alexander Feklissov, *Beyond the Ocean and on the Island* (Moscow: DEM, 1994), pp. 112–15.

7. File 84490, Vol. 1, pp. 264–71.
8. Ibid.
9. Ibid., p. 384.
10. Ibid., p. 316.
11. Ibid., pp. 336–37.
12. Ibid., p. 343.
13. Ibid., p. 345.
14. Ibid., p. 356.
15. Ibid., p. 393.
16. Ibid.
17. Ibid., pp. 408–409.
18. Ibid., pp. 424–26.
19. Ibid., p. 468.
20. File 86194, Vol. 2, p. 169.
21. Ibid., pp. 157, 185.
22. Ibid., pp. 188, 190.
23. Ibid., pp. 219–22, 237.
24. Ibid., p. 232.
25. Ibid., pp. 227–28.
26. Ibid., p. 252.
27. Ibid., pp. 246, 252.
28. File 84490, Vol. 2, p. 60.
29. File 86194, Vol. 2, p. 257.
30. Ibid., p. 260.
31. File 84490, Vol. 3, pp. 27–30.
32. File 86194, Vol. 2, pp. 263–64.
33. Ibid., p. 266.
34. Ibid., p. 272.
35. Ibid., p. 392.
36. File 84490, Vol. 2, pp. 151–53, 171–72.
37. Ibid., p. 245.
38. Ibid., pp. 288–90.
39. File 84490, Vol. 3, pp. 46–50.
40. File 84490, Vol. 2, p. 280.
41. Ibid., p. 292.
42. File 84490, Vol. 3, p. 190 (in the envelope). Photostats of the original MI-5 document are contained in an envelope attached to p. 190 of this file.
43. Ibid.
44. File 86194, Vol. 2, p. 301.
45. File 84490, Vol. 3, pp. 129–30.
46. File 84490, Vol. 6, p. 20.
47. Ibid., p. 31.
48. Ibid., pp. 38–41.
49. Ibid., pp. 43–47.

50. Ibid.

51. File 86192, Vol. 1, p. 70.

52. Ibid., p. 71.

53. Ibid., pp. 77, 82, 85.

54. Ibid., p. 86.

55. Ibid., p. 92.

56. Ibid., p. 97.

57. Ibid., p. 103.

58. Ibid., p. 107.

59. Ibid., p. 104.

60. Ibid., p. 109.

61. Ibid., pp. 109–10.

62. Ibid., p. 113.

63. Ibid., p. 114.

64. Ibid., pp. 114–15.

65. Ibid., p. 116.

66. Ibid., p. 118.

67. Ibid., p. 121.

68. Ibid., pp. 130–31.

69. Ibid., p. 131.

70. Ibid., p. 132.

71. Ibid., p. 159.

72. The most thorough and accurate account of the Rosenberg case is found in Ronald Radosh and Joyce Milton, *The Rosenberg File*, rev. ed. (New Haven, Conn.: Yale University Press, 1997).

73. File 86192, Vol. 1, pp. 163–65.

74. File 84490, Vol. 5, pp. 329–30.

75. File 84490, Vol. 6, pp. 71–72.

76. Ibid., pp. 75–76.

77. Ibid., pp. 77, 79, 80.

78. Feklissov, *Beyond the Ocean and on the Island*, p. 177.

79. Joseph Albright and Marcia Kunstel, *BOMBSHELL: The Secret Story of America's Unknown Atomic Spy Conspiracy* (New York: Times Books, 1997), p. 289.

80. File 40129, Vol. 3a, pp. 287–88.

81. Markus Wolf, *Man Without a Face* (New York: Times Books, 1997), p. 146.

Epilogue: Aftermath and Legacy

1. Allen Weinstein, *Perjury: The Hiss-Chambers Case* (New York: Knopf, 1968), pp. 105–10, 171, 204, 281.

2. Commission on Protecting and Reducing Government Secrecy, *Report of the* . . . , Appendix A, p. 37.

3. Ronald Radosh and Joyce Milton, *The Rosenberg File* (New Haven, Conn.: Yale University Press, 1997), p. 472.

4. Allen Weinstein, "The Symbolism of Subversion: Notes on Some Cold War Icons," *Journal of American Studies*, vol. 6, no. 2 (August 1972): 170–74.

5. Ibid., pp. 165–70; Weinstein, *Perjury*, pp. 450–513.

6. Earl Latham, *The Communist Controversy in Washington* (New York: Atheneum, 1966), p. 10.

7. Quoted in Weinstein, *Perjury*, p. 473.

8. Herodotus, *The Persian Wars* (New York: Random House, Modern Library, 1942), p. 3.

BIBLIOGRAPHY

❖

Abt, John. *Advocate and Activist: Memoirs of an American Communist Lawyer*. Urbana: University of Illinois Press, 1993.

Albright, Joseph, and Marcia Kunstel. *BOMBSHELL: The Secret Story of America's Unknown Atomic Spy Conspiracy*. New York: Times Books, 1997.

Aldrich, Richard J. *British Intelligence, Strategy, and the Cold War, 1945–1951*. London: Routledge, 1992.

Andrew, Christopher. *For the President's Eyes Only*. New York: Harper-Collins, 1995.

Andrew, Christopher, and Oleg Gordievsky. *KGB: The Inside Story*. New York: HarperCollins, 1990.

Barron, John. *KGB: The Secret Work of Soviet Secret Agents*. Pleasantville, N.Y.: Reader's Digest Press, distributed by E. P. Dutton Co., New York, 1974; London: Hodder and Stoughton, 1974.

Barros, James. *No Sense of Evil: The Espionage Case of E. Herbert Norman*. New York: Ballantine Books, 1987.

Benson, Robert Louis, and Michael Warner, eds. *VENONA: Soviet Espionage and the American Response, 1939–1957*. Washington, D.C.: National Security Agency & Central Intelligence Agency, 1996.

Bentley, Elizabeth. *Out of Bondage: The Story of Elizabeth Bentley*. New York: Ballantine, 1988.

Berle, Beatrice B., and Travis B. Jacobs, eds. *Navigating the Rapids, 1918–1971: From the Papers of Adolf A. Berle*. New York: Harcourt Brace Jovanovich, 1973.

Blum, Richard H. *Surveillance and Espionage in a Free Society*. New York: Praeger, 1972.

Boveri, Margret. *Treason in the Twentieth Century*. New York: Putnam, 1963.

Budenz, Louis F. *This Is My Story*. Dublin: Browne and Nolan, 1948.

Burnham, James. *The Web of Subversion: Underground Networks in the U.S. Government*. New York: John Day and Co., 1954.

Carr, Robert Kenneth. *The House Committee on Un-American Activities, 1945–1950*. Ithaca: Cornell University Press, 1952.

Caute, David. *The Fellow-Travellers*. New York: Macmillan, 1973.

Cave Brown, Anthony. *Wild Bill Donovan: The Last Hero*. New York: Times Books, 1982.

Cecil, Robert. *A Divided Life: A Personal Portrait of the Spy Donald Maclean*. New York: Quill/William Morrow, 1989.

Chambers, Whittaker. *Witness*. New York: Random House, 1952.

Chase, Harold. *Security and Liberty: The Problem of Native Communists*. Garden City, N.Y.: Doubleday, 1955.

Cole, Wayne S. *Senator Gerald P. Nye and American Foreign Relations*. Minneapolis: University of Minnesota Press, 1962.

Commission on Protecting and Reducing Government Secrecy. *Report of* . . . Washington, D.C.: U.S. Government Printing Office, 1997.

Conquest, Robert. *The Great Terror: Stalin's Purge of the Thirties*. London: Macmillan, 1968.

Cooke, Alistair. *A Generation on Trial*. Baltimore: Penguin, 1952.

Costello, John. *Mask of Treachery*. New York: William Morrow, 1988.

Costello, John, and Oleg Tsarev. *Deadly Illusions*. New York: Crown, 1993.

Crossman, Richard, ed. *The God That Failed*. New York: Bantam, 1954.

Dallin, David Y. *Soviet Espionage*. New Haven, Conn.: Yale University Press, 1955.

Davis, Hope Hale. *Great Day Coming: A Memoir of the 1930s*. South Royalton, Vt.: Steerforth Press, 1994.

Delaney, Robert Finley. *The Literature of Communism in America*. Washington, D.C.: Catholic University Press, 1962.

De Toledano, Ralph. *Lament for a Generation*. New York: Farrar, Straus and Cudahy, 1960.

Deutscher, Isaac. *The Prophet Outcast*. London: Oxford University Press, 1963.

Diamond, Sander A. *The Nazi Movement in the United States, 1924–1941*. Ithaca: Cornell University Press, 1974.

Draper, Theodore. *American Communism and Soviet Russia*. New York: Viking, 1960.

———. *The Roots of American Communism*. New York: Viking, 1957.

Epstein, Edward Jay. *Dossier: The Secret History of Armand Hammer*. New York: Random House, 1996.

Feklissov, Alexander. *Beyond the Ocean and on the Island*. Moscow: DEM, 1994. (Russian edition.)

Gaddis, John Lewis. *We Now Know: Rethinking Cold War History*. New York: Oxford University Press, 1997.

Goodman, Walter. *The Committee*. New York: Farrar, Straus and Giroux, 1968.

Goulden, Joseph C. *The Best Years, 1945–1950*. New York: Atheneum, 1976.

Harper, Alan D. *The Politics of Loyalty: The White House and the Communist Issue, 1946–1952*. Westport, Conn.: Greenwood, 1969.

Hirsch, Richard. *The Soviet Spies*. New York: Duell, Sloan, and Pearce, 1974.

Hiss, Alger. *In the Court of Public Opinion*. New York: Knopf, 1957.

———. *Recollections of a Life*. New York: Seaver Books/Henry Holt, 1988.

Holloway, David. *Stalin and the Bomb: The Soviet Union and Atomic Energy, 1939–1956*. New Haven, Conn.: Yale University Press, 1994.

Howe, Irving, and Lewis Coser. *The American Communist Party: A Critical History*. New York: Praeger, 1957.

Hutton, J. Bernard. *Women in Espionage*. New York: Macmillan, 1971.

Isserman, Maurice. *Which Side Were You On?: The American Communist Party During the Second World War*. Middletown, Conn.: Wesleyan University Press, 1982.

Jaffe, Philip J. *The Rise and Fall of American Communism*. New York: Horizon, 1975.

Kahn, David. *The Codebreakers*. New York: Macmillan, 1967.

Kempton, Murray. *Part of Our Time: Some Monuments and Ruins of the Thirties*. New York: Dell, 1967.

Kessler, Ronald. *Spy Versus Spy: Stalking Soviet Spies in America*. New York: Scribner, 1988.

Klehr, Harvey. *The Heyday of American Communism: The Depression Decade*. New York: Basic Books, 1984.

Klehr, Harvey, and John Earl Haynes, with Fridrikh Igorevich Firsov. *The Secret World of American Communism*. New Haven, Conn.: Yale University Press, 1995.

Klehr, Harvey, John Earl Haynes, and Kyrill M. Anderson. *The Soviet World of American Communism*. New Haven, Conn.: Yale University Press, 1998.

Klehr, Harvey, and Ronald Radosh. *The Amerasia Spy Case: Prelude to McCarthyism*. Chapel Hill: University of North Carolina Press, 1996.

Knightley, Phillip. *The Master Spy*. New York: Knopf, 1989.

Koch, Stephen. *Double Lives: Spies and Writers in the Secret Soviet War of Ideas Against the West*. New York: Free Press, 1994.

Koestler, Arthur. *Darkness at Noon*. New York: Macmillan, 1941; Signet ed., 1950.

Krasnov, Vladislav. *Soviet Defectors: The KGB Wanted List*. Stanford, Calif.: Hoover Institution Press, 1986.

Krivitsky, Walter. *In Stalin's Secret Service*. New York: Harper and Brothers, 1939.

Lamphere, Robert J., and Tom Schachtman. *The FBI-KGB War: A Special Agent's Story*. New York: Random House, 1986.

Latham, Earl. *The Communist Controversy in Washington*. New York: Atheneum, 1966.

Leuchtenburg, William E. *Franklin D. Roosevelt and the New Deal.* New York: Harper & Row, 1963.

Levine, Isaac Don. *Eyewitness to History.* New York: Hawthorn, 1973.

Lewis, Flora. *Red Pawn: The Story of Noel Field.* Garden City, N.Y.: Doubleday, 1965.

Marmorstein, Gary. *Hollywood Rhapsody.* New York: Schirmer Books, 1997.

Massing, Hede. *This Deception.* New York: Duell, Sloan, and Pearce, 1951.

Modin, Yuri. *My Five Cambridge Friends: Burgess, Maclean, Philby, Blunt and Cairncross.* New York: Farrar, Straus & Giroux, 1994.

Morris, Roger. *Richard Milhous Nixon: The Rise of an American Politician.* New York: Holt, 1990.

Morros, Boris (as told to Charles Samuels). *My Ten Years as a Counter-Spy.* New York: Viking Press, 1959.

Myers, Constance. *The Prophet's Army: Trotskyists in America, 1928–1941.* Westport, Conn.: Greenwood Press, 1977.

Newton, Verne W. *The Cambridge Spies: The Untold Story of Maclean, Philby and Burgess in America.* Lanham, N.Y.: Madison Books, 1991.

O'Neill, William L. *A Better World: The Great Schism—Stalinism and the American Intellectuals.* New York: Simon and Schuster, 1982.

Orlov, Alexander. *Handbook of Intelligence and Guerrilla Warfare.* Ann Arbor: University of Michigan Press, 1965.

O'Toole, G. J. A. *Honorable Treachery: A History of U.S. Intelligence . . .* New York: Atlantic Monthly Press, 1991.

Ottanelli, Fraser M. *The Communist Party of the United States: From the Depression to World War II.* New Brunswick, N.J.: Rutgers University Press, 1991.

Packer, Herbert L. *Ex-Communist Witnesses.* Stanford, Calif.: Stanford University Press, 1962.

Page, Bruce, David Leitch, and Phillip Knightley. *The Philby Conspiracy.* Garden City, N.Y.: Doubleday, 1968.

Parrish, Michael. *Soviet Security and Intelligence Organizations, 1917–1990: A Biographical Dictionary and Review of Literature in English.* New York: Greenwood Press, 1992.

Peterson, Neal H. *American Intelligence, 1775–1790: A Bibliographic Guide.* Claremont, Calif.: Regina Books, 1992.

Philby, Kim. *My Silent War.* New York: Grove, 1968.

Poretsky, Elisabeth K. *Our Own People. A Memoir of "Ignace Reiss" and His Friends.* Ann Arbor: University of Michigan Press, 1970.

Powers, Richard Gid. *The Life of J. Edgar Hoover.* New York: Free Press, 1987.

Primakov, E. M., chief editor. *Essays on the History of Russian Foreign Intelligence.* Volume 2, 1917–1933; Volume 3, 1933–1941. Moscow: International Relations Publishers, 1997. (Russian edition.)

Pritt, D. N. *Spies and Informers in the Witness Box*. London: Bernard Harison, 1958.

Radosh, Ronald, and Joyce Milton. *The Rosenberg File*, rev. ed. New Haven, Conn.: Yale University Press, 1997.

Ranelagh, John. *The Agency: The Rise and Decline of the CIA*. New York: Simon and Schuster, 1986.

Rees, David. *Harry Dexter White: A Study in Paradox*. New York: Coward, McCann and Geoghegan, 1973.

Reuben, William A. *The Atom Spy Hoax*. New York: Action Books, 1960.

Rhodes, Richard. *Dark Sun: The Making of the Hydrogen Bomb*. New York: Simon and Schuster, 1995.

———. *The Making of the Atomic Bomb*. New York: Simon and Schuster, 1986.

Richelson, Jeffrey T. *The U.S. Intelligence Community*. Cambridge, Mass.: Ballinger, 1985.

Rocca, Raymond G., and John J. Dziak. *Bibliography on Soviet Intelligence and Security Services*. Boulder, Co.: Westview, 1985.

Romerstein, Herbert, and Stanislav Levchenko. *The KGB Against the "Main Enemy": How the Soviet Intelligence Service Operates Against the United States*. Lexington, Mass.: Lexington Books, 1989.

Rositzke, Harry. *The CIA's Secret Operations: Espionage, Counterespionage, and Covert Action*. New York: Reader's Digest Press, 1977.

Ryan, James G. *Earl Browder: The Public Life of an American Communist*. Tuscaloosa: University of Alabama Press, 1997.

Schlesinger, Arthur M., Jr. *The Coming of the New Deal*. Boston: Houghton Mifflin, 1959.

———. *Crisis of the Old Order*. Boston: Houghton Mifflin, 1956.

———. *The Politics of Upheaval*. Boston: Houghton Mifflin, 1960.

Schneir, Walter, and Miriam Schneir. *Invitation to an Inquest*. Garden City, N.Y.: Doubleday, 1965.

Schrecker, Ellen. *Many Are the Crimes: McCarthyism in America*. Boston: Little, Brown, 1998.

Shannon, David A. *The Decline of American Communism*. New York: Harcourt, Brace and Company, 1959.

Shils, Edward Albert. *The Torment of Secrecy: The Background and Consequences of American Security Policies*. Glencoe, Ill.: Free Press, 1956.

Smith, R. Harris. *OSS: The Secret History of America's First Central Intelligence Agency*. Berkeley: University of California Press, 1972.

Starobin, Joseph R. *American Communism in Crisis, 1943–1957*. Cambridge, Mass.: Harvard University Press, 1972.

Stettinius, Edward R., Jr. *Roosevelt and the Russians*. Garden City, N.Y.: Doubleday, 1949.

———. *The Diaries of Edward R. Stettinius, Jr., 1943–1946*. Edited by Thomas M. Campbell and George C. Herring. New York: New Viewpoints, 1975.

Straight, Michael. *After Long Silence*. New York: William Morrow, 1983.

Stripling, Robert. *The Red Plot Against America*. Edited by Robert Considine. Drexel Hill, Pa.: Bell, 1949.

Sudoplatov, Pavel, and Anatoli Sudoplatov, with Jerrold L. Schecter and Leona P. Schecter. *Special Tasks: The Memoirs of an Unwanted Witness—A Soviet Spymaster*. New York: Little, Brown, 1995.

Tanenhaus, Sam. *Whittaker Chambers: A Biography*. New York: Random House, 1997.

Theoharis, Athan G., ed. *Beyond the Hiss Case: The FBI, Congress and the Cold War*. Philadelphia: Temple University Press, 1982.

Troy, Thomas F. *Donovan and the CIA: A History of the Establishment of the Central Intelligence Agency*. Frederick, Md.: University Publications, 1981.

Ulanovskaya, Nadezhda, and Maya Ulanovskaya. *Istoriia Odnoi Semyi* [The Story of One Family]. Benson, Vt.: Chalidze, 1982.

Vassiliev, A., and A. Koreshkov. *Station Chief Gold*. Moscow: Andropov Red-Banner Institute, 1984.

Waller, J. Michael. *Secret Empire: The KGB in Russia Today*. Boulder, Colo.: Westview Press, 1994.

Waller, John H. *The Unseen War in Europe: Espionage and Conspiracy in the Second World War*. New York: Random House, 1996.

Weinstein, Allen. *Perjury: The Hiss-Chambers Case*. New York: Knopf, 1978; Random House paperback, 1997.

West, Nigel (pseud.). *MI6: British Secret Intelligence Service Operations, 1909–1945*. New York: Random House, 1983.

———. *Games of Intelligence: The Classified Conflict of International Espionage*. London: Nicholson Ltd.; New York: Crown Publishers, Inc., 1989.

———. *The Illegals*. London: Hodder & Stoughton, 1993.

West, Nigel and Oleg Tsarev. *The Crown Jewels: The British Secrets at the Heart of the KGB Archives*. London: HarperCollins, 1998.

West, Rebecca. *The New Meaning of Treason*. New York: Viking, 1967.

Williams, Robert Chadwell. *Klaus Fuchs, Atom Spy*. Cambridge, Mass.: Harvard University Press, 1987.

Wiltz, John E. *In Search of Peace: The Senate Munitions Inquiry, 1934–36*. Baton Rouge: Louisiana State University Press, 1963.

Wise, David, and Thomas B. Ross. *The Espionage Establishment*. New York: Random House, 1967.

Wolf, Markus. *Man Without a Face*. New York: Times Books, 1997.

INDEX

❖

AAA (Agricultural Adjustment Administration), 39–41, 43

Abakumov, Victor, 308

Abraham (code name). *See* Soble, Jack

Abt, John, 39, 48, 223, 224

Academy of Sciences, 181, 209–10, 335

Acheson, Dean, 48, 129, 131, 134

Acorn (code name). *See* Gold, Bella

Actor (code name), 30

Adam (code name), 106

Addis, Thomas, 216

Adler, Solomon, 78, 158

Agriculture Department, U.S.: early Soviet probes into, 37. *See also* AAA

Akhmerov, Helen. *See* Lowry, Helen

Akhmerov, Itzhak, 117, 236, 340, 341; agents' relationships with, 166; and Arena, 235; and Bentley/Golos, 93, 95, 96–98, 99, 102, 107, 157, 170, 224, 226; on blending into American identity, 35–36; and Browder, 95, 96–97, 304; and Chambers, 43; code names for, 35, 43, 156, 165; cover identity for, 155–56, 170–71; and Dan, 262; and Dodd case, 60; and Duggan, 8, 9, 13, 14–17, 18–19, 42, 44, 82, 156, 170; and early probes into U.S. government, 36–37; entry into U.S. of, 35; and Field, 44; and Glasser, 267; and Hiss, 79, 80; and ideology versus professionalized imperatives, 166; Mally's opionion of, 75; and Markin's death, 36; and Morros, 120; and OSS-NKGB cooperation, 243; and Perlo Group, 95, 96–97, 156, 224–25, 226; personal life of, 36, 341; recall to Moscow of, 17, 36, 82, 107, 170, 171, 235; and reestablishment of U.S. networks, 155–56, 157; and Reiss's threats to reveal U.S. agents, 10, 11; and selling of documents, 43; and Silvermaster, 96, 98, 157, 162, 163, 164–66, 167, 168, 169, 170; Soviet opinions about and honors for, 165; and Soviet penetration of OSS, 252; and Stern, 120; and Straight, 76–82, 83, 156, 170; as survivor, 340; and Ware Group, 80; and Wheeler, 259

Aksenov, N., 137–38
Al (code name). *See* Slack, Alfred
Alben, Jacob, 138
Albert (code name). *See* Akhmerov, Itzhak
Ales (code name). *See* Hiss, Alger
Alexsey (code name). *See* Yatskov, Anatoly
Allakhverdov, Colonel, 253
Allen (code name), 263, 264
American Communist Party (CPUSA). *See* Communist Party of the United States
Ames, Aldrich, 340
Amtorg Trading Corporation, 23, 99, 243
Ant (code name). *See* Heineman, Mrs.
Antenna (code name). *See* Rosenberg, Julius
Anti-Semitism, 32, 88
Anton (code name). *See* Kvasnikov, Leonid
Archimedes (code name), 113
Arena (code name), 106n, 235–37
Argot (code name), 273
Arno (code name). *See* Gold, Harry
Art (code name), 107
Atomic bomb: exploding of, 211. *See also* Atomic research
Atomic Energy Commission (AEC), 132–33, 134
Atomic research: anonymous material delivered to Soviets about, 193; characteristics of agents involved with, 29–30; early Soviet information about, 172, 178, 179–81; and exploding of atomic bomb, 211; and Gorsky-Wallace meeting, 284; and Great Britain, 178, 180, 181–83, 188, 193–94, 209, 214, 313; memo from scientists to American government about, 215–16; and Morros, 132–33, 137, 138; in postwar world, 211–22; Soviet coordination of work on, 181; Soviet penetration of U.S., 340; Soviet priority for information about, 181; in Soviet Union, 211, 283, 316–17, 335;

and Soviet-U.S. relations, 284; VENONA project exposes Soviet penetration of, 291, 325; and XY Line, 173–76, 177, 178, 191–92, 194–95, 203, 219, 220. *See also* Fogel; Fuchs, Klaus; Greenglass, David; Hall, Theodore; Rosenberg, Julius
August (code name). *See* Rosenberg, Julius

Baker, Nicholas (*aka* Niels Bohr), 187
Baldwin, Roger, 76, 78
Balkans, 241–42, 248
Bark (code name), 156
Barkley, Alben, 129
Barkovsky, Vladimir, 180, 181, 183
Barr, Joel, 217, 218, 333
Baruch, Bernard, 129
Bazarov, Boris, 8, 9, 10, 12, 37
Beck (code name). *See* Kurnakov, Sergei
Bedacht, Max, 42, 43
Bentley, Elizabeth: and Akhmerov, 96–98, 99, 102, 107, 157, 224, 226; alienation from Soviet espionage of, 97; and American Communist Party, 92; attitude about NKGB of, 95–96; biography of, 88; and Browder, 95, 96, 97, 98, 99, 102, 105, 107, 224, 301, 304, 308; code names for, 84; criticism of Golos by, 93–94; defection of, 68, 84, 103–9, 124, 170, 216, 217–18, 220, 226, 234, 235, 237, 256, 264, 271, 280, 283, 285, 286–87, 289, 296, 298, 306, 311, 318, 340, 341, 342, 344; and Dimitrov, 303; and FBI, 84, 91, 99, 100, 102, 103–9, 216, 218, 248; and Glasser, 266; Golos' relationship with, 84, 86, 87–94, 99, 102, 103, 157, 341; and Gorsky, 100–102, 103–4, 106–7, 108; and Heller, 100–101, 102, 103; and HUAC, 292; importance of, 84; memoir of, 88; and Merkulov, 102–3, 104–6, 107, 108; moral dilemma of, 341; and OSS list of

communists, 254; and Perlo Group, 96–97, 224–25, 226, 227, 229, 237, 262; personal life of, 98, 99, 101–4; post-Golos career of, 94–109; proposed recall to Moscow of, 106; and Silvermaster, 94, 95, 96, 97, 98, 157, 161, 170, 262; Soviet honors for, 99; Soviet opinions about, 97–98, 99, 100–101, 102–3; and Soviet penetration of OSS, 251, 252, 254, 257, 259, 260, 262; Soviet proposals killing of, 102–3, 108; style of, 84–85; unknown whereabouts of, 109; and Zarubin, 96, 97

Berg (code name). See Koral, Alexander

Beria, Lavrenty: arrest and execution of, 334–35; and atomic research, 181; and Bentley defection, 108; as Commissar of Internal Affairs, 30; and Fuchs's exposure, 335; and Golos, 87, 90; and Hoettl case, 248; and Morros, 116, 122, 125, 131; and OSS-NKGB cooperation, 240, 246, 248; Philby's material sent to, 107; and reestablishment of U.S. networks, 155; and Trotskyites, 30

Berkman, Raissa, 301

Berle, Adolf, 17, 18, 48, 239, 240

Bill (code name). See Akhmerov, Itzhak

Bissell (U.S. official), 236

Black (code name), 174, 176

Blerio (code name Shumovsky), 26

Blin (code name), 31

Blum, Leon, 56

Blunt, Anthony, 72, 73, 74, 81, 83, 230, 290

Bob (code name). See Krotov, Boris

Bogdan (code name), 234

Bohlen, Charles, 129, 228

Bohr, Niels, 187

Bokhara rugs: as gifts to Soviet agents, 12, 44

Boris (code name), 105

Borodin, Norman, 9–10, 11, 12, 13, 19, 20

Bowers, Claude, 60–61

Boy (code name). See Dodd, William (brother)

Boyd, Helen, 4, 6, 7–8, 9, 10

Brit (code name), 32–33

British intelligence, 104, 107, 315, 322–23, 335

Brodsky (lawyer for Communist Party), 87

Brothman, Abraham, 176, 177, 189, 218–21, 311, 318, 319

Browder, Bill, 302, 304

Browder, Earl: activities and responsibilities of, 302–3; and Akhmerov, 95, 96–97, 304; and atomic espionage, 190, 191; Bentley's relationship with, 84, 95, 96, 97, 98, 99, 102, 105, 107, 224, 301, 304, 308; biography of, 301; code names for, 84, 309; and Dodd case, 55; expulsion of, 300–301, 302, 304, 305–6, 341; and FBI, 99, 308; and FBI's anonymous letter, 274; and Feklissov, 301; Golos's relationship with, 84, 89, 90, 92, 93, 95, 157, 224, 256, 257, 301–2, 304; and HUAC, 102; and intelligence operations, 302–4, 305–6, 309; Lowry as niece of, 36, 155; Moscow trip of, 305, 306–8; motivation of, 341; payments to, 301–2, 309; and Perlo Group, 96–97, 224, 229, 237; and Peter, 38, 225, 302; plan to regain CPUSA leadership of, 304–5; as possible informant, 304; in prison, 92, 300, 301; as publisher, 307, 308, 309; and reform of CPUSA, 301; Roosevelt amnesty for, 300, 306–7; and Silvermaster, 96, 158, 162; Soviet opinions about, 99, 302–3, 309–10; and Soviet penetration of OSS, 251, 256, 257; and Straight, 78; and Zarubin, 96, 302. See also Communist Party of the United States (CPUSA)

Bruslov, Yuri, 289–90, 291, 292

Buben (code name). See Budenz, Louis

Buby (code name), 141–42
Buchbinder, 255
Buck (code name), 235
Budenz, Louis, 30, 103, 105, 107, 298
Bukhartsev (Soviet agent), 51, 52, 53–54
Bulgaria, 245, 259
Bullitt, William, 9, 15, 36–37, 53, 56
Bumblebee (code name). See Greenglass, David
Burgess, Guy, 71, 72, 73, 83, 105, 210, 230, 290, 344
Bykov, Boris, 12, 43, 44, 45
Byrnes, James F., 234, 285

C-II (code name), 27
Cairncross, John, 172, 194, 230, 290, 344
Caliber (code name). See Greenglass, David
Cambridge University, 15, 72, 73, 75, 76, 82–83
Camp 1 (code name), 213
Camp 2 (code name), 195, 197, 199, 200, 202, 213, 221
Camp Y (code name). See Los Alamos, New Mexico
Cannon, James, 30
Cantwell, Robert, 45, 47
Captain (code name). See Roosevelt, Franklin D.
Careful (code name). See Joseph, Julius
Chambers, Esther Shemitz, 42, 44, 45
Chambers, Whittaker, 153, 223; with AAA, 40; and Akhmerov, 35; and Bentley, 89; Berle's meeting with, 17, 18; biography of, 41–42; code names for, 39, 48, 294; contact procedures used by, 14; as courier, 37, 38–41, 158; defection of, 17, 43, 44–49, 223, 235, 298, 341, 344; and early Soviet probes into U.S. government, 37; and FBI, 47, 342; and gifts to key Soviet operatives, 12; and Herbst, 40; and Hiss, 14, 21, 38–44, 294, 342, 344; and HUAC, 292; as informant, 17, 18; legacy of, 342–43,

344; moral dilemma of, 341; and Nye Committee, 40–41; and Panyushkin's disinformation proposal, 294–95; personal life of, 341; recruitment of, 42, 43; Soviet career of, 43; and Wadleigh, 14; and Ware group, 38–41
Chap (code name). See Zelman, Franklin
Chaplin, Charlie, 137
Charles (code name). See Fuchs, Klaus
Cherny (code name), 174
Chester (code name). See Oppenheimer, J. Robert
Chevalier, Haakon, 216
Chicago Bread Exchange, 25
Child of the Danube (film), 132–33
China, 258, 289
Chita (code name), 27–28
Chord (music publishing house) (code name), 66, 70, 118–19, 120–23
Churchill, Winston, 160, 210, 212, 230, 234, 258, 272
Civil Service Commission, 161, 235
Clark, Tom, 285, 291
Clay, Lucius, 126–27, 129
Clayton, Will, 270
Code names, change in Soviet, 276–77
Codes, Soviet, 247, 286, 291–93
Coe, Frank, 48, 158, 162, 169, 229
Cohen, Lona, 207, 208, 209, 211, 213, 221
Cohen, Morris, 190, 207, 221
Colleague (code name), 251
Collins, Henry, 39, 224
Columbia University, 35, 41, 178, 179, 182
Comintern, 38, 43, 55, 75, 85, 86, 87, 157, 165, 278, 303
Communist Party of the United States (CPUSA): Browder's plans to regain leadership of, 304–5; Browder's proposal for reform of, 301; dues for, 39; and early Soviet probes into U.S. government, 38; exposure of Nazis' activities

against, 31; financing of, 43; and
intelligence operations, 8, 13, 87,
235, 249, 256, 257, 266, 300,
302–4, 305–6; and OSS list of
communists, 254; and Smith Act,
309; and Ware group, 38, 39, 40.
See also U.S. Shipping
Corporation; *specific person, espe-
cially* Browder, Earl
Compton, Arthur, 182, 210
Condenser (code name), 191, 301
Congress, U.S., 227. *See also*
Dickstein, Samuel; HUAC;
Kramer, Charles
Connison, Emil, 174
Conquest, Robert, 339
Constructor (code name). *See*
Brothman, Abraham
Coplon, Judith, 91, 216, 226, 261,
277–79, 280, 298, 317
Corcoran, Thomas, 80
Cornford, John, 73–74
Cosmos Club, 17
Council of Foreign Relations, 287
CPUSA. *See* Communist Party of the
United States
Crook (code name). *See* Dickstein,
Samuel
Cuban missile crisis, 275
Currie, Lauchlin, 48, 106, 157, 159,
161–62, 163, 168, 243, 274

Daily Worker, 42, 76, 77, 105
Dan (code name), 261, 262–64
Daniel (code name), 34–35
Davis (code name). *See* Markin,
Valentin
Davis (U.S. official), 56
Dean, John, 241, 244–47
DeGaulle, Charles, 163
Dekanozov, Vladimir, 239
Dennis, Gene, 266
Deputy (code name). *See* Wallace,
Henry
Deutsch, Arnold, 15, 75, 76, 155
Dewey, Thomas E., 126, 127, 131
Dickstein, Samuel, 140–50, 228, 341
Dies, Martin, 141
Dies Committee, 144, 146, 147, 148

Dimitrov, Georgy, 303
Dir (code name). *See* Price, Mary
Dodd, Martha, 122, 136, 341; and
Akhmerov, 60; and Bentley defection, 68; and Browder, 55; code
name for, 51; defection of, 69–71;
and Dodd case as fiction, 50–51;
and elections of 1948, 68–69;
exile of, 71, 344; and FBI, 51, 68,
69, 70, 71; as guilty of espionage,
70; handling of, 57–58, 59–60;
material provided to Soviets by,
53–54, 58, 66; Soviet memo of,
55–57, 58; Soviet opinions about,
62, 68–69, 72, 228; Soviet recruitment of, 51–52, 57; and Stern, 60,
61–62, 63–64, 65–66, 68–71; studies of communism by, 53–54; and
Vinogradov relationship, 51–53,
54–55, 57–60, 61, 62, 63, 64, 65,
70; Zelman memo about, 63–65
Dodd, William (brother), 66–68
Dodd, William (father), 51, 52, 53,
56–57, 58, 59, 60, 62, 66, 67, 68
Dolbin, Grigory, 287–89
Dolliway (Comintern worker), 55
Donovan, William J.: concerns about
Soviet postwar activities of, 255;
Lee as protegé of, 257, 259; and
Lee's fears of exposure, 259; and
OSS-NKGB cooperation, 238,
240–49, 259, 264; on Stalin, 243
Dora (code name). *See* Silvermaster,
Helen
Douglas, William O., 333
Douglas Aircraft Corporation, 26–27
Duclos, Jacques, 301
Duggan, Helen. *See* Boyd, Helen
Duggan, Laurence, 34, 42, 265; and
American Communist Party
work, 8, 13; code names for, 19,
20, 295; concerns about events in
Soviet Union of, 12–14, 15, 21;
death of, 21, 344; exposure of,
10–11, 15, 16–17, 18, 19, 48, 49,
82, 192; and FBI, 18, 21, 295–96;
Field's relationship with, 4–8; as
Hull aide, 17; material provided
to Soviets by, 9–10, 11–12, 14–15,

Duggan, Laurence (cont'd):
16, 19–20; motives for cooperation of, 4, 12–13, 19, 20; payments for, 12, 44; re-recruitment
of, 18–19, 20, 156, 170, 295–96;
recruitment of, 3, 4–8, 35; resignation from State Department of,
19, 20, 48, 49; Soviet opinion
about, 11, 13–14, 15, 16, 18–19;
and Straight, 78, 79; UN position
of, 19

Dulles, Allen, 241, 247, 250
Dumbarton Oaks Conference, 164
Dunn (U.S. official), 56
Dunning, Professor, 182
Dupont Company, 29, 37, 284
Durmashkin, Ilya (Soviet agent), 90

Eastman Kodak Company, 28, 176
Echo (code name). See Schuster,
Bernard
Eck (code name). See Perlo, Victor
Economic espionage, 24, 25–30
Eisenhower, Dwight D., 126, 130,
248, 270
Eisenhower, Milton, 126, 129
Election campaigns: Soviet contribu-
tions to, 145
Eleron (code name). See Silverman,
David
Elitcher, Max, 333
Elsa (code name). See Lowry, Helen
Emir (code name). See Bukhartsev
Enemy (code name). See Krivitsky,
Walter
Enormoz (code name). See Atomic
research
Eric (code name), 181–83, 193, 283,
336, 342
Ernst (code name). See Field, Noel
Export-Import Bank, 232

Falcon (code name), 27
Farm Security Administration, 161
FBI (Federal Bureau of Investigation):
anonymous letters to, 274–75;
appropriations for, 148; and
Chord venture, 119; Coplon's
materials about, 278; and Fuchs's

arrest, 322–23, 325; Heller as
agent for, 100–101, 102, 103; as
high Soviet priority for information, 228, 230; increased counterintelligence activity by, 175, 261,
275–80, 283, 287, 293–300;
Justice Department's files about,
278; Kramer's information about,
234; Morgenthau's views about,
239; OSS's relationship with,
242–43, 245; and Soviet attempts
to reestablish U.S. networks, 156;
and Soviet codes, 247; and Soviet
coordination of information, 160;
Soviet views about, 275–76. See
also Hoover, J. Edgar; specific
agent

Fedotov, Peter, 126, 130, 131, 315
Feklissov, Alexander, 264, 280, 334,
340, 341; and atomic espionage,
189, 191–92, 194–95, 198,
199–200, 201–2, 206, 221; and
Browder, 301; cover for, 191; and
FBI increased counterintelli-
gence activity, 275; and Fuchs,
313–18, 320, 324, 326, 335; and
Rosenberg's security, 217, 222; on
Semyonov, 173; and Soviet pene-
tration of OSS, 264; views about
FBI of, 275–76
Feldman, Armand Lavis (aka I. V.
Volodarsky), 33, 91
Fermi, Enrico, 183, 210, 314
Field, Frederick Vanderbilt, 8
Field, Herta, 10
Field, Noel, 4–8, 10–11, 34, 35, 44,
48, 80, 265
"Fifth column," 239
Finnish intelligence, 247
Fischer, Louis, 59
Fitin, Pavel: and atomic espionage,
182–83, 188, 190, 193–94, 197,
198, 199, 200–201, 208, 212–13;
and Bentley, 97–98; and
Browder's expulsion, 305, 308;
Donovan passes Soviet codes to,
247; and FBI's anonymous letter,
275; and Glasser, 267, 268, 271;
and Golos, 90, 93; and Hoettl

case, 248; and OSS-NKGB cooperation, 241, 242, 243, 244, 245, 246, 247–48; and possible German and Anglo-American peace agreement, 247; and reestablishment of U.S. networks, 155; on Roosevelt's death, 248; and Rosenbergs, 333; and Silvermaster, 163–64, 165; and Soviet penetration of OSS, 253; and Trotskyites, 30

Fitzgerald, Edward "Ted," 224, 225, 227, 231, 261–62

Flato, 97, 224

Fogel (code name), 190–91, 192, 194, 203, 212, 336, 342

Foreign agents: registration of, 141

Foster, William Z., 305, 308

France, 163, 241, 258, 272, 299

Frank (code name). See Duggan, Laurence

Frankfurter, Felix, 41, 48

Frenchman (code name), 28

Frost (code name). See Morros, Boris

Fry, D., 228

Fuchs, Klaus: arrest and confession of, 320–27, 330, 335, 342, 343; "arrest" of, 220, 221; biography of, 312; code names for, 311; controlled schizophrenia of, 324–25; death of, 335; in East Germany, 326, 335, 336; in England, 184–85, 189–90, 193, 220, 221, 311–18, 320–26; exposure of, 320–23, 325–26, 335; and Feklissov, 313–18, 320, 324, 326; and German Communists, 312, 321; and Gold, 186–88, 189–90, 203–5, 207–9, 210–11, 213–15, 318, 320–21, 325–26, 327; importance of, 185, 213–14; as informant, 326, 327; materials passed by, 185, 188, 193, 214–16, 219, 313, 315–16, 317, 320; meetings with, 186–88, 189, 190, 207–8, 210–11, 214–15, 312–13, 314–16, 317–18; motivation of, 324; in New Mexico, 203–4, 205, 208, 210–11, 213–15, 219; payments for, 204, 205, 313, 324; personal life of, 316, 326; in postwar world, 211, 213–16, 219, 220, 221, 311–18, 326–27; recruitment of, 185; and Semyonov, 187, 188; sentence of, 321; Soviet honors for, 335; Soviet misinformation about, 321–22; Soviet opinions about, 185, 187, 188, 190, 208–9, 214; Soviet visit of, 326–27; Soviets restore relationship with, 311–13; and Yatskov, 316

Fuchs, Margaret, 335

Fuller, Helen, 67

Fyodor (code name). See Sokolov, Gyorgi

Galeazi, Enrico, 128

Gapon (code name), 27

Gardner, Meredith, 291

General Electric Company, 25, 132, 284

General Motors Corporation, 77

George (code name). See Ovakimyan, Gaik

German Communists, 312, 321

Germany: allegations about Zarubina working for, 274; atomic research in, 179; Dickstein's interest in Nazi, 141; future of, 164; Glasser material about, 270, 271, 272; invasion of Soviet Union by, 158–60, 174, 223; occupation zones of, 232, 271; and OSS-NKGB cooperation, 238–39, 241, 242, 245–46, 247; possible Anglo-American peace agreement with, 247, 249, 250; and Soviet penetration of OSS, 250, 253–54, 255, 256, 262; Soviet priority for information about, 24, 28–29, 31–32, 34, 175, 233; surrender of, 247–48. See also Dodd, Martha

Gershwin, Ira, 137

Gestapo, 204, 294–95

Getsov, Eva, 106

Glan (code name), 17–18, 173

Glasser, Harold, 106, 225, 229, 265–72, 286

Global Tourist, 104

Gnedin (Soviet agent), 54

Gnome (code name), 177

Göering, Hermann, 64

Gold, Bella, 167

Gold, Harry: arrest and sentence of, 325–26, 330, 332, 342; biography of, 176; and Brothman, 218–20, 311, 318, 319; code names for, 321, 326; as courier, 176–77; exposure of, 218–20, 326, 327; and FBI, 219, 220, 319; and Fuchs, 185, 186–88, 189–90, 203–5, 207–9, 210–11, 213–15, 318, 320–21, 325–26, 327; and Golos, 319; grand jury appearance of, 319; and Greenglasses, 198, 208, 209, 210, 211, 328, 332; importance of, 176; as informant, 320–21, 325–26, 328, 332, 333, 342; initial assignment of, 176; and military espionage, 27; payments to, 177; post-imprisonment years of, 336; in postwar world, 211, 216, 218–20, 311, 318–20, 325–27; in prison, 133; proposed flight plans of, 319, 321; restoration of connection with, 220; restoration of relationship with, 318–19; and Semyonov, 177; and Slack, 176, 177, 189; Soviet honors for, 195; Soviet opinions about, 176–77, 320–21; and Sulpho operation, 177; Yatskov as controller of, 189

Gold, Sonya, 167

Golos, Jacob: and Akhmerov, 157, 224; and American Communist Party, 92; arrest and conviction of, 87, 89, 93; and atomic espionage, 174, 177, 178; Bentley's relationship with, 84, 86, 87–94, 99, 102, 103, 157, 341; biography of, 85–87; and Browder, 89, 90, 92, 93, 157, 224, 256, 257, 301–2, 304; and Buck, 235; and Budenz, 103; code names for, 84; death of, 84, 89, 93–94, 95, 96, 97, 102, 103, 157, 177, 224, 256; and FBI,

86, 90, 91, 93, 94, 104, 278; and Gold, 319; health of, 92; and ideology versus professionalized imperatives, 166; and Ovakimyan, 85, 89; and Perlo Group, 156, 229; proposed recall of, 89–90; and Rosenberg, 174, 177, 197, 217, 218; and Silvermaster's network, 91, 94, 157, 158, 161, 162; Soviet honors for, 93; Soviet monitoring of, 91; Soviet opinions about, 89–90, 94, 105, 165; and Soviet penetration of OSS, 251, 256, 257, 258; style of, 84–85, 189; vulnerability of, 93; World Tourist as cover for, 84–86, 87, 94

Goodman, Walter, 141

Goose (code name). See Gold, Harry

Gore (code name), 106

Gorsky, Anatoly, 285, 340, 341; and Arena, 236; and atomic espionage, 172, 181, 184–85; as Bentley handler, 99, 100–102, 103–4, 106–7, 108; and Browder, 304; and FBI, 107; and freezing of operations, 296–97; and Glasser, 265–66, 267, 268, 269, 271; and Hiss background, 269; and Kramer, 233–34; and Maclean, 230; and Morros, 122; Panyushkin criticized by, 297; and Perlo Group, 227, 228, 229, 231, 237; recall to Moscow of, 107; and Soviet penetration of OSS, 255, 259, 260–61, 262, 263; and U.S. breaking of Soviet codes, 286; views about FBI of, 276; Wallace's meeting with, 283–85

Gouzenko, Igor, 104–5, 124, 218, 283, 285, 287, 297, 306, 311, 340, 342

GPU, 22, 23–24, 43, 85, 194, 223. See also specific agent

Granite (code name). See Borodin, Norman

Graur, Andrei, 242

Great Britain: and atomic research, 178, 180, 181–83, 188, 193–94, 209, 214, 313; Glasser material about, 270, 271, 272; intelligence in, 263; and OSS-NKGB cooperation, 242; possible German and American peace agreement with, 247, 249, 250; and Soviet penetration of OSS, 249; Soviet relations with, 210, 263, 270

Greece, 242

Green (code name), 28–29

Green, Joseph C., 11, 12

Green, Michael (code name). See Akhmerov, Itzhak

Greenglass, David: arrest and trial of, 327–34; code names for, 328; and FBI, 330, 331; and Fuchs, 326; guilt of, 333–34; as informant, 331–32, 342; materials passed to Soviets by, 328; in New Mexico, 199–203, 206, 208, 209, 210; payments for, 331; post-imprisonment years of, 336; in postwar world, 211, 212, 213, 221, 311, 327–34; proposed flight of, 328–31; recruitment of, 198–99; and Rosenberg, 132, 311, 329, 330–31, 332, 333, 336; sentence of, 333; Soviet reaction to trial of, 333–34

Greenglass, Ruth, 198–203, 206, 208, 209, 210, 213, 221, 326, 327, 328, 329, 332, 334, 336

Gromov, Anatolij Borisovich, 269

Gromyko, Andrei, 239, 240, 247, 265, 287, 309

Gross, A., 48

Groves, Leslie, 173

GRU (Soviet military intelligence): and Bentley defection, 105; lack of availability of archives of, 44; legal covers of agents for, 23–24; and OSS-NKGB cooperation, 245; priority of intelligence for, 160; and Soviet penetration of OSS, 254; and U.S. recognition of Soviet Union, 23–24. See also specific agent

Gubitchev, Valentin, 298, 317

Guennady (code name). See Ovakimyan, Gaik

Gumperz, Hedda, 4–10, 13, 35, 44, 48, 249, 250, 251, 298

Guron (code name), 203, 216

Gutzeit, Peter, 24, 29, 334, 341; and Dickstein, 143, 144–45, 147, 149; and Dodd case, 66–67; and Duggan's recruitment, 4, 5; and early Soviet probes into U.S. government, 37; and Golos, 86, 89; and monarchists, 31; and Morros, 110, 111–13, 114, 115–16; purging of, 114, 147, 153; recall to Moscow of, 89, 114, 146

Halifax, Lord, 230

Hall, Theodore, 195–98, 203, 208–9, 211, 212, 213, 221, 283, 311, 336–37, 342

Halperin, Maurice, 106, 254, 256

Hammer, Armand, 23

Hammer, Julius, 23

Hare (code name). See Halperin, Maurice

Harnack, Arvid, 53

Harriman, Averill, 129, 130, 159, 246

Harry (code name). See Rabinovitz

Harvard University, 41, 197, 273

Haskell, John H. F., 241, 246

Hearst, William Randolph, 31

Heifetz, Grigory, 183, 184

Heineman, Mrs. (Fuchs's sister), 203, 207, 208, 219, 220, 313

Heisenberg, Professor, 185

Helen (code name), 250

Heller, Peter, 100–101, 102, 103

Helmsman (code name). See Browder, Earl

Hemingway, Ernest, 239, 273

Henderson, Loy, 239

Herbert (code name). See Markin, Valentin

Herbst, Josephine, 39–40

Herrmann, John, 39, 40

Hicks (code name). See Burgess, Guy

Hiroshima, Japan, 211

Hiskey, Clarence, 179–80, 181, 182, 183

Hiss, Alger: and AAA, 39, 41, 43; biography of, 41; and Chambers, 14,

Hiss, Alger (cont'd):
17, 21, 38–44, 46–47, 48–49, 294,
342, 344; code names for, 43, 165;
denial of covert deeds by, 341; and
Duggan, 21, 265; and FBI, 21,
267–68; and Field, 5–8, 44, 80,
265; and Glasser, 267–69; in
Justice Department, 5, 44; legacy
of, 342–43; motivation of, 341;
Nye connections of, 29, 40–41, 43;
and Peter, 8, 38, 80, 165; sentence
for, 344; Soviet activities of, 269;
Soviet gifts to, 12, 44; Soviet hon-
ors for, 269; Soviet opinion about,
10, 11, 40; as State Department
employee, 29, 44, 48–49, 267–68,
269; and Straight, 78, 79–80; and
Ware group, 38–41, 80, 165
Hiss, Donald, 48
Hiss, Priscilla, 40, 41, 44, 46–47
Hitler, Adolph, 3, 118, 141, 160, 210,
250, 324
Hoettl, William, 248
Hollywood: purge of communists in,
125. See also Morros, Boris
Homer (code name). See Maclean,
Donald
Hook, Sydney, 46
Hoover, Herbert, 131, 134
Hoover, J. Edgar, 67, 104, 148,
242–43, 244, 248, 274, 275, 343
Hopkins, Harry, 74, 154, 159, 160, 243
Howard, Roy, 23
HUAC (House Committee on Un-
American Activities), 102, 129,
143, 149, 161, 292, 294, 295
Hull, Cordell, 12, 17, 34, 36, 56, 57,
239
Hut (code name). See FBI
Hydrogen bomb, 313, 327

Ickes, Harold, 287
Ida (code name). See Greenglass, Ruth
Igor (code name), 60–61, 82, 142, 143,
144
Industrial espionage, 24, 235
Institute of International Education
(IIE), 4, 20–21, 295
Intelligence agents, Soviet: as anony-
mous writers to FBI, 274–75;

bleak times for, 293–300; change
in code names of, 276–77; characteristics of, 29–30; covers for,
23–24, 155–56; and CPUSA, 8,
13, 87, 235, 249, 256, 257, 266,
300, 302–4, 305–6; effects of
defections on, 105–6, 216,
217–18, 235, 237, 256, 264, 271,
285, 286–87, 289, 290, 296, 298,
306, 311, 340, 342; freezing of
operations of, 218, 280, 285–86,
287, 293–300; and ideology versus
professionalized imperatives, 166;
and increase in U.S. security, 175,
205, 215, 216, 261, 275–80, 283,
287, 293–300; instructions for
passing materials to, 317; and
legacy of "Golden Era," 339–44;
"legality" of, 4, 23–25, 32; and
media as source of information,
286–87; mercenaries as, 340; and
misinformation, 190–91; moral
dilemma of, 340–41; motivations
of, 29–30, 76, 324–25, 336–37,
340; OSS cooperation with,
238–49; OSS list of, 254;
Panyushkin's proposals concerning, 290, 291, 295–96; and political and scientific-technical
separation, 173; priority of information gathered by, 24, 25–30,
220, 223, 227–28, 230, 287–88;
recruitment of, 3–4, 298–300,
322; Savchenko's proposals for,
297–99; shortage of cash for, 175;
shortage of, 153–55, 227–29,
286–89, 298–300; and Stalin's
purges, 89, 153–54, 189, 223; and
U.S. recognition of Soviet Union,
4, 23–25, 32. See also specific person or organization
Interior Department, U.S., 227
International Brigades, 64, 86, 253
Irma (code name), 100
Italy, 19, 255
Izra (code name). See Wheeler,
Donald

Jack (code name), 299
Jackson, Robert, 251

James (code name), 35, 37

Japan, 24, 32, 34, 211, 258, 259, 271, 272, 274, 275

Jimenez (code name), 254

John (code name). *See* Morros, Boris

Johnson (code name), 105

Johnson, Edwin, 284

Johnston, Eric, 128

Joint Chiefs of Staff, U.S., 180, 240, 243–44, 271

Joseph, Julius, 251

Josephson, B., 305

Journalists, 145, 146

Julia (code name), 164

Juliet #1 (code name), 58

Juliet #2 (code name). *See* Dodd, Martha

Julius, Emil, 322

Justice Department, U.S.: Golos inquiry by, 87; as high Soviet priority for information, 227, 230; Hiss in, 44; Silvermaster investigation by, 161–62. *See also* Coplon, Judith; FBI; Hiss, Alger

Kaganovich, Mikhael, 174

Kalistrat (code name). *See* Feklissov, Alexander

Kamenev (Soviet agent), 318, 319, 320, 326

Kapitza, Peter, 284

Kaplan, Irving, 229

Karl (code name). *See* Chambers, Whittaker

Karo (code name). *See* Kuchinsky, Urgen

Kasenkina, Oksana, 150

Katya (code name). *See* Zarubin, Vassily

Katz, Joseph, 106, 108, 227, 229, 236, 237, 259, 260–61

Katz, Otto, 46, 55

Kaufman, Irving R., 332–33

Kellex, 190–91

Kellogg Construction Company, 182, 190–91

Kessler, Frank (code name). *See* Gold, Harry

KGB: *See also* Cheka; GPU; NKGB; NKVD; OGPU

Khrushchev, Nikita, 70, 334, 335

Kilgore, Harley, 184–85, 232

King (code name). *See* Rosenberg, Julius

King, Mackenzie, 107

Kirillov (code name), 330–31

Kistiakowsky, George, 201

Klopshtock, Hanna, 312–13

Knox, Frank, 159

Kokh (code name). *See* Lee, Duncan

Koltsov (Soviet agent), 168

Konstantin (code name), 235

Koral, Alexander, 107, 293, 298

Koral, Helen, 107

Korneev, Colonel, 70

Korotkov, Alexander, 126, 127, 128, 131, 132, 134, 136

Kostrov (code name), 69

Koussevitzky, Serge, 118

Kramer, Charles, 96, 106, 156, 184–85, 224, 225, 231, 232–35

Kremer, Simon Davidovich, 185

Krivitsky, Walter, 47, 148, 153

Krotov, Boris, 289–91, 321, 325–26, 330, 331

Kuchinsky, Urgen, 185, 312

Kuchinsky, Ursula, 312, 315

Kuhn, Fritz, 147

Kurchatov, Igor, 181, 211

Kurnakov, Sergei, 195–97, 336

Kurt (code name), 173

Kvasnikov, Leonid, 334, 341; and atomic espionage, 180, 188, 194–95, 198, 199, 200–201, 202, 203, 205, 207–8, 209, 211; and Fuchs, 326–27; on Greenglass's sentence, 332; and Rosenbergs, 216–17, 333; and Soviet penetration of OSS, 255

Laboratory #2 (Soviet Union), 181

Larry (code name). *See* Statskevich, Nikolai

Latham, Earl, 39, 343

Lavr (code name), 173

Lawrence, Ernst, 210

Lawyer. *See* Hiss, Alger; White, Harry Dexter

Leahy, William D., 243

Lee, Duncan, 242, 254, 257–61, 264, 341

Lend-Lease agreement, 159–60, 163, 164, 270, 271, 272
Lenin, V. I., 11, 253
Leo (code name), 35–36
Leonid (code name), 276
Leslie (code name). *See* Cohen, Lona
Leuchtenberg, William, 23
Lever (code name), 27
Levine, Isaac Don, 47–48
Liberal (code name). *See* Rosenberg, Julius
Lieber, Maxim, 45
Lisa/Liza (code name). *See* Dodd, Martha
List (code name). *See* Cairncross, John
Litvinov, Maxim, 23, 239
Lomakin, Jacob, 150
Los Alamos, New Mexico: early information about, 183; and Fogel, 192; Soviet penetration of, 340; VENONA project exposes Soviet penetration in, 291. *See also* atomic research; Fuchs, Klaus; Greenglass, David; Greenglass, Ruth; Hall, Theodore
Lot (code name). *See* Kramer, Charles
Louis (code name). *See* Stern, Alfred
Lovestone, Jay, 85
Lowry, Helen, 36, 95, 155, 165, 170, 171, 341
Lozovsky, Solomon, 307–8
Lubyanka Prison, 89, 115, 147
Luka (code name). *See* Pastelnyak, Pavel

MacArthur, Douglas, 271, 272
McCarthy, Joseph, 136, 343
McCarthy committee, 136
McCormack, John, 141
McIntyre, Marvin, 48
Maclean, Donald, 71, 72, 86, 107, 230, 286, 290–91, 336, 344
Maclean, Melinda, 230
Mad (code name). *See* Gold, Harry
Magdoff, Harry, 224, 225, 231
Magnate (code name), 28
Mally, Theodore, 72–75
Man (code name). *See* Mally, Theodore

Manhattan Project, 192, 330. *See also* Atomic research
Marcantonio, Vito, 69
Marietta Company, 27
Markin, Valentin, 33, 34, 35, 36, 37, 38, 42, 43
Marshall, George, 248
Marshall Plan, 129
Massachusetts Institute of Technology (MIT), 178, 181, 182
Massing, Paul, 8, 10, 35, 249, 250, 251
Matthews, T. S., 47
Maxim (code name). *See* Zarubin, Vassily
May, Allan Nunn, 313
Mechanic (code name), 16
Media: as source of Soviet information, 287
Mensheviks, 90
Mer (code name). *See* Akhmerov, Itzhak
Merkulov, Vsevolod: arrest and execution of, 334, 335; and atomic espionage, 182–84, 193–94, 212–13; and Bentley case, 102–3, 104–6, 107, 108; and Browder's expulsion, 305–6; and Chord venture, 118; and Glasser, 268, 269; and Gorsky-Wallace meeting, 284; and Hoettl case, 248; and increased FBI counterintelligence activity, 276–77; and Morros, 132; and OSS-NKGB cooperation, 239; and Silvermaster, 163, 164, 165
Meter (code name). *See* Barr, Joel
Mielke, Erich, 335
Mikoyan, Anastas, 277
Military espionage, 25–30
Mironov, Colonel, 274, 276
Misinformation, 190–91
Mlad (code name). *See* Hall, Theodore
Modin, Yuri, 82–83
Mole (code name). *See* Kramer, Charles
Molotov, Vyacheslav, 16, 25, 87, 104, 107, 122, 128, 240, 246, 259, 275, 280, 284
Monarchists, 30–31, 153

Mora (code name), 166

Morgenthau, Henry, 74, 234; and Glasser's activities, 265, 269, 270, 271; and Silvermaster Group, 159, 161, 163–64, 166, 167, 168; views about FBI of, 238–39

Moroz, Alexander, 116

Moroz, Mendel, 117

Moroz, Savely, 117

Moroz, Yuli, 117

Morros, Boris: and Akhmerov, 120; and atomic energy, 132–33, 137, 138; biography of, 110–11; and Chord venture, 66, 70, 118–19, 120–23; code names for, 66, 112, 126; death of, 139; and Dodd case, 66, 70, 71; as double agent, 70, 110, 122, 123–24, 134, 136, 138; and FBI, 66, 70, 110, 119–20, 122, 126, 133, 135, 136, 137, 138; film company partnership proposed by, 123–26, 127, 128, 131–32, 133; and Gutzeit, 110, 111–13, 114, 115–16; indictment of, 138; memoir of, 138; in Moscow, 130–31; motivation of, 341; with Paramount, 111–15, 125, 132; payments to, 341; recruitment of, 110–12; and Soble, 120, 121–22, 123–27, 128–29, 130, 134, 135, 136–37, 138; Soviet opinions about, 113, 114–15, 116, 127–28, 131, 132, 133, 134, 135, 136; and Stern, 118, 120–21, 122–23, 124; and world figures in Soviet Union proposal, 137; and Zarubin, 111, 112, 113–15, 117–18, 119–20, 121, 122, 128

Morros, Boris Jr., 132–2

Morros, Richard, 123

Moynihan, Daniel Patrick, 340

Mr. X (code name). See Chambers, Whittaker

Mrs. D. (code name). See Heineman, Mrs.

Muse (code name). See Tenney, Helen

Myrna (code name). See Bentley, Elizabeth

Nabob (code name). See Morgenthau, Henry

Nagasaki, Japan, 211

National Association of Manufacturers, 287

National Resources Board, 75

Navy, U.S.: Arena passes information about, 235–36; and Chambers's defection, 45; and Duggan as agent, 11; early Soviet probes into, 37; Justice Department's files about, 278; and OSS-NKGB cooperation, 245; as Soviet priority, 26, 27–28; and Ware group, 38

Nazar (code name), 305

Nazi-Soviet Pact (1939), 81

Needle (code name). See York, Jones Orrin

Nelly (code name). See Lowry, Helen

Neumann, Franz, 249–51, 254, 261

New Deal agencies: as attraction for romantics, 3–4; early Soviet probes into, 32–38; efforts to discredit, 343; Soviet intelligence agents in, 29–30; and Straight, 74; and Ware group, 38. See also specific agency

New Masses, 42

New Republic, 72, 73, 76, 82

Nigel (code name). See Straight, Michael

Nil (code name), 217, 218, 333

Nixon, Richard, 343

NKGB: and Bentley defection, 105–7; Bentley's attitude about, 95–96; opinion about FBI of, 244–45; OSS cooperation with, 238–49; and OSS list of communists, 254; penetration of OSS by, 240, 248, 249–64

NKVD: and Chambers's defection, 45; effect of purge on, 153–54; Reiss as head of European operations of, 10. See also specific agent

Nora (code name), 117

Nord (code name). See Bazarov, Boris

Norma (code name), 86

Norman, Bob, 60
Northrop Corporation, 26
Novikov, Kiril, 287
Nye, Gerald, 28, 40, 43
Nye Committee, 28–29, 40–41, 43

Oak Ridge facility, 183
O'Dwyer, Paul, 70
OGPU, 22
Okhrana (Czarist), 90
Old (code name), 135
Old man (code name). *See* Trotsky, Leon
Oppenheimer, Frank, 184
Oppenheimer, J. Robert, 133, 137, 138, 183–85, 201, 216
Orlov, Alexander, 153, 207
OSS (Office of Strategic Services): creation of, 240; FBI's relationship with, 242–43, 245; Glasser material about, 269, 270; investigations of Soviets within, 259; Justice Department's files about, 278; NKGB cooperation with, 238–49; NKGB opinions about, 244–45; Soviet codes passed to, 247; and Soviet coordination of information, 160; Soviet penetration of, 225, 240, 248, 249–64, 303; as Soviet priority for information, 228, 230; Truman disbands, 248, 256, 263. *See also specific person*
Ossip (code name), 110, 111
Ossipov, Alexander (code name). *See* Ovakimyan, Gaik
Ostap (code name), 70, 132, 134
Ovakimyan, Gaik, 154, 166, 334, 341; arrest of, 154, 173, 176; and Bentley, 88; and Browder, 306–7, 308; and Dickstein, 142, 144, 149; and Dolbin's appointment, 289; expulsion of, 276; and FBI, 91, 154, 276; and Golos, 85, 89; and Morros, 116; and OSS-NKGB cooperation, 241, 242, 244, 245–46; on Semyonov, 173; and Slack, 176; suspicions of, 90; and Trotskyites, 272–73

Page (code name). *See* Currie, Lauchlin
Pal (code name). *See* Silvermaster, Nathan Gregory
Panyushkin, Alexander: and Browder, 304, 305, 309; Chambers's disinformation proposal of, 294–95; and Dodd case, 68–69; and Duggan, 20, 295; Gorsky criticism of, 297; as head of Soviet intelligence, 297; and increased FBI counterintelligence efforts, 293; and Kramer, 234–35; and Morros, 131–32, 137; personal life of, 341; and proposals for re-recruitment of agents, 290, 291, 295–96; on Savchenko's proposal, 299; and Soble, 137; as U.S. ambassador, 289–90; as Washington station chief, 289–90
Paramount Pictures, 111–15, 125, 126, 132
Passov, Zinovy, 147
Pastelnyak, Pavel, 91, 172
Pavel (code name). *See* Bruslov, Yuri
Pavlov, V., 137
Peierles, Rudolph, 187
Pepper, Claude, 233, 234
Perlo Group: and Akhmerov, 95, 96–97, 156, 224–25, 226; and Bentley, 96–97, 106, 224–25, 226, 227, 229, 237, 262; and Browder, 96–97, 224, 229, 237; and Chambers's defection, 223; closing down of, 231; freeze on operations of, 226–27; and Golos, 156, 229; and Gorsky, 227, 228, 229, 231, 237; members of, 224–25; priority of information gathering for, 227–28, 230; Soviet opinions about, 225, 227–28, 229–30, 231; and Soviet penetration of OSS, 251, 252, 253, 254, 256, 262, 263; style of operations of, 227, 229, 231, 233
Perlo, Katherine Wills, 226–27, 231, 251, 341

Perlo, Victor, 39, 223, 225, 226–27, 231, 232–33, 236, 259, 266, 267, 341. *See also* Perlo Group

Perseus (code name), 190–91

Persian. *See* Fogel

Peter, Joszef: and Browder, 225, 302; and Chambers, 42, 45, 48; codes names of, 39; deportation of, 38; and FBI, 38, 225; and Hiss, 8, 38, 80, 165; and Soviet penetration of OSS, 262; and Ware group, 38–39, 42; Weinstein's interview of, 38

Pettigrew, M. W., 247–48

Philby, Harold "Kim," 72, 104–5, 107, 108, 155, 230, 290, 335, 344

Phillips (U.S. official), 56

Photon (code name). *See* Kamenev

Pick (code name). *See* Coe, Frank

Pilot (code name). *See* Ullman, William Ludwig

Pioneer (code name), 54

Pol (code name), 269

Poland, 246, 255, 270

Polecats (code name), 273

Political funding, 145

Pollitt, Harry, 73, 74

Polo (code name). *See* Ullman, William Ludwig

Potsdam Conference (1945), 211, 234, 235, 272

Poyntz, Juliette Stuart, 88–89

Pravdin, Vladimir: and Bentley defection, 104, 107; and Browder, 304; and Coplon, 277–78; and Maclean, 230; personal life of, 341; recall to Moscow of, 107, 286; and Silvermaster, 167–68, 169–71; and White, 169

President (code name). *See* Dodd, William (brother)

Pressman, Lee, 39, 48, 234

Price, Mary, 224, 257, 259

Prince (code name). *See* Duggan, Laurence

Pronsky, D., 326–27

Rabinovich (Soviet agent), 86

Rachmaninoff, Sergey, 130

Raid (code name). *See* Perlo, Victor

Ramzai (code name). *See* Hiskey, Clarence

Ray (code name). *See* Oppenheimer, Frank

Raymond (code name). *See* Reiss, Ignatz

"Red Spy Queen." *See* Bentley, Elizabeth

Redhead (code name). *See* Gumperz, Hedda

Reed (code name). *See* White, Harry Dexter

Reed, John, 207

Reina (code name), 304

Reiss, Ignatz, 10–11, 153, 203

Rest (code name). *See* Fuchs, Klaus

Richard (code name). *See* White, Harry Dexter

Rina (code name), 236–37

Robert (code name). *See* Silvermaster, Nathan Gregory

Robeson, Paul, 137

Romanticism, 76, 324–25

Roosevelt, Eleanor, 50, 62, 72, 74, 83, 228

Roosevelt, Franklin D.: and Browder's amnesty, 300, 306–7; Chambers requests meeting with, 47–48; code name for, 119; Currie's information about, 163; death of, 167, 248; and Dodd case, 50, 56, 57, 72, 228; Duggan provides Soviets with materials about, 12; and elections of 1944, 284; Glasser material about, 270; and leaks, 160; Morgenthau as influence on, 159; and OSS-NKGB cooperation, 238–39, 240, 242–44, 245, 247; and Silvermaster Group, 160; on Soviet codes, 247; Soviet need for information about, 154, 160–61; and Soviet penetration of OSS, 258; and Straight, 72, 74, 81, 82, 83; and threats to expose Perlo, 226; and U.S. recognition of Soviet Union, 22, 23; and Wallace, 284. *See also* New Deal agencies

Rosenberg, Allen, 106
Rosenberg, Ethel, 217, 326, 331, 332–33, 336, 342, 343, 344
Rosenberg, Julius: arrest and trial of, 133, 332–33, 343; and Bentley's defection, 217–18; code names for, 177, 197, 328, 329; death sentence for, 333, 336, 342, 344; denial of covert deeds by, 341; exposure of, 222, 326; and FBI, 206, 217, 222; and Feklissov, 191, 217–18; freezing of activities of, 206–7, 216–17, 222; and Golos, 174, 177, 197, 217, 218; and Greenglasses, 198–202, 206, 221, 311, 329, 330–31, 332, 333, 336; at Los Alamos, 197–98; motivation of, 341; in postwar world, 216–17, 222; proposed flight of, 330; and Semyonov, 177–78; Soviet opinions about, 198, 205–6, 217; Soviet reaction to trial of, 333–34; on Tal-1 agent, 174; and Zarubin, 177–78
Rosenman, Samuel, 270
Rote Kapelle ring, 53
Ruble (code name). *See* Glasser, Harold
Ruff (code name). *See* Neumann, Franz
Russian Foreign Intelligence Service (SVR), xv–xix, 190–91

Sakharovsky, A., 335
Satyr (code name), 273
Saushkin (code name), 20–21, 295–96
Savchenko, Sergei, 133, 134, 135, 297–99
Sax (code name). *See* Adler, Solomon
Sax, Saville, 195, 197, 203, 208, 209, 221
Sayre, Francis B., 44, 48
Scali, John, 275
Schapiro, Meyer, 46–47
Schuster, Bernard, 107, 177, 217, 218, 303
Scientific espionage, 24. *See also* Atomic research
Sebastian, George, 116

Sedov, Lev, 273
Semyon (code name). *See* Aksenov, N.
Semyonov, Semyon, 173, 174, 175, 177, 178, 183, 187, 188, 189, 190–91, 195, 207, 209–10
Serebryansky, Jacob, 89
Sergei (code name). *See* Pravdin, Vladimir
Shaman (code name), 309
Shelepin, Alexander, 326
Sherman, John Loomis, 42, 45
Shipley, Ruth, 134–35
Shumovsky (code name Blerio), 26–27
Sibert, Hans, 312
Sid (code name). *See* Rosenberg, Allen
Silverman, David, 158, 162–63, 167, 169, 235
Silverman, A. George, 47
Silvermaster, Helen, 158, 163, 164, 341
Silvermaster, Nathan Gregory: and Akhmerov, 96, 98, 157, 162, 163, 164–66, 167, 168, 169, 170; and Bentley, 94, 95, 96, 97, 98, 107, 157, 161, 162, 170, 262; biography of, 157–58; and Browder, 96, 158, 162; code names for, 90, 107, 165; denial of covert deeds by, 341; with Farm Security Administration, 161; and FBI, 161, 162, 164–65, 170; and German invasion of Soviet Union, 158–60; and Glasser, 266, 267; and Golos, 94, 157, 158, 161, 162; investigations of, 161, 170; payments to, 164–65; and Perlo Group, 224; personal life of, 164, 167, 169, 226, 231, 259, 341; and Pravdin, 167–68, 169–71; Soviet opinions about, 91, 157, 159, 162, 163–64, 165, 166, 167–68; and Soviet penetration of OSS, 262; Treasury Department discharges, 161; and Zarubin, 158, 159, 161–62
Sima (code name). *See* Coplon, Judith
Skinner, Herbert (code name), 316, 317

Slack, Alfred, 175–76, 177, 189, 213

Slutsky, Abram, 55, 57, 86

Smith, Bradley, 244

Smith (code name), 154

Smith Act, 309

Sobell, Morton, 332–33

Soble, Jack: code name for, 119; and Dodd, 70, 136; and FBI, 134; indictment of, 138; "kidnapping" of, 135–36; leaves France, 134–35; McCarthy investigation of, 136; and Morros, 120, 121–22, 123–27, 128–29, 130, 134, 135, 136–37, 138; Soviet opinions about, 135–36

Soble, Myra, 119, 138

Söhnchen. See Philby, Harold "Kim"

Sokolov, Gyorgi, 297

Solid (code name), 175

Solidny (code name), 175

Solow, Herbert, 46, 47

Sorokin, Valentin, 68–69

Sound (code name). See Golos, Jacob

Soviet Union: atomic research in, 211, 283, 316–17, 335; British relations with, 210, 263, 270; coordination of atomic espionage in, 182–83; Donovan receives codes of, 247; German invasion of, 158–60, 174, 223; "mole" in, 316–17; OSS information about activities in, 255, 263; and possible German and Anglo-American peace agreement, 247, 249, 250; purges in, 10, 12–13, 15, 16, 29, 54, 89, 91, 114, 147, 189, 223, 273, 339, 340; U.S. document about inevitability of war with, 232; U.S. loan to, 270, 271, 272; U.S. as main adversary of, 300; U.S. recognition of, 22–25, 32–33; U.S. relations with, 168, 210, 216, 224, 248, 262, 263, 283, 284, 285, 300; and World War II, 91, 92, 271

Sovinformbureau, 307, 309

Spain, 9, 12, 27, 74, 86, 239, 249, 253, 300

Spellman, Francis (Cardinal), 122, 124, 125, 126, 127, 128, 130, 131, 134, 250

Spiguelglass, Michael, 15

Stalin, Joseph: and atomic research, 181, 211; and Browder's expulsion, 300, 304, 305–6, 307, 308, 309; death of, 334; and Dodd case, 57, 63; Donovan's views about, 243; and Fuchs's arrest, 320; and German reparations, 234; and Golos, 87; and Gorsky-Wallace meeting, 284; and Gouzenko's defection, 104; and Hoettl case, 248; materials given to, 16, 107, 159, 225, 230, 268, 270; Mironov's letter to, 274; and monarchists, 31; and motivation of intelligence agents, 337; and OSS-NKGB cooperation, 246, 247, 248; and possible German and Anglo-American peace agreement, 247, 250; and Potsdam Conference, 211; and Reiss's defection, 11; timely forwarding of information to, 164; and Trotskyites, 24, 30, 273; and U.S.-Soviet relations, 262. See also Soviet Union

Standard Oil Corporation, 25

Stanley (code name). See Philby, Harold "Kim"

Star (code name). See Sax, Saville

Starikov (Soviet agent), 326

State Department, U.S.: and Chambers's defection, 45; code name for, 5, 7; Dickstein's attempts to infiltrate, 148; Duggan's activities known to, 16–17; early Soviet probes into, 33, 34–35, 37; European Division of, 4; exposure of Nazi agents in, 31; Glasser's materials about, 266–68, 270, 271, 272; Latin American Division of, 4, 9–10, 13; Markin as recruiter within, 33; NKGB cooperation with, 239–40; and OSS-NKGB cooperation, 244; and Soviet coordina-

State Department, U.S. (cont'd):
tion of information, 160; and
Soviet penetration of OSS, 255,
256, 257, 263; as Soviet priority
for information, 227, 230; Soviet
retreat from recruitment of agents
within, 34–35; and Ware group,
38. See also Daniel; Dodd,
Martha; Duggan, Laurence;
Field, Noel; Hiss, Alger; Straight,
Michael; Willie
Station chiefs: beleaguered, 285–91.
See also specific person
Statskevich, Nikolai, 292, 293
Steinhardt, Lawrence, 16
Stepan (code name), 293
Stephan (code name). See Deutsch,
Arnold
Stephenson, William, 104
Stern, Alfred: and Akhmerov, 120; and
Dodd case, 60, 61–62, 63–64,
65–66, 68–71; exile of, 71, 344;
and FBI, 120; and McCarthy
committee, 136; and Morros,
118, 120–21, 122–23, 124
Stettinius, Edward, 246, 247, 267–68
Stokowski, Leopold, 118, 121–22
Storm (code name). See Peter, Joszef
Straight, Michael, 72–83, 140, 155,
156, 170, 228, 253, 265, 344
Stravinsky, Igor, 118
Sudoplatov, Pavel, 11, 245, 274, 275
Sulpho (operation code name), 177
Surrogate. See State Department, U.S.
SVR (Russian Foreign Intelligence
Service), 190–91
Sweden, 247, 330

Taft Hotel (New York City), 33, 35
Tal-1 (code name), 174
Talent (code name), 174, 181
Tan (code name), 106, 113–14, 229,
237
Tannenhaus, Sam, 41
Taran (code name), 26
TASS News Agency, 68, 321
Ted (code name). See Fitzgerald,
Edward
Teller, Edward, 314

Tenney, Helen, 106, 225, 251, 256,
261
TEZHE (Soviet cosmetics firm), 25
Tina (code name), 194
Tito, Marshall, 242, 310
Treasury Department, U.S.: and
Chambers's defection, 45; as high
Soviet priority for information,
227; information forwarded to
Soviets about, 163. See also Adler,
Solomon; Glasser, Harold
Trilling, Lionel, 46
Trotsky, Leon, 14–15, 24, 30, 76, 143,
272–73, 274
Trotskyists, 30, 37, 76, 89, 90, 116,
153, 223, 272–74, 278, 303
Troyanovsky, Alexander, 142
Truman, Harry S: and atomic
research, 211, 212, 215; and
German reparations, 234; Glasser
material about, 271, 272; and
Gorsky-Wallace meeting, 284–85;
Kramer's information about, 234;
and Morros, 128–29, 131; OSS
disbanded by, 248, 256, 263; and
Perlo Group, 233; and Potsdam
Conference, 211, 234; Soviet
need for information about,
167–68; and U.S.-Soviet relations,
283; and VENONA project, 291
Truman, Margaret, 128, 129, 131
Tuk (code name). See Trotsky, Leon
Tulip (code name), 273
Turkey, 11, 241, 245–46
Twen (code name). See Semyonov,
Semyon

Ulanovski, Alexander, 43, 339
Ulanovskaya, Nadya, 339
Ullman, William Ludwig, 157, 158,
162, 163, 164, 165, 167, 169, 170
Ulrich (code name). See Ulanovski,
Alexander
Umansky, Konstantin, 60, 62, 238, 239
Union Carbide Corporation, 284
United Nations, 168, 235, 284
United Nations Relief and
Rehabilitation Administration
(UNRRA), 19, 228, 235

University of California, 182, 184, 187
University of Chicago, 182, 183, 221, 313, 314, 327–28
Urey, Harold, 172, 174, 181
U.S. Shipping Corporation, 99, 100, 101, 102, 103, 104

Vadim (code name). *See* Gorsky, Anatoly
Vardo (code name), 250
Vassilevsky, Colonel, 236
Vassiliev, Alexander, 180
VENONA program, 286, 287, 291–93, 325, 336, 339
Vinogradov, Boris, 51–53, 54–55, 57–60, 61, 62, 63, 64, 65, 66, 70
Vinson, Fred, 168, 234, 271, 272
Vladimir (code name). *See* Panyushkin, Alexander
Volodarsky, I. V., 32–33, 91. *See also* Feldman, Armand Lavis
Volunteer (code name). *See* Cohen, Morris
Vonsyatsky (Russian Fascist leader), 142
Voroshilov, Kliment, 16, 87, 131
Vyshinskij, Andrei, 269

Wadleigh, Henry Julian, 14, 47, 48
Walker family, 340
Wallace, Henry A., 68–69, 74, 119, 120, 168, 234–35, 283–85, 287
War Department, U.S.: and atomic research, 284; early Soviet probes into, 37; Glasser's materials about, 266–67, 272; and OSS-NKGB cooperation, 245; Soviet agents in, 236; and Soviet penetration of OSS, 263; as Soviet priority for information, 230
War Production Board, 227, 228, 230, 231, 232, 262. *See also* Perlo, Victor
Ware Group, 38–41, 43, 80, 140. *See also specific member*
Ware, Harold (Hal), 5, 37, 38, 39, 40, 43, 140, 223
Warren, Earl, 127, 130, 131
Wasp (code name). *See* Greenglass, Ruth

Weisband, William, 286, 291–93, 294
Weyl, Nathaniel, 39
Wheeler, Donald, 106, 225, 251–56, 257, 259, 261, 264, 286
White, Harry Dexter: and Akhmerov, 157; and Chambers's defection, 44, 47, 48; code names for, 90, 157, 165; denial of covert deeds by, 341; and FBI, 161; fears of exposure of, 158, 168; and Glasser, 265–66, 267; importance of, 161, 169; material forward to Soviets by, 163–64, 168; and Morgenthau, 166; and Silvermaster, 157, 158, 159, 163, 166, 167, 168; Soviet gifts to, 44; Soviet opinions about, 157, 158, 167; with World Bank, 168; and Zarubin, 158
"Whites." *See* Monarchists
Willie (code name), 34–35, 36–37
Winant, Joseph, 270
Wise, Miss (code name). *See* Bentley, Elizabeth
Witt, Nathan, 39, 48, 224
Wolf, Markus, 337, 344
World Bank, 168
World Tourist, 85–86, 87, 94, 99, 105
World War II: Soviet intelligence agents in, 29–30; Soviet losses in, 271; Soviet Union during, 91, 92; U.S. counterintelligence during, 90. *See also* Germany; *specific agent*

X (code name). *See* Chambers, Whittaker; Katz, Joseph
XY Line, 173–76, 177, 178, 191–92, 194–95, 203, 219, 220

Yakov (code name), 134, 136, 217
Yalta Conference, 269
Yasha (code name), 244, 256
Yatskov, Anatoly, 222, 316, 334, 341; and atomic espionage, 189–90, 192, 194–95, 197, 202, 203, 208, 210, 213, 215, 216, 218, 219; and Gold's security, 218–19, 220
Yezhov, Nikolay, 55, 57, 142
York, Jones Orin, 26–27, 174

Young Communist League, 195, 197, 198

Yugoslavia, 249, 309–10

Yung (code name), 35

Yuz (code name), 154

Z (code name), 245

Zarubin, Vassily: anonymous letters about, 274–75, 276; and atomic espionage, 177–78, 179–80, 182, 183; and Bentley, 96, 97; and Browder, 96, 302, 306–7, 308; and Chord venture, 66, 118–19; code names for, 111, 117, 239; and Dodd case, 65–66, 67–68; expulsion of, 276; and FBI, 276; and Golos, 92–93, 94; and Morros, 111, 112, 113–15, 116, 117–20, 121, 122, 128; and Perlo Group, 224, 228; personal life of, 341; and possible State Department–

NKGB cooperation, 239–40; and Silvermaster, 158, 159, 161–62; and Soviet penetration of OSS, 250, 251; and Straight, 82; style of, 276; views about FBI of, 276; and White, 158

Zarubina, Elizabeth, 162, 249–50, 251, 274, 276, 303, 341

Zborovsky, Mark, 273

Zelman, Franklin, 63–65, 179, 180, 181, 182

Zero (code name), 28–29

Zhemchuzhina, Polina, 25

Zhenya (code name). See Gold, Sonya

Zhora (code name). See Weisband, William

Zinger (code name). See Greenglass, David

Zora (code name), 277–78

Zubilin (code name). See Zarubin, Vassily

ABOUT THE AUTHORS

Historian ALLEN WEINSTEIN has held professorships at Boston University, Georgetown University, and Smith College. He is founder and president of The Center for Democracy, a Washington-based nonprofit foundation created in 1985 to work internationally in helping democratic development. His international awards include the United Nations Peace Medal (1986) and the Council of Europe's Silver Medal (1990). Weinstein has been a director of the congressionally chartered United States Institute of Peace since 1985. His books include *Perjury: The Hiss-Chambers Case*; *Freedom and Crisis: An American History*; and *Prelude to Populism*. He serves as chairman of the judging panel for the International IMPAC/Dublin Literary Award, the world's largest annual prize for a single novel. His other awards and fellowships include two Senior Fulbright Lectureships, an American Council of Learned Societies Fellowship, and the Commonwealth Fund Lectureship. He has written for a number of scholarly and popular publications. He is married and lives with his family in Washington, D.C.

ALEXANDER VASSILIEV graduated from Moscow State University's Faculty of Journalism and, in 1984, worked for *Komsomolskaya Pravda* as a reporter. The following year, he joined the KGB and, in 1987, after two years of training, worked as an operative in the U.S. department of the KGB's First Directorate. He retired in 1990 over disagreements with the policy of the Soviet Communist Party and returned to work at *Komsomolskaya Pravda*, first as a reporter and later as a columnist dealing with international politics and espionage issues. During this period, he also presented a number of political programs on Russian television's First Channel. He began working with Allen Weinstein on *The Haunted Wood* in 1993. Since 1996, he has lived in Western Europe with his family, working as a correspondent for *The Express Gazette*, a Russian weekly.

ABOUT THE TYPE

This book was set in Electra, a typeface designed for Linotype by W. A. Dwiggins, the renowned type designer (1880–1956). Electra is a fluid typeface, avoiding the contrasts of thick and thin strokes that are prevalent in most modern typefaces.